IRISH BIRMINGHAM

John +
Angela
x x

Irish Birmingham

A History

James Moran

Liverpool University Press

FOR THE 'ROBIN' MORANS

First published 2010 by
Liverpool University Press
4 Cambridge Street
Liverpool
L69 7ZU

British Library Cataloguing-in-Publication data
A British Library CIP record is available

ISBN 978-1-84631-474-2 cased
      978-1-84631-475-9 limp

Typeset by Carnegie Book Production, Lancaster
Printed and bound by CPI Group (UK) Ltd, Croydon, CR0 4YY

Contents

Abbreviations

BBC	British Broadcasting Corporation
BCL	Birmingham Central Library
BG	*Birmingham Gazette* (alternatively known as *Aris's Birmingham Gazette* from 1746, *Birmingham Daily Gazette* from 1862, *Birmingham Gazette & Express* from 1904, and *Birmingham Gazette* from 1912 until 1956).
BL	British Library
BM	*Birmingham Mail* (alternatively known as *Birmingham Daily Mail* from 1871, *Birmingham Mail* from 1918, *Evening Mail and Despatch* from 1963, *Birmingham Evening Mail* and *Evening Mail Birmingham* from 1967, and *Birmingham Mail* from 2005 to the present).
BP	*Birmingham Post* (alternatively known as *Birmingham Daily Post* from 1857, *Birmingham Post* from 1918, *Birmingham Post & Birmingham Gazette* from 1956, and *Birmingham Post* from 1964 to the present).
BRCAA	Birmingham Roman Catholic Archdiocesan Archives
IRA	Irish Republican Army
NAI	National Archives of Ireland
NLI	National Library of Ireland
NYPL	New York Public Library
RTÉ	Radio Telefís Éireann
SCUB	Special Collections, University of Birmingham

Acknowledgements

THIS BOOK could not have been written without the generous assistance of a number of friends and colleagues. I would particularly like to express my thanks to Donald MacRaild and Janette Dillon, who have made detailed and intelligent suggestions about my draft manuscript, and also to Neal Alexander, Carl Chinn, Billy Cowan, Brian Crowley, Fintan Cullen, Andrew Downes, Tom Murphy, David Rudkin, Clare Short, Annie Smith, and David Worrall, who have each been kind enough to pass on their valuable advice and ideas.

In addition, I have been greatly helped by Victor Merriman and Nicholas Grene's invitations to try out some of these ideas before academic audiences, and by John Sharpe's assistance in getting to grips with the records of the Birmingham Archdiocese. I would also like to express my gratitude to Anthony Cond at Liverpool University Press for his encouragement and assistance in preparing the final version of the book, and to Jean Chothia and Brean Hammond for helping to me to secure the time away from teaching that I needed to write the manuscript. I have also been assisted by the staff at a number of libraries and research centres, and would particularly like to thank Kathleen Dickson of the British Film Institute and Stephen Crook of the Berg Collection at New York Public Library.

Closer to home, I am obliged to Angela Moran, who offered helpful comments on the manuscript and whose work on Irish music in Birmingham showed how my idea for this book might lead to a viable research project in the first place. I am grateful, too, for the hints, memories, and suggestions provided by Elizabeth, Michael, Alana, and Thérèse Moran, as well as for the support of those in the Shannon, Cahill, Tomlinson, Keefe, and wider Moran families: I have repeatedly found myself returning to and reflecting on their experiences in the English midlands when writing this book. My thanks also go to those Birmingham-Kerrymen, Andrew and Stephen Griffin, who have kept me up to date about the city on our occasional restorative visits to Vaughan's.

Finally, I would like to express my thanks to Maria for her constant support and affection, and to Thomas, who arrived as I was finishing the first draft, and who has not only proven to be extremely good at sleeping but has also provided me with a great set of excuses for taking a break from the laptop.

Copyright permissions

Extracts from *Error of Judgement* are reprinted by permission of United Agents on behalf of Chris Mullin; the section of Seán O'Casey's *Autobiographies* is reproduced by kind permission of the Estate of Seán O'Casey; Department of Foreign Affairs records are reprinted by permission of the National Archives of Ireland and the Director of the National Archives; extracts from the correspondence of W. B. Yeats are published by permission of Oxford University Press and the Henry W. and Albert A. Berg Collection of English and American Literature, the New York Public Library Astor, Lenox and Tilden Foundations; part of David Lodge's *Small World* is reproduced with permission of Curtis Brown Group Ltd., London, on behalf of David Lodge, copyright © David Lodge 1984. The Board of the National Library of Ireland, the British Library, University of Birmingham Special Collections, the Archdiocese of Birmingham, and Birmingham Libraries and Archives have also kindly given permission to quote from material in their possession.

Introduction

It is the entitlement and birthright of every person born in the island of Ireland, which includes its islands and seas, to be part of the Irish Nation [...] Furthermore, the Irish nation cherishes its special affinity with people of Irish ancestry living abroad who share its cultural identity and heritage.

Constitution of the Irish Republic, Article 2[1]

One has not great hopes from Birmingham. I always say there is something direful in the sound.

Jane Austen[2]

Ireland in Birmingham

In the book *Wherever Green is Worn*, the journalist Tim Pat Coogan ambitiously attempts to examine why emigrants left Ireland in such large numbers, where they went, and what happened to them when they reached their various destinations. He discusses, for instance, the triumphant progress of Irish communities in the USA, and confirms the narrative that has been popularized by numerous dewy-eyed films and memoirs, declaring, 'The story of the Irish in America is a chronicle of the triumph of the human spirit over adversity.'[3]

---

[1]   This amended version of Article 2 was agreed in 1998 as part of the constitutional changes proposed by the Good Friday-Belfast Agreement. 'Bunreacht na hÉireann' <http://www.taoiseach.gov.ie/upload/static/256.htm> [accessed 29 January 2010] ('the Nation', Article 2 of 3), p. 26.

[2]   Jane Austen, *Emma*, ed. James Kinsey (Oxford: Oxford University Press, 1995), p. 280.

[3]   Tim Pat Coogan, *Wherever Green Is Worn: The Story of the Irish Diaspora* (London: Random House, 2000), p. 254.

But when Coogan describes the Irish in England he has a different picture to paint, as he highlights the problematic history that has long existed between the two neighbouring countries as well as the discrimination often faced by those from Ireland who came to live amongst the English. Nevertheless, he portrays the wealth and success of the Irish in London, and mentions the close ties that have existed between Ireland and other English urban centres, detailing Ireland's connection with Liverpool from 1819, and with Manchester from 1830.[4] However, Coogan saves his most scathing description for Birmingham, where he acknowledges an Irish influence only from the 1950s, and declares that 'the dull tide of grey, rather than green, which is emblematic of so much of the Irish community in Birmingham, will not readily evaporate'.[5]

There are two main reasons why Coogan should write in this way about Birmingham. For one thing, Coogan remembers the treatment of the 'Birmingham Six', those Irishmen unjustly imprisoned and horribly abused after the pub bombings of the 1970s. As we shall see, the fate of the 'Birmingham Six' became closely connected to the fortunes of the Irish in the city during a significant part of the twentieth century. For another thing, earlier anti-Irish sentiments had been expressed in Birmingham during the middle of the century. In the 1950s and 1960s social scientists observed the 'sense of grievance' directed against aggressive Irish 'tinkers' in Sparkhill, the tendency of Birmingham landlords to 'double-let' the beds for different Irish day- and night-shift workers, and the notices on display at various hostels in the city that declared 'no coloured; no Irish'.[6]

Yet to dismiss the Irish experience of Birmingham because of such evidence is to ignore the wider context of two centuries of Irish life in the area. Birmingham housed a large and dynamic Irish population from the early nineteenth century, with the town becoming a hub for Irish communities in other parts of the English midlands, such as Wolverhampton and Coventry. Although Liverpool and urban areas in the north of England tend to dominate the perception of Irishness in Britain during the Victorian era, by the 1850s, after the first large wave of Irish immigration, Birmingham boasted the fourth highest Irish-born population of any town in England and Wales,

---

4   Coogan, *Wherever Green Is Worn*, pp. 181, 183, 168.

5   Coogan, *Wherever Green Is Worn*, p. 199.

6   John Rex and Robert Moore, *Race, Community and Conflict: A Study of Sparkbrook* (London: Oxford University Press, 1967), p. 99; John Archer Jackson, *The Irish in Britain* (London: Routledge and Kegan Paul, 1963), p. 63.

and for many subsequent years the Irish formed the biggest ethnic minority in the area.[7]

In the twentieth century, Birmingham grew to become the second-largest conurbation in the United Kingdom, and when the rise of post-war 'clean' industries in 1951 to 1961 brought a new wave of arrivals, the Irish came to the city in greater numbers than those large groups from the West Indies or from India-Pakistan. In fact, during the mid-1960s, 16.5 per cent of all births in Birmingham were to couples where at least one parent had been born in Ireland.[8]

By the 1990s, the flow of Irish immigration to England had been staunched by the impressive performance of Ireland's own economy, but at the time of the 2001 census, Birmingham's population still contained more than two and a half times more Irish-born residents than the rest of England, with the proportion of those from Ireland proving particularly high in areas such as Hall Green, Acocks Green, and Erdington.[9] Indeed, shortly after Coogan's book was published, his analysis was contradicted by a crowd estimated at around 80,000, whose members gathered in the centre of Birmingham for the annual St Patrick's Day march. That year an outbreak of foot-and-mouth disease caused the postponement of a similar pageant in Dublin, leaving the Birmingham organizers proudly claiming that the English event would be the second largest St Patrick's Day procession in the world, ranked only behind the festivities in New York City.

Surveying the Bookshelf

Yet until now there has been no major, book-length study of the Irish in England's second city. Birmingham's Irish story is largely overlooked in key civic histories such as Robert K. Dent's 626-page Victorian study *Old and New Birmingham* and the two volumes of Asa Briggs and Conrad Gill's 1954 *History of*

---

7   *Census of England and Wales for the Year 1861, Volume III, General Report, Appendix to the Report* (London: HMSO, 1863), p. 160.

8   Gordon E. Cherry, *Birmingham: A Study in Geography, History and Planning* (Chichester: Wiley, 1994), p. 204. Corporate Statistician, BCL, 'The Nationality of Children born in 1964, table 11' and 'Trends, The Nationality of Children Born in 1965', in *Ethnic Origins of Birmingham Children 1966–81*, Birmingham Central Statistical Office, LF 40–41.

9   Birmingham City Council, *2001 Population Census in Birmingham: Cultural Background: Ethnic and Religious Groups, Country of Birth* (Birmingham: Birmingham City Council, [2007]), table 2.11.

Birmingham.[10] In the same way, important recent studies of Birmingham, such as those by Victor Skipp, Chris Upton, and Roger Ward, only touch lightly upon the Irish population of the area.[11]

This study of Birmingham, then, builds on the kind of approach with which previous scholars have approached the Irish communities located in other parts of the United Kingdom. John Archer Jackson made one of the earliest scholarly attempts to analyse the country's Irish in his work *The Irish in Britain*, which appeared in 1963.[12] In the ensuing years, the 'Troubles' pushed the relationship between the two neighbouring countries to the top of the news agenda, with the Irish in England becoming a booming topic for scholarly enquiry. In 1979 Lynn Hollen Lees published *Exiles of Erin: Irish Migrants in Victorian London*, the first full-length book to explore the Irish experience of a particular English city, and this work was followed in 1985 by Francis Finnegan's study of the Irish in York, as well as Roger Swift and Sheridan Gilley's landmark volume, *The Irish in the Victorian City*, which contained articles on the Irish in Bristol, York, London, Wolverhampton, Stockport, and Liverpool.[13] In the wake of this latter publication, scholars increasingly examined the Irish in various English locations, situating such migration from Ireland in a global context of population movement, and popularizing such research far beyond the ivory tower. In 1990 Mary Robinson began her presidency of the Irish Republic by dwelling on her role as figurehead for those of Irish descent around the world, introducing the

10   Robert K. Dent, *Old and New Birmingham: A History of the Town and Its People*, 3 vols (Birmingham: Houghton and Hammond, 1880; repr. Wakefield: EP Publishing, 1973), vol. III, p. 450; and Asa Briggs and Conrad Gill, *History of Birmingham*, 2 vols (London: Oxford University Press, 1952). A 1974 supplementary volume to Briggs and Gill does include some fleeting descriptions of Irish migration to Birmingham: see Anthony Sutcliffe and Roger Smith, *History of Birmingham, Volume III, Birmingham 1939–1970* (London: Oxford University Press, 1974).

11   Victor Skipp, *Victorian Birmingham* (Birmingham: Studio Press, 1983), p. 115; Chris Upton, *Living Back to Back* (Trowbridge: Cromwell, 2005); Roger Ward, *City-State and Nation: Birmingham's Political History 1830–1940* (Chichester: Phillimore, 2005).

12   Earlier studies include Arthur Redford's *Labour Migration in England, 1800–1850* (Manchester: Manchester University Press, 1926), and the more sympathetic analysis of the Irish in Scotland by James Edmund Handley, *The Irish in Scotland 1798–1845* (Cork: Cork University Press, 1943) and *The Irish in Modern Scotland* (Cork: Cork University Press, 1947).

13   Lynn Hollen Lees, *Exiles of Erin: Irish Migrants in Victorian London* (Manchester: Manchester University Press, 1979), p. 4; Frances Finnegan, *Poverty and Prejudice: Irish Immigrants in York, 1840–75* (Cork: Cork University Press, 1985); Roger Swift and Sheridan Gilley (eds), *The Irish in the Victorian City* (London: Croom Helm, 1985).

theme later explained to the *Oireachtas* (Irish parliament) as 'cherishing the diaspora'.[14] At the same time, the English and Welsh Joint Matriculation Board began offering a history syllabus that allowed teenage students to follow A-level courses on the Irish in Britain.[15]

In the 1990s, books such as Graham Davis's *The Irish in Britain* and Donald MacRaild's *Irish Migrants in Modern Britain* paid closer attention to the historiography of dispersed Irish groups and to the diversity of the Irish-British experience.[16] At the same time, several more book-length studies were published about Irish migration to different parts of England, most notably MacRaild's *Culture, Conflict and Migration: The Irish in Victorian Cumbria* and Frank Neal's *Sectarian Violence: The Liverpool Experience*.[17] However, there remained a general silence about England's second largest city until, in the late 1990s, the historian Carl Chinn wrote an intelligent article about mid-nineteenth-century Birmingham for inclusion in *The Irish in Victorian Britain: The Local Dimension*, an edited collection of essays that explored the Irish in hitherto overlooked locations such as Cornwall, Hull, and Stafford.[18]

Chinn later reproduced parts of his article in a newspaper read by the Irish in Birmingham, and supplemented his research to create the 2003 survey *Birmingham Irish: Making Our Mark*, published by Birmingham Libraries as something of a *mea culpa* to the local Irish.[19] After all, for many years,

14 Catherine Nash, *Of Irish Descent: Origin Stories, Genealogy, and the Politics of Belonging* (Syracuse, NY: Syracuse University Press, 2008), pp. 26, 29.

15 Roger Swift, *Irish Migrants in Britain, 1815–1914: A Documentary History* (Cork: Cork University Press, 2002), p. xvii.

16 Graham Davis, *The Irish in Britain, 1815–1914* (Dublin: Gill and Macmillan, 1991); Donald MacRaild, *Irish Migrants in Modern Britain, 1750–1922* (Houndmills: Macmillan, 1999).

17 Donald MacRaild, *Culture, Conflict and Migration: The Irish in Victorian Cumbria* (Liverpool: Liverpool University Press, 1998); Frank Neal, *Sectarian Violence: The Liverpool Experience, 1819–1914: An Aspect of Anglo-Irish History* (Manchester: Manchester University Press, 1988). Other publications appearing at about this time include W. J. Lowe, *The Irish in Mid-Victorian Lancashire: The Shaping of a Working-Class Community* (New York: Lang, 1989); Steven Fielding's book about the Irish Catholic experience of Manchester, *Class and Ethnicity* (Milton Keynes: Open University Press, 1992); and Roger Cooter, *When Paddy Met Geordie: The Irish in County Durham and Newcastle* (Sunderland: University of Sunderland Press, 2005).

18 Carl Chinn, '"Sturdy Catholic Emigrants": The Irish in Early Victorian Birmingham', in *The Irish in Victorian Britain: The Local Dimension*, ed. Sheridan Gilley and Roger Swift (Dublin: Four Courts Press, 1995), pp. 52–74.

19 Carl Chinn, 'The Voice of the Irish in Brum', *The Harp*, May 2007, p. 23; Carl Chinn, *Birmingham Irish: Making Our Mark* (Birmingham: Birmingham Libraries, 2003).

Birmingham's libraries had collected almost no archival material about this community. Indeed, the two volumes of the *Catalogue of the Birmingham Collection* show that in more than half a century of acquiring material up until 1931, only three scraps of information relating to the Irish had been gathered.[20] By contrast, during the same period the local libraries had acquired a great deal of information on the Welsh and Scottish communities in Birmingham, collecting reports by *Undeb y Brythoniaid, Birmingham* (the Birmingham Welsh Society), as well as the accounts, lectures, and concert details of the Birmingham and Midland Scottish Society.[21] By the 1990s, however, Birmingham's library service set about making amends, and, at the same time as printing Chinn's work, catalogued two folders of material about the local Irish that had been compiled by the librarian Joe McKenna.[22] During the past two decades, students at Birmingham University have also written some valuable dissertations on the local Irish population, whilst Enda Delaney has included several insightful pages on Birmingham in his 2007 volume *The Irish in Post-War Britain*.[23]

Politics, Literature, and Performance

In recent years, scholars such as Delaney have moved beyond the blunt facts provided by census statistics to explore the cultural significance of England's Irish population. Where such research has been conducted, the results have often been illuminating, with those who study the influence of the Irish in

---

20   Walter Powell and Herbert Maurice Cashmore, *Birmingham Public Libraries Catalogue of the Birmingham Collection* (Birmingham: Cornish Brothers, 1918), p. 511.

21   Herbert Maurice Cashmore, *Birmingham Public Libraries Catalogue of the Birmingham Collection: Supplement 1918–1931* (Birmingham: Public Libraries Committee, 1931), pp. 751–52, 849. Powell and Cashmore, *Birmingham Public Libraries Catalogue of the Birmingham Collection*, pp. 881, 1011–12.

22   BCL, Local Studies Collection, Two Irish Studies boxes, LF 21.7. The library also holds a bound copy of some of this material: Joe McKenna, 'The Irish in Birmingham: A Scrapbook 1643–1989', BCL, Local Studies Collection, Birmingham Collection 21.7; Joe McKenna, 'The Irish in Birmingham 1990', BCL, Local Studies Collection, LF 21.7.

23   Kaja Irene Ziesler, 'The Irish in Birmingham 1830–1970' (unpublished doctoral thesis, University of Birmingham, 1989); Nuala Katherine Killeen, 'Culture, Identity and Integration: The Case of the Irish in Birmingham' (unpublished doctoral thesis, University of Birmingham, 2002); Patsy Davis, 'Green Ribbons: The Irish in Birmingham in the 1860s: A Study of Housing, Work and Policing' (unpublished master's thesis, University of Birmingham, 2003); Enda Delaney, *The Irish in Post-War Britain* (Oxford: Oxford University Press, 2007), pp. 95–102.

Liverpool, for example, highlighting Merseyside's history of Irish festivities and religious tensions, as well as the development of Irish music, dance, and singing in the area.[24] In addition, John Belchem's excellent study *Irish, Catholic and Scouse* has demonstrated how Liverpool has often proved 'the pivot of Irish politics in Britain', with the region electing Irishmen to the town council and returning a nationalist MP to Westminster for over forty years.[25] Meanwhile, Manchester has been subject to similar investigations, with recent books charting the lives of those from Ireland who engaged in Gaelic games, Irish dancing, or other sports in the region, as well as the work of the Irish who assisted Manchester's Chartist, Fenian, and Trade Union movements.[26]

Of course, the English city whose Irish residents have become best known is probably London, that vast metropolis where an impressive array of different activities have been undertaken by the Irish, and where a number of upper- and middle-class émigrés have played a significant part in legal, journalistic, and artistic life ever since the Victorian era. In recent years, publishers have highlighted the dancing, sporting, and musical accomplishments of the Irish in London: in 2003 Catherine Dunne's volume *An Unconsidered People: The Irish in London* charted the experiences of the immigrants of the 1950s; whilst in 2005 Fintan Cullen and Roy Foster wrote the book *'Conquering England': Ireland in Victorian London* to emphasize Ireland's earlier contribution to the politics, literature, and drama of the English capital, and to accompany a significant exhibition of related art at Britain's National Portrait Gallery.[27] Even those who know little about the recent books on such topics may well have heard popular reports about the exploits of London-Irish controversialists from

---

24   Neal, *Sectarian Violence*; Matthew J. Gallman, *Receiving Erin's Children: Philadelphia, Liverpool, and the Irish Famine Migration 1845–1855* (Chapel Hill: University of Carolina Press, 2000); Kevin McManus, *Ceílís, Jigs and Ballads: Irish Music in Liverpool* (Liverpool: Institute of Popular Music, 1994).

25   John Belchem, *Irish, Catholic and Scouse: The History of the Liverpool Irish 1800–1939* (Liverpool: Liverpool University Press, 2007), p. 157.

26   Fielding, *Class and Ethnicity*; Michael Herbert, *The Wearing of the Green: A Political History of the Irish in Manchester* (London: Irish in Britain Representation Group, 2001); Alan Keegan, *Irish Manchester* (Stroud: Sutton, 2004); Alan Keegan and Danny Claffey, *More Irish Manchester* (Stroud: Sutton, 2006); Lawrence W. McBride (ed.), *The Reynolds Letters: An Irish Emigrant Family in Late Victorian Manchester* (Cork: Cork University Press, 1999).

27   John Cullinane, *Aspects of Irish Céilí Dancing 1897–1997* (Cork: [n. pub.], 1998); Peter Bills, *Passion in Exile: 100 Years of London Irish RFC* (Edinburgh: Mainstream, 1998); Catherine Dunne, *An Unconsidered People: The Irish in London* (Dublin: New Island, 2003); Fintan Cullen and Roy Foster, *'Conquering England': Ireland in Victorian London* (London: National Portrait Gallery, 2005).

Oscar Wilde to Shane MacGowan; the succession of Irish soccer players at
Old Trafford and Anfield; or the achievements of Merseyside and Mancunian
musicians of Irish descent such as Noel and Liam Gallagher, or John Lennon
and Paul McCartney.[28]

This book seeks to recover the significant, if little examined, role that the
Irish have also played in Birmingham. Whilst I have conducted my research
for this book, I have repeatedly encountered evidence of the way that Irish
men and women have taken part in mass political movements in Birmingham,
with members of this population campaigning on issues that include electoral
reform and Home Rule, as well as Northern Irish civil rights and radical
republicanism. Birmingham has thus witnessed a sustained tradition of Irish
political meetings, processions, and protests, with today's massive St Patrick's
Day festivities ultimately developing out of the region's 1869 campaign for Irish
independence. Such events in Birmingham have influenced a number of literary
writers in the nineteenth and twentieth centuries, particularly inspiring some
significant dramatists who have offered a kind of corollary to the less rehearsed
spectacles and speeches that the Irish have repeatedly coordinated in the city.
On numerous occasions, both the orator's platform and the playhouse stage
have therefore provided Birmingham's residents with the opportunity to enact,
contest, and parody different kinds of Irish nationality in particularly graphic
and deliberate ways, even in the face of hostile or disapproving voices. Indeed,
to use Foucault's term, such spaces have often proved a kind of 'heterotopia',
or a site that somehow speaks of other sites.[29] People may have been driven

---

28   Wilde's and MacGowan's London-Irish identity is highlighted, for instance, by the
Museum of London's webpage on 'Irish London' <http://www.museumoflondon.org.uk
/English/Collections/Onlineresources/RWWC/themes/1295/1151> [accessed 4 March
2009] (paras 8 and 18 of 18). The Irish footballers of Liverpool FC have been celebrated by
various commemorative matches and by supporters groups, see for example David Prentice,
'Irish Eyes Smiling as Liverpool Stars Boost Charity', *Liverpool Echo*, 5 February 2009
<http://www.liverpoolecho.co.uk/liverpool-fc/liverpool-fc-news/2009/02/05/irish-
eyes-smiling-as-liverpool-stars-boost-charity-100252-22859043/> [accessed 4 March 2009].
Manchester United's Irish players are remembered by Chris Moore's *United Irishmen:
Manchester United's Irish Connection* (Edinburgh: Mainstream, 2000). Meanwhile, the Irish
roots of Oasis are discussed in, for example, Ronan McGreevy's article, 'Oasis to Come
"Home" to Slane', *Irish Times*, 16 October 2008 <http://www.irishtimes.com/newspaper
/ireland/2008/1016/1224069691647.html> [accessed 4 March 2009]; whilst the Irish
background of Lennon, McCartney, and Harrison is described by Michael Lynch and
Damian Smyth in *The Beatles and Ireland* (Cork: Collins Press, 2008).
29   Michel Foucault, 'Different Spaces', in *Aesthetics, Method, and Epistemology*, ed. James
Faubion (London: Penguin, 2000), pp. 175–85.

to such 'heterotopias' by crises such as starvation, unemployment, or political instability, yet here various ideas about Ireland or Britain might be represented, contrasted, and inverted. Indeed, Foucault claims that the ultimate example of 'heterotopia' is a ship, a paradoxical space that is enclosed and self-contained but that allows passengers the possibility of various global movements, contacts, and conquests. For most of the past two centuries, those who travelled between Birmingham and Ireland knew perfectly well that the boat might be a location that at once represented and contained many other places. The Holyhead ferry could somehow be both Irish and British; a place to hear about the unknown; and a site invested with numerous hopes and dreams for the future, as well as a place to confront the reality of migrant life. And when these men and women reached Birmingham, various spaces in the city also allowed groups to continue negotiating between Britain and Ireland, between actuality and imagination, and between the tendency to close together and the impulse to reach out towards the wider community.

Each chapter of this chronological study therefore begins with a key public spectacle associated with Ireland in Birmingham, designed to be witnessed by a large audience of people, and containing elements of what the theatre anthropologist Eugenio Barba labels the 'extra-daily'.[30] Barba's work refines Erving Goffman's sociological observation that everyday life can in many ways be considered theatrical, with each of us rehearsing and acting out various behaviours for different audiences.[31] In the 'extra-daily' situation, the individual is particularly conscious of his behaviour, and engages in stylized actions that are not simply functional but are notable for the energy that they involve. So whilst an Irish person in Birmingham might be conscious of behaving in various 'Irish' ways during his day-to-day life in the town, on certain occasions he may go to special lengths to demonstrate such characteristics, for example by singing, orating, parading, or dancing. The Irish in Birmingham have often engaged in forms of self-conscious public display in order to attract attention or to make a particular point, and my book revolves around such moments. Thus, in addition to the playhouse drama and the political meeting, this study includes related events such as the religious lecture, the public procession, the interrupted cinema show, and – most horrifyingly – the fatal pub bombings of 1974.[32] Each individual

---

30   Eugenio Barba, *The Paper Canoe: A Treatise on Theatre Anthropology*, trans. Richard Fowler (London: Routledge, 1995), pp. 15–16.
31   Erving Goffman, *The Presentation of the Self in Everyday Life* (New York: Doubleday, 1956).
32   Of course, it scarcely needs to be spelled out that IRA attacks have some key

chapter then echoes Eugenio Barba's approach by analysing the culture and cultural practices that have produced these events, narrating the spectacle and emphasizing a set of wider contexts and significances. By placing such moments here in chronological order I hope to show how the idea of Ireland has emerged, evolved, and recurred in Birmingham over the course of two centuries.

A Birmingham-Irish Chronology

This history begins with an extravagant playhouse show organized in 1803 by William McCready, the first high-profile immigrant from Ireland to settle in Birmingham. At a time when the small Irish population of the town could be counted in tens rather than hundreds, McCready premiered a play called *The Magic of British Liberty*, presenting an onstage vision of his fellow countrymen for an audience of Englishmen and women. Ever since the mid-1600s, the English had been alarmed by the 'wild' Irish, who constituted a dangerous Catholic threat, and who tended to be portrayed as a rabble of potentially murderous lunatics. But as the historian D. W. Hayton has argued:

> In 1708, 1715 and 1745 the actual danger to the English establishment came from Scotland rather than Ireland, with the result that in the eighteenth century the Scottish highlander took over from the Irish 'kerne' as the Jacobite bogyman [...] From the Restoration onwards English attitudes towards Ireland were settling into a more-or-less permanent sneer. The 'wild Irishman' was a contemptible fool; even if a cunning cut-throat, at heart a coward: the emphasis throughout was on the inferiority of all things Irish.[33]

---

differences to the other political and theatrical spectacles that this book discusses, not least in that those who witnessed such explosions were scarcely willing participants, and that the Birmingham bombings involved death and injury on a massive scale. Yet the bombings also involved pre-planned action, an awareness of the importance of venue and setting, and the participation of an audience that would see the spectacle reproduced on television and in the newspapers. For more on the connections between literary drama and non-theatrical events, see Manfred Pfister, *The Theory and Analysis of Drama*, trans. John Halliday (Cambridge: Cambridge University Press, 1988), p. 11.

33   D. W. Hayton, 'From Barbarian to Burlesque: English Images of the Irish c.1660–1750', *Irish Economic and Social History* 15 (1988), pp. 13–15. See also G. C. Duggan, *The Stage Irishman: A History of the Irish Play and Stage Characters from the Earliest Times* (Dublin and Cork: Talbot, 1937).

Correspondingly, from the 1660s we can find the origins of the 'Irish joke' in popular jest books, which tend to treat the Irish as poverty-stricken idiots much given to amusing speech and bizarre religious beliefs.[34] But in Birmingham, William McCready avoided adhering either to this tradition or to the earlier, more threatening Irish stereotype, even though local newspapers reported real-life bloodshed in Ireland during the period when McCready wrote and rehearsed *The Magic of British Liberty*. In this Birmingham show the onstage character of 'Patt' appeared as a brave and loyal character who worked hard to protect his English brother from the barbarous French, onto whom various uncivilized traits could be projected instead. McCready thus anticipated the tendency of Victorian cartoonists to depict Hibernia standing supportively alongside her sister Britannia, rather than the unflattering newspaper caricature of the Irish simian thug.[35] Furthermore, McCready's Birmingham production displayed technological complexity and ambition, typifying the contribution to the development of local drama that he made through his fastidious work as manager of the Theatre Royal on New Street. Indeed, McCready left a lasting influence on the English stage by using the Birmingham playhouse as a training ground for his son, who was destined to become one of the most famous actors of the nineteenth century.

The early 1800s saw a great deal of Irish migration to Birmingham, and although no official census figures were kept at this time, local residents variously estimated the Irish population of the town to have reached somewhere between 6,000 and 11,000 by the mid-1830s.[36] At this stage, the most famous Irish politician of the era, Daniel O'Connell, had successfully campaigned for Catholic emancipation, and his work had impressed members of both the

---

34   See for example, *The Irish Miscellany; or Teagueland Jests* (London: R. Adams, 3rd ed., 1749), which contains stories such as the tale of an Irishman (a 'Bog-trotting Son of a Whore') who went to a brothel and awoke in the arms of a black woman: '[H]e started out of Bed, ran down the Stairs naked, crossing himself over and over; feeling for his Beads, when he had never a Rag about him; and skipping up and down like one of the most frantick in Bedlam, roaring and bellowing; Whoo! whoo! boo! boo! vat vill I doe? be Chreesht mine owne moder vill kill me for mauking Child upon the Dee'ls awne shelf: Vat vill I shay to mine Confeshor indeed, ven I come for de Absholoushion?' (p. 62).

35   To contrast these images of Ireland as depicted by Victorian cartoonists see the pictures reproduced in R. F. Foster, *Paddy and Mr Punch* (London: Allen Lane, 1993), pp. 177 and 188.

36   *Reports from Commissioners: Fifteen Volumes (13) Poor Laws (Ireland): Supplement II, Vol. XXXIV, 1836 (Appendix G: Report on the State of the Irish Poor in Great Britain), Evidence Taken 4–7 January 1834* (London: House of Commons, [n.d.]), pp. 477–78, 475.

Irish and non-Irish populations of Birmingham. During the months following his triumph in 1829, Birmingham's radicals founded their own organization to demand increasing voting rights, the Birmingham Political Union, which was based upon O'Connell's campaign. These Birmingham radicals invited O'Connell himself to visit the town, and he duly arrived to address this English organization in 1832. It is difficult to tell what proportion of the town's Irish population supported the Birmingham Political Union, although the organization was spearheaded by a prominent leader of the local Irish Catholics, Father Thomas McDonnell, and did pass a number of pro-Irish resolutions at a public meeting in June 1832. Indeed, even after the 'great' reform act of 1832 had granted some of the radicals' demands, O'Connell repeatedly came back to Birmingham during the following years.

However, some of those in the Birmingham Political Union opposed these visits to the town, with O'Connell and the local reform campaigners eventually quarrelling and parting company in 1837, perhaps offering a hint of the anti-Catholicism that Birmingham would witness during the ensuing years. Nevertheless, there would be a significant adjunct to the town's links with O'Connell later in the century, when a young stone carver named James Pearse worked in the city and embraced Birmingham's tradition of radical politics. Perhaps we should not be surprised, then, to find that James's Irish-born son Pádraic went on to become the most famous leader of the Dublin insurrection at Easter 1916.

Since the start of the nineteenth century, many of Birmingham's residents had been impressed by William McCready's work in the local theatre and had supported Daniel O'Connell's campaign for improved conditions in Ireland. But such enthusiasm for Irish causes had flagged by the mid-1800s, with the town experiencing large-scale immigration as a result of the potato famine. Census returns, which undoubtedly underestimate the true figure, show the number of Irish-born residents of Birmingham rising from 4,683 in 1841 to 9,341 in 1851 (or from 2.56 per cent to 4.01 per cent of the town's population), and then increasing further to 11,332 by 1861.[37] It would take until the 1950s for the official Irish-born population to grow so large again, and if the historian Patsy Davis is correct to assert that multiplying the figures by 2.5 gives a better representation of the true size of the Irish population, the number becomes about 28,000 in 1861, or 10 per cent of those living in the town.[38] However, this

---

[37]   See appendix for census figures.

[38]   Patsy Davis, 'Birmingham's Irish Community and the Murphy Riots of 1867', *Midland History* 31 (2006), p. 38.

surge in immigration during the mid-1800s was accompanied by an upsurge in racism and religious tension. In particular, when the divisive preacher William Murphy delivered a controversial series of lectures in Birmingham during 1867, he deliberately sought to goad many of the area's impecunious Irish Catholics, and successfully initiated a great deal of violence. Such disruption affected the work of two of the town's English Catholic priests, John Henry Newman and Gerard Manley Hopkins, whilst the victimized Irish laymen and women felt disillusioned with the English authorities for apparently colluding in the onslaught. Many now showed an increasing enthusiasm for the Irish revolutionary organization, the Fenians, provoking opposition from members of the local Orange Order and inspiring the police to arrest potential Irish insurrectionists in the town, including another future revolutionary leader of 1916, Thomas Clarke. The Catholic Church in Birmingham looked on with alarm, and attempted to divert the local Irish residents away from insurgency by organizing a large St Patrick's Day meeting at the town hall, with the event soon becoming a well-attended annual gathering in the region.

These town hall meetings became increasingly politicized during the late nineteenth century in reaction to the work of Birmingham's famous mayor and MP, Joseph Chamberlain, whose activities encouraged Irish Catholics to jeer his name at the town hall but English imperialists to cheer in approval elsewhere in Birmingham. The historian Ian Chambers has recently pointed out that most of the published biographies of Chamberlain tend to 'devote very little attention to his involvement with Irish affairs', and there is a particular dearth of work detailing the politician's interaction with Birmingham's Irish population.[39] Yet from the 1880s Chamberlain became Britain's foremost Unionist, and used the English midlands as the base from which to promote his view that Ireland and Britain should remain as one conjoined state. As British political discourse during the late nineteenth century became dominated by arguments about whether Ireland should be granted self government, many of the Irish residents of Chamberlain's city expressed opposition to the way that he had transformed Birmingham into a bastion of Unionism, and in return Chamberlain held pro-union meetings in the area, as well as scripting a play called *The Game of Politics* that satirized Irish nationalists in the style of the melodramatic fare offered at the local theatres. Birmingham's enthusiastic embrace of Unionism, as well as the improved economic conditions that existed in Ireland after the famine, meant the rate of Irish migration to the

---

[39]   Ian Chambers, *The Chamberlains, the Churchills and Ireland: 1874–1922* (New York: Cambria, 2006), p. 3.

area now decreased markedly: census enumerators recorded 11,332 men and women from Ireland living in Birmingham during 1861, but that figure grew smaller in every survey for the next fifty years, leaving Birmingham with only 3,165 Irish-born residents by 1911. Chamberlain's opponents could, however, claim at least one kind of lasting victory over him, with the politician being mocked by James Joyce in the pages of *Ulysses*.

By the time that Chamberlain died in 1914, Birmingham had settled into a pattern of consistently voting for Unionist MPs, and the local census showed that the number of Irish-born residents had dwindled to a mere 0.38 per cent of the city's population, compared to 1 per cent of the total population of England and Wales as a whole.[40] As a result, the old political debates in the area cooled down, and Irish influence upon the region could instead be found in the development of the Birmingham Repertory Theatre, whose English founder, Barry Jackson, consciously emulated the theatre of Dublin. Although writers such as William Butler Yeats and George Bernard Shaw might be more commonly associated with London, Yeats's plays and visit to the city in 1910 led Barry Jackson and other enthusiasts to develop the new Birmingham company, whilst Shaw later spent a significant period of time in collaboration with Jackson. However, the Birmingham Repertory Theatre's adoption of an Irish repertoire would prove contentious, and in 1917, after Irish politics became an incendiary matter during the First World War, rioters arrived at the playhouse to protest against the onstage portrayal of Ireland.

If the theatre of the English midlands had thus taken its cue from Ireland in the early decades of the twentieth century, during the ensuing years a reversal occurred, as the condition of Birmingham in turn prompted Irish playwrights to write several dramatic scripts concerning the city, where once again census figures show that the Irish-born population had started to rise (up from 3,165 in 1911 to 6,055 by 1921). In 1939 the IRA attacked Birmingham for the first time, setting off explosions in local cinemas and elsewhere, and one of those who lived in the city and assisted the organization during that year was the seventy-seven-year-old grandmother of the playwright Brendan Behan. After her arrest and the hanging of two other IRA men in the city, Behan himself remained haunted by events in Birmingham, and repeatedly described those executions in fictional form throughout his later writings. However, the wider European conflict of 1939 meant that local residents had little time to dwell on the IRA campaign, with the ensuing war bringing destruction to Birmingham

---

40   For national figures see Colin Holmes, *John Bull's Island: Immigration and British Society, 1871–1971* (Houndmills: Macmillan, 1988), p. 21.

as well as heralding another massive increase in Irish immigration to the area. Whilst census figures record that the Irish-born residents had numbered 6,470 in 1931, the figure reached 36,349 twenty years later, and 58,961 (or 5.31 per cent of the city) by 1961.

Amongst those who arrived from Ireland during this period were the playwrights David Rudkin and Tom Murphy, and the poor standard of living that they saw being endured by the local Irish population gave both writers the subject matter for their early work, with each man expressing new ideas about cruelty and emigration on the British and Irish stage. At the same time, the condition of the Irish in Birmingham also stirred Ireland's prime minister, Eamon de Valera, to make attempts at intervention, and after he visited Birmingham in person, some of those in the city decided to project a more positive view of emigrant life by organizing the area's first ever St Patrick's Day parade.

These parades soon became a fixed event on the civic calendar, and the Irish grew increasingly prosperous, settled, and confident during the 1960s and early 1970s. But in 1974 the IRA placed bombs at two crowded pubs in the city centre, inflicting the worst death toll of any IRA attack during the 'Troubles'. These explosions exerted a deadening effect on the political and cultural life of the Irish in Birmingham, with the city witnessing a spate of revenge attacks and unjust imprisonments. Indeed, the most notorious part of this backlash saw the jailing and torturing of those innocent men who became known as the 'Birmingham Six', whose treatment eventually came to overshadow the original bombings.

Only in 1991 did a television campaign of investigative reporting and docudrama culminate in the release of the six men, and following this turn of events, the wider Irish population in Birmingham began to recover a sense of self confidence. The ensuing decade saw the restoration of the St Patrick's Day parades that had been abandoned after the explosions, as well as a renaissance of Irish cultural activity in the city. Yet during the final years of the twentieth century, Ireland itself underwent a process of dynamic social and economic change, leaving many of the emigrants of the 1950s and 1960s scarcely recognizing the country, and with Birmingham's theatre becoming one of the places that attempted to make sense of such transformations, staging new works that debated Irish violence, sexuality, and national allegiance. By the start of the new millennium, large numbers of those who had settled in Birmingham during the previous century were dying away, leaving the city with only 28,933 Irish-born residents according to the census of 2001. Yet at the same time, those who had previously been given little opportunity to speak about Irish matters in Birmingham also began to find their voices, with the city producing plays by women writers such as Anne Devlin and Kaite O'Reilly, as well as drama about Irish homosexuality by Billy Cowan.

Problematic Concepts

There remain, however, a number of problems when piecing together the kind of chronology that I have outlined. The first is that many of the Irish who arrived in England during the Victorian and post-1945 periods often worked as seasonal labourers or viewed themselves as temporary residents, and so did not leave children in the area, census returns, nor archives of written material. Secondly, those families that did remain in Birmingham during the second half of the twentieth century faced a more hostile situation than those who settled elsewhere. Whilst the conflict in Northern Ireland and the concomitant public debate about multiculturalism helped to foster scholarly interest in the Irish of many other locations, the scale of the 1974 IRA attack and the reprisals that followed made those of Irish birth or ancestry wary of discussing Ireland in Birmingham. Scholars may have developed some sophisticated ways of analysing Irishness in the late twentieth century, but for a number of years the legacy of the pub bombings served to gag debate in this city.

In addition, anyone attempting to understand the history of Ireland in Birmingham must realize that the term 'Irish' is scarcely uncomplicated, and has shifted and changed in meaning and significance over time. During the past two centuries different groups on the island of Ireland have held mutually incompatible political and social outlooks, spoken different languages, and maintained separate systems of religious belief. Indeed, since 1921 two distinct political states have coexisted on the island, with many of those in the province of Northern Ireland preferring to maintain British rather than Irish allegiances. As a result, any discussion of those from the island arriving in Birmingham must acknowledge both the diversity of the group under examination and the difficulty of recovering some of these varying voices. It is, for instance, difficult to trace the lives of women in England's Irish communities, and these women's roles have been characterized as 'especially invisible' by the social scientist Bronwen Walter.[41] Although my study highlights the work of Irish women in Birmingham since the First World War, surviving records can

---

41   Bronwen Walter, *Outsiders Inside: Whiteness, Place and Irish Women* (London: Routledge, 2001), p. 1.

unfortunately offer very few details of the lives led by such female residents in earlier times.

Similarly, Protestants from the island of Ireland who settled in Birmingham have tended not to show demonstrative evidence of belonging to a distinct Irish community in the way that Irish Catholics have done. As the Irish Studies scholar Brian Walker argues, Protestant arrivals have usually integrated 'easily into mainstream British society, given the absence of religious barriers for them', whereas Catholic emigrants have shown 'a greater tendency to create separate communities thanks to their larger numbers and the impact of religious divisions in society'.[42] In a great deal of popular discourse the term 'Irish' has simply been assumed to incorporate the term 'Catholic', even though, as we shall see, the notion of Irishness in Birmingham has been considerably shaped by, and represented in, the work of individual Irish Protestant residents, including the theatre manager William McCready, the preacher Thomas Finigan, and the dramatist David Rudkin. Of course, even the use of such religious labels can be crudely reductive, with Rudkin and Finigan, for instance, scarcely sharing the same range of theological beliefs and devotional practices.[43] Indeed, the Palestinian academic Edward Said, when based in the USA, warned about the dangers of making generalizations about emigrants, as such men and women may hold complex and contrasting feelings as a result of living simultaneously in two imagined communities, and as a result there may be little 'homophony' even in one individual's experience of exile.[44]

When the Duke of Wellington was reminded of his own Irish birth he reputedly remarked, 'Just because one is born in a stable does not make one a horse', and in the same way, others from Ireland have at times chosen to downplay those characteristics perceived as Irish when living in Birmingham, particularly in the face of persecution or for reasons of personal and economic advantage.[45] Some have remained proud of their Irish homeland, but have

---

42   Brian Walker, '"The Lost Tribes of Ireland": Diversity, Identity and Loss among the Irish Diaspora', *Irish Studies Review* 15:3 (2007), p. 274.

43   In terms of Irish Catholics, David Miller has suggested that at least 50 per cent of Catholics who immigrated because of the Famine did not regularly attend religious services, in 'Irish Catholicism and the Great Famine', *Journal of Social History* 9 (1975), pp. 81–98.

44   Bonnie Marranca, Marc Robinson, and Una Chaudhuri, 'Criticism, Culture, and Performance: An Interview with Edward Said', in *Interculturalism and Performance: Writings from PAJ*, ed. Bonnie Marranca and Gautam Dasgupta (New York: PAJ, 1991), p. 43.

45   Quoted by Dermot Moran, 'Review – A History of Irish Thought', *Notre Dame Philosophical Reviews* (1 September 2003) <http://ndpr.nd.edu/review.cfm?id=1165>

nonetheless undergone various unconscious changes in behaviour and outlook. As James Clifford points out in *The Predicament of Culture*, different groups in modern world societies may be so interconnected by a 'kind of cultural incest' that it would be very difficult to separate out entirely the Irish experience of Birmingham from that of other residents in the area.[46] Those of Irish birth in the city have long lived alongside a range of people from an assortment of backgrounds, with personal and collective memories of Ireland consequently being shaped and affected by the media, discussions, and symbols that predominate in this particular part of England. One only has to hear the changed voice of an Irish-born person who has spent a protracted period of time abroad to realize how emigrants can scarcely be described as having maintained entirely the same kind of life as if they had remained in Ireland.

Conversely, for a number of years Birmingham has also housed those who were born in the English city, but who also lay claim to an Irish identity. So far, the census figures used in this introduction have tended to foreground those men and women born on the island of Ireland. Yet this is not the full story of the Irish in the city. Particularly since the 1950s, a great many people in Birmingham have been born into families that at some stage emigrated from Ireland, and such English-born residents boast varying levels of attachment to their ancestral homeland. Naturally, some believe themselves to be entirely English. But others have attended schools or churches alongside those born in Ireland, have socialized and worked with predominantly first- and second-generation Irish people, and have spent lengthy periods of time in Ireland for holidays, weddings, or other family events. As the human-geographer Catherine Nash points out, for a number of families the very notion of a 'second generation' is scarcely applicable anyway, given the complex cross-generational 'patterns of migration that led to family members' births in England and lives in Ireland, and births in Ireland and lives in England'.[47]

Of course, in general, those who made the initial journey across the sea to England are likely to maintain a more dense network of affinities with the island of Ireland than any descendants, yet the large numbers of people who

---

[accessed 21 May 2008] (para. 1 of 16). For the way that the Irish in Birmingham might at other times adopt more 'English' behaviour, see Iestyn Williams, Máiréad Dunne, and Máirtín Mac an Ghaill, *Economic Needs of the Irish Community in Birmingham* (Birmingham: Birmingham City Council, 1996), p. 58; also Kaite O'Reilly, *Belonging* (London: Faber, 2000), p. 74.

[46]   James Clifford, *The Predicament of Culture: Twentieth-Century Ethnography, Literature, and Art* (Cambridge, MA: Harvard University Press, 1988), pp. 4, 14, 231.

[47]   Nash, *Of Irish Descent*, p. x.

attend the modern St Patrick's Day parades in Birmingham, who particularly seek out the Irish pubs and clubs of the area, and who claim an Irish ethnic background on official forms, indicate that there may be a kind of inadequacy in considering only the Irish-born population to encompass the totality of Ireland in Birmingham. In the 2001 census, for instance, 31,467 people in Birmingham claimed that they belonged to the Irish ethnic group, even though only 22,828 had been born in Ireland.[48] However, this survey does not tell us whether the members of this self-identified ethnic group were attempting to claim a cultural kind of Irishness, or whether they intended to evoke the notion of a migration 'home' that might characterize various other 'diasporic' communities. The cultural theorist David Lloyd has observed that in the USA, where the Irish are now fully integrated into mainstream white society and often display little desire to return to Ireland, those who claim the title 'Irish American' do so in order to seek 'the cultural distinctiveness that they have learnt to see as the "privilege" of ethnic minorities'.[49] The Irish in Birmingham of course experienced a very different history to those who ended up in the USA, and yet there is something of Lloyd's observation that also rings true in the English midlands, particularly since the arrival of a newly fashionable and wealthy Ireland in the 1990s.

In order to incorporate and include all of these multifarious aspects of Irishness, this study will use 'Irish' as a relatively broad term to refer to an identity that is underpinned by some individual or familial experience of living on the geographical island of Ireland, with 'Irish-born' describing that subset of individuals who personally originated from the island. In addition, my discussion will at times require greater specificity, and will indicate, for instance, when I am talking about a person emigrating from Ireland during a certain period, born or living in a particular part of Ireland or Birmingham, or enacting certain kinds of behaviour associated with Irishness. Of course, for a group of arrivals in Birmingham who generally look physically indistinguishable from the pre-existing white English population, various kinds of outward behaviours have usually indicated what sort of connection, if any, a person enjoys with Ireland. But these supposedly Irish characteristics are scarcely fixed and unalterable, just as the Irishness that they signify is not a homogeneous and unchanging concept. By examining those moments of public spectacle when Irish behaviour has been particularly marked or contested, this

---

48   Birmingham City Council, *Cultural Background: 2001 Population Census*, tables 2.11 and 3.1.

49   David Lloyd, *Ireland after History* (Cork: Cork University Press, 1999), p. 102.

book will show that Birmingham's Irish identity has encompassed quite distinct things in different historical contexts, and as we shall see, being associated with Ireland in Birmingham has undergone some profound shifts in meaning between the first part of the nineteenth century and the opening years of our current millennium.

1

Curtain up on 'Brother Paddy'

*The audience, the Birmingham audience, gave me a reception such
as I have never witnessed out of London, and very, very rarely
even there. They stood up all through the house, waving hats and
handkerchiefs, till I was anxious to proceed. I thought to myself:
'Will I not act for you!'*

William Charles Macready[1]

*I look upon Birmingham to be the great Toy Shop of Europe [...]
the most proper Place in England to have a licenced Theatre.*

Edmund Burke[2]

The Grand National Pantomime

By Tuesday, 5 September 1803, William Charles McCready could consider
himself a successful man. The forty-eight-year-old Dubliner had already
pursued an acting career in Ireland and London, had mingled with some of
the leading thespians of the day, and for the past eight years had worked as
manager of the only theatre in Birmingham. To McCready's satisfaction, this
last career move had been the most lucrative part of his life so far, and he
now sat beneath the decorative image of Apollo in his playhouse, the Theatre
Royal on New Street, for the final show of the year's theatrical season.
That evening, before the performance began, he may have looked with
satisfaction at the patrons pushing their way into the expensive boxes, which
were decked out with crimson seats, apple green cushions, and cut-glass

---

1   William Charles Macready, *The Diaries of William Charles Macready, 1833–1851*, ed.
William Toynbee (London: Chapman and Hall, 1912), vol. II, p. 430.

2   'Birmingham, Monday, March 31', *BG*, 31 March 1777, p. 3.

chandeliers.[3] These spectators had made McCready a wealthy man, allowing him to become one of Birmingham's most prominent citizens and to send his two sons to the prestigious Rugby school for the past six months.[4]

On that September evening, McCready might also have glanced down at the pit, where those in the cheaper seats perched in front of the wide proscenium arch, having been drawn to the theatre by the boastful promises of scenic effects that McCready had advertised in that week's local newspaper.[5] Birmingham itself had undergone an unprecedented expansion during the previous century, quadrupling from a modest population of somewhere between 5,000 and 7,000 at the start of the eighteenth century to 23,688 fifty years later, and then roughly tripling in size again to leave the town with 73,670 residents by 1801.[6] Such growth had been based on abundant mineral fuel, supplies of finished iron from the nearby Black Country, and local manufacturers with particular skill at working with metal, allowing the town to supply the booming upper-class predilection for showy ornaments as well as the military's seemingly insatiable demand for guns.[7] McCready knew that Birmingham's workers enjoyed seeing something of their own skill reflected back at them from the stage, with previous plays at the theatre having praised machinery, described the interlinked nature of industry and art, and featured scenes especially designed to reward the 'industrious artisan'.[8] The publicity for McCready's latest production therefore emphasized the play's technical wizardry, proudly making clear that very little on this scale could be seen by audiences outside the English capital. He had asked a number of his metropolitan friends to

3   The rebuilt Birmingham theatre is described in 'The Theatre', *BG*, 15 June 1795, p. 3. See also NYPL, Lincoln Center Library, MWEZ+NC 27,695, folder marked 'no dates', clipping about Birmingham Theatre marked 'Aug 12 20'.

4   Richard Foulkes, 'Macready [M'cready], William (1755–1829)', *Oxford Dictionary of National Biography*, ed. H. C. G. Matthew and Brian Harrison (Oxford: Oxford University Press, 2004), vol. XXXVI, p. 15.

5   R. Crompton Rhodes, *The Theatre Royal, Birmingham, 1774–1924: A Short History* (Birmingham: Moody, 1924), p. 49. *BG*, 5 September 1803, p. 2.

6   Eric Hopkins, 'The Birmingham Economy during the Revolutionary and Napoleonic Wars 1793–1815', *Midland History* 23 (1998), pp. 105–20. London, of course, still dwarfed Birmingham: in 1775, for example, when Birmingham had a population of 40,000, the capital was home to 775,000 people. Eric Hopkins, *The Rise of the Manufacturing Town: Birmingham and the Industrial Revolution* (Phoenix Mill: Sutton, 1998), pp. 26–27.

7   Hopkins, *The Rise of the Manufacturing Town*, pp. 25–26.

8   John Money, 'Taverns, Coffee House and Clubs: Local Politics and Popular Articulacy in the Birmingham Area, in the Age of the American Revolution', *The Historical Journal* 14:1 (1971), p. 20.

arrange new scenes, costumes, and technological innovations for this piece, which featured some complex staging, including at one point a panorama of London that showed the kind of architectural glories that might one day appear in Birmingham if the aspiring town continued to grow and develop. Indeed, the performance culminated with a series of complicated shifts in setting during which the stage displayed 'many mechanical changes and entertaining transformation[s]'.[9] As McCready looked down at those packed into the pit, he saw that these scenic contrivances pleased his Birmingham audience, and in all likelihood anticipated winning further plaudits from the local critics. At this time, provincial journalists could be notoriously catty about regional theatre, but McCready had inspired genuine devotion in Birmingham, where he received repeated praise for his 'liberal and high spirited exertions' and his 'spirit and liberality'.[10] He also won admiration for holding fundraising nights in aid of the local hospital, and in 1802 Admiral Horatio Nelson, the British naval hero, visited the Theatre Royal for a production of *The Merry Wives of Windsor* and praised McCready for being held in 'universal esteem'.[11]

Five years later, from Lancaster Castle prison, McCready must have looked back on such halcyon days in Birmingham with nostalgia. Shortly after that complex performance of September 1803, McCready's wife would die, he would lose his fortune, and he would end up locked inside a jail cell.[12] Yet on that late summer evening, it looked as though the theatre manager should feel nothing but self-satisfaction, with the show onstage giving him cause for particular pride. After all, he celebrated the completion of his eighth season in New Street with a 'grand national pantomime', and although McCready required the actor Andrew Cherry to set down the final script, the entire piece was 'arranged, selected, and invented' by the manager himself; which meant that McCready had formulated the original idea for the production, commissioned the work for the theatre, and produced the play on the stage.[13] As a result, throughout the different parts of the fan-shaped auditorium, up to 2,000 people excitedly peered to see a play composed especially for them

---

9   William Charles Macready and Andrew Cherry, *The Magic of British Liberty*, in John E. Cunningham, *Theatre Royal: The History of the Theatre Royal Birmingham* (Oxford: Ronald, 1950), p. 108.

10   'Birmingham, July 25, 1803', *BG*, 25 July 1803, p. 3; 'Birmingham, September 12, 1803', *BG*, 12 Sept 1803, p. 3; Alan S. Downer, *The Eminent Tragedian: William Charles Macready* (London: Oxford University Press, 1966), p. 10.

11   *BG*, 10 August 1807, p. 4; Rhodes, *The Theatre Royal, Birmingham*, p. 10.

12   Foulkes, 'Macready [M'cready], William (1755–1829)', p. 15.

13   *BG*, 5 September 1803, p. 2.

in Birmingham, rather than the usual hand-me-down versions of pieces made famous in theatres elsewhere.

At this time, of course, a pantomime was a very different kind of affair to the cross-dressed world of Christmas camp with which the form is usually associated today. At the start of the nineteenth century, a pantomime usually still showed more of a debt to the Italian improvised comedy, *commedia dell'arte*, and would often revolve around the tomfoolery, trickery, and disguises of the character Harlequin, who was usually called to the stage by some kind of immortal or magical figure. Over the course of the nineteenth century, the opening sequences that summoned Harlequin gradually gave way to fairytale stories, and Harlequin found himself relegated from the shows altogether. But in 1803 such developments all lay in the future, and the Birmingham pantomime began, as expected, with some conjuring from a Prospero-like stage magician, who with his magic wand summoned Harlequin to face the audience. These two characters then engaged in some knockabout fun, with the magician commanding a group of imps to drag the shrieking figure of Napoleon across the stage. This was topical stuff. At the time of the show, the British fleet was fighting in the Napoleonic wars, and McCready, who had already arranged patriotic performances of *The Threatened Invasion* and *The Surrender of Calais*, decided to conclude the summer with one last anti-French hurrah.[14] Thus the end-of-season pantomime, entitled *The Magic of British Liberty*, saw Napoleon being rudely abused, before the arrival onstage of the play's two main characters: an English mariner called Bill Breeze, and a sailor from Ireland, Patt Bowling.

Patt Bowling

The portrayal of Patt Bowling helped introduce the denizens of Birmingham to a nationality that, until then, had seldom been seen in the town. A handful of soldiers from Ireland had unsuccessfully helped defend Aston Hall from parliamentary forces in 1643, and later parish records describe travellers occasionally passing from Ireland through Birmingham, but only in the second half of the 1700s did Irish people begin to settle in the area.[15] At the start of the nineteenth century, the town boasted a scattering of skilled tradesmen bearing Irish names, including the varnisher Francis Byrne, the cabinetmaker

14   'Theatre, Birmingham', *BG*, 8 August 1803, p. 2.
15   McKenna, 'The Irish in Birmingham: A Scrapbook', pp. 1, 3; Alex Peach, 'Poverty, Religion and Prejudice in Britain' (unpublished doctoral thesis, De Montford University, 2000), pp. 78–79.

William Ryley, the ivory turner Daniel Ryley, the metal plater John Magenis, and the shoemaker Francis Mackaness.[16] However, by far the most famous of Birmingham's Irish residents was William McCready of New Street.

In creating the character of Patt Bowling for *The Magic of British Liberty*, William McCready of course revealed little about what people from Ireland were like in real life. Instead, just as Oscar Wilde would do later in the century, McCready developed an outsider's acute sense of English humour, prejudice, and theatrical taste, and drew on this knowledge to attract audiences to the playhouse. McCready presented an impression of Irishness that Birmingham's spectators would find palatable, and in *The Magic of British Liberty* Patt Bowling and the English shipmate Bill Breeze arrive outside the gates of Calais on a mission to seize the town, before meeting a cowardly and comic Frenchman whom they greet with boasts about Nelson, patriotic songs about the greatness of Britain, and vows to kill the 'Frogs'.[17]

Anyone in the audience who had previously been to the theatre in London would have known that fictional depictions of men from Ireland were hardly a rarity. Ever since the 1600s, the English stage had seen depictions of the 'wild' Irish, and although such portrayals had gradually become less murderous as real-life fears about the threat posed by Irish Catholicism had diminished, by the start of the nineteenth century the Irish character onstage remained an easily recognisable type.[18] He generally enjoyed singing, speaking with a thick brogue, and displaying inordinate loyalty to his master. Although often lazy, the 'stage Irishman' would willingly use his shillelagh in a fight, appreciated food and whiskey, and displayed a comic ability to mangle and confuse the English language.[19]

William McCready may have known little of this stereotype when growing up and working as an upholsterer alongside his father, who ran the family business from Bride Street in Dublin.[20] But the youthful McCready soon

---

16   *Chapman's Birmingham Directory* (Birmingham: Chapman, 1800), pp. 54, 16, 73, 54.

17   Macready and Cherry, *The Magic of British Liberty*, p. 104.

18   See Hayton, 'From Barbarian to Burlesque', p. 13, and Annelise Truninger, *Paddy and the Paycock: A Study of the Stage Irishman from Shakespeare to O'Casey* (Bern: Francke, 1976), p. 23.

19   In the 1700s Irish dramatists themselves found inventive ways of recycling and reinventing the stereotype, with the Irish footman Teague featuring in George Farquhar's *The Twin Rivals*, the talkative and brave Captain O'Blunder appearing in Thomas Sheridan's *The Brave Irishman*, and the rascally character of Lucius O'Trigger starring in *The Rivals* by Sheridan's son Richard Brinsley.

20   Samuel Watson (ed.), *Gentleman's and Citizen's Almanack* (Dublin: Powell, 1770), p. 50;

decided to abandon this career and instead become an actor in Waterford and Dublin, eventually befriending and performing alongside the elderly player Charles Macklin, who had scripted characters 'of Irish distraction' for the London theatre.[21] Macklin warmed to McCready and in 1785 persuaded the young thespian to abandon Ireland for the more remunerative English stage, and then helped McCready to secure engagements in Liverpool and Manchester.[22] In 1786 Macklin eased McCready into employment at the heart of the British dramatic world, the Theatre Royal at Covent Garden in London, and here McCready was welcomed as an actor who 'comes from [...] Dublin, and promises to please in the light and airy parts of comedy', before duly acting in plays that featured comic servants from Ireland.[23] In 1797, for instance, McCready found himself in a production of *The Honest Thieves*, although he avoided playing the obvious part and instead took the role of an English captain who insults a comic 'Irish brute' across the stage.[24] McCready also acted in the 1795 Covent Garden play *The Irish Mimic*, where he again acted as an English captain who insults an Irish immigrant. McCready must have found no little irony in playing this latter role, which required him, using his most cut-glass English tones, to declare that anyone from Ireland, even in disguise, would always be betrayed by innately Irish behaviour, and that although the play's mimic 'fancies he speaks or sings a variety of voices, you can only think yourself in a debating society at Tipperary'.[25]

The fact that McCready himself avoided playing the Irish part on these occasions perhaps indicates something of his feeling for the stereotype, and when he brought the character of Patt Bowling to the Birmingham stage,

John Watson Stewart (ed.), *The Treble Almanack, for the Year MDCCXCVIII* (Dublin: Watson, 1798), p. 75.

21   For example, at the start of Charles Macklin's 1746 play, *A Will or No Will; or, a Bone for the Lawyers*, an Irish character introduces himself by saying, 'My name is Laughlinbullrude rrymackshoughlinbulldowny, at your service ...' Quoted by Owen Dudley Edwards, 'The Stage Irish', in *The Creative Migrant*, ed. Patrick O'Sullivan (London: Leicester University Press, 1994), p. 109; J. C. Trewin, *Mr Macready: A Nineteenth-Century Tragedian and His Theatre* (London: Harrap, 1955), p. 14; Christopher Morash, *A History of Irish Theatre, 1601–2000* (Cambridge: Cambridge University Press, 2002), pp. 52–53.

22   Trewin, *Mr Macready*, p. 14.

23   'Theatre: Covent Garden', *The Times*, 9 September 1786, p. 2; William Archer, *William Charles Macready* (London: Kegan Paul, 1890), p. 3; Trewin, *Mr Macready*, p. 14.

24   Thomas Knight, *The Honest Thieves: A Farce* (London: G. Cawthorn, 1797), pp. 27–28.

25   John O'Keeffe, *The Irish Mimic; or, Blunders at Brighton* (London: Longman, 1795), p. 12.

McCready again avoided the familiar caricature. For one thing, in *The Magic of British Liberty* Patt avoids any servile relationship with his English companion, Bill Breeze. Rather, the two characters are portrayed as brave equals, with Patt boasting of being reliable 'Brother Paddy!' whilst Bill refers to 'Brother Patt'.[26] When a French soldier attempts to draw his sword on the unarmed Englishman, Patt retaliates swiftly to ward off the threat; but this is no display of Ireland's hot-headedness contrasted with English reserve, as Bill quickly joins in beating the Frenchman with considerable vigour.

For another thing, Patt's speech is neither mangled nor ridiculed, and instead the French character is the object of mockery, stuttering and stammering in broken English.[27] This depiction of Irishness perhaps contradicted the audience's presumptions. After all, when G. C. Duggan published a history of *The Stage Irishman* in 1937, he pointed out that although he could find only two main examples of the Irish sailor as a type, on both occasions the Irish character showed either 'a touch of brogue' or that 'Blunders, and bulls are his stock-in-trade'.[28] Indeed, in the years before McCready had moved to Birmingham, London audiences had seen him mocking the 'invincible brogue' of Ireland's speech.[29] Yet in Birmingham's pantomime Patt Bowling draws attention to the 'brogue' as a source of pride rather than shame, punningly highlighting the foot that will help stamp upon the French enemy.[30] McCready clearly enjoyed toying with audience expectations of voices in this way, as he showed when he wrote the farce *The Irishman in London* for Covent Garden in the early 1790s, a work in which he played an Irish immigrant who speaks with such eloquence that the others onstage describe the character as 'an elegant and polite well bred man', whilst a confused and verbose English rival is conversely mistaken for a 'wild Irishman'.[31] Indeed, the critic Christopher Flynn has argued that this earlier play contrasts an 'emptied-out version of Englishness' with Irish and African identities that are rooted in cultural distinctiveness and 'notable histories'.[32] McCready

---

[26]   Macready and Cherry, *The Magic of British Liberty*, pp. 101–2.

[27]   In Macready's earlier play, *The Irishman in London*, an African housemaid speaks in similar broken English. William Charles Macready, *The Irishman in London; or, the Happy African* (Dublin: Perrin, 1793), p. 30.

[28]   Duggan, *The Stage Irishman*, pp. 214–16.

[29]   O'Keeffe, *The Irish Mimic*, p. 12.

[30]   Macready and Cherry, *The Magic of British Liberty*, p. 106.

[31]   Macready, *The Irishman in London*, pp. 25, 17–18.

[32]   *The Irishman in London* proved popular with audiences in the English capital, first appearing at Covent Garden in April 1792, and being performed frequently over the ensuing years, with a final show recorded at the Grecian in December 1844. Christopher

thus attempted to disturb any simplistic national distinctions, showing that someone from Ireland might be just as likely to display refined, serious, and gentlemanly characteristics, whilst an Englishman could equally well exhibit bewilderment, garrulousness, and a lack of self control.

When McCready came to stage *The Magic of British Liberty* in Birmingham, he again shunned the familiar stage servant, and instead tried to show something altogether more courageous. In *Henry V*, Shakespeare had depicted an Irishman called MacMorris assisting British forces in laying siege to Harfleur in France. Shakespeare drew the character crudely, as MacMorris fills the stage with oaths and enthusiasm for violence. But this Irishman also proves one of the bravest characters of *Henry V*, impatient with merely talking about military methods, keen to recommence the fight against the French, and disdainful of the idea that Ireland's interests might be different from those of Britain. William McCready wished to demonstrate a similar kind of Irish identity in Birmingham's pantomime, where the siege of Harfleur is replaced by the siege of Calais, and in which Patt Bowling echoes his Shakespearean predecessor in eagerness for waging war. Just like MacMorris, Patt swears oaths, happily uses violence, and assumes that an Irishman should risk life and limb in loyalty to the Crown. Indeed, even Patt Bowling's name has some distinctly Anglophile connotations. In the pantomime's seafaring context his surname gives an echo of Francis Drake's apocryphal nonchalance before the Spanish Armada, whilst also recalling 'Tom Bowling', that heroic English sailor 'of the manliest beauty' who was the subject of a popular song written by the London theatre composer Charles Dibdin.[33]

Rebellion in Ireland

The fraternal relationship between Patt Bowling and Bill Breeze had an unmistakable political resonance for the audience in Birmingham in 1803, helping to reassure spectators that the French would find it difficult to gain

Flynn, 'Challenging Englishness from the racial margins: William Macready's *Irishman in London; Or; The Happy African*', *Irish Studies Review* 16:2 (2008), pp. 161, 169.

[33] The lyrics of 'Tom Bowling' declared: 'His form was of the manliest beauty, / His heart was kind and soft; / Faithful below he did his duty, / But now he's gone aloft'. Dibdin himself had acted in Birmingham during the 1760s and was composer at Covent Garden shortly before Macready arrived at the theatre. Charles Dibdin, *The Songs of Charles Dibdin* (London: Howe and Parsons, 1842), p. 97; Jon A. Gillaspie, 'Dibdin, Charles', *Oxford Dictionary of National Biography*, ed. H. C. G. Matthew and Brian Harrison (Oxford: Oxford University Press, 2004), vol. XVI, pp. 25–30.

a toehold in Patt's homeland during the current wars. But in reality, many peasants in Ireland felt alienated by the harsh penal laws that prevented Catholics from attending school, voting, and purchasing land. The danger for England was that, given the opportunity, this disaffected population would rally to the French banner, and indeed, from 1791 a separatist group called the United Irishmen grew ever more inspired by continental republicanism, and sought help from Paris to overthrow British rule.[34] In 1796 the French attempted to land in Ireland, and even if this invasion proved abortive, more than 1,000 French soldiers returned two years later and joined with Irish revolutionaries to win a celebrated victory at Castlebar, although here the French soon surrendered, and British forces went on to slaughter some 2,000 Irish rebels.[35]

The Magic of British Liberty alludes to this bitter episode, but insists that the problems were of France's making and that without such interference Ireland would be at peace. The English sailor in the play lambastes the French for having 'ravaged unoffending nations' and for 'marching uncontroul'd through countries, where, for ages, a musquet has never been shoulder'd, or a canon heard to roar'.[36] Meanwhile, Patt threatens to beat the Frenchman 'if ever you shew your dirty whiskers at t'other side of the water'.[37] Such sentiments, alongside McCready's vision of Patt singing 'Rule Britannia', helped to reassure Birmingham that any earlier rebelliousness had been an aberration, and that Ireland would now prove just as stout in defending against France as any other part of the British Isles. Indeed, the appearance of Patt and Bill as mutually supportive sailors, united in fighting for the same cause, provided a theatrical version of the Act of Union, which prime minister William Pitt had pushed through after the events of 1798 and meant Ireland's affairs being managed from the parliament at Westminster rather than from College Green in Dublin.

The Theatre Royal's staging of *The Magic of British Liberty* may therefore have revealed McCready's heartfelt British patriotism during a time of war, but more cynical audience members might also have suspected that the playhouse manager was cannily looking out for his own interests. Although Birmingham had enjoyed an economic boom between 1781 and 1791, the town's valuable export trade had dried up as a result of the Napoleonic wars, and McCready knew that if local businesses suffered, the amount spent on nearby entertainment

---

34   Stuart Semmel, *Napoleon and the British* (New Haven: Yale, 2004), pp. 57–58.

35   Michael J. Turner, *The Age of Unease: Government and Reform in Britain, 1782–1832* (Stroud: Sutton, 2000), p. 99; S. J. Connolly (ed.), *The Oxford Companion to Irish History* (Oxford: Oxford University Press, 2002), p. 264.

36   Macready and Cherry, *The Magic of British Liberty*, p. 101.

37   Macready and Cherry, *The Magic of British Liberty*, p. 105.

correspondingly declined.[38] Although the Theatre Royal could take £200 when full, in that wartime season of 1803 McCready felt hamstrung, and so the play condemned French militarism for disturbing the 'commerce' of old England, with the onstage characters lauding the kind of seafaring bravery that might soon end the hostilities and restore full houses to this playhouse.[39] In addition, when the theatre manager decided how to stage the pantomime, he may have thought carefully about his own personal welfare as well as his financial affairs. During the month before *The Magic of British Liberty*, local newspapers reported another 'Rebellious Conspiracy in Ireland' and 'barbarity unexampled in these kingdoms for ages', as Robert Emmet's United Irishmen reacted against the Act of Union by attempting to capture a number of symbolic buildings in Dublin.[40] These insurgents hoped that their action would inspire revolt across the whole of Ireland, but the attempt proved rushed and ill prepared, with only a small number of the expected participants turning out. When the situation calmed, the authorities found about fifty people dead, including the Lord Chief Justice and his nephew, who had both been gored by revolutionary pikes.[41] Birmingham learned of these events in blood-chilling newspaper reports, which focussed particularly on the way that this murdered pair had been dragged through the streets and 'inhumanly butchered'.[42] In such a climate, William McCready felt little desire to emphasize the kind of Irishness that might have encouraged attacks upon himself, his theatre, or his family. With journalists having described the brutality with which Ireland's revolutionaries had stabbed a Crown official, the Theatre Royal instead portrayed such ferocity being directed towards the French, with Patt Bowling declaring a willingness to thrust a sword down the 'ugly throttle' of England's enemy.[43]

In real life, Ireland's insurrectionists of 1803 had again looked to Paris for assistance, but McCready felt no such Gallic affinities; indeed, during the week that news of the rebellion broke, he and his collaborator Andrew Cherry acted in the Theatre Royal's production of *John Bull's Old Friends*, in which they joined in the song 'French invasion a farce'.[44] When *The Magic of British Liberty* subsequently appeared at the theatre, the performance coincided with the trial

---

38   Hopkins, 'The Birmingham Economy', pp. 105–20.

39   Macready and Cherry, *The Magic of British Liberty*, p. 101; Rhodes, *The Theatre Royal, Birmingham*, p. 49; 'Birmingham, September 12, 1803', *BG*, 12 September 1803, p. 3.

40   'Rebellious Conspiracy in Ireland', *BG*, 1 August 1803, p. 2.

41   Connolly (ed.), *Oxford Companion*, p. 180.

42   'Rebellious Conspiracy in Ireland', *BG*, 1 August 1803, p. 2.

43   Macready and Cherry, *The Magic of British Liberty*, p. 103.

44   'Theatre, Birmingham', *BG*, 8 August 1803, p. 2.

of the pro-French rebels in Dublin, and on the same day that Patt Bowling proclaimed his Anglophilia in the playhouse, Birmingham's newspapers carried news about death sentences for Ireland's revolutionaries.[45] McCready, eager to preserve his popularity with the Birmingham public, showed no fondness for the rebels and had few reservations about reminding the town of Ireland's allegiance to England. After all, Ireland and Scotland sent disproportionately large amounts of men to do battle against Napoleon, and if few in Ireland could feel communal pride in this contribution – with Catholics resenting the penal laws, and Protestants fearing that praise for Irish Catholic combatants might encourage demands for civil rights – McCready enjoyed the exilic status of living in England, and accordingly used his playhouse to celebrate Ireland's contribution to Britain's fighting force.[46]

The Worthy Manager

William McCready took the business of theatre seriously. He became known as a stickler for discipline and timeliness, and whilst the familiar stage stereotype of Irishness might have been that of comic disorder, away from the footlights McCready proved an exacting manager, instilling a strong sense of professionalism in his Birmingham actors. He knew the importance of preparing a show thoroughly, and devised an elaborate system of fines to punish cast members who stumbled onstage at the wrong time during rehearsals, those who refused to take an assigned part, and those who paid no heed to his directions. McCready also extended his sanctions to the performance itself, warning actors that they would receive docked wages for forgetting their lines, for appearing at the front of the house in costume, or for altering any allocated stage garments. The theatre manager subsequently printed and posted his regulations in order that his Birmingham cast knew to meet the exacting standards of the London stage or else face retribution.[47] After all, if things were done with savvy and sophistication at Covent Garden, McCready could see no reason why his aspiring theatre in Birmingham should fail to emulate these same qualities.

In bringing such theatrical professionalism to the English midlands, McCready rejuvenated the Birmingham stage. Before McCready arrived, the banausic town had consistently struggled to support a permanent playhouse, with the Theatre Royal being destroyed by arsonists in 1792, and adjoining a

---

45   'Monday's Post, from the London Gazette', *BG*, 5 September 1803, p. 3.

46   Turner, *Age of Unease*, p. 98.

47   Downer, *The Eminent Tragedian*, pp. 11–12.

slum so dark that even the local law-enforcers walked there in groups of three.[48] The area also contained far fewer leisured middle-class inhabitants than places like London, Bath, or York, and although an assortment of enthusiasts had ensured that at least one venue had been regularly used for dramatic work in Birmingham since 1730, attempts to open a second playhouse had repeatedly bitten the dust.[49] From the mid-1700s the London comedian Richard Yates had brought a professional company to Birmingham during the summer months, in an arrangement that McCready emulated at the turn of the century, but when Yates requested a licence for the Theatre Royal, which would have increased opening times and lengthened the theatrical season, parliament rejected the petition.[50] Although Yates initially gained support from Edmund Burke, who declared a playhouse in Birmingham 'the best Place, that it is probable a Blacksmith's idle Moments will carry him to', the Theatre Royal did not win such a licence until 1807, after McCready had furthered the reputation of the playhouse and put the venue on a firmer footing.[51]

As part of this quest to establish a successful playhouse in Birmingham, McCready knew that he needed to instil a disciplined attitude in his actors. But he also realized that his theatre lacked the glamour of the London stage, and so set about drawing in an ambitious number of star actors. When he arrived in Birmingham he promised the Theatre Royal a stock company that would be complemented with 'a succession of the most capital performers on the London stage', and, with the hint of a threat, declared that he would only remain in Birmingham whilst his efforts met with the 'favour and protection' of the public.[52] His earlier acting career had been tinged with disappointment, as he had failed to live up to the early promise noted by Charles Macklin, and in London had remained in the second tier of roles rather than becoming

---

[48]   Downer, *The Eminent Tragedian*, p. 5; Derek Salberg, *Ring Down the Curtain* (Luton: Cortney, 1980), p. 17.

[49]   Hopkins, *The Rise of the Manufacturing Town*, p. 135.

[50]   Fred Norris, *Birmingham Hippodrome, 1899–1999* (Birmingham: Birmingham Hippodrome Theatre Trust, 1999), p. 60; Rhodes, *The Theatre Royal*, pp. 11, 14.

[51]   'Birmingham, Monday, March 31', *BG*, 31 March 1777, p. 3; P. T. Underdown, 'Religious Opposition to the Licensing of the Bristol and Birmingham Theatres', *University of Birmingham Historical Journal* 6 (1957–58), pp. 149–60; House of Commons, *An Act to Enable His Majesty, His Heirs and Successors to Grant Letters Patent for Establishing a Theatre or Playhouse, under Certain Restrictions, in the Town of Birmingham, in the County of Warwick, Anno Quadragesimo Septimo, Georgii III Regis, Sess. 2, Cap. 44* (London: George Eyre and Andrew Strahan, 1807).

[52]   'Theatre, Birmingham', *BG*, 15 June 1795, p. 3.

a leading light, playing Malcolm in *Macbeth*, Tybalt in *Romeo and Juliet*, and Edmund in *Lear*.[53] Nevertheless, McCready made a number of useful friends at Covent Garden, and when he began work at Birmingham's Theatre Royal he decided to call in some favours. As a consequence, playgoers in Birmingham saw a great variety of different productions during the summer months and grew acquainted with famous London actors such as John Philip Kemble, Sarah Siddons, Sir Peter Teazle, and William T. Lewis.[54] During McCready's first season at Birmingham, he received praise from the local newspaper for bringing 'a Company of Performers superior to any that ever yet left the metropolis, we hope the exertions that have been made, and the great expenses incurred for the public's accommodation and amusement, will not be unremunerated'.[55]

As well as shepherding established stars to Birmingham, McCready also scoured around for newly developing talent. He brought the great tragedian Edmund Kean to Birmingham when Kean remained relatively unknown, and also introduced the town to 'Young Roscius', an actor who at the age of twelve played Shakespearean heroes. Birmingham thus saw the first English appearance of Roscius, and spectators proved so appreciative of McCready's efforts to present such novelty that the theatre manager organized another successful visit of the young actor in the following year.[56] McCready also used his London contacts to bring to Birmingham a number of plays that had recently proved successful at Covent Garden, including works with comic Irish characters such as his own *The Irishman in London*, the piece called *The Irish Mimic* that he had previously acted in whilst at London, and a drama in which McCready himself now played a faithful servant from Ireland, *Honest Thieves*.[57]

---

53 Downer, *The Eminent Tragedian*, p. 6. Macready gained a reputation in London for accurately knowing his lines, but being rather uninspiring, summed up in the couplet: 'Tho' than Macready there are many better, / Who, pray, like him, so perfect to a letter?' (Archer, *William Charles Macready*, p. 4).

54 Trewin, *Mr Macready*, p. 15; and Downer, *The Eminent Tragedian*, p. 8.

55 'The Theatre', *BG*, 15 June 1795, p. 3.

56 Archer, *William Charles Macready*, p. 9.

57 'Theatre, Birmingham', *BG*, 20 July 1807, p. 3; 'Theatre, Birmingham', *BG*, 17 August 1807, p. 3; 'Theatre, Birmingham', *BG*, 24 August 1807, p. 3. Birmingham's spectators also saw Macready playing the Irish haymaker, Darby Leary, in a Birmingham production of *Rosina*, as well as watching the reappearance of a work that Richard Yates had brought to Birmingham's King Street Theatre as early as 1776, *The Irish Widow*. 'Theatre, Birmingham', *BG*, 1 June 1807, p. 3; 'Theatre, Birmingham', *BG*, 30 July 1804, p. 2; *BG*, 19 August 1776, p. 3.

In addition to importing famous actors and popular plays, McCready knew that his audiences appreciated technically advanced stage business, and so paid close attention to scene design and lighting effects.[58] The kind of impressive display that he arranged for *The Magic of British Liberty* appeared in his other productions, and indeed the surviving promptbook from a later McCready show staged outside Birmingham reveals how he drove his stage manager to distraction by demanding that the audience should see cliffs with icicles, a frozen lake with 'islands of frost', and even an Aurora Borealis.[59] Nevertheless, such hard work ensured that when the playhouses in London closed during the summer months, some of the biggest stars, the best shows, and the most elaborate scenic devices of the day travelled up to Birmingham. Little wonder that a local guidebook noted that the New Street theatre would be 'open during four months in the summer, viz. June, July, August, and September, and the most eminent London and Provincial performers are usually engaged for the season. The machinery and scenery are excellent, and the Manager spirited and attentive'.[60] As a result, when the curtain fell on both *The Magic of British Liberty* and the theatrical season of 1803, the audience applauded the efforts of the manager, hoping that he would stay in town during the following year and offer more of the same.

McCready did indeed remain in Birmingham for the time being, but disaster struck in 1807 when the landlord of the Theatre Royal decided to take advantage of McCready's success by doubling the rent.[61] In response, McCready took umbrage and, having already toured for short seasons to nearby towns, now decided to abandon the region altogether and work instead at a theatre in Manchester.[62] However, this new venture soon proved a professional and financial catastrophe. Although he tried to reproduce his Birmingham accomplishments by inviting actors such as 'Young Roscius' to his playhouse, McCready had now been away from English capital for a decade and no longer enjoyed the kind of intimacy with the London stage that might tempt the brightest new performers to travel northwards. Indeed, Roscius's own star was now on the wane, and the Manchester audience criticized McCready's tired-looking fare. After the impresario had failed to impress with his imported actors he decided

58   Downer, *The Eminent Tragedian*, p. 8.

59   Kathleen Barker and Joseph Macleod, 'The Macready Prompt Books at Bristol', *Theatre Notebook* 4:4 (1950), p. 76.

60   James Bisset, *A Poetic Survey Round Birmingham* (Birmingham: Swinney and Hawkins, 1800), p. 25.

61   Salberg, *Ring Down the Curtain*, p. 18.

62   Foulkes, 'Macready [M'cready], William (1755–1829)', p. 15.

to win the public over by force of personality, but when he took to the boards he found his own Irish accent criticized. Worst of all, as the economic climate worsened, McCready's business partner demanded repayment of some £3,500 invested in the Manchester playhouse, and when McCready proved unable to pay, the theatre manager was promptly thrown into jail.[63]

In McCready's absence, the Theatre Royal in Birmingham lay unoccupied before being rented by the manager of a playhouse in Worcester, who attempted to take advantage of New Street's newly licensed status by installing stoves and running a winter as well as summer season.[64] But the new manager singularly failed to put the Birmingham playhouse back into the black, and he soon abandoned the entire enterprise. By 1810 McCready had been released from prison, and the owners of the Theatre Royal attempted to revive their fortunes by reinstalling the former favourite and hoping to recreate his earlier triumphs. However, McCready now lacked the lustre that once coaxed the best London actors, musicians, and stage designers to the English midlands, and he found increasing difficulty in trying to fill the playhouse as the Napoleonic wars dragged on. When in 1812 he again considered leaving the town to pursue some improvident ventures elsewhere, the local newspaper encouraged its readers to attend a special benefit show for the manager, asking for 'one grand effort [to] fill the house', and reminding Birmingham of 'what sums of money have been exhausted, what industry and fatigue have been borne, and what anxious care our worthy Manager has displayed'.[65] Nevertheless, despite such exhortations, when the theatre opened for the 1813 season the worthy manager had indeed departed. During the ensuing years Birmingham saw the Theatre Royal being run by an assortment of different actors and entrepreneurs, until in the 1830s the stage manager Mercer Simpson took charge, and he and his family ran the playhouse until the 1890s, restoring the venue's flagging fortunes by following McCready in building a stock company and using pantomimes to draw in the Birmingham crowds.[66] Meanwhile, McCready himself roved haphazardly from theatre to theatre in a vain and impecunious bid to repeat his earlier Birmingham success, travelling to Carlisle, then to Berwick, then Dumfries, and on to Newcastle-upon-Tyne, before quitting the north of the country to settle in Bristol. Here in the southwest he did finally recreate some of the eminence that he had enjoyed in Birmingham, and also returned to Irish comedy, at one point

---

63   Archer, *William Charles Macready*, p. 10.

64   Salberg, *Ring Down the Curtain*, p. 18; 'Theatre Royal, Birmingham', *BG*, 15 August 1808, p. 5.

65   'Birmingham, September 28, 1812', *BG*, 28 September 1812, p. 3.

66   Rhodes, *The Theatre Royal*, pp. 17–20; Salberg, *Ring Down the Curtain*, pp. 19–21.

giving detailed instructions to M. R. Carroll, then a favourite in such shows, on how to exploit the slapstick potential of various stage scenes.[67] Having revived his fortunes, McCready finally died, a respected Freemason, on 11 April 1829, and was buried in Bristol Cathedral one week later.[68]

McCready's Influence

Despite the maverick course that McCready's career had followed, by the time of his death he had left a lasting impression on the local and national stage. His tenure at New Street's Theatre Royal had established Birmingham as a location that could attract the major stars of the day, and he had left the region with a licensed venue that was no longer restricted to performing on only 60 nights a year. Aside from two or three short-lived ventures, the Theatre Royal remained the only place to show drama in the town until the second half of the nineteenth century, and encouraged those in the English midlands to develop higher expectations of what they ought to find in a playhouse.[69]

In 1808, when McCready had taken charge of the Birmingham theatre for the second time, his straitened circumstances led to another important development for the nineteenth-century stage. The theatre manager's initial move to the town had seen him bringing his five-year-old son, William Charles, from prep school in Kensington to attend boarding school at St Paul's Square, Birmingham. When the boy reached ten, he was sent to Rugby, but during the holidays he practically lived at the New Street playhouse, seeing top-class actors and carefully rehearsed shows.[70] However, the theatre manager's losses in Manchester forced his son to abandon Rugby, and the boy resorted instead to training for the stage, making an acting debut in Birmingham in June 1810 as Romeo. The Theatre Royal audience, already so well disposed to the name of McCready, gave the debutant such a good reception that a life on the boards beckoned, with Birmingham's newspaper predicting his 'future fame and prosperity', and with the young actor expressing his 'gratitude to a liberal Public for the fostering Encouragement and cheering Applause bestowed on his first Dramatic Efforts'.[71]

The young William Charles Macready (who generally spelt his surname with an extra 'a') went on to develop his own distinctive acting style during

---

67   Barker and Macleod, 'The Macready Prompt Books at Bristol', p. 79.
68   Foulkes, 'Macready [M'cready], William (1755–1829)', p. 14.
69   Salberg, *Ring Down the Curtain*, pp. 18, 38–39.
70   Trewin, *Mr Macready*, p. 19.
71   Downer, *The Eminent Tragedian*, p. 29.

the next decade, and toured around Britain's theatres to great acclaim.[72] He became friends with Charles Dickens, enjoyed being praised as 'sublime' by Tennyson, and far surpassed his father's London achievements by managing both the Covent Garden and Drury Lane theatres.[73] But, like other children born to parents from Ireland, the younger William Charles Macready may sometimes have felt the tug of two national identities. He appeared sufficiently English for his 1849 *Macbeth* in New York to be surrounded by an angry mob protesting at London's callous attitude to Ireland's potato famine, and for his performance to be interrupted by cries of 'Down with the English hog!'[74] Yet Dublin audiences might also 'feel satisfaction in his success' and he could be associated with characteristics felt to be typically Irish: Dickens paired the actor with the Cork-born painter Daniel Maclise when referring to the duo as 'the two Macs'; John Ruskin may have hinted at Macready's ethnic origin in referring to 'the Irish ruffian who appeared in "Hamlet"'; and a later theatre historian J. C. Trewin wrote of Macready, 'Half a Celt, he had certain racial traits: intolerance, a long memory, acute touchiness, a way of smouldering over ancient or fancied wrongs. But he was also affectionate and generous, loyal to his friends, creatively imaginative'.[75]

When the younger Macready acted as Macbeth in 1835, he in turn inspired another second-generation Irishman to begin a celebrated acting career. The fourteen-year-old Barry Sullivan had been born in Birmingham to parents from Cork, but after seeing *Macbeth* decided to travel to his parent's homeland and commence a life on the stage that would see Sullivan become known as once of the most famous Shakespearean actors of the day across Ireland, Britain, and Australia.[76] And in a roundabout way, this theatrical baton eventually passed back to Birmingham, as the founder of the Birmingham Repertory Theatre (who

---

72   Downer, *The Eminent Tragedian*, p. 81.

73   Tennyson quoted by Trewin, *Mr Macready*, p. 8.

74   Michael Dobson, 'Let him be Caesar!', *London Review of Books*, 2 August 2007, p. 17; Nigel Cliff, *The Shakespeare Riots: Revenge, Drama, and Death in Nineteenth-Century America* (New York: Random House, 2007), p. xviii.

75   John Finlay, *Miscellanies: The Foreign Relations of the British Empire, the Internal Resources of Ireland, Sketches of Character, Dramatic Criticism, etc, etc, etc.* (Dublin: Cumming, 1835), p. 276; Dickens and Ruskin quoted by Fintan Cullen, 'Maclise and Shakespeare', in *Daniel Maclise 1806–1870: Romancing the Past*, ed. Peter Murray (Kinsale: Gandon, 2008), p. 175; Trewin, *Mr Macready*, p. 24.

76   Robert M. Sillard, *Barry Sullivan and His Contemporaries* (London: Fisher Unwin, 1901), vol. I, pp. 1, 18, 23. Sullivan found particular fame in Liverpool, where he was championed as an Irish Catholic performer. See Belchem, *Irish, Catholic and Scouse*, p. 230.

we shall encounter in chapter five) would owe his initial attraction to the stage, as well as his Christian name, to his parent's enthusiasm for Barry Sullivan.[77]

Hence William McCready's work at the start of the 1800s continued to impact the local theatre for many years after the actor-manager himself had died, with later audiences having good cause to feel affection for his name, and to remember how their quondam theatre manager had helped enhance the reputation and prestige of the town. When the younger William Charles Macready in turn grew old and planned his retirement from the stage, he found himself rewarded with a proud send-off from the audience at the Theatre Royal, and the tail-end of his career in 1849 saw Birmingham's spectators giving him just as hearty a standing ovation as they had done when he trod the boards under his father's tutelage almost four decades earlier. The elderly star now noted gratefully, 'The applause was fervent, the attention deep, and the reception, when I was called on, equal to the first appearance'.[78]

---

[77]   J. C. Trewin, *The Birmingham Repertory Theatre 1913–1963* (London: Barrie and Rockliff, 1963), p. 3.

[78]   Macready, *Diaries*, vol. II, p. 430.

2

The Birmingham Political Union

*It was my first effort in the Council of the Birmingham Union, to
enlist the virtuous feelings of Englishmen in the cause of injured
Irishmen, and, to the honour of Englishmen, I am happy to say,
that I completely succeeded.*

Thomas McDonnell [1]

*Above all, Ireland owed a debt of deepest gratitude to the men of
Birmingham, but for whose exertions — and he spoke the language of
undoubted truth — the Reform Bill would never have been passed.*

Daniel O'Connell [2]

New Arrivals

Early one morning at the start of 1832, Father Thomas Michael McDonnell
must have felt a surge of panic. The Catholic priest had arranged for the
people of Birmingham to be addressed by a famous speaker from Ireland who
would be arriving in only a few hours. But at the last moment the plans of
this lanky cleric had started unravelling. Nightmarishly, the local hotels had
one by one refused to host the gathering, and McDonnell started to run out
of options about where to turn next. As a final resort, he decided to approach
the owner of Birmingham's largest indoor venue, a vast hall usually used
to sell horses, close to the central market area. The hall's dandyish owner
was one of Birmingham's wealthy self-made men, who strutted around the
town dressed fashionably in nankeen trousers, cut-away coat, and stovepipe

---

1   Thomas McDonnell, 'The Rambler in Ireland', *Catholic Magazine* 5:37 (1834),
p. 114.
2   'Mr O'Connell in Birmingham', *BG*, 18 December 1837, p. 2.

hat.[3] But with time ticking away, he took sympathy on the priest. After all, public meetings and boxing matches had occurred at the hall in the past, and no horse sale had been scheduled for that day.[4] A presumably thankful Father McDonnell then dashed away to drum up an audience by printing a number of last-minute posters, and as he did so, the venue's owner may have smiled in puzzlement about these arrangements, wondering why a crowd of people with no hope of making a penny from any commercial transactions would, at such late notice, flock to see a speaker from faraway Kerry in a building that reeked so strongly of damp hay, fresh manure, and the tang of horse piss.[5]

Part of the reason for the orator's popularity was that, in the early years of the 1800s, immigrants from Ireland had arrived in Birmingham in significant numbers for the first time. During this period, of course, the town filled with all kinds of newcomers, as England experienced a general population movement from the countryside to urban areas. Yet for those from Ireland, a move to Birmingham was all too often a dire necessity, with many being compelled to leave their homes by desperate hardship, and with most of the immigrants hailing from the impoverished areas of Mayo and Roscommon.[6] Centuries of colonial settlement had left peasants farming the thin and rocky soil of western Ireland, and by the nineteenth century the country's rising population struggled to subsist on small plots of land that had often been subdivided by families many times. In some places, the poor harvests of 1816 to 1817 and 1822 brought starvation. On top of all this, the 1800 Act of Union had imposed a doctrinaire free-trade philosophy on Ireland, ignoring the fact that the country's small manufacturers could scarcely compete with their larger English counterparts. By 1816 the first regular steamboat service had therefore begun operating between Ireland and Britain, with many poor men and women journeying across the sea. During the next decade, news of public works or industrial projects in England spread quickly around the west of Ireland, and unskilled labourers travelled to lay roads or dig canals.[7]

---

3   See John Frederick Herring's portrait of Beardsworth, 'Birmingham, with Patrick Conolly up, and his Owner John Beardsworth (1830)', in *The Tate Gallery: Illustrated Catalogue of Acquisitions 1978–80* (London: Tate Gallery, 1981), pp. 29–30.

4   Pierce Egan, *Pierce Egan's Book of Sports* (London: Tegg, 1832), p. 119.

5   'Mr O'Connell in Birmingham', *Birmingham Journal*, 21 January 1832, p. 3.

6   The 1851 census documents that well over half of those aged over twenty in the town had been born elsewhere. Davis, *The Irish in Britain*, p. 90; Hopkins, *The Rise of the Manufacturing Town*, p. 58.

7   Chinn, *Birmingham Irish*, pp. 39–41; Barbara M. Kerr, 'Irish Seasonal Migration to Great Britain, 1800–38', *Irish Historical Studies* 3 (1943), pp. 370, 374; David Fitzpatrick,

Unlike William McCready, the majority of migrants who followed him to Birmingham belonged to the Roman Catholic Church, and the priest at St Chad's in Shadwell Street estimated that although no more than 100 Irish could be found amongst the faithful when the venue was founded in 1807, by about 1826 there had been such an increase that 'my chapel would not hold my congregation by many hundreds'.[8] In the mid-1830s, when Birmingham's total population had grown to somewhere in excess of 107,000, residents variously estimated the Irish population of the town at somewhere between 6,000 and 11,000.[9] Of course, such figures must be treated with caution: the higher estimates doubtless include the second generation on top of the original arrivals from Ireland, as well as the seasonal workers who lived in Birmingham for only part of the year. The census of 1841 gives the far lower figure of 4,683 Irish-born residents in the town.[10] But whatever the true number, the situation in Birmingham had undoubtedly transformed since the time when the town's inhabitants had been less likely to encounter Irishness in the streets than in the fictional creations of the Theatre Royal.

Those real-life men and women who arrived from Ireland generally boasted little material wealth, and a parliamentary enquiry heard that the newcomers were heavy drinkers, brawlers, and 'the very pests of society'.[11] In turn the Irish developed their own stereotypes of the English, with a correspondent for the *Cork Examiner* describing how many in Birmingham 'live as brutes'.[12] Yet the experience of those English workers who grew to know the Irish population could contradict the idea that the two groups necessarily felt antagonistic towards one another, and that the immigrants had reprehensible habits and morals. For example, one English plasterer in Birmingham stated:

'Irish Emigration in the Later Nineteenth Century', *Irish Historical Studies* 22 (1980), pp. 136–37.

[8]   McCready married his wife at the Anglican collegiate church in Manchester, which later became Manchester Cathedral, his son was baptised at the Anglican St Pancras parish church on Euston road, and the elder William McCready was buried in the Church of England cathedral in Bristol. Foulkes, 'Macready [M'cready], William (1755–1829)', pp. 14–15; Richard Foulkes, 'Macready, William Charles (1793–1873)', *Oxford Dictionary of National Biography*, ed. H. C. G. Matthew and Brian Harrison (Oxford: Oxford University Press, 2004), vol. XXXVI, p. 15; *Reports from Commissioners: Poor Laws (Ireland)*, p. 475.

[9]   *Reports from Commissioners: Poor Laws (Ireland)*, pp. 477–78, 475.

[10]   Chinn, *Birmingham Irish*, p. 39.

[11]   *Reports from Commissioners: Poor Laws (Ireland)*, p. 480.

[12]   Comments reprinted in 'How the Irish Fought at Birmingham', *The Nation*, 6 July 1867, p. 724.

If it was not for the Irish we could not get the work done. I never observed that they taught bad habits; nothing of the kind. I think that the prejudice in England against the Irish labourers arises from not being acquainted with them [...] The work of this town could not be done without the Irish labourers.[13]

Another person who felt deeply impressed by the Irish people he met in Birmingham was Father Thomas McDonnell, the priest of St Peter's Church off Broad Street. This cleric bore an Irish name, but as he had been born in Surrey and adopted when young by an English family in Oxfordshire, he actually had little connection with Ireland until he moved to Birmingham in 1824 and met the recent arrivals.[14] Yet once in Birmingham, the cleric found himself enjoying the company of those who packed his chapel, and as a result he worked hard to help them, with his church taking particular care to clothe and educate a group of local Irish orphans whom the congregation labelled 'The children of St Patrick'.[15] In addition, Father McDonnell became concerned with Ireland's political worries, and soon befriended the most famous Irishman of that generation.

At that time, the major issue which inflamed Ireland was Catholic emancipation. Across the islands, McDonnell's co-religionists were banned from holding senior government offices, acting as judges, or sitting in parliament, an injustice felt particularly keenly in Ireland, where four-fifths of the population were Catholic.[16] However, the Kerry lawyer Daniel O'Connell had begun to wage an influential campaign against such discrimination, setting up a popular organization called the Catholic Association, and coordinating hundreds of mass meetings and petitions. During the 1828 parliamentary elections in county Clare, for instance, he arranged 1,600 simultaneous rallies.[17] News of the campaign soon reached Birmingham, and Father McDonnell decided to meet the Irish hero, probably seeing O'Connell for the first time at a meeting of the Catholic Association in London, after which the two men enjoyed a firm friendship. As time went by, the priest repeatedly travelled to address

---

13   *Reports from Commissioners: Poor Laws (Ireland)*, pp. 479–81.

14   Joseph Gillow, *A Literary and Biographical History, or Bibliographical Dictionary of the English Catholics*, 4 vols (New York: Burt Franklin, 1969), vol. IV, p. 372.

15   'Records of Catholicity in the Midland Districts from Penal Times', *Birmingham Catholic Magazine*, September 1913, pp. 353–54.

16   Connolly (ed.), *Oxford Companion*, p. 79.

17   Kevin Whelan, 'Daniel O'Connell: The Kerry Proteus', in *Daniel O'Connell*, ed. Kevin Whelan (Dublin, Keough-Notre Dame Centre, 2003), p. 27.

O'Connell's gatherings in the English capital, and the politician expressed feelings for McDonnell of 'personal regard, identity of political sentiments' and 'veneration for his sacerdotal functions'.[18] McDonnell soon established a branch of the Catholic Association in Birmingham, with O'Connell arriving in town to address this new offshoot in 1825.[19] Eventually, as a result of O'Connell's campaign, Westminster granted the relief measure, allowing Catholics to hold public office from 1829.[20] Accordingly, O'Connell himself took a seat in the London parliament, and became popularly acclaimed by the title of 'Liberator', with Father McDonnell urging the Irish in Birmingham to 'come forward, and cheer on the patriot in his career of glory'.[21]

The Monster Meetings

At this stage Birmingham had no MP of its own, and many in the town felt that this situation paralleled the lack of representation that had encouraged Ireland's Catholics to join O'Connell's crusade. Indeed, Birmingham had less of a parliamentary voice than some of England's deserted villages, but the town had long been a centre of advanced political thinking and radical residents now became obsessed by the idea of emulating the way that O'Connell had achieved Catholic emancipation.[22] Local reform leaders decided to set up their own organization called the Birmingham Political Union, modelled on O'Connell's earlier Catholic Association, and they described the need for 'Union – such as the Irish exhibited', remembering how 'the Irish people refused to break the law, and yet they moved onward in a sullen, patriotic, and determined course, until they had accomplished their objective'.[23]

---

18   Daniel O'Connell, *Correspondence of Daniel O'Connell*, ed. Maurice R. O'Connell, 8 vols (Dublin: Irish Manuscripts Commission, 1972–80), vol. VII, p. 109.

19   O'Connell addressed a gathering at the Royal Hotel in May 1825. J. Langford, *A Century of Birmingham Life; or, A Chronicle of Local Events, from 1741 to 1841*, 2 vols (Birmingham: Osborne, 1868), vol. II, pp. 460, 464.

20   Alvin Jackson, *Home Rule: An Irish History 1800–2000* (London: Weidenfeld and Nicolson, 2003), p. 13; Judith Champ, 'Priesthood and Politics in the Nineteenth Century: The Turbulent Career of Thomas McDonnell', *Recusant History* 18:3 (May 1987), p. 291.

21   'Mr. O'Connell', *Catholicon* 1:6 (1836), p. 303.

22   Chris Upton, *A History of Birmingham* (Chichester: Phillimore, 1993), p. 111. Nonconformists had flooded to Birmingham ever since the Five Mile Act of 1665 had forbidden their preaching in other towns, and these settlers brought with them Leveller ideas of religious toleration and an extended franchise. British Association for the Advancement of Science, *Handbook of Birmingham* (Birmingham: Hall and English, 1886), p. 105.

23   'Birmingham Reform Meeting', *BG*, 14 May 1832, p. 1.

It was little surprise, then, to find Birmingham's reform leaders making overtures to Father McDonnell, flattering him and his Church in an attempt to persuade the one local man who enjoyed a close relationship with O'Connell to help with the region's new political enterprise.[24] In the event, McDonnell proved eager to assist, soon acting as one of the new union's most prominent orators, and according to the local press becoming 'perhaps better known as a public political disputant, than as a member of the Roman Catholic priesthood'.[25] In fact, for McDonnell, the Birmingham Political Union was a kind of continuation of the earlier Catholic Association. After all, Birmingham's radicals wanted parliamentary representation for their own town, but also campaigned for a much more widespread electoral reform that would allow all men to vote and enable the poor to become MPs. Meanwhile, Daniel O'Connell wholeheartedly supported such ideas, wishing to make the Irish and British representation in parliament more equitable, and campaigning to make Westminster increasingly democratically accountable. In the month after the Birmingham reformers had formed their union, they sent a delegate to meet O'Connell in person, and he quickly announced his affinity with their cause. Indeed, when he learned about the Birmingham Political Union, the Irishman felt impressed enough to enquire about paying a subscription, and then joined the new organization, writing to Birmingham:

> I am quite convinced that the British and Irish nations cannot retain their stations amidst the powers of the world; neither can their people be restored to plenty and prosperity without a radical reform of the law and of the present corrupt state of representation. To these great objects I devote all my faculties, and I beg, with the view to the attaining of these great objects, to have my humble name enrolled on the Birmingham Reform Union.[26]

Those in Birmingham realized that during the previous emancipation campaign, Daniel O'Connell's mass meetings had allowed the 'Liberator' to demonstrate Catholic numerical superiority in Ireland and to highlight the absurdity of excluding this bulk of politically active people from representation in government. The Birmingham reformers now decided to coordinate similar gatherings, and held a series of monster meetings at Newhall Hill (today a concreted part of the Jewellery Quarter). Just like William McCready at the

---

[24] 'Mechanics Institute', *Birmingham Journal*, 9 January 1830, p. 2.

[25] 'Birmingham, Jan 23, 1832', *BG*, 23 January 1832, p. 3.

[26] O'Connell, *Correspondence*, vol. IV, pp. 128–29.

start of the century, the local reformers knew that the residents of their drab town appreciated the sight of impressive scenery and colourful display, and in October 1831, the Birmingham Political Union organized probably the largest political gathering ever seen in Britain, in an effort to persuade the House of Lords to pass electoral reform measures. Birmingham's church bells summoned between 50,000 and 150,000 men, women, and children to Newhall Hill, where bands played, banners waved, and the Birmingham Political Union formed grand processions.[27]

When the meeting failed to move the peers in London, Father McDonnell next invited Daniel O'Connell himself to Birmingham, and this was the occasion on which the priest had to utilize the town's cavernous horse market, as local hoteliers feared that the cleric and the 'Liberator' might inspire a Roman Catholic jamboree. The historian D. G. Paz has argued that by 1850 Birmingham would be 'officially on the anti-Catholic side', and that the attacks on local Irish Catholics in 1867 (which we shall encounter in the following chapter) were the culmination of 'a thirty-year history of well-organized anti-Catholicism' in the town.[28] In Birmingham's reluctance to provide a venue for O'Connell in the early 1830s there is perhaps a hint of that nationwide anti-Catholicism that would become so particularly pronounced in Birmingham during the ensuing years. Yet despite these organizational tribulations, a crowd of 15,000 to 20,000 did congregate to cheer and welcome the politician in January 1832.[29] Many of these supporters doubtless came from the Irish population of Birmingham, who would consistently turn out in large numbers to applaud later high-profile visitors from Ireland.[30] But O'Connell also attempted to appeal to a wider circle of radicals, declaring the town's lack of an MP 'monstrous' and stating that his mission 'was to assist in putting an end to such a fraudulent system'. Some of the leading Birmingham reformers had stayed away from this meeting, fearing, like the hoteliers, that O'Connell's visit might become a 'Romish' event with only a 'scanty sprinkling of respectability', but nevertheless O'Connell

---

[27] Carlos Flick, *The Birmingham Political Union and the Movements for Reform in Britain* (Folkestone: Dawson, 1978), pp. 59, 62; Edward Pearce, *Reform!: The Fight for the 1832 Reform Act* (London: Jonathan Cape, 2003), p. 165.

[28] D. G. Paz, *Popular Anti-Catholicism in Mid-Victorian England* (Stanford: Stanford University Press, 1992), pp. 195, 257.

[29] 'Birmingham, Jan 23, 1832', *BG*, 23 January 1832, p. 3.

[30] For instance, when Father Mathew, the famous temperance reformer, arrived in Birmingham in 1843 he was greeted by crowds of Irishmen, and during the Home Rule debates a number of Irish politicians received a warm welcome in the town. See chapter 4 of this study, and Ziesler, 'The Irish in Birmingham', p. 68.

generously described how he endorsed the Birmingham campaign for political change with all his 'heart and soul'.[31] At the end of the meeting, throngs of supporters escorted both O'Connell and Father McDonnell through the streets, and as the horse-drawn carriage of the 'Liberator' set forth to Westminster, McDonnell lead cheers from the doorway of the Swan Hotel.[32]

Two months after O'Connell's visit, the House of Commons decided to pass a new bill that would grant the changes requested by Birmingham's reformers. But the House of Lords remained intransigent and looked likely to block any such move. In response, the Birmingham reformers decided to organize another meeting at Newhall Hill for 7 May, which became one of the most famous public meetings of the nineteenth century. Excellent weather brought out – according to the official estimate, which was undoubtedly exaggerated – 'at least 200,000 persons' onto the hill and into the adjoining streets, with marchers stretching out for four miles, and with the reformers attracting cross-community support.[33] As well as being attended by O'Connell's supporters, the meeting also attracted members of the Orange movement, founded in Armagh during the 1790s to commemorate William of Orange's victories over Catholics in Ireland, and first appearing in Birmingham in 1807, with six lodges being established here by 1830.[34] Unsurprisingly, the Orangemen had opposed Daniel O'Connell's Catholic emancipation campaign, and consistently attempted to bolster the existing Protestant ascendancy. Yet, possibly because the Birmingham reform cause had generally proved friendly to Protestantism and hostile to insurrection, the small group of Birmingham Orangemen attended this Newhall Hill gathering in a show of support for reform. Of course, such a display was highly unusual, as Donald MacRaild has explained, '[O]ne of the early and persistent selling-points for Orangeism was its utility as a bulwark against radicalism and a restive, protean working class'.[35] These enthusiasts subsequently found themselves lambasted by their wider Orange brethren for showing such 'un-orange and improper conduct', and the organization in the town then withered away until a revival in the 1860s.[36]

---

[31]   'Mr O'Connell in Birmingham', *Birmingham Journal*, 21 January 1832, p. 3.

[32]   'Birmingham, Jan 23, 1832', *BG*, 23 January 1832, p. 3.

[33]   Flick, *The Birmingham Political Union*, p. 80; Pearce, *Reform!*, p. 273; 'Second Reform Meeting at Newhall Hill', *BG*, 14 May 1832, p. 2.

[34]   Davis, 'Birmingham's Irish Community', p. 41.

[35]   Donald M. MacRaild, 'Networks, Communication and the Irish Protestant Diaspora in Northern England, c.1860–1914', in *Irish Migration, Networks and Ethnic Identities Since 1750*, ed. Enda Delaney and Donald M. MacRaild (Abingdon: Routledge, 2007), p. 167.

[36]   *Report from the Select Committee Appointed to Inquire into the Origin, Nature, Extent and*

At Newhall Hill, resolutions in favour of reform passed amidst hearty applause, after which a deputation took the documents to Daniel O'Connell in London for presentation to Parliament.[37] The House of Lords now began to fear that agitation such as that in Birmingham might be leading England towards revolution, and grudgingly allowed the 'great' reform bill to become law in June 1832. As a result, Birmingham received direct parliamentary representation for the first time, and at the ensuing election, delighted voters returned two leaders of the Birmingham Political Union as MPs for the new parliamentary borough.[38] Father McDonnell made sure to highlight Daniel O'Connell's contribution to these developments, stating that England 'owes him a tribute of gratitude for her truly popular charter of rights – the Reform Bill' and observing that the residents of Birmingham 'hailed him as their deliverer, from a conviction that the Catholic Association was not only the prototype but the parent of their Union, which exacted from the fears of the Government what a sense of justice would never have conceded'.[39]

Birmingham's Irish Campaign

Such was the popularity of O'Connell and McDonnell at this moment amongst radicals in the town that even though the English reformers had won a great victory, the Birmingham Political Union continued to campaign so that Ireland might share in this success. Unfortunately, despite earlier parliamentary promises that O'Connell's homeland would be treated the same as Scotland, in the event Ireland had not been granted the same settlement that the reform bill granted to the rest of the kingdom because ministers felt uneasy about granting additional powers to a large number of Catholics.[40] So Father McDonnell, prompted by O'Connell, spent time concentrating the minds of the Birmingham Political

Tendency of Orange Institutions in Great Britain and the Colonies; with the Minutes of Evidence, Appendix and Index. Reports from the Committees: Sixteen Volumes (13) Orange Lodges: Great Britain and Colonies, Session 19 February–10 September 1835 (Vol. XVII) 1835 (London: House of Commons, [n.d.]), minutes of evidence, p. 43 and report, p. 19.

37   Flick, *The Birmingham Political Union*, p. 80; 'Second Reform Meeting at Newhall Hill', *BG*, 14 May 1832, p. 2.

38   W. B. Stephens (ed.), 'Political and Administrative History: Political History to 1832', in *A History of the County of Warwick: Volume 7: The City of Birmingham* (1964) <http://www.british-history.ac.uk/report.aspx?compid=22971> [accessed 22 May 2008] (para. 77 of 77).

39   'Mr. O'Connell', *Catholicon* 1:6 (1836), p. 302.

40   Oliver MacDonagh, *The Emancipist: Daniel O'Connell 1830–1847* (London: Weidenfeld and Nicolson, 1989), p. 55; Pearce, *Reform!*, p. 216.

Union on the unequal treatment that Ireland had received, and in June 1832 the organization therefore adopted a petition to parliament calling for an improved Irish bill. The radicals appreciated that O'Connell had supported reform measures that would primarily help England, apparently putting his concerns about his homeland to one side for the sake of reform across the islands, and the Birmingham radicals now wanted to return the favour by championing Ireland's cause. Those in Birmingham saw how their previous mass meeting had successfully aided the passage of that original reform legislation, and now decided to repeat the tactic in order to press for more equitable measures for Ireland. Consequently, at Newhall Hill that June, thousands of people gathered to endorse strongly worded motions that declared:

> 1st – That this Meeting had anticipated that the Reform Bill for Ireland would have been assimilated to that for England and that the same measure of justice and liberty would have been extended to both countries; but they have learned, with sentiments of disgust and indignation, that the Irish Bill of Reform is by no means calculated to confer upon Irishmen those constitutional rights which Englishmen now enjoy, and to which Irishmen are equally entitled.

> 2nd – That the People of England are deeply indebted to the noble and disinterested conduct of many distinguished Irishmen, particularly of Daniel O'Connell, Esq., and of the people of Ireland generally, who so generously forgot their own wrongs, when the rights of Englishmen were in jeopardy, in order to devote themselves to the achievement of the constitutional regeneration of England, and this Meeting deems it to be the duty of Englishmen to repay that debt of gratitude, by the most strenuous exertions in behalf of the people of Ireland.[41]

Of course, we might have reason to feel suspicious about the apparent altruism of the Birmingham Political Union here. The historian Dorothy Thompson describes how, seven years later, the leading Birmingham radical Thomas Attwood would oppose giving the Irish too much political clout at Westminster, and she also points out that the working people may have supported justice for Ireland so as to rid the English workingman of competition from Irish immigrants, with such radicals turning 'their attention to the achievement of

41   'Irish Reform Bill', *Birmingham Journal*, 30 June 1832, p. 2; Thomas McDonnell, 'The Rambler in Ireland', *Catholic Magazine* 5:37 (1834), p. 114.

political power which they hoped would give them the control needed to protect their jobs and their wages'.[42] John Belchem puts it more bluntly:

> The radical appeal for social justice to Ireland was remarkably persistent, precisely because a programme of Catholic Emancipation, repeal, tithe abolition, poor relief, security of tenure and the like, implied a cessation of Irish immigration and competition in the English labour market.[43]

In any case, the passing of the English reforms had inspired hubris amongst the members of the Birmingham Political Union, and this Newhall Hill gathering had no particular effect at Westminster. The government pressed ahead with its plans for Ireland, apparently without politicians having noticed that anything had happened in Birmingham at all, and the London press shared this indifference, with *The Times* and *Morning Chronicle* failing to print a single line about Birmingham's pro-Irish event. Following this defeat, the morale of the Birmingham Political Union suffered badly, as the organization's members increasingly bickered amongst themselves. Indeed, Father McDonnell now resigned from the organization, although he remained its *éminence grise*.[44]

In effect, 1832 had marked the high-water mark both for the political influence enjoyed by local reformers and for Birmingham's affinity with Irish grievances. Following the failed Newhall Hill meeting, O'Connell did return to the town in January 1833 for a public dinner in his honour, with the Birmingham Political Union launching a new campaign for Ireland during the following month. But by this time most Westminster politicians had learned to turn a deaf ear to the town, and parliament now took exactly the opposite course to that recommended by the radicals in the English midlands, passing a severe coercion bill for Ireland in April that temporarily suspended *habeas corpus*, imposed military courts, and banned meetings.[45] In May, O'Connell again visited Birmingham, to be hailed as the liberator of Ireland at another meeting on Newhall Hill, where *The Times* estimated the attendance at 80,000 and the reformers claimed 230,000. However, on this wonderfully sunny day, the

---

42   Dorothy Thompson, 'Ireland and the Irish in English Radicalism before 1850', in *The Chartist Experience: Studies in Working-Class Radicalism and Culture, 1830–60*, ed. James Epstein and Dorothy Thompson (Houndmills: Macmillan, 1982), p. 131.

43   John Belchem, 'English Working-Class Radicalism and the Irish, 1815–50', in *The Irish in the Victorian City*, ed. Roger Swift and Sheridan Gilley (London: Croom Helm, 1985), p. 87.

44   Flick, *The Birmingham Political Union*, pp. 95, 98.

45   Flick, *The Birmingham Political Union*, p. 103; MacDonagh, *The Emancipist*, pp. 90–92.

attendance of many had little to do with deep-seated political convictions. After all, 53 ale booths had been stationed on the hill by nine in the morning, and the press responded scornfully, with *The Times* labelling the event 'a good and merry fair'.[46] Following this meeting, the members of the Birmingham Political Union realized that they were making little headway; that the organization lacked funds, unity of purpose, and wider support in the country; and that the most sensible course of action would be to disband the association in the summer of 1834. Although O'Connell returned to the town in 1836 and had the pleasure of being the first Irish celebrity to speak in the magnificent 3,000-seat town hall rather than the smelly old horse market, and although Father McDonnell continued to hail the 'Universal Emancipator', in reality the town's view of O'Connell was undergoing a sea change, and would never again offer the kind of effusive reception that had been seen in the early 1830s.[47]

Alienating O'Connell

Nevertheless, Daniel O'Connell remained keen to associate himself with the town that had previously expressed such sympathy with his cause, and after the Birmingham Political Union revived in 1837 he returned to speak to reformers at the town hall. However, the situation had deteriorated since the early days of the organization, as local radicals now lacked the unified focus of 1832, and the working class seemed suspicious of reformers who seemed to offer little more than a stale rerun of the battles fought half a decade earlier.[48] Likewise, O'Connell's campaign for Irish reform had stalled during those five years, and he returned to the town in 1837 to whip up popular pressure for the bills still needed to improve the system of electoral representation in Ireland. However, the previous few months had been disastrous for him, marked by damaging allegations of corruption and complaints that he supported religious persecution and intolerance. To cap it all, he even found himself persistently trailed by a woman who claimed he had fathered her child.[49]

Birmingham's reformers now looked on O'Connell with newfound misgivings, particularly as, on top of everything else, they suspected he was

46   Quoted by Flick, *The Birmingham Political Union*, p. 107.

47   'Reform Dinner', *BG*, 1 February 1836, p. 2; Angus Macintyre, *The Liberator* (London: Hamish Hamilton, 1965), pp. 77–78; 'O'Connell at Oscott', *Catholicon* 1:6 (1836), pp. cxx–cxxii; 'Mr O'Connell in Birmingham', *BG*, 8 February 1836, p. 4; Thomas McDonnell, 'O'Connell's Visit to Birmingham', *Catholicon* 1:3 (1836), pp. 136–37.

48   Upton, *A History of Birmingham*, p. 118.

49   MacDonagh, *The Emancipist*, pp. 155–56, 139–47.

abandoning the cause of English reform in order to advance solely the ambitions of Ireland. In truth, O'Connell had aligned with a Whig government that looked sympathetically on Irish reform, but which had recently alienated Birmingham's radicals by ruling out some of their key demands.[50] O'Connell could of course point out that in 1832 he had supported the reform bill not because the measures promised anything 'great' for his own homeland but in order to advance the wider cause of enfranchisement, and he felt that his fellow radicals in Birmingham should now take a reciprocal approach. But the members of the Birmingham Political Union refused to see things this way, only viewing the Whig government as an obstacle to reform, and making their concerns clear at a rally in the town hall on the afternoon of 14 December 1837, where O'Connell was due to be the guest of honour.[51]

This meeting started awkwardly, with the Irishman arriving an hour late. But in truth his timekeeping in Birmingham had never been good, and Father McDonnell still introduced the MP warmly, with O'Connell responding by again praising the Birmingham Political Union for helping to pass the famous bill of 1832. O'Connell also flattered his audience by stating that further reform depended on determined action and agitation in the town, and explaining that tomorrow he would be in his homeland where he would tell his countrymen of the 'deep sympathy for Ireland' currently felt by the men of Birmingham.[52]

However, the mood of O'Connell's audience soured when he praised the Whig government. Amongst other things, he said, this administration had given Ireland a number of 'upright and high-minded' judges, and appointed liberal sheriffs throughout his homeland. Such sentiments caused tumult in the hall, confirming that O'Connell wished Birmingham's reformers to ditch their fundamental disagreements with the Whig government for the sake of Ireland. As O'Connell finished speaking, several members of the Birmingham Political Union council pushed forward, and although some tried to pass a quick vote of thanks and rush the orator from the hall, he realized that the situation had grown hostile and refused to depart until he knew exactly what the leaders of the assembly intended to say. One local leader then told O'Connell that the local reformers had no confidence in the Whigs, and lambasted the Irishman for praising the government.

---

[50] MacDonagh, *The Emancipist*, p. 161.
[51] 'Town-Hall Meeting – O'Connell', *Birmingham Journal*, 16 December 1837, p. 1.
[52] 'Town-Hall Meeting – O'Connell', *Birmingham Journal*, 16 December 1837, p. 1; 'Mr O'Connell in Birmingham', *BG*, 18 December 1837, p. 2.

O'Connell must have felt horrified to find his one-time collaborators speaking against him in this way, and after an exchange of insults he declared, 'Well, do as you please – throw us overboard if you like – despise use – ridicule and blame us', continuing, 'The present government enacts good and equitable and just laws for Ireland, and therefore I will support it, as I think you are all bound to support it, until you get a better'. He concluded, 'Reserve your "lip service" for others. I work for Ireland, you work for England', and in this fit of pique O'Connell quit the hall, leaving town on the next train, and evidently feeling estranged from the union that he had once supported.[53]

As O'Connell stormed out, Thomas McDonnell loyally attempted to instigate an ovation for the MP, and then berated the remaining spectators for their discourteous behaviour. Although most of the audience trailed out after O'Connell, about 500 stayed to hear McDonnell hark back to the town's affinity with the 'Liberator' during the campaign for the 1832 bill, and recall the long-ago meeting at the local horse showroom, when O'Connell had supported the English electoral changes despite knowing the government had prepared a substantially less satisfactory measure of reform for Ireland.

However, despite McDonnell's words, Birmingham's other influential reformers felt little inclination to dwell on the past. T. C. Salt had decided before the meeting that O'Connell had proved a 'turncoat', P. H. Muntz decided that the Whigs would only put 'Ireland in chains', and Joshua Scholefield warned O'Connell to 'be guarded when you meet us again and say rather less in praise of the present Administration'.[54] In any case, the Birmingham Political Union would soon become an irrelevance, superseded by the working-class activism of the Chartists, whose increasingly violent rhetoric troubled and alienated many of Birmingham's reformers.[55] By the late 1830s the Chartists had displaced the Birmingham Political Union in the vanguard of radical politics, and when Chartist agitation led to violent rioting in the town during 1839, the dreams of a united Birmingham reform movement lay in ruins, heralding years of political stagnation in the area. O'Connell sadly realized that Birmingham could no longer help him achieve anything for Ireland, and when he returned to the town he came for an anti-slavery meeting in August 1838 and for a nostalgic meeting about British constitutional liberties in March 1844, when polite applause greeted his reminiscences about the influential Newhall Hill

---

53   'Mr O'Connell in Birmingham', *BG*, 18 December 1837, p. 2.

54   'Mr O'Connell in Birmingham', *BG*, 18 December 1837, p. 2; MacDonagh, *The Emancipist*, p. 162; O'Connell, *Correspondence*, vol. VI, p. 106.

55   Ward, *City-State and Nation*, p. 36.

gatherings of the past.[56] Daniel O'Connell's final visit to Birmingham, at the age of seventy-one in August 1846, saw him simply attending the celebration of the Eucharist at St Chad's Cathedral, where he perhaps prayed for the victims of the recent crop failures in Ireland. Afterwards, a deputation of Birmingham's Irishmen met him at the Queen's Hotel, and had the opportunity of presenting an address of praise one last time in the town, for O'Connell was to die the following year.[57]

Thomas McDonnell

After the debacle of O'Connell's clash with the Birmingham reformers in the town hall, Father Thomas McDonnell nonetheless continued to wage an increasingly impassioned and solitary campaign for Irish justice. When the priest's chapel was redecorated in 1833, he toured Ireland and visited O'Connell's Kerry home, feeling 'sickened by the evidence, which the face of the country almost universally bore, of the fatal influence of the oppressor [England]'.[58] McDonnell declared his own 'ardent devotion to the cause of Ireland' and from Birmingham he broadcast his views in the *Catholic Magazine*, where he described an assortment of abominable cruelties that had been perpetrated for centuries by the English in Ireland.[59]

However, Father McDonnell's outspokenness increasingly worried his local bishop, Thomas Walsh, himself the London-born son of an Irish merchant.[60] Walsh wrote to McDonnell's co-editor at the magazine:

> I have had several heavy complaints made against it [the *Catholic Magazine*] by influential and most respectable priests & some of the respectable Catholic gentry [...] I as B[isho]p of the District, in which it is composed and printed should express my disapprobation of it. I have reason to think that, unless

56   O'Connell, *Correspondence*, vol. VI, p. 174, 194; 'Daniel O'Connell, Esq., M. P., in Birmingham', *BG*, 11 March 1844, p. 1.

57   *BG*, 3 August 1846, p. 3; MacDonagh, *The Emancipist*, p. 318.

58   Thomas McDonnell, 'Narrative of a Few Weeks in Ireland', *Catholic Magazine* 4 (1833), p. 247; Thomas McDonnell, 'The Rambler in Ireland', *Catholic Magazine* 5:42 (1834), p. 467.

59   Thomas McDonnell, 'The Rambler in Ireland', *Catholic Magazine* 5:37 (1834), pp. 109–10.

60   John J. Delaney and James Edward Tobin, *Dictionary of Catholic Biography* (London: Hale, 1962), p. 1184.

it be conducted in a very different manner, whatever may be the circulation in Ireland, the sale of it will decrease in England.[61]

A chastened McDonnell then agreed to avoid including 'combustible matter' in the publication, and abandoned writing a fulsome review of O'Connell's life and work planned for inclusion in a later edition.[62] However, a short time afterwards McDonnell established the *Catholicon*, a journal that he edited alone and printed in his church, allowing him again to start excoriating 'Eight centuries of tyranny and misrule' by English 'murderers' who ruled over an Ireland 'loaded with chains' and covered 'with blood'.[63]

Aside from Bishop Walsh, others in Birmingham also felt troubled by such rhetoric. McDonnell's congregation included aspiring English Catholic businessmen, and they scarcely wanted to become associated with controversial causes that might frighten away potential customers. The most powerful entrepreneur amongst the local flock was John Hardman, a wealthy Englishman who ran an important church-furnishing firm and had become Birmingham's biggest donor to Catholic causes. Hardman had given money for construction work at McDonnell's chapel, as well as for various nearby Catholic schools, orphanages, and convents.[64] But he strongly disapproved of McDonnell's political activism, and conspired with Bishop Walsh to rid Birmingham of this turbulent priest. In 1833, the bishop tried removing McDonnell from the town, but in response received more than 1,500 signatures of objection from McDonnell's congregation, as well as petitions from local Protestants who testified that the priest had consistently 'advocated the cause of the poor and oppressed' and had ensured that non-Catholics 'were no longer prejudiced against the Catholic religion'.[65] In the face of such opposition, Bishop Walsh had little choice but to back down, and he spoke personally in McDonnell's church to proclaim that 'your pastor should never be separated from you'.[66] Yet Hardman remained resentful, probably influencing McDonnell's resignation from the Birmingham Political Union's council, and ensuring the banishment

61   Thomas Walsh, BRCAA, letter dated 23 August 1834, B185.

62   Thomas McDonnell, 'Renewal of the Magazine', *Catholic Magazine* 5:45 (1834), p. 610; Thomas McDonnell, 'The Rambler', *Catholic Magazine* 5:44 (1834), p. 598.

63   'O'Connell's Visit to Birmingham', *Catholicon* 1:3 (1836), p. 139; William Greaney, *A Guide to St. Chad's Cathedral* (Birmingham: Canning, 1877), p. 23.

64   Gillow, *A Literary and Biographical History*, vol. III, pp. 128–29.

65   Quoted by Gillow, *A Literary and Biographical History*, vol. IV, p. 374; Champ, 'Priesthood and Politics', p. 296.

66   Quoted by Champ, 'Priesthood and Politics', p. 296.

of the man known locally as the 'priest's protégé', the Catholic radical speaker Matthew Priestman Hayes.[67] Hardman also liaised conspiratorially with Walsh when the peeved bishop realized in 1833 that McDonnell was again making speeches for the Birmingham reformers despite assurances to the contrary, and before long the businessman discovered a more effective way of punishing the priest.[68]

By the 1830s the English clergy had realized that the newcomers from Ireland had permanently increased the Catholic population of Birmingham, so decided to build a cathedral in the town, naturally looking to Hardman for financial support. He agreed with the decision, but scarcely wanted to honour his adversary by enlarging Father McDonnell's church of St Peter's into a prestigious new venue, and instead arranged with the architect Augustus Pugin to use the nearby church of St Chad's as the site of the cathedral. Predictably enough, this decision left McDonnell heartbroken. After all, his chapel was Birmingham's mother church, founded two decades before St Chad's, and greatly enhanced by his efforts to refurbish the dilapidated presbytery, add side galleries to the chapel, establish a church school, and purchase adjoining land for a graveyard.[69] His chapel now found itself perfectly positioned for an expansion that would never come, but nonetheless, when McDonnell learned about the cathedral site he first attempted to disguise his feelings and assist with the rebuilding of St Chad's. However, John Hardman, who ruled the cathedral committee, now decided to twist the knife by debarring McDonnell from co-operation in the project altogether.[70] At this point the priest began wholeheartedly to oppose the new construction, and Augustus Pugin noted that 'Mr. McDonnell is acting shamefully here and has got up a party which is

---

[67]   Catholic Education Committee, BRCAA, Journal of the Catholic Sunday School Established in Birmingham 1809, Meeting of the committee held on 16 July 1832, P1/60/1, fol. 230. The 'priest's protégé' label appears in 'Mr O'Connell in Birmingham', *Birmingham Journal*, 21 January 1832, p. 3.

[68]   Thomas Walsh, BRCAA, letter dated 20 February 1833, B133; Gillow, *A Literary and Biographical History*, vol. IV, p. 375; and Eileen Groth Lyon, *Politicians in the Pulpit* (Aldershot: Ashgate, 1999), p. 115.

[69]   'Records of Catholicity in the Midland Districts from Penal Times', *Birmingham Catholic Magazine*, September 1913, pp. 353–54; W. B. Stephens (ed.), 'Religious History: Roman Catholicism', *A History of the County of Warwick: Volume 7: The City of Birmingham* (1964), pp. 397–402 <http://www.british-history.ac.uk/report.aspx?compid=22977> [accessed 22 May 2008] (para. 5 of 12).

[70]   Gillow, *A Literary and Biographical History*, vol. IV, p. 375; Lyon, *Politicians in the Pulpit*, p. 115.

doing mischief and giving scandal'.[71] Amongst other things, the priest scheduled a church fête to coincide with the opening of the cathedral, interrupted the celebratory dinner held in the town hall, and ended up barricading himself in his parochial house.[72] Inevitably, such contumacy provoked another belt from the crosier, with Walsh finally deciding to transfer the loose cannon out of Birmingham for good, this time ignoring another petition of allegedly 7,000 names requesting McDonnell's retention. The dismissed priest placed the blame for his downfall squarely on the shoulders of Hardman, and felt like a martyr when asked to clear out of the chapel in July 1841.[73] McDonnell's Parthian shot came in the form of a meeting of Catholics at the Mechanics Institute where Walsh's actions were criticized, and when the editor of the Dublin *Freeman's Journal* heard of this gathering the newspaper took up the story, noting that:

> We have long been accustomed to look upon that gentleman [McDonnell] as one of the most useful auxiliaries of the friends of Ireland resident in Britain [...] It is not denied that the proceedings taken against the Rev. Mr. McDonnell are founded upon his *political* views alone.[74]

This comment provoked an angry letter of denial in the Irish newspaper from Walsh's new coadjutor in Birmingham, which in turn spurred McDonnell into writing to the *Freeman's Journal* and asserting that 'In the tumult of popular assemblies I have encountered yells, execrations, the threats, and even the infliction of personal violence in the cause of Ireland; and I boldly claim the whole people of Ireland as my friends'.[75] But regardless of this escalation of hostilities in the Dublin press, McDonnell found himself placed in a dead-end chaplaincy near Torquay, never again to reside in Birmingham. By contrast, John Hardman continued to make numerous donations to the new cathedral, and on

[71]   Pugin wrote his letter in mid-June 1841, see *The Collected Letters of A. W. N. Pugin*, ed. Margaret Belcher, 2 vols (Oxford: Oxford University Press, 2001), vol. I, p. 245.

[72]   Judith Champ, *William Bernard Ullathorne 1806–1889: A Different Kind of Monk* (Leominster: Gracewing, 2006), p. 142.

[73]   Gillow, *A Literary and Biographical History*, vol. IV, p. 375; Champ, 'Priesthood and Politics', p. 299.

[74]   'The Catholics of Birmingham – Extraordinary Document', *Freeman's Journal*, 11 November 1841, p. 1; 'The Rev. T. M. MacDonnell', *Freeman's Journal*, 11 November 1841, p. 2.

[75]   N. Wiseman, 'To the Editor of the Freeman's Journal', *Freeman's Journal*, 19 November 1841, p. 2; McDonnell, *The Case of the Rev. T. M. McDonnell, Late of St. Peter's Mission, Birmingham, Stated by Himself in a Series of Letters: Letter First* (London: Brown, 1842), p. 15.

his death in 1844 was laid in splendour in St Chad's crypt to acknowledge his generosity.[76]

Pádraic Pearse

There is an important coda to these Birmingham events. In the years after the St Chad's controversy, John Hardman's firm of church furnishers employed a young stone carver named James Pearse. This Unitarian Englishman had been born to a picture-frame maker in London, lived in Birmingham since childhood, and in 1863, at the age of twenty-two, married an eighteen-year-old Birmingham woman.[77]

James Pearse had come from poor, nonconformist stock, and when he heard about the famous history of Newhall Hill he came to admire the area's political radicalism.[78] Indeed, the sculptor himself developed a number of advanced views on Ireland, republicanism, and religion. He journeyed towards an eventual conversion to Catholicism whilst also becoming an enthusiastic follower of the freethought movement, whose leader dismissed the main tenets of Christianity and advocated causes such as self-government for Ireland, universal suffrage, and votes for women.[79]

Although Pearse had been little more than a child at the time of the town's hieratic arguments and had missed the area's monster meetings, he could scarcely have avoided learning about the town's recent history as he mingled with those who remembered the reformers and had attended the rallies. Indeed, from 1851 Pearse's employer operated from premises on Newhall Hill, the site of the Birmingham Political Union's most triumphant gathering that – to local minds at least – had forced the government to pass the 1832 reform bill.[80] In addition, Pearse came to work for Hardman's ecclesiastical

---

[76]   Gillow, *A Literary and Biographical History*, vol. III, p. 130.

[77]   Brian Crowley, '"His Father's Son": James and Patrick Pearse', *Folk Life: Journal of Ethnological Studies* 43 (2004–5), p. 73; BCL, St Thomas Bath Row, Marriages vols. 3–5, 1 October 1853–13 July 1868, p. 184; Michael J. Lennon, 'James Pearse', *BP*, 21 August 1947, p. 2.

[78]   Crowley, '"His Father's Son"', p. 72.

[79]   Bishopsgate Institute London, Bradlaugh papers, quoted by Crowley, '"His Father's Son"', p. 74.

[80]   Archives of John Hardman and Company, BCL, 'The House in the Park – John Hardman Studios', MS 175; St Chad's Cathedral staff, 'Our Heritage: Pugin & the Hardmans' <www.stchadscathedral.org.uk/heritage.php> [accessed 21 May 2008] (para 3 of 3).

outfitters in the decade following the St Chad's imbroglio, and the ghost of Thomas McDonnell must have felt near at hand every time a member of the firm argued over religious architecture, particularly as Hardman's son collaborated ever more closely with Pugin, the cathedral architect, on taking charge of the firm.[81]

Furthermore, whilst James lived in Birmingham the area experienced something of a revival in reforming sentiment. John Bright, an anti-imperialist from Manchester, became Birmingham's MP from 1857 to 1889, and he rejuvenated the town's dormant radicalism. He encouraged the formation of a new Reformers' Union at the town hall in spring 1858, and pointed out that an electoral system which still, at that time, excluded five out of every six men from the franchise, was a 'disgraceful fraud'. From 1858, Bright spoke in Birmingham once or twice a year, addressing large assemblies at the town hall or Bingley Hall exhibition centre, where he would tell the enthusiastic crowds about the issues that faced radicals in the year ahead.[82] James Pearse evidently heard some of Bright's oratory, as in 1886 Pearse himself wrote a pamphlet called 'England's Duty to Ireland', which remembered Bright giving a 'large and most touching appeal for justice to this country [Ireland]' in 1868.[83] James Pearse also recalled another:

> Speech made by John Bright – although I cannot call to mind the occasion, and perhaps not the exact words – he said: If it were possible to unlode [sic] Ireland from her moorings, and let her float some thousand miles away from England, the then – to us – humiliating state of that country [Ireland] could not be maintained for twenty-four hours.[84]

Pearse remembered such sympathetic words about Ireland, and also wrote in that same Birmingham tradition, praising Daniel O'Connell as a 'Reformer' and 'Agitator', and insisting that 'without Reform you would have a state of affairs which may be described as: dark, unwholesome stagnation'.[85] Of course, James Pearse advocated lawful means of achieving Irish reform, but in his writing we can find some intriguing ideas that would prove influential in future years.

---

81   Roderick O'Donnell, *The Pugins and the Catholic Midlands* (Leominster: Gracewing, 2002), p. 14.

82   Ward, *City-State and Nation*, pp. 57–58.

83   James Pearse, NLI, Pearse Papers, 'England's Duty to Ireland', MS 21,079, fol. 16.

84   Pearse, 'England's Duty to Ireland', fol. 19.

85   Pearse, 'England's Duty to Ireland', fols 27, 47.

For example, he asserted that Irishmen working in Birmingham had the right to send weaponry back to Ireland, as many in the gun-manufacturing town certainly attempted to do during the 1860s.[86] Pearse declared that 'I maintain that a working man in England who sends a rifle home, to help in the work of establishing self-government; is by that much remedying the evils caused by Absenteeism'.[87] He also argued that Ireland needed to take drastic action to ensure that the country would no longer be controlled from London. He believed in Ireland's 'unalienable right to be free and self governed, which the very constitution of England sanctions, which the lives of Reformers and Patriots of all times sanctify'.[88] And he declared that:

> This intense and unquenchable desire to be free, is – coupled with Catholicism – the one great trait of the Irish character. It asserts itself at all points, and at all times. The history of Ireland since its connection with England, is the history of one long struggle for 'Faith and fatherland'. That struggle is not yet finished.[89]

In future years, James Pearse's son would echo this rhetoric, by famously declaring that 'Ireland unfree shall never be at peace' and that 'it is a goodly thing to see arms in Irish hands'.[90]

Pearse's son was born and raised in Ireland because between about 1859 and 1864 the Hardman company had run a stone-working operation in Dublin, which later became known as Earley and Powell's.[91] At some point in the 1860s James Pearse transferred to the Irish operation in order to help with a business that was then booming, and by 1870 he and his wife had converted to Catholicism in a Dublin church. However, following the death of this first wife, he married again in Dublin in 1877, this time to Margaret Brady, the nineteen-year-old daughter of a native Irish speaker.[92] In 1879 Margaret gave birth to Pádraic, who in childhood may have been drawn to the abstract glamour of weaponry after hearing about his paternal uncle William's work as a gun maker

---

[86]   'Fenianism in Birmingham', *The Nation*, 21 May 1870, p. 629.

[87]   Pearse, 'England's Duty to Ireland', fol. 104.

[88]   Pearse, 'England's Duty to Ireland', fol. 54.

[89]   Pearse, 'England's Duty to Ireland', fol. 23.

[90]   P. H. Pearse, 'O'Donovan Rossa' and 'The Coming Revolution', in *Political Writings and Speeches* (Dublin: Phoenix, 1924), pp. 137, 98.

[91]   BCL, The Archives of John Hardman and Company, MS 175.

[92]   NLI, Pearse Papers, Letter re. James Pearse's conversion to Catholicism, MS 21,077.

in Birmingham, and may also have developed a taste for oratory after James schooled the boy in how to give lectures about sculpture work.[93]

In 1877, James set up his own ecclesiastical furnishings business at Great Brunswick Street, with workshops at Townsend Street. Here he made over 500 altars, as well as communion railings, rood screens, fonts, carvings, and busts of all descriptions, as well as various monuments, tombs, and headstones.[94] Indeed, the *Irish Builder* observed that 'works of his are to be found in well nigh every church in Ireland'.[95] Yet James Pearse also maintained links with the English midlands, made significant investments of over £1,118 in bonds and stocks from the Borough of Birmingham, and instructed architects to design him a large two-storey business premises on the corner of Bristol Street and Great Colmore Street.[96] But if James had been considering relocating back to Birmingham, history took a different turn when, whilst staying at his brother's home at the back of 158 Great Russell Street in the city during September 1900, the sculptor suffered a cerebral haemorrhage and dropped dead, leaving the younger members of the family in Dublin rather than the English midlands.[97]

Although Pádraic and his younger brother attempted to continue their father's work, the siblings had little business acumen, and abandoned the career in stone carving by 1910.[98] Instead, Pádraic grew increasingly involved in the secretive work of revolutionary nationalism for which he is remembered today, becoming a powerful orator and advocating violent rebellion for Irish independence. James Pearse had bequeathed views to his offspring about the necessity of Ireland struggling for self-governance, and Pádraic saw that working for drastic political change could be a divinely inspired cause, writing plays with revolutionary connotations, sometimes, with a nod to James, set

---

93   P. H. Pearse, 'The Coming Revolution', p. 98; Charles Townshend, *Easter 1916: The Irish Rebellion* (London: Allen Lane, 2005), p. 15; Lennon, 'James Pearse', p. 2; Mary Brigid Pearse, *The Home Life of Pádraig Pearse* (Dublin: Browne and Nolan, 1934), p. 108.

94   NLI, Pearse Papers, Account book of James Pearse's sculpting business, MS 21,075; NLI, Pearse Papers, Envelope addressed to William Pearse, MS 21,078 (1).

95   Quoted by Ruth Dudley Edwards, *Patrick Pearse: The Triumph of Failure* (Dublin: Poolbeg, 1990), pp. 44–45.

96   By comparison with the £1,118 in Birmingham, James Pearse had only £697 in Ireland by 1888. NLI, Pearse Papers, Bank books of James Pearse 1889–98, MS 21,07; NLI, James Pearse's Diary, ACC 5153; NLI, Pearse Papers, Plans of business premises to be erected in Bristol Street Birmingham, MS 21,078 (3).

97   Crowley, '"His Father's Son"', p. 83.

98   Dudley Edwards, *Patrick Pearse*, pp. 46, 112.

against a backdrop of ecclesiastical architecture.[99] Ultimately, both of James Pearse's Irish-born sons inscribed their names in the annals of Ireland's history by participating and dying in the Easter Rising of 1916, with Pádraic Pearse leading the revolt against English rule, assuming the presidency of the newly proclaimed independent republic, and becoming the most widely remembered of all Irish rebels.

According to the mantra of forensic science, every touch leaves traces, and in Pádraic Pearse's work for Irish independence there lingers something of that same political radicalism that had been found in Birmingham so many years before. Although history has largely forgotten James Pearse, his son emphasized:

> [W]hen my father and my mother married there came together two very widely remote traditions – English and Gaelic. Freedom-loving both, and neither without its strain of poetry and its experience of spiritual and other adventures. And these two traditions worked in me, and […] made me the strange thing I am.[100]

In 1916, Pádraic Pearse commanded his revolutionary forces to requisition the General Post Office as their headquarters, the main building that dominated Dublin's central thoroughfare. In selecting this exposed venue he demonstrated little military nous, but showed an unerring sense for where the public's eye would be drawn, perhaps realizing that bomb and bullet would carve the memory of his iconic sacrifice into the masonry just as surely as his father's chisel had once etched religious imagery into the stone of church and chapel. If Pádraic Pearse's Dublin mother had first taught him to love Ireland, his Birmingham father had guided the boy into becoming a rebel.

---

99 P. H. Pearse, 'The King' and 'The Master', in *Plays, Stories, Poems* (Dublin: Talbot, 1966), pp. 47, 71.

100 P. H. Pearse, 'Childhood and Youth', in Mary Brigid Pearse, *The Home Life of Pádraig Pearse* (Dublin: Browne and Nolan, 1934), p. 18.

3

The Murphy Riots

I am in hot water. For two years past there has been a Fenian conspiracy in this place to alienate the Irish people from me.

William Bernard Ullathorne [1]

Send them back to Paddy Land.

William Murphy [2]

William Murphy

At three in the afternoon, on Sunday, 16 June 1867, a travelling preacher from Limerick, William Murphy, readied himself, stood upon a platform, and began to give the first of two sermons that he would deliver in the centre of Birmingham that day. As a result of what Murphy would say, the English and Irish residents of the area would come to regard one another with newfound hostility and suspicion, with parts of the town being ransacked and reduced to rubble during the ensuing week.

Murphy's own origins are obscure, but according to the preacher himself, he had been born in Castletown-Conyers in 1834 to a father and mother who secretly converted to Protestantism, along with their seven children. When this conversion was revealed, the family moved to Mayo, where the elder Murphy became the head of a Protestant school. Meanwhile, the new faith captivated his son William, who had once been an altar boy but who eagerly became a scripture reader at the age of eighteen for an evangelical Protestant organization. By 1862, after an abortive attempt at running a Dublin shoe shop,

1 Ullathorne quoted by Cuthbert Butler, *Life and Times of Bishop Ullathorne*, 2 vols (London: Burns, Oates and Washbourne, 1926), vol. II, p. 141.
2 'Mr Murphy in Birmingham: Serious Disturbances', *BP*, 17 June 1867, p. 8.

William Murphy sailed to Liverpool and then walked to London, to become an evangelist in England.[3] Although a number of evangelical organizations wanted little to do with him, he did become the star lecturer of the small Protestant Electoral Union, speaking in London, Wales, and the South of England between 1862 and 1866.[4] Alarming reports of these events reached the Catholic bishop of Birmingham, who decided to warn his flock about what usually happened when Murphy arrived in a place:

> There suddenly comes into that town a man who is an utter stranger to its people, to its Catholic as well as Protestant inhabitants. He gets upon a platform, pours out a railing accusation, discharges upon his hearers a whole volume of obscenity, such as would be hissed and howled away from off the stage of any theatre in the world, and declares that this is a picture of the life and maxims of the priests, nuns, and Catholic people to be found within the precincts of their town.[5]

But the bishop's words scarcely affected Murphy's growing popularity as the Protestant preacher drew closer to Birmingham. In February 1867 Murphy gained national notoriety by delivering such 'obscenity' in Wolverhampton, where he urged devout Catholic women to attend a talk in which he delivered semi-pornographic stories about what happened behind the closed door of the confessional. With each seat costing only a penny, many Catholics from Ireland had indeed accepted the invitation, and felt so outraged that pandemonium broke out in the hall, accompanied by scuffles in the streets outside.[6]

These disturbances provided only a tame warm-up for the summer of 1867, which across Britain would be marked by agitation for electoral reform just like the start of 1832 had been. Murphy opposed the idea of increasing the number of voters in Ireland, as he felt this would increase the danger posed by Catholicism, and so he planned a five-week series of political meetings in Birmingham to coincide with the height of the reform demonstrations in June.[7] Birmingham's mayor heard of events in nearby Wolverhampton, and refused

---

3   These biographical details are uncovered in Walter Arnstein's 'The Murphy Riots: A Victorian Dilemma', *Victorian Studies* 14:1 (1975), p. 52.

4   Paz, *Popular Anti-Catholicism*, p. 257.

5   William Ullathorne, *The Confessional: An Address, Delivered in the Catholic Churches, Walsall* (London: Richardson, 1867), p. 11.

6   Paz, *Popular Anti-Catholicism*, p. 257; Roger Swift, 'Anti-Catholicism and Irish Disturbances', *Midland History* 9 (1984), pp. 94–98.

7   Donald C. Richter, *Riotous Victorians* (Athens: Ohio University Press, 1981), p. 37.

the preacher's request for the town hall, a decision that particularly angered Murphy because the venue had previously been granted to the English Catholic leader and convert from Anglicanism, Archbishop Henry Manning.[8] However, Murphy's supporters were not so easily dissuaded, and set up the portable wooden structure, that he had used many times already, on waste ground in Carr's Lane. Even before Murphy had spoken in the town, locals vandalized this 'tabernacle', and on the night before the opening lecture the entire roof was pulled off.[9] Nevertheless, 3,000 spectators arrived for the lecture on the afternoon of Sunday, 16 June, and when this hall began to fill, groups of hostile Irish Catholic men and women congregated in the street outside, making repeated efforts to push into the building despite nervous attempts to keep order by a handful of policemen, whose numbers had deliberately been kept low in order to avoid adding to the excitement.[10] As Murphy spoke from a platform in the gas-lit hall, his audience could hear the disturbance outside, and panic broke out when smoke from a nearby chimney blew in, as some spectators believed they might be burned alive.

Nevertheless, the apparently unruffled preacher attempted some biblical exegesis whilst the offstage commotion grew louder and as stones started hitting the roof of the building. Those standing towards the back of the hall inched nearer the doors to peer at the protestors, and scuffles inevitably broke out between those on either side of the threshold. Inside the hall, those doormen who traded blows with the demonstrators found themselves being praised, with one such hero being passed forward on the shoulders of the spectators to reveal a large gash in his forehead. Murphy himself now stoked the audience's desire for retribution, telling them:

> You have this day witnessed what Popery is – it is the same today as it was in days gone by. If she had the power what would she do to you, and what would she do to me? She would roast me as she did Latimer and Ridley and Cranmer. Then our duty is this – to stand firm and steadfast, and let our cry be 'no surrender'.[11]

The preacher then described how Catholics had beaten his own father to death, saying 'No wonder, then, that I speak against that system which killed my

---

8   Arnstein, 'The Murphy Riots', p. 57.

9   Richter, *Riotous Victorians*, p. 38.

10   Arnstein, 'The Murphy Riots', p. 56; 'Mr W Murphy in Birmingham', *BG*, 17 June 1867, p. 3.

11   'Mr W Murphy in Birmingham', *BG*, 17 June 1867, p. 3.

nearest and dearest friend on earth'.[12] The audience gasped at this revelation, even though in reality Murphy's father had died of a heart attack.[13]

The crowd of rowdy demonstrators now sounded increasing murderous to those inside the hall. One protestor, Michael McNally, yelled in that, if he got the chance, he would kill Murphy. In addition, a plain-clothes policeman stoked up the tension outside by apprehending a protestor from Ireland, and consequently infuriating the other agitators so much that the arresting officer found himself being chased along the road.[14] The demonstrators then fought running battles with the authorities throughout the rest of the day, as the police were reinforced by colleagues who found themselves repeatedly set upon by Irish opponents armed with an arsenal of stones from the waste ground next to Murphy's building.[15] By the end of the day 25 people had been arrested, and ten injured, mostly as a result of being hit by police cutlasses. Two men lost their elbow joints.[16] Amidst the hurly burly, one group smashed the windows of a house belonging to a prominent Protestant in Dale End, before eventually three local Catholic priests walked through the district and managed to calm the situation.[17] However, this lull would only prove temporary, and the situation deteriorated dramatically during the next 24 hours.

The Irish Parson

Catholicism already had a turbulent history in Birmingham. An angry mob had razed the Masshouse Lane chapel to the ground in 1688, and ever since then the residents of the town had been wary of showing any open signs of allegiance to the old faith.[18] Indeed, when Franciscans built the new church of St Peter's in 1786 following the Relief Act, they cautiously erected the construction to look like a factory in order to avoid attracting attention.[19] Anti-Catholic feeling persisted in the 1800s, and although in 1829 a radical petition in favour of Catholic emancipation gained 5,000 signatures in

---

12   'Mr Murphy in Birmingham: Serious Disturbances', *BG*, 17 June 1867, p. 8.
13   Murphy's own supporters later admitted as much: see 'Funeral of Mr. W. Murphy', *BG*, 19 March 1872, p. 8.
14   Davis, 'Birmingham's Irish Community', p. 47.
15   'The Scene outside the Tabernacle', *BP*, 17 June 1867, p. 8.
16   Davis, 'Birmingham's Irish Community', p. 47.
17   'Mr W Murphy in Birmingham', *BG*, 17 June 1867, p. 3.
18   St Chad's Cathedral clergy, *A History of St. Chad's Cathedral Birmingham, 1841–1904* (Birmingham: Cornish Brothers, 1904), p. 2.
19   Stephens (ed.), 'Religious History', para. 5 of 12.

Birmingham, a counter-petition boasted 36,000 names, with Father Thomas McDonnell being jostled and heckled when he abortively attempted to speak to an anti-emancipation rally in late February that year.[20] Nevertheless, McDonnell's work at St Peter's did help to mollify anti-Catholic sentiment in the 1820s and 1830s. He gave weekly lectures explaining ideas and doctrines of the faith, usually well-attended by other denominations; in 1827 he conducted a series of public debates with a well-known Baptist minister from Cork; and he later held a large public meeting at the town hall to discuss theology with two itinerant preachers from Ireland.[21] Indeed, as a result of McDonnell's work, for a time Birmingham reportedly became 'the most liberal towards Catholics of all our towns and cities', and the Protestants of St Martin's chapel in the centre of Birmingham even invited him to become the congregation's churchwarden.[22]

McDonnell was not however the only religious minister to help heal Birmingham's religious divisions in the period before the Murphy riots. In June 1837 Thomas Austin Finigan, a convert from Catholicism, left Dublin in order to work as an Anglican preacher at the Birmingham Town Mission. He visited people in their own homes rather than giving sermons in the street, and trod a beat around London Prentice Street, where many arrivals from Ireland had settled, even though he initially gained an icy welcome here from Catholics who disliked his evangelical predecessors at the mission. Yet despite this reception, he managed to charm his audience by speaking in the Irish language, which meant that eventually he found himself 'received with civility in every house, and with marked attention even to tears'. One household of 14 indigent Irish-born lodgers, for instance, at first tried to throw a pan of water over him, only to beg his pardon when he later returned and reasoned with them. Increasingly, as time went by, he became known to the Birmingham immigrants as 'the Irish Parson', and they grew protective of him, threatening to smash the head of one local drummer who unadvisedly insulted the preacher.[23]

---

20   Ward, *City-State and Nation*, p. 13; Champ, 'Priesthood and Politics', p. 292.
21   Carl Chinn, 'The Voice of the Irish in Brum', p. 23; 'Records of Catholicity in the Midland Districts from Penal Times', *Birmingham Catholic Magazine*, November 1913, p. 428; Thomas McDonnell and John Burnet, *Authentic Report of the Discussion which Took Place between the Rev. John Burnet (of Cork), and the Rev. T. M. McDonnell (of Birmingham)* (Birmingham: Hudson, 1827).
22   Gillow, *A Literary and Biographical History*, vol. IV, pp. 373–74; Champ, 'Priesthood and Politics', p. 93.
23   Thomas Austin Finigan, BCL, Journal of Austin Finigan, MS 3255, no. 12749, fols I–1, I–7, I–3, I–99, I–108, I–170, I–132.

On Finigan's part, he developed great affection for the Irish-born residents of Birmingham and their families, savouring religious discussion with them because of their 'shrewdness', 'intellect and argumentative faculty', and 'patience and attention'. Finigan read and prayed with the dying members of this population, risked illness himself by visiting their sick, and helped them to gain admittance at the general hospital. However, the abject living conditions he found left him deeply upset, and led him to launch a humanitarian appeal in the local press.[24] He wrote to *Aris's Birmingham Gazette*:

> I assure you that not a day passes without my seeing several families who are nearly destitute [...] If any lady or gentleman should feel disposed to contribute a little assistance, either in bread, soup, potatoes, or food of any kind, or by clothes or bedding, and will favour me with a note to that effect, I will either send the sufferers to them, or distribute the contributions in the best way that I can.[25]

Finigan realized that the Irish-born residents of Birmingham needed particular help because, whilst the native English could find aid at the workhouse, his fellow countrymen and women were being refused assistance by that very institution on the grounds of nationality. Such callousness made Finigan particularly frustrated, as he witnessed the results of the institution's indifference during his daily visits to the penniless. He wrote:

> I challenge all England to produce a single instance, where a distressed native of England received such treatment at the hand of an Irishman in any part of Ireland – tho' they have neither workhouses nor rates to provide for the poor – I have seen poor English men and women treated with kindness, lodged and fed and assisted on their journey without any reflection on their country or their creed.[26]

As a result of Finigan's humanitarian efforts, many poor residents of Birmingham received food, and his work even gained the respect and approval of those local Catholic clergymen more accustomed to warning the faithful away from rival preachers. A priest from St Chad's church praised the 'moral change' that Finigan had effected in the district, acclaiming the

---

24   Finigan, Journal of Austin Finigan, fols I–22, I–23, I–196, I–58, II–33, II–65.

25   *BG*, 15 January 1838, p. 2.

26   Finigan, Journal of Austin Finigan, fol. II–25.

Protestant's Christological views and giving 'full assent' to Finigan's mode of preaching. In return, although Finigan had little time for Rome's sacramental theology, he nevertheless felt pleased when he inspired lapsed Catholics to return to St Chad's, and attempted to maintain good relations between Catholics and Protestants in the town. However, his attempts to 'steer my course apart of all sectarian or denominational interests' brought him into increasing conflict with his managers at the mission, and when he complained in a private conversation that the organization's setup 'was sectarian' he found his words reported back to his superintendents, and his work in Birmingham at an end.[27]

Fleeing Famine

In the years after both Thomas Finigan and Thomas McDonnell had been forced from the town by clashes with their superiors, the area experienced a renewed paroxysm of religious strife. By the end of the 1830s the Vatican had started planning the establishment in Birmingham of the first Catholic cathedral in England since the Reformation, and when news of this construction at St Chad's emerged, between 12,000 and 14,000 protestors arrived at the town hall, heralding a backlash against Catholicism that would characterize the ensuing decades.[28]

A period of renewed immigration now played a part in inflaming the situation. At the end of 1845, a calamitous potato famine hit Ireland, ravaging the native population and reducing the average number of inhabitants in each square mile of the country from 335 in 1841 to only 231 ten years later.[29] In horrifying scenes, many of the most frail and needy succumbed to disease or starved to death. But those who could raise the necessary strength and money often managed to escape to the USA or Britain, and if Birmingham had an official Irish-born population of 4,680 in 1841, by the next decade that figure had risen to 7,980, although the true figure is likely to have been far higher.[30]

Those who fled famine usually arrived at Birmingham in penury, and crammed disproportionately into the older, overcrowded, central parts of the

27   Finigan, *Journal of Austin Finigan*, fols II–8, II–34, II–72, II–108, I–48, I–195.

28   Ward, *City-State and Nation*, p. 13.

29   Paul Bew, *Ireland: The Politics of Enmity 1789–2006* (Oxford: Oxford University Press, 2007), p. 206.

30   Carl Chinn calculates that the Irish-born population of Birmingham was 9,340 by 1851: see his *Birmingham Irish*, pp. 39, 48–49; Patsy Davis estimates that the figure was probably 28,000 by 1861: see her 'Birmingham's Irish Community', p. 38.

town, which often lacked clean water and sanitation. One Birmingham doctor examined the Irish arrivals and reported, 'It is with these that fever mostly prevails [...] They are badly clothed, miserably fed, and miserably lodged, and in every respect exhibit a striking contrast to their more fortunate neighbours'.[31] Another visitor saw 'ragged Catholic children who squat among the dust-heaps and gutter', whilst one of the Irish-dominated streets bore the stigma of a murder committed in 1835 and so inspired observers to condemn the area as 'notoriously infested with bad characters of every description'.[32] The smaller number of Irish-born Protestants tended to disperse elsewhere in the town, and Birmingham usually equated Irishness with Catholicism.[33] Indeed, with half of the new arrivals hailing from Connacht and often speaking little English, local priests from Ireland were left struggling to remember scraps of the Irish language in order to absolve penitents in the confessional.[34]

The existing inhabitants of Birmingham scarcely welcomed the arrival of so many impoverished newcomers, and some English residents may even have felt a sense of *schadenfreude* at the struggles of Catholic Ireland. After all, the Reverend Thomas Malthus had advised that 'the land in Ireland is infinitely more peopled than in England: and to give full effect to the natural resources of the country a great part of the population should be swept from the soil'.[35] Even those in Birmingham who felt horrified by the famine still sometimes excoriated the religion of the victims, and when the town hall hosted a meeting of the London Hibernian Society in 1846 one orator described Catholicism as 'an apostate religion, and the great curse of Ireland and every country where it was'.[36] Indeed, at Birmingham's Theatre Royal, where audiences had once

---

[31]   The opinion of Dr Darwall, quoted by T. P. Heslop, 'Medical Aspects of Birmingham', in *The Resources, Products, and Industrial History of Birmingham and the Midland Hardware District*, ed. Samuel Timmins (London: Cass, 1967), p. 696.

[32]   The murder had occurred in London Prentice Street. Comments quoted by Raphael Samuel, 'The Roman Catholic Church and the Irish Poor', in *The Irish in the Victorian City*, ed. Swift and Gilley, p. 273.

[33]   In the 1830s Thomas McDonnell gave the figure of 1,000 non-Catholic Irishmen in Birmingham, and Thomas Finigan also mentions seeing Irish Protestants here, although Carl Chinn has since failed to find evidence of large numbers living in the town. McDonnell also states that those from the predominantly Protestant north of Ireland tended to live apart from the other Irish immigrants. *Reports from Commissioners: Poor Laws (Ireland)*, p. 475; Chinn, *Birmingham Irish*, pp. 69, 51.

[34]   John Denvir, *The Irish in Britain: From the Earliest Times to the Fall and Death of Parnell* (London: Kegan Paul, 1892), p. 259.

[35]   Quoted by Davis, *The Irish in Britain*, p. 11.

[36]   'The London Hibernian Society', *BG*, 27 April 1846, p. 2.

cheered for William McCready, spectators now laughed at those from Ireland. In November 1846, the year in which three quarters of Ireland's potato crop failed, the playhouse staged a one-act farce called *The Irish Lion*, with a storyline that repeatedly poked fun at Irish eating habits.[37] When the fictional English characters of the piece hear that they are to welcome a guest from Ireland they joke 'mind there are plenty of potatoes', and the Irish character himself repeatedly makes jokes and weak puns about his stomach and about 'praties'.[38] As people starved in the fields and cottages of Connacht during the worst depredations of the famine in December 1847, playgoers in Birmingham also giggled at the Theatre Royal's *Christmas Comic Pantomime*, featuring the character of Harlequin paying an amusing visit to Ireland, with the English nation personified as 'a sprightly youth' and the neighbouring island 'a potato salesman'. Indeed, this disconcerting production proved so popular that the theatre reprised the show at Christmas the following year.[39]

Of course, those who had recently arrived in Birmingham from Ireland scarcely had money to waste upon visiting the theatre, and in any case local Catholic opinion frowned on the playhouse. Father Thomas McDonnell's friend and fellow reform leader, the Leicestershire man Matthew Priestman Hayes, had lost his job as master of a Birmingham school in 1832 after the local Catholic education committee 'learned that Mr Haynes has been in the habit of frequenting the theatres and has thereby disqualified himself as a teacher in a Catholic school where Christian morality must always be considered as paramount importance'.[40] A disaffected Haynes, under the influence of McDonnell's Hibernophilia, instead left for Ireland where he married a woman from Tuam and became editor of the *Mayo Telegraph*.[41] But whilst it is unlikely that Catholics from Ireland comprised any significant amount of the town's theatre audience, they regularly witnessed other kinds of performances, such

37   *BG*, 16 November 1846, p. 3. The work had previously been performed at Birmingham in 1841. John Alfred Langford, *Modern Birmingham and Its Institutions*, 2 vols (London: Simkin, Marshall and company, 1873), vol. I, p. 139.

38   John Baldwin Buckstone, *The Irish Lion* (London: Chapman and Hall, 1838[?]), pp. 17, 6, 8, 16.

39   *BG*, 27 December 1847, p. 3; *BG*, 10 January 1848, p. 3. Birmingham audiences were also capable of demonstrating sympathy for Ireland, and the Theatre Royal's performance of *As You Like It* on 24 February 1847 was given in aid of a relief fund for Ireland's destitute. *BG*, 22 February 1847, p. 3.

40   BRCAA, Catholic Education Committee, Meeting of the committee held on 16 July 1832, P1/60/1, fol. 230.

41   Gillow, *A Literary and Biographical History*, vol. IV, pp. 231–32.

as the baptisms, weddings, and funerals at St Peter's or St Chad's, teaching by the Sisters of Mercy, and sermons or public lectures organized by an assortment of local groups. Indeed, one man who moved from Ireland to Birmingham complained, 'Ten or twelve times a day we have religion cram'd down our throats as it were with a drum stick'.[42] Some newcomers preferred instead to find their spiritual comfort at the local pubs, or to consider the passion in Birmingham's nearby brothels.[43] Others played cards in their lodging houses, a particularly popular activity amongst families from Ireland at the weekends, or watched cock fights, dog fights, and sometimes human fights as well. Just as brawls occurred amongst the English population in some quarters of Birmingham, so labourers from Ireland also locked horns in the town, and at the start of 1838, for example, hundreds of people turned out to watch a bout between two 'stout athletick fellows': one an Irishman and the other a Scot who had cast aspersions upon 'Patt's poverty and his country'. With fever and smallpox periodically sweeping through the Irish homes, a wake would also bring the people together to reminisce, sing, and share treats such as alcohol, tobacco, and snuff.[44]

It was the Catholics who lived in these conditions that in June 1867 William Murphy and his supporters set out to goad and provoke. In particular, the organizers of the preacher's visit sought to antagonize those living around Park Street, the centre of Irish immigration to the town, by locating Murphy's talk on nearby Carr's Lane. Before the lectures began, the Catholic Church advised its flock in Birmingham to steer well clear of Murphy, 'so you will be kept from danger, and from the temptation of being harried beyond the limits of your patience'.[45] But the site chosen for Murphy's oration meant that local Irish Catholic residents could scarcely avoid encountering his supporters. In 1867 families from Ireland occupied most houses on Park Street, and for the previous two decades the road also housed a number of Catholic support services, including a school and a chapel.[46] Park Street backed onto London Prentice

---

42   Quoted by Finigan, Journal of Austin Finigan, fols I–129, I–30.

43   Finigan, Journal of Austin Finigan, fols II–22, II–40. There is, however, little evidence that Irish women engaged in prostitution when in Birmingham. See *Reports from Commissioners: Poor Laws (Ireland)*, p. 475.

44   Finigan, Journal of Austin Finigan, fols I–221, II–39, I–117, I–194, I–205, II–52, I–79, II–55, II–8, II–33, I–137.

45   Ullathorne, *The Confessional*, p. 23.

46   'Mr Murphy in Birmingham', *BP*, 19 June 1867, p. 5; 'Records of Catholicity in the Midland Districts from Penal Times', *Birmingham Catholic Magazine*, October 1913, p. 389.

Street, the area once so often visited by Thomas Finigan, and where by 1851, according to Carl Chinn, almost two-thirds of the residents enjoyed a first- or second-generation connection with Ireland, with other neighbouring streets boasting a similarly high proportion of such inhabitants.[47] Murphy's citing of his wooden hall in this vicinity encouraged his audience to see and deplore the most impoverished Irish Catholics, or even better, witness a violent response, and he astutely chose a weekend for his lecture so that the enemy would be visible and time available for rioting.

Anti-Catholicism

According to the Scottish Reformation Society, in the build up to Murphy's visit Birmingham had become home to 'some of the most zealous Protestants in the empire'.[48] These included the leader of Birmingham's Anglican evangelicals, Thomas Ragg, who edited a monthly periodical, the *Protestant Watchman*, which boasted a circulation of 3,000 in the late 1840s and included the regular feature, 'Romish Doings in Birmingham and Neighbourhood'.[49] As if the construction of St Chad's Cathedral in 1841 was not bad enough, Ragg and his supporters felt incensed when in 1848 rumours began to circulate that the Pope would re-establish the hierarchy of the Catholic Church in England, which meant Birmingham would have diocesan and parish organization rather than the missionary arrangements that had been in place since the Reformation. This change may have been a sensible administrative decision for an English Church swelled by Irish immigration, but when the Vatican confirmed the plan at the end of September 1850 many Protestants believed that a belligerent Rome was trying to claim jurisdiction over the country, and Birmingham saw 8,000 people turn out for a 'No Popery' meeting in the town hall.[50] Rumours also circulated that a Catholic priest had burned a bible in the Irish area of the town, and that a Protestant scripture reader in the region had been assaulted by an Irishman madly hollering 'Break his neck!'[51]

Another Irish Protestant immigrant, John Frederick Feeney, did his best to mitigate such sectarian feeling. After Feeney arrived in Birmingham from Sligo, where he had a number of Catholic relatives, he took control of the old

47   Samuel, 'The Roman Catholic Church', p. 273; Chinn, *Birmingham Irish*, pp. 49–50.

48   Quoted by Paz, *Popular Anti-Catholicism*, p. 118.

49   Paz, *Popular Anti-Catholicism*, p. 118.

50   John Henry Newman, *Lectures on the Present Position of Catholics in England* (Notre Dame, IN: University of Notre Dame Press, 2000), p. x–xiv.

51   Samuel, 'The Roman Catholic Church', p. 273.

radical publication the *Birmingham Journal*, and revived its flagging sales from
1,200 to 12,000 copies. Nevertheless, Feeney felt willing to risk unpopularity
in 1850, when his newspaper responded to increasing anti-Catholic sentiment
by making statements of support for Rome.[52] As a result, the satirical local
periodical, the *Town Crier*, would later joke about Birmingham's 'Feeney-an
Newspaper'.[53] But despite the mollifying attitudes promoted by Feeney, during
the mid-1800s the Birmingham Protestant Association organized a series of
public lectures in the town, given by speakers such as George Stringer Bull,
who condemned 'The moral system of Popery'; Charles Newdegate, an MP who
made a parliamentary career out of denouncing converts; and Giancinto Achilli,
a defrocked Dominican priest who abandoned the Catholic Church after being
accused of both assault and sexual immorality.[54]

In the summer of 1867, William Murphy therefore became the latest in a
line of anti-Catholic preachers to visit the town at the behest of the Birmingham
Protestant Association, but this speaker behaved far more truculently than
his predecessors. After his first talk in Birmingham had inflamed local Irish
Catholics, he returned later that day and for an audience of 3,000, now
under heavy police protection, began a second lecture. He had learned of
that afternoon's attack on a Protestant house in Dale End, and described this
vandalism to his audience as a 'dastardly outrage' for which they 'must blame
the Papists'.[55] He gave barely disguised instructions for revenge, telling his
spectators that they needed to 'band together as Protestants and Englishmen'
and tell the Catholic immigrants that, 'We have given you liberty of conscience,
you can go to your chapels, and worship God on the top of your heads if you
like, but if you interfere with the rights of an Englishman, then John Bull will
…', at which point Murphy concluded his sentence by violently stamping on
the ground. His audience cheered uproariously, and continued to show approval
as he declared that 'every Popish priest was a murderer, a cannibal, a liar, and

52 In 1857 Feeney founded the *Birmingham Post* to complement the weekly *Birmingham Journal*, and his son John would later print the *Birmingham Mail* as a late afternoon newspaper, thus establishing two of the most important and enduring Birmingham publications of the twentieth century. Feeney's son also became one of the area's greatest benefactors, bequeathing thousands of pounds to hospitals, chapels, and the local art gallery. Andrew McCulloch, *The Feeneys of the Birmingham Post* (Birmingham: University of Birmingham Press, 2004), pp. 27–30, 31, 122, 132–33.
53 *Town Crier*, October 1865, p. 14.
54 Paz, *Popular Anti-Catholicism*, pp. 257, 118; Ian Ker, *John Henry Newman* (Oxford: Oxford University Press, 1988), p. 372.
55 'Mr W Murphy in Birmingham', *BG*, 17 June 1867, p. 3.

a pickpocket' and proclaimed that those who had opposed him in Birmingham should be deported back to 'Paddy Land'.[56] His supporters, stirred by this rhetoric, shouted for vengeance, and many went away to organize against the Irish of the town.

The title 'Murphy Riots' has long tended to describe the events on that first day of the disturbances, Sunday 16 June, perhaps because English chroniclers could denigrate the Irish by pointing out that the disturbances had been instigated by those who protested outside Murphy's lecture. However, the major affray took place on the following day, and had causes and consequences that were far less easy to assimilate into a straightforwardly anti-Irish version of events.[57] On Monday, those living in the Irish areas seem to have anticipated trouble following Murphy's initial lectures, and crowded the roads from early in the morning. In Freeman Street, some men defiantly raised a large, if short-lived, wooden cross decorated with green ribbons.[58] Other Irishmen continued to fling bricks and other missiles in the vicinity of Murphy's lecture hall.[59] According to the *Birmingham Post*, which took a notably less anti-Irish line than the other local newspapers, Murphy's supporters soon appeared in Park Street as expected, with their ranks swollen by those who felt a sense of English patriotism, indignation, and religious fervour, as well as by those who were simply opportunists, troublemakers, and thieves. This self-styled 'party of order' entered the Irish neighbourhood, confronted a group of residents, and a brawl began, with Birmingham's mayor estimating the number in the streets at anywhere between 50,000 and 100,000.[60]

Unfortunately, the upper part of Park Street had recently been covered with tarmac, and Murphy's supporters now tore up the road to hurl at the houses. As this supply ran out, the rioters wrenched bricks from the walls of the Park Street burial ground to lob instead.[61] One woman was crushed so badly in the mayhem that she died a few days later.[62] Yet the residents appear to have defended the area stoutly, and according to the *Birmingham Post* remained in control of the street throughout the morning, until finally the situation changed

---

56   'Mr Murphy in Birmingham: Serious Disturbances', *BP*, 17 June 1867, p. 8.

57   See Davis, 'Birmingham's Irish Community', p. 49.

58   'Mr Murphy in Birmingham: Renewed Disturbances Yesterday', *BP*, 18 June 1867, p. 4.

59   Arnstein, 'The Murphy Riots', p. 57.

60   'Mr Murphy in Birmingham', *BP*, 19 June 1867, p. 5; Arnstein, 'The Murphy Riots', p. 57.

61   'Yesterday's Proceedings', *BG*, 18 June 1867, p. 3.

62   Davis, 'Birmingham's Irish Community', p. 48.

with the arrival of the police.[63] The local constabulary had grown infuriated by the behaviour of the Irish on the previous day, and now in all likelihood nursed an assortment of cuts, bruises, and grudges. In any case, Birmingham's policemen appear to have shown a distinctly anti-Irish prejudice, treating Irish Catholic youths in a similar way to that experienced by black youths under the infamous 'sus' laws of the late twentieth century.[64] Patsy Davis has conducted some compelling research into the composition of the Birmingham force, and finds that the town often recruited veterans from the Royal Irish Constabulary, middle-class Protestants such as the chief constables Rafter and Moriarty, who were accustomed to opposing nationalist campaigns and rural unrest in Ireland.[65] Murphy had in any case reassured more than forty policemen that his camp would defend 'the local authorities against the Popish mob', and so these local policemen, bolstered by the support of colleagues from neighbouring boroughs as well as from the military, probably had little doubt about whom to attack.[66] On that Monday morning, the mayor and magistrates also began to swear in special constables who were described by Father Thomas Leith of St Chad's as 'roughs'.[67]

On that Monday, large numbers of this force appeared in the Park Street area at about three in the afternoon, quickly setting about the Irish with truncheons and other weapons, and dragging in handfuls of prisoners. Patsy Davis argues that the 450 special constables soon became 'subordinate to the mob', and provides evidence that these men conspired with the English rioters to attack the Irish. For example, when one man in involved in the disturbances, James Drinkwater, was arrested the following day on his way to pelt stones at 'the Catholics' he felt indignant because he was 'on the Protestant side' and had earlier been stopped and commended by a police constable. Meanwhile, Birmingham's chief constable described the end of Monday's riot by telling of how the 'respectable' portion of the English mob 'formed up in front of the police and stoned the Irish with such force that the police became entire masters of the street'.[68] According to an Irish journalist, some of the residents, in desperation, climbed onto the roofs to push chimney pots onto

63   'Mr Murphy in Birmingham', *BP*, 19 June 1867, p. 5.
64   See Barbara Weinberger, 'Law Breakers and Law Enforcers in the Late Victorian City: Birmingham 1867–1877' (unpublished doctoral thesis, University of Birmingham, 1989), pp. 176, 196; cited by Davis, 'Birmingham's Irish Community', p. 44.
65   Davis, 'Birmingham's Irish Community', p. 45.
66   'Mr W Murphy in Birmingham', *BG*, 17 June 1867, p. 3.
67   Leith quoted by Davis, 'Birmingham's Irish Community', p. 50.
68   Davis, 'Birmingham's Irish Community', pp. 50–51.

these assailants below.[69] Realistically, these exhausted and hungry inhabitants could hardly hope to hold out against the combined force of armed police and local hooligans, although the *Birmingham Post* reported that the resistance took another six hours to crumble.[70] Finally, however, the police gained control and expelled all the remaining male residents of the street, most of whom were so drenched with blood that they looked like butchers emerging from an abattoir.[71]

The *Birmingham Post* described how, for the remaining women, children, and elderly inhabitants, the situation now took a decided turn for the worse.[72] The victorious 'party of order' started determinedly looting and destroying the neighbourhood, under the watchful gaze of the policemen supposedly guarding the area. Indeed, some of the police were seen lobbing stones and smashing windows.[73] Most of the homes had already been badly damaged during the fighting, but the winners now sealed the triumph by kicking in all of the remaining doors and windows, and – at least according to the Irish *Nation* newspaper – beating any children found sheltering inside.[74] Only the houses in the road owned by English families remained intact. At the others, Murphy's supporters smashed tables and chairs, stole whatever money could be found, and tore up the bedding, strips of which the victors wore as signs of their conquest whilst chanting loud choruses of 'Glory, Glory Hallelujah'. Anything that could not be carried off was simply strewn in the street, with one man delightedly emptying a bag of flour amidst the flotsam and jetsam of the road.[75] The gang also made assaults on the recently established St Michael's Catholic Church in Moor Street, as well as on the home of a priest responsible for converting St Joseph's in Nechells from being a Unitarian chapel into a Catholic church.[76]

Those Irish families who remained at their homes tried to shelter in the ruins that night as best they could, but most must have felt utterly shocked and distraught, and sat on the doorsteps, presumably lamenting the loss of those possessions that were stolen or scattered around in a heap of broken

---

69   'How the Irish Fought at Birmingham', *The Nation*, 6 July 1867, p. 724.

70   'Mr Murphy in Birmingham', *BP*, 19 June 1867, p. 5.

71   See Davis, 'Birmingham's Irish Community', p. 48.

72   'Mr Murphy in Birmingham', *BP*, 19 June 1867, p. 5.

73   Davis, 'Birmingham's Irish Community', p. 48.

74   'How the Irish Fought at Birmingham', *The Nation*, 6 July 1867, p. 724.

75   'Mr Murphy in Birmingham', *BP*, 19 June 1867, p. 5.

76   Chinn, *Birmingham Irish*, pp. 70, 49; Peter Fanning, 'The Irish in England', *The New Age: A Weekly Review of Politics, Literature, and Art*, 31 July 1913, p. 387.

images.[77] Many of these residents had fled famine in Ireland and worked hard in Birmingham as labourers, in the metal trade or domestic service, determined to improve the lives of their families and to save money for the few meagre pieces of furniture that the 'party of order' now carried in fragments up and down the streets.[78]

On the following day, Tuesday 18 June, large crowds again gathered in the streets, with rumours circulating that Murphy's supporters would attack a High Church Anglican venue or the local synagogue, and that a number of men from Ireland plotted to kill Murphy.[79] Nevertheless, the large number of soldiers and policemen who had been deployed in the streets managed to keep order, and Murphy lectured to his cock-a-hoop supporters in relative peace for the rest of the week. The night after the destruction of Park Street he mocked local Catholics, with his supporters yelling to him that if anyone attacked, 'we will protect you'.[80] His audience also booed and jeered the mention of Joseph Frederick Feeney's *Birmingham Post* newspaper, which condemned the anti-Catholic brutality. Yet Murphy remained entirely unrepentant, and the following Friday he gave the same sexually explicit lecture on the Catholic confessional that had already proved so contentious in Wolverhampton, with 6,000 tickets apparently being sold for the Carr's Lane hall holding only 3,000 people.[81] Indeed, Murphy began to enjoy his time in Birmingham so much that he decided to remain in the town, founding a chapel in Wrottesley Street as 'a standing protest against Popery', whilst continuing to needle the residents of Park Street, by, for example, preaching that 'In the North of Ireland the people had plenty to eat; they were clean and happy, because they were a Bible-reading people; but in the South of Ireland there was poverty, misery, sloth, and degradation. It was because Popery prevailed'.[82] Meanwhile, as Murphy's audience celebrated, those living in the damaged quarter set about dealing with the aftermath.[83]

---

[77] 'Mr Murphy in Birmingham: Renewed Disturbances Yesterday', *BP*, 18 June 1867, p. 4.

[78] Davis, 'Birmingham's Irish Community', p. 39; 'Mr Murphy in Birmingham', *BP*, 19 June 1867, p. 5.

[79] Arnstein, 'The Murphy Riots', p. 58; 'Yesterday's Proceedings', *BG*, 18 June 1867, p. 3.

[80] 'Mr Murphy in Birmingham', *BP*, 19 June 1867, p. 5.

[81] Arnstein, 'The Murphy Riots', p. 59.

[82] T. H. Aston, *Truth Versus Error: Facts about the Recent Riots in Birmingham* (Birmingham: Underwood, 1867), pp. 6, 8; 'Mr William Murphy in Birmingham', *BG*, 29 June 1867, p. 5.

[83] 'State of the Town Yesterday', *BP*, 21 June 1867, p. 4.

Residents requested £1,562 in compensation, but local magistrates deemed only two claims valid and awarded less than £72.[84] By contrast, after Chartist riots in the Bull Ring in 1839, similar claims from local tradesmen resulted in £15,000 compensation.[85] In addition, the courts also charged 25 men with riot in 1867, 14 of whom came from Park Street.[86] Finally, one last tragic footnote to the Irish disturbances came the following month, when the twenty-four-year-old man who had yelled threats at Murphy, Michael McNally, entered the Dale End pub owned by one of the English mob leaders, only to be shot and suffer an agonizing death during the following hours. Somewhat predictably, the authorities failed to convict the gunman of murder.[87]

Meanwhile, William Murphy moved on to tour the north of England, inspiring smaller brawls at Irish areas in Rochdale, Stalybridge, Bolton, Ashton, and Oldham. But Murphy's antics made him a number of English as well as Irish enemies, and he soon reaped what he had sown.[88] Various towns began to clamp down on the preacher, and although, armed with a gun and a knuckleduster, he continued lecturing between 1869 and 1871, he found himself excluded from large centres of population.[89] Indeed, in Bradford in June 1868, only 12 people turned up to hear him.[90] When he attempted to give another controversial lecture at Birmingham in 1869 the new mayor instructed his chief of police to keep Murphy away, and then locked up the preacher until after the scheduled meeting, which ended in disorder anyway. Murphy subsequently sued the mayor and won the case, although any satisfaction was short-lived.[91] The Warwickshire jury limited Murphy's damages to forty shillings and a few months later, in September 1871, a group of Irish miners gave him a severe beating at Cumberland, throwing him down a flight of stairs and then repeatedly

---

84   Langford, *Modern Birmingham*, vol. II, p. 300; Chinn, *Birmingham Irish*, p. 71.

85   Davis, 'Birmingham's Irish Community', p. 55.

86   For details of the bias of the court see Davis, 'Green Ribbons', p. 169.

87   Davis, 'Birmingham's Irish Community', pp. 54–55.

88   In Birmingham, for example, the *Town Crier* journal satirized the anti-Catholic paranoia of Murphy's lectures, advertising a sham lecture at the hall on Carr's Lane, about 'an eminent Jesuit, who recently disguised himself as a nursemaid [...] and successfully undermined the sound Protestant principle of two little girls, ages respectively, one-and-a-half and three years'. *Town Crier*, August 1867, p. 6.

89   'Murphy Bound Over to Keep the Peace', *Manchester Guardian*, 2 September 1868, p. 6.

90   Carolyn Steedman, *Policing the Victorian Community: The Formation of English Provincial Police Forces, 1856–80* (London: Routledge, 1984), p. 34.

91   Arnstein, 'The Murphy Riots', p. 66; 'The Mayor and Murphy', *Town Crier*, July 1869, p. 8.

striking the bleeding orator until he lost consciousness. His supporters then kept a vigil outside his chambers, occasionally bursting into hymns, but although Murphy rallied enough to attend court and identify his assailants, he never fully recovered from the assault.[92] When he died the following March, the Birmingham surgeons who conducting his post mortem concluded that Murphy's death was the direct result of his recent battering. Yet even at the end Murphy would not go gentle, and his funeral in Birmingham on 18 March 1872 was marred by chaotic scenes and spectators throwing bricks along the route of the cortège.[93]

Newman and Hopkins

At the time of the Murphy riots, the town's most famous Catholic priest was John Henry Newman, the thinker, writer, and high-profile convert from Anglicanism who had set up home with his group of Oratorian Fathers in a disused gin distillery on Alcester Street at the start of 1849, before moving to a more permanent home on the Hagley Road three years later.[94] For Catholics from Ireland, Newman's presence was a real boon, as the Oratorians ministered to the poor and Newman preached brilliantly.[95] Soon after he arrived, congregations of 600 attended the Oratorians' Sunday evening services, often with too many worshippers appearing for the priests to accommodate.[96] Newman may have had little time for Irish political aspirations but he maintained a high regard for those from Ireland, as he worked in Birmingham alongside the theologian John Stanislas Flanagan, who proved indispensable to running the Oratory. Newman also spent much of the 1850s travelling between Birmingham and the new Catholic University of Ireland (now University College Dublin), which he helped to establish in the Irish capital, and where he observed 'the great cleverness of the Irish, which far surpasses any thing I ever saw elsewhere'.[97]

---

92   Donald M. MacRaild, 'William Murphy, the Orange Order and communal violence: The Irish in West Cumberland, 1871–84', in *Racial Violence in Britain, 1840–1950*, ed. Panikos Panayi (Leicester: Leicester University Press, 1993), p. 50.

93   Donald Richter, *Riotous Victorians*, pp. 48–49.

94   Upton, *A History of Birmingham*, p. 103.

95   Louis McRedmond, *Thrown Among Strangers: John Henry Newman in Ireland* (Dublin: Veritas, 1990), p. 1.

96   R. H. Kiernan, *The Story of the Archdiocese of Birmingham* (West Bromwich: Wones, 1950), p. 31.

97   Ker, *John Henry Newman*, pp. 419, 469–70, Newman quoted by Ker p. 379.

Yet Newman's arrival in Birmingham infuriated zealous Protestants. After all, he was English Catholicism's most high-profile convert, and seemed to demonstrate how the tentacles of Popery reached deep into the country. At the time of the restoration of the hierarchy in 1850, hostile crowds gathered outside the Oratory to attack him before being dispersed by police, and when the riots of 1867 broke out, Newman received another set of threatening warnings, informing him that those wreaking havoc in Park Street also intended to target the Oratory.[98] Consequently, Newman again requested protection from the police, who assured him that in the event of any trouble the telegraph system would swiftly send mounted soldiers galloping up to the Oratory. In any case, the policemen felt content to let the mob expend all of its energy in Park Street, and told Newman that those from Ireland had already borne such a beating that the authorities now expected no further disturbances anywhere else.[99] Nevertheless the threat had not entirely fizzled out, as on the following Tuesday a Wesleyan minister, who had acted as chairman at the Carr's Lane lectures, gave a talk advising Protestants to defend themselves aggressively, declaring that he 'would not give much more than the price of old bricks for the Oratory in Birmingham'.[100]

Three months later, Newman brought Gerard Manley Hopkins, a fellow Englishman and Oxford graduate who had recently converted to Catholicism, to teach at the Birmingham Oratory school.[101] Hopkins spent only a few forlorn months in the post, leaving in April 1868 after finding that teaching took up all the time that he wanted to spend reading, and that he greatly missed his university studies. Whilst in Birmingham he also received a hefty kick during a football game, and was left sulking over his injured leg.[102] Nevertheless, his lodgings on the Plough and Harrow Road showed the sensitive poet from Oxford the condition of the poor in this manufacturing district, and he later wrote, '[I]t is a dreadful thing for the greatest and most necessary part of a very rich nation to live a hard life without dignity, knowledge, comforts, delight, or

---

98   Ker, *John Henry Newman*, p. 361.

99   John Henry Newman, *The Letters and Diaries of John Henry Newman, vol. XXIII*, ed. Charles Stephen Dessain (Oxford: Clarendon Press, 1973), p. 255.

100   Aston, *Truth Versus Error*, p. 11.

101   Ker, *John Henry Newman*, p. 464.

102   Gerard Manley Hopkins, *The Letters of Gerard Manley Hopkins to Robert Bridges*, ed. Claude Colleer Abbott (London: Oxford University Press, 1935), p. 18; Gerard Manley Hopkins, *Further Letters of Gerard Manley Hopkins*, ed. Claude Colleer Abbott (London: Oxford University Press, 1956), pp. 43–44; Gerard Manley Hopkins, *Selected Poetry*, ed. Catherine Phillips (Oxford: Oxford University Press, 1998), p. xvii.

hopes in the midst of plenty – which plenty they make'.[103] Religious hostilities continued to flare up during Hopkins's time in Birmingham, with the autumn of 1867 seeing English mobs chanting pro-Murphy slogans, attacking the High Church Anglican venue of St Alban's, and attempting to vandalize an assortment of Catholic buildings, including the Oratory.[104] Hopkins could scarcely have avoided learning about the recent riots that had triggered these troubles, and in this environment he may have developed the sensitivity to religious persecution that marks one of his most famous works. In a poem of 1875, 'The Wreck of the Deutschland', he describes a shipwreck off Harwich that killed five Franciscan nuns who had been driven out of their homes by Bismarck's anti-Catholicism in Germany.[105] Hopkins praises the fleeing nuns, but in describing their struggle his poem also carries an echo of the anti-Catholicism that he had discovered in Birmingham. At the start of the poem, Hopkin's God appears as a kind of local artisan who has 'bound bones and veins in me, fastened me flesh', and who acts like a blacksmith, forging 'with fire' and 'With an anvil-ding'. The poem then portrays the shipwreck with the language of human combat ('beat', 'Crushed', 'fought', 'death at a blow') and conjures up the lamentations of 'a heart-broke rabble, / The women's wailing, the crying of child without check'.[106] The poem remained in obscurity until the twentieth century, but if any of the Irish Catholics in Birmingham who witnessed the destruction of 1867 could have read Hopkins's manuscript they might have found particular resonance in these lines and sympathized with those nuns so traumatically exiled from home.

Orangemen and Fenians

In the wake of the Murphy riots, many residents of Birmingham became increasingly militant, and the town experienced an upsurge in support for the local Orange Order. Unlike in Liverpool, Orangism had largely disappeared from Birmingham in the mid-nineteenth century, and only emerged again in June 1864, following the controversies around the Catholic revival and Irish immigration, with sympathizers generally meeting once a month for prayers, toasts to William of Orange, scripture reading, and singing 'God Save

103   Norman White, *Hopkins: A Literary Biography* (Oxford: Clarendon Press, 1992), p. 154; Hopkins, *The Letters*, pp. 27–28.

104   Chinn, *Birmingham Irish*, p. 72; 'The Condemned Fenians at Manchester: Disturbances in Birmingham', *Birmingham Journal*, 23 November 1867, p. 8.

105   John E. Keating, *The Wreck of the Deutschland: An Essay and Commentary* (Kent, OH: Kent State University, 1963), p. 12.

106   Gerard Manley Hopkins, *Selected Poetry*, pp. 98–107.

the Queen'.[107] As Donald MacRaild has pointed out, the Orange Order's
Loyalism may have had a particularly strong resonance in Ulster, but when
transplanted to English locations the organization's message struggled against
widespread hostility and indifference.[108] In Birmingham, then, the renewed
Orange Order at first operated on a small scale. As few as eight members
attended the snowbound New Year celebrations in January 1865, only 30 sat
down for the annual supper that June, and in the spring of 1866 the turnout
for meetings was so small that the group was prevented from discussing any
scheduled business. Only after the message of anti-Popery gained greater
popularity in Birmingham following the Murphy riots did the organization
thrive, and in the ensuing six months more than 80 new recruits joined the
Order, with members seeking to establish three new lodges in the area.[109]
Indeed, the local Orangemen may have deliberately helped to cultivate the
Murphy riots, as the original lodge enjoyed close links with the Birmingham
Protestant Association, which arranged Murphy's visit to the region.[110] As
early as summer 1865, one prominent member of both organizations, the
master of Birmingham's Orange lodge, had declared at a meeting of local
Orangemen that 'The day was coming when men would have to declare
under what colours they fought; and the hour was not far distant when truth
would stand face to face with error – Protestantism as opposed to Popery'.[111]
Subsequently, the Protestant Association had become known to opponents in
the town as 'an ultra-bigoted section of the Orange faction'.[112]

Many of the members of Birmingham's Orange Order may have had
little personal experience of Ireland, but the country loomed large in their
thoughts.[113] Soon after the Birmingham lodge had been revived in the 1860s,
its members commemorated the Battle of the Boyne on the lawn of Aston Park,
celebrated William of Orange's landing in Ireland, and expressed concern

---

[107] Belchem, *Irish, Catholic and Scouse*, p. 189; Orange Order, BCL, Minute Book of the
Orange Order Birmingham, MS 1250/1, fols 2ᵛ, 19ʳ, 3ᵛ, 14ʳ.

[108] Donald M. MacRaild, *Faith, Fraternity and Fighting: The Orange Order and Irish Migrants
in Northern England, c.1850–1920* (Liverpool: Liverpool University Press, 2005), p. 17.

[109] Orange Order, Minute Book, fols 10ᵛ, 14ʳ, 20ᵛ–21ʳ, 64ʳ, 70ʳ–70ᵛ. See also Peach,
'Poverty, Religion and Prejudice in Britain', pp. 298–301.

[110] Peach, 'Poverty, Religion and Prejudice in Britain', pp. 298–314.

[111] 'Yesterday's Proceedings', *BG*, 18 June 1867, p. 3.

[112] Aston, *Truth Versus Error*, p. 4.

[113] In *Sectarian Violence*, Frank Neal argues that, in Liverpool, the Orange Order was a
kind of English grouping built up in reaction to large numbers of Irish Catholic migrants,
and something similar appears to have been the case in Birmingham.

over 'the scandalous manner in which the Orangemen of the North of Ireland and their principles were misrepresented'. The Birmingham organization also learned about conditions in Ireland from John Bruton, an Orangeman who moved to the town from Dublin, whilst the Birmingham group was also supported by English-born MP George Whalley, who penned an anti-Catholic tract titled *Popery in Ireland* under the pseudonym Patrick Murphy.[114] After the rioting of 1867, the local Orange Order showed an increasing interest in Ireland, with the lodge's members pledging themselves to the suppression of disorder caused by local Irish nationalists.[115] Indeed, although the high profile enjoyed by these particular Orangemen would fade away in the ensuing years, Orange sentiment would come to resonate more widely in Birmingham. The historian H. J. Hanham has argued that the Murphy riots ultimately undermined support for pro-Irish Catholic politicians in England, and that 'the riots encouraged Conservative controversialists, and particularly clerical controversialists, to go much farther than they would otherwise have done'.[116] Certainly in Birmingham, when Joseph Chamberlain worked to convert the town into a hotbed of Unionism later in the century, the politician would use that 'Orange card' – the suspicion of Ireland's Catholics and loyalty towards Ulster Protestants – in order to mobilize local English opinion in favour of his cause.

By contrast with the Orange Order, many of those Catholics who had emigrated from Ireland in the 1840s and 1850s blamed England for inaction or even deliberate genocide during the famine, and after the rioting they felt further alienated from a country that permitted the destruction of their dwellings, theft of their property, and assault and murder of their compatriots. In consequence, Birmingham became 'one of the most active centres' of the Fenian movement, a secret revolutionary group established in 1858 that spread rapidly and boasted a widespread membership in Irish areas by 1865.[117] In spring 1867 the organization in the north of England made a major assault on Chester Castle, whilst Fenians in Ireland launched an abortive insurrection, at which time Birmingham boasted 'considerable numbers' of sympathizers who took part in drilling, and who realized that the local gun industry made the English

---

114   Orange Order, Minute Book, fols 4ᵛ, 33ᵛ, 14ʳ, 48ᵛ; Mary C. Sullivan (ed.), *The Friendship of Florence Nightingale and Mary Clare Moore* (Philadelphia: University of Pennsylvania Press, 1999), p. 136.

115   Orange Order, Minute Book, fol. 74ᵛ.

116   H. J. Hanham, *Elections and Party Management: Politics in the Time of Disraeli and Gladstone* (London: Longmans, 1959), p. 307.

117   Graham Davis, *The Irish in Britain*, p. 260.

midlands strategically important for such insurgent activity. Indeed, local police seized 'considerable quantities of ammunition and arms' from Birmingham *en route* to Ireland's 1867 rebellion, the nationalist leader Michael Davitt visited the town on several occasions to procure arms, and at least one Fenian gun maker lived in Birmingham for more than three decades.[118]

On 20 November 1867 a number of the town's men and women held an open-air meeting to support Fenian prisoners who had been condemned in Manchester for killing a policeman.[119] The convicted men were due to hang in three days' time, and so their supporters in Birmingham set up a wagon next to the town hall to call for clemency. However, when opponents learned of this assembly they furiously attacked the orators, throwing stones and breaking up the gathering in chaos. With memories of the recent riots still fresh, the anti-Fenian mob then marched through the area's main streets to St Alban's Church, where they cheered the name of William Murphy, threw stones and bricks through the windows, and demolished a fence. The next day this faction returned to the town hall to campaign in favour of hanging the Manchester Fenians, and then marched to St Chad's, making an attempt to attack the cathedral before being repelled by a mob of young Irish Catholic men and women.[120] Indeed, one woman launched herself at the cathedral's assailants with such force that she could only be overpowered by the combined efforts of half a dozen men.[121]

Eventually the police arrived, and partly regained the trust of the Irish by repelling the English attackers and helping to guard the town's Catholic venues throughout the evening. Up to 3,500 anti-Fenian demonstrators roved around the town looking for another symbol of Popery to assault, but when they eventually made for the Oratory the police fulfilled the pledge made to Newman and successfully dispersed the would-be vandals with a sabre charge. The next day a group of Irish Catholics stood guard at St Chad's Cathedral, and then made their own march through the town to St Michael's Church on Moor Street. The local Orangemen ringed William Murphy's chapel on Wrottesley Street in anticipation of attacks, and unsuccessfully asked the mayor if all members

---

118 'Fenianism in Birmingham', *The Nation*, 21 May 1870, p. 629; 'The Fenians in London', *The Nation*, 4 June 1870, p. 659.

119 Richard English, *Armed Struggle: The History of the IRA* (London: Macmillan, 2003), p. 8; Gary McGladdery, *The Provisional IRA in England: The Bombing Campaign 1973–1997* (Dublin: Irish Academic Press, 2006), p. 231.

120 Langford, *Modern Birmingham*, vol. II, p. 301.

121 'The Condemned Fenians at Manchester', *Birmingham Journal*, 23 November 1867, p. 8.

of the local Orange lodges could be sworn in as special police constables to combat the Fenians.[122] However, unlike the anti-Fenian mob of the night before, the Catholic group did no damage whilst traversing the town, being content instead to boo the name of William Murphy and to cheer for Ireland and for Rome.[123]

Nevertheless, the English authorities hanged the Manchester Fenians as scheduled, and in response a number of those from Ireland organized a memorial service at St Joseph's Church. This venue proved far enough away from the town centre to avoid protestors, but did allow local Irish nationalists to demonstrate the broad appeal of the revolutionary cause, with about 2,500 people in attendance.[124] However, at St Chad's, the Bishop of Birmingham, William Bernard Ullathorne, viewed these developments with alarm. He felt repelled by the idea of an insurrectionary group operating amongst his flock, and expressed worries about how support for the Fenians had fused with professions of Catholic piety. At Advent 1868 Ullathorne tried to restrain the faithful by issuing a pastoral letter against Irish revolutionaries, asserting the Catholic duty to obey the law and civil authority, condemning Fenianism along with Freemasonry, and labelling the supporters of such secret societies as 'dupes'.[125] But this approach could scarcely hope to win him widespread support. Many of those listening to the letter had seen precisely what the civil authorities were capable of doing in Park Street, and did not want a lecture on Irish politics from a conservative English patriot like the bishop. Ullathorne found himself shunned by Catholics from Ireland and abused for several months in the letters pages of a Catholic newspaper called the *Universal News*.[126]

To an extent, Ullathorne had been misrepresented. During the 1850s he had shown great sympathy with the poor of Ireland, having drawn attention to the country's 'Famine, utter want, cold, nakedness, pestilence', and having asked 'Can any of us be so hardened as to indulge in superfluities or luxuries, unneedful for health, whilst our poor unhappy brethren die daily by so many

122 Orange Order, Minute Book, fols 72ᵛ, 74ᵛ.

123 Langford, *Modern Birmingham*, vol. II, p. 301. 'The Condemned Fenians at Manchester', *Birmingham Journal*, 23 November 1867, p. 8.

124 Chinn, *Birmingham Irish*, p. 72. Militant Birmingham Protestants staged their response the following April, when a government attempt to disestablish the Church of Ireland brought up to 4,000 protestors to a lively and frequently violent gathering at the town hall. 'Meeting in the Town Hall', *Birmingham Journal*, 18 April 1868, p. 3.

125 Quoted by Butler, *Life and Times*, vol. II, p. 142.

126 Edward Norman, *The English Catholic Church in the Nineteenth Century* (Oxford: Clarendon Press, 1984), p. 194; Butler, *Life and Times*, vol. II, p. 142.

hundreds?'[127] His public pronouncements still expressed profound distress about the general condition of Ireland, blamed English misgovernment for Ireland's plight, and professed admiration for the Irish people. Furthermore, he had made a bitter enemy of the Birmingham Orange Order five months before Murphy came to town by publicly challenging the anti-Catholic MP Charles Newdegate.[128] But despite such credentials, Ullathorne had little time for any ideas of Irish independence that might weaken the British empire, and deplored the idea of political violence.

Ullathorne also expressed fears about what might happen next in Birmingham, telling friends about the 'nest of Fenians here who are giving us some trouble'. After some deliberation, he decided to pre-empt his enemies' next move by putting out another pastoral, which priests read aloud in local churches during January 1869. This letter began by firmly declaring that Fenianism did indeed constitute a secret society of the kind condemned by the Church, and that members of such a group would be banned from receiving the sacraments. But thereafter Ullathorne pulled his punches, being careful to denounce only the Fenian leaders rather than the Irish *en masse*. He explained that 'for nearly forty years I have been the devoted servant of the Irish people', citing his earlier work as chaplain to convicts in Australia, where he assisted men who had been transported for Irish revolutionary activities. 'I conversed with these men, knew their inmost hearts as well as their histories, and they altogether represented some three-quarters of a century of the history of the Irish people', declared Ullathorne. 'Those men were wont to say that if I looked like an Englishman I felt like an Irishman'.[129]

After this extraordinary claim to kinship with Irish political prisoners, Ullathorne went on to describe how he wished to help the thousands of their countrymen driven to exile in Birmingham, and concluded with warm words of praise for Daniel O'Connell.[130] Of course, many of those who listened to this letter remained highly dubious about the bishop. But the Birmingham Church then made an intelligent move in order to defuse the situation, organizing a major St Patrick's Day celebration in March 1869. Naturally, the feast day had

---

[127] Quoted by Butler, *Life and Times*, vol. I, p. 145.

[128] The Birmingham Orangemen wished to unite in action 'to counteract if possible a "Dirty Conspiracy" on the part of the Popish Bishop Ullathorne'. Orange Order, Minute Book, fol. 31ʳ. For more on Newdegate's activities see Walter L. Arnstein, *Protestant Versus Catholic in Mid-Victorian England: Mr. Newdegate and the Nuns* (London: University of Missouri Press, 1982), pp. 74–87.

[129] Quoted by Butler, *Life and Times*, vol. II, pp. 141, 143.

[130] Butler, *Life and Times*, vol. II, p. 144.

been commemorated in local homes and hostelries on many previous occasions, and three decades earlier Thomas Finigan had lamented that many of those who had come from Ireland to Birmingham celebrated in a stupor.[131] But 1869 saw a far more formal event. More than 2,000 people arrived at the town hall to listen to a speech by the Irish-born Vicar General of Birmingham, Eugene O'Sullivan, in which he linked history, politics, and religion, and compared the successful struggle for Catholic emancipation with the modern campaign for Ireland's independence.[132] Audience members frequently applauded and cheered the priest as he nudged them toward constitutional rather than revolutionary politics, and after the speech there followed a concert of Irish music that included a wide range of orchestral, choral, and solo turns. A rump of 130 men and women did take the opportunity to protest against Bishop Ullathorne, but the majority of those in attendance simply applauded the show. With enthusiasm for Fenianism now flagging in Ireland, and with William Murphy under close mayoral supervision in Birmingham, the period of riots and demonstrations came to an end. Instead, in the ensuing years, this annual March event in the middle of Birmingham became one of the most important opportunities for the Irish to articulate, contest, and share a sense of nationality, with the meetings inspiring much political debate in the later Victorian period and providing a template for the St Patrick's Day celebrations in the area that survive to the present day.

Nevertheless, it would be wrong to believe that Fenianism had entirely disappeared from the town after 1869. In 1883, for instance, under the guise of a paint and wallpaper business, the Irish-American John Cadogan-Murphy and his Irish-born assistant Thomas Clarke set up a factory to make nitro-glycerine bombs in Ledsam Street, Ladywood, although both men found themselves arrested when a sharp-eyed chemist in the Bull Ring tipped off the police.[133] The following year, the Fenian John Daly was staying at the home of his friend James Egan in Kyotts Lake Road, Sparkbrook, when police raided the house and dug up the garden, where detectives apparently found a bottle containing

---

131 Finigan, Journal of Austin Finigan, fol. II-54.

132 Twenty years earlier, an Irish priest in Liverpool had similarly organized a 'refined evening soirée' to draw attention away from that town's more boisterous celebrations of the feast day. Belchem, *Irish, Catholic and Scouse*, p. 125; 'St. Patrick's Day Celebrations: Concert at the Town Hall', *BP*, 18 March 1869, p. 8; Ziesler, 'The Irish in Birmingham', p. 108.

133 Chinn, *Birmingham Irish*, p. 73. The Bull Ring is Birmingham's central market area, named after the bull baiting that once took place there. Tony Collins, *Encyclopedia of Traditional British Rural Sports* (London: Routledge, 2005), p. 52.

traces of nitro-glycerine.[134] After all, the newspapers boasted that, under 'the practised eyes of the detective police', the 'Fenians have been innocently working their ends under almost as complete a surveillance as if their movements were carried on in the detective office'.[135]

However, although Clarke and Cadogan-Murphy had indeed been making explosives, the authorities had deliberately framed Daly and Egan. In the latter case, policemen discovered traces of explosives where none had existed, thanks to the detectives who planted an incriminating bottle in Egan's garden.[136] Ultimately, of course, such deception was always likely to damage the British establishment, and the Birmingham arrests indeed rebounded in spectacular style. John Daly's unjust imprisonment would never be forgotten by his family, with his nephew and niece going on to play key roles in the Irish revolution that drove Britain out of Southern Ireland.[137] Daly, Egan, and Thomas Clarke also found themselves imprisoned together and thus managed to maintain one another's spirits, with Clarke being particularly fortified in revolutionary enthusiasm by this time in jail.[138] Later on, after release, Clarke joined Pádraic Pearse in leading the Easter Rising against the British in Dublin, and became the first signatory of Ireland's proclamation of independence.

When 1916 brought widespread popular support for independence in Ireland, thoughtful imperialists may have wondered if the forces of British patriotism could have trodden more lightly in Dublin, Birmingham, and elsewhere. Yet the authorities learned few long-term lessons from this incident, and the framing of Daly and Egan offered an eerie premonition of England's notorious Irish fit-up almost a century later, when policemen again discovered traces of explosives where none had existed during investigations into the Birmingham pub bombings.

---

134   Kathleen Clarke, *My Fight for Ireland's Freedom* (Dublin: O'Brien, 1997), p. 12.

135   'Fenianism in Birmingham', *The Nation*, 21 May 1870, p. 629.

136   Chinn, *Birmingham Irish*, p. 73; Clarke, *My Fight*, p. 12.

137   Daly's nephew Ned became one of the celebrated martyrs of Easter 1916, whilst Daly's niece Kathleen became one of Ireland's most influential nationalist women, working to defeat Britain during the Anglo-Irish War. Clarke, *My Fight*, pp. 19, 11, 175.

138   For example, the three men passed each other with lines such as 'Here's to our land / May she withstand / The might of England vile'. Thomas Clarke, *Glimpses of an Irish Felon's Prison Life* (Dublin: Maunsel, 1922), p. 25.

4

Joseph Chamberlain

Take my word for it, if you live to be a hundred you'll never comprehend the idiosyncrasies of a warm hearted and impulsive people like the Irish.

Joseph Chamberlain[1]

Brummagem England was toppling already and her downfall would be Ireland.

James Joyce[2]

Town Hall and Grand Theatre

On 17 March 1900, about 3,000 men and women packed Birmingham's town hall for the annual St Patrick's Day meeting. This gathering had proved continually popular with local Irish Catholics ever since the turbulent 1860s, when the Church established the event in order to steal support away from the revolutionary nationalism of the Fenian movement, and in the ensuing years those in attendance had consistently endorsed constitutional means of achieving Ireland's separation from Britain. The event of 1900 would be no different, and the evening began with a rendition of Thomas Moore's melody 'Let Erin Remember', celebrating Ireland's long-lost independence:

> Let Erin remember the days of old,
> Ere her faithless Sons betrayed her […]

---

1   Joseph Chamberlain, SCUB, Austen Chamberlain Archive, *The Game of Politics*, AC 1/5/1–1/6/1/5, fol. 22.

2   James Joyce, *Ulysses* (London: Folio Society, 1998), p. 599.

> Ere the emerald gem of the western world
> Was set in the crown of a stranger.[3]

After this song, speakers stood up to praise the notion of Ireland's self-government, to excoriate the cruelty of the British regime, and to urge all of those present to work for Irish separatism.[4] With Moore's song having nostalgically described the 'days of old', the speeches then emphasized that the days to come should be filled with the most strenuous efforts to restore Irish sovereignty.[5]

The main speaker was an MP from the Irish parliamentary party, an organization that now campaigned at Westminster for Ireland's self-government. He reminded those listening that their primary loyalty lay with Ireland's interests, and declared, 'What did the Irish people who were in Birmingham come there for? It was not because they loved England better than Ireland, but because they could make a better living'. The assembled crowd cheered these sentiments, musicians played stirring music, and one particularly excitable old lady repeatedly untied her bonnet to wave in the air. But the following day, a storm of disapproval erupted in Birmingham's newspapers, denouncing the town hall gathering as being 'anti-English' and full of 'wild speech'.[6]

The newspapers noted disapprovingly that the town hall had been crammed 'almost full of Irishmen and women'.[7] But local journalists also observed that, happily, Birmingham had also seen a more palatable celebration of St Patrick's Day amongst those from 'outside essentially Irish circles'.[8] At the same time as the first audience of 3,000 had gathered in the town hall, in a nearby part of Birmingham another crowd of 2,200 had filed into Birmingham's largest theatre. Those in the second camp also spent the evening in high spirits, wore similar celebratory costumes, and proved willing to applaud, sing, and cheer; yet these revellers loathed the very ideas being celebrated by the Irish at the town hall.

3   Thomas Moore, *Moore's Irish Melodies: with Symphonies and Accompaniments by Sir John Stevenson*, ed. J. W. Glover (Dublin: Duffy, 1859), pp. 87–91.
4   'The Wearing of the Green', *BP*, 18 March 1900, p. 11.
5   'St. Patrick's Day in Birmingham: A Discordant Irish Note', *BG*, 18 March 1900, p. 4. For more on this song see Leith Davis, *Music, Postcolonialism, and Gender* (Notre Dame: University of Notre Dame Press, 2006), p. 152.
6   'The Wearing of the Green', *BP*, 18 March 1900, p. 11; 'St. Patrick's Day in Birmingham: A Discordant Irish Note', *BG*, 18 March 1900, p. 4.
7   'The Wearing of the Green', *BP*, 18 March 1900, p. 11.
8   'St. Patrick's Day in Birmingham: A Discordant Irish Note', p. *BG*, 18 March 1900, p. 4.

On that St Patrick's Day, the second audience had gathered at the Grand Theatre, a building that stood massively in Corporation Street since November 1883 and grandiosely styled itself 'the Drury Lane of the Midlands'.[9] Usually this Birmingham playhouse offered a popular programme of melodrama as well as regular operatic productions, but on this particular evening the audience members arrived in carnival mood. The theatre was giving a performance of the comic play *Niobe, All Smiles*, which had been one of the longest running dramas in London, where the actors had notched up some 600 performances at the Strand Theatre, and where a tradition had developed of wedding parties attending the show.[10] When the work transferred to Birmingham, the actors planned for the play's connection with festivity to continue by performing on St Patrick's Day, even if the plot had little connection with Ireland. Indeed, the script revolves around a Greek statue that comes alive in a well-to-do English Victorian home, with numerous comic misunderstandings occurring before the final revelation of the statue's identity.[11] Nevertheless, the Grand Theatre advertised that evening's performance as a special St Patrick's Day gala that would commemorate British war victories and celebrate the bravery of Ireland's soldiers currently fighting for her majesty's army. Accordingly, those taking their seats in the bustling theatre received a sprig of shamrock that had been especially shipped over from Ireland, and as the silk curtain crimped and folded, the spectators saw the cast also decked out with similar leaves.[12] At the end of the play the lead actor burst onto the stage brandishing a large green flag, and to the accompaniment of music from the theatre's orchestra he then sang a specially adapted Irish melody, before the audience responded by cheering wildly and then joining in songs that praised the British empire.

The spectators hollered most enthusiastically when the cast concluded the evening by singing a version of 'The Wearing of the Green', a song praising Irish rebellion against British rule, first widely heard in Birmingham thirty-five years earlier as part of a popular Boucicault play.[13] Of course, in 1900 those in

---

9   Salberg, *Ring Down the Curtain*, p. 68.

10   Phyllis Hartnoll (ed.), *The Oxford Companion to the Theatre* (London: Oxford University Press, 1957), p. 773; Edward Paulton, *The Stone Lady* (New York: French, 1926), p. 3.

11   Harry and Edward Paulton, *Niobe, All Smiles* (London: French, 1904), p. 4.

12   'The Wearing of the Green', *BP*, 18 March 1900, p. 11.

13   *Arrah-na-Pogue* received its British premiere in 1865 at London's Princess's Theatre and appeared in Birmingham's New Adelphi later that year. Deirdre McFeely, 'Dion Boucicault's "The Wearing of the Green"', in *Irish Theatre on Tour*, ed. Nicholas Grene and Chris Morash (Dublin: Carysfort, 2005), p. 148; 'The Theatres', *Town Crier*, November 1865, p. 14.

the Grand Theatre did not hear the old lyrics, but instead listened to a revised version that had been written especially for the occasion by the play's leading man. The original words of the song had berated England for shedding Ireland's blood, and promised that the shamrock – symbolizing the Irish nation – would take root and flourish despite being brutally trodden underfoot.[14] However, those who attended the Grand Theatre listened to no such revolutionary sentiments, but instead heard:

> So we'll take the four-leaved shamrock for the luck which never fails,
> And its leaves shall stand for England, Ireland, Scotland, and for Wales;
> While the Empire's voice is lifted high to cheer our well-loved Queen,
> And a hundred million Britons are a Wearin' of the Green.[15]

Thus, at the same time as those in the town hall celebrated the idea of Ireland's independence, the Grand Theatre glorified the yoking of Ireland with Britain.

The reason why such a schism had opened up between Birmingham's two audiences on that spring evening in 1900 was that Britain had declared another war, with Crown forces now fighting an internationally unpopular conflict to end the independence of the two Boer republics in South Africa. Consequently, those in the stalls at the Grand Theatre wished to give a hearty display of patriotism and to conclude their evening with a rousing rendition of 'God Save the Queen'. This audience cheered with particular gusto when the cast mentioned Frederick Roberts, the Anglo-Irish commander currently leading British troops in what wrongly looked like being a rapid victory against the Boers.[16] Roberts had recently reversed the early humiliations of the conflict by relying on the bravery of his Irish regiments, and the appalling losses amongst those battalions left Queen Victoria mourning 'my brave Irish soldiers'.[17]

---

14   David Krause (ed.), *The Dolmen Boucicault*, (Dublin: Dolmen, 1964), p. 134.

15   Rudyard Kipling also rewrote 'The Wearing of the Green' in much the same vein during March 1900; see Rudyard Kipling, *The Sussex Edition of the Complete Works in Prose and Verse of Rudyard Kipling*, vol. 35 (London: Macmillan, 1939), p. 213.

16   'The Wearing of the Green', *BP*, 18 March 1900, p. 11; 'St. Patrick's Day in Birmingham: A Discordant Irish Note', p. 4; Peter Galloway, *The Most Illustrious Order of St. Patrick, 1793–1983* (Shopwyke Hall: Phillimore, 1983), p. 81; Brian Robson, 'Roberts, Frederick Sleigh', *Oxford Dictionary of National Biography*, ed. H. C. G. Matthew and Brian Harrison (Oxford: Oxford University Press, 2004), vol. XLVII, pp. 156–61.

17   Thomas Pakenham, *The Boer War* (London: Weidenfeld and Nicolson, 1997), p. 358; Brian Moynahan, *The British Century: A Photographic History of the Last Hundred Years* (London: Weidenfeld and Nicolson, 1997), p. 14.

On 7 March the public learned that the queen herself would visit Ireland in April, and that Irish soldiers in the British army would be permitted to wear the shamrock, something that had long been banned.[18] These announcements meant that the shamrock appeared throughout the streets of England during the following ten days, with many, like the cast at the Grand Theatre, embracing the plant as an emblem of British patriotism. In Birmingham, women donned green dresses, retailers decorated shops with shamrocks, and numerous emerald flags fluttered in company with the Union Jack.[19] Some residents probably remembered a pleasing show by Walter Howard at the Aston Theatre Royal the previous July, which revealed how the shamrock's green leaves symbolized the love linking Ireland to England, with the actors indicating that, despite occasional disagreements, supportive Hibernians would still appear whenever the empire 'wanted men to fight her battles'.[20]

Yet the idea of Ireland's men sacrificing their lives on behalf of the Crown inflamed Irish nationalist opinion, and that year's St Patrick's Day parades in New York and Chicago featured Boer flags, whilst a procession in Dublin witnessed violent protests against Queen Victoria.[21] During the course of the war, branches of Ireland's Gaelic League increased nearly fourfold, Catholic gangs in Belfast took the names of Boer generals, and bands of men from Ireland travelled to fight alongside Britain's adversaries.[22] Many Irish nationalists in Birmingham thought in a similar way, and at the St Patrick's Day meeting at the town hall they linked the Boer and Irish desire for independence, lamenting the 'vilest calumnies' that had been circulated in Britain about the empire's enemies. Those at the town hall also condemned the British army which fought for 'vindictive diabolical' reasons, declaring that all of those present 'must deplore' the current campaign in South Africa.[23]

But feeling ran particularly high in Birmingham because the local MP, Joseph Chamberlain, acted as Britain's colonial secretary and had been a major driving force towards military deployment. Indeed, the hostilities were variously

---

[18] James H. Murphy, *Abject Loyalty: Nationalism and Monarchy in Ireland During the Reign of Queen Victoria* (Cork: Cork University Press, 2001), pp. 278–79.

[19] 'The Wearing of the Green', *BP*, 18 March 1900, p. 11.

[20] Walter Howard, BL, Lord Chamberlain's Collection, *The Wearing o' the Green: A Story of the Irish Rebellion*, 53,607, scene III, fol. 6; scene IV, fol. 11; and scene I, fol. 7; 'Aston Theatre', *BM*, 25 July 1899, p. 2.

[21] 'St. Patrick's Day Celebrations in Birmingham', *BM*, 19 March 1900, p. 3.

[22] Donal P. McCracken, *MacBride's Brigade: Irish Commandos in the Anglo-Boer War* (Dublin: Four Courts Press, 1999), p. 74.

[23] 'St. Patrick's Day in Birmingham: A Discordant Irish Note', *BM*, 19 March 1900, p. 4.

characterized as 'Joe's war' or 'Chamberlain's war'.[24] Furthermore, his tactics towards the Boers formed only the latest piece in his larger political jigsaw, as by 1900 Chamberlain had become Britain's foremost advocate of empire, and long before his interventions in South African he had cut his teeth on the issue of Ireland. During the preceding years, Chamberlain had spent much of his political life attempting to strengthen Britain by damaging the prospects of Irish sovereignty, and thus became a hate figure for Irish nationalists at the same time that he proved a hero for English patriots.

Birmingham Joe

Joseph Chamberlain had been born in London, and adopted Birmingham as his home in 1854 at the age of eighteen, when he came to work in the Broad Street office of a screw manufacturing company. As one of his first activities in the English midlands, he enrolled in the local debating society, and participated in a discussion where, perhaps ominously for the Irish, he strongly defended the man still widely reviled for atrocities in Ireland, Oliver Cromwell.[25] Nevertheless, after the Murphy riots of 1867 Chamberlain showed concern for the wrecked district, and when visiting the scene the following day noted that 'The roofs were gone, the fronts of the houses also; the remains of the fires were still to be seen'.[26]

However, the realm of provincial screw manufacturing could scarcely contain Chamberlain's exceptional talents for very long, and after mastering the convolutions of local business he entered the town council, where he associated himself with Birmingham's traditional radicalism. In 1873 he successfully stood as a candidate for the mayoralty of Birmingham on behalf of the Liberals, a political party that had morphed out of the radicals and Whigs, and after being elected he proved the most successful and visionary mayor that the area has ever seen. In previous years, cities like Leeds, Manchester, and Liverpool had led the field in terms of civic improvement, but Chamberlain soon established Birmingham as the trailblazer, motivated by the kind of egalitarianism that had caused an earlier generation of local politicians to campaign for franchise reform. He began by taking the region's two gas companies out of private ownership and putting them into the hands of the council, an example of

---

24   Ward, *City-State and Nation*, p. 137.

25   In later years this defence was publicized in a commemorative booklet about Chamberlain, *The Man and the City* (Birmingham: Silk and Terry, 1906[?]).

26   Quoted by N. Murrell Marris, *Joseph Chamberlain: The Man and the Statesman* (London: Hutchinson, 1900), p. 65.

'municipal socialism' that quickly repaid the initial investment, improved the quality of gas, and reduced the bill for consumers.[27]

Next, Chamberlain turned his attention to the area's stomach-churning water supply. In 1869, 150,000 people in Birmingham depended on open wells that could scarcely be distinguished from sewers, and so Chamberlain repeated the trick that he had performed with the gas companies, setting up a non-profit-making monopoly that ensured a cheap supply of clean water. He also greatly improved the local landscape by purchasing and redeveloping slum areas in Birmingham's centre, replacing much of the unsanitary and mazy Irish quarter with a wide, shop-lined boulevard called Corporation Street.[28] In addition, he organized the surfacing of roads, laying of pavements, and careful landscaping of the town's main open spaces – even donating his own money towards the improvements – and kick-starting the development of a new council house (1879), reference library (1882), art gallery (1885), four public parks (from 1873), and a range of board schools and branch libraries.[29] As a result, Birmingham became one of the healthiest of Britain's industrial regions, winning Chamberlain a solid base of local support that would stay with him until the end of his life and remain with his offspring until the 1940s. Indeed, even during his mayoralty, grateful admirers made plans to develop the area between the town hall and the council house into 'Chamberlain Square', with an Italianate fountain commemorating the man who established the region's clean water supply.[30] Chamberlain then decided to run as a Liberal party candidate for parliament, with his local popularity ensuring that he was a shoo-in for the Birmingham constituency, and he quit the council house for Westminster in 1876.

By contrast, at the same time as industrial workers in Birmingham marvelled at Chamberlain's revivified town, the tenant farmers of Ireland endured great hardship and frustration. Irish landowners had long been able to set rates of rent without reference to agricultural prices, making conditions difficult for the impecunious labourers who worked and lived on the land, with poor harvests, low prices, and bad weather compounding the problem in the 1870s, and triggering horrifying memories of the potato famine.[31] In response,

27   Peter T. Marsh, *Joseph Chamberlain: Entrepreneur in Politics* (New Haven: Yale University Press, 1994), pp. 79, 86.

28   Briggs and Gill, *History of Birmingham*, vol. II, pp. 75, 73; Chinn, *Birmingham Irish*, p. 51.

29   Ward, *City-State and Nation*, p. 78.

30   Marsh, *Joseph Chamberlain*, pp. 94–95, 100–2.

31   Jackson, *Home Rule*, p. 40.

constitutional Irish nationalists, aware that such desperate conditions bred sympathy for violence, sought to alleviate the situation and avert a full-scale rebellion by demanding Home Rule, whereby Irish affairs would be managed in Ireland rather than being controlled at a distance from London. Home Rule always remained a relatively nebulous concept, but the key features included giving Ireland and Scotland their own parliaments for dealing with domestic matters, whilst Westminster would maintain a council to co-ordinate any business of mutual concern across the islands. This idea found fertile soil amongst those from Ireland who had settled in Birmingham, as one teacher and journalist from Wexford observed:

> We are in one of the most active centres of English political thought – a town as noted for the freedom and spirit of its people, as for the variety of its productions in art and manufactures. Here the Irish population is large, amounting to over 30,000 souls; and here the political influence which the Irish people exercise is most marked and beneficial. There is no interest, local or national, in which that influence is not felt – [...] Birmingham was one of the first towns in England in which a Home Rule Association was formed – *the* first, I believe, so publicly pledged itself to the principle and purpose of the movement.[32]

The Fenianism of the 1860s had prepared the way for increased Irish nationalist sentiment in Birmingham, and after a Home Rule convention took place at the town hall in February 1873 the nationalist cause in Birmingham reignited, with delegates raising the profile of the independence campaign and establishing a common set of rules for Home Rule groups across Britain.[33] On the following St Patrick's Day, Irishmen and women in the town hall gave forthright affirmations of the importance of political action, and in March 1874 gathered again to cheer the idea that 'There was one thing that must spring to the lips of every Irishman on the present occasion, and that was Home Rule'.[34] Very soon, the St Patrick's Day commemorations in Birmingham were regularly attracting Irish MPs to speak about the progress being made towards legislative independence, whilst elsewhere in Birmingham, nationalists attended weekly meetings of the

[32]   Hugh Heinrick, *A Survey of the Irish in England*, ed. Alan O'Day (London: Hambledon, 1990), pp. 41–42.
[33]   Denvir, *The Irish in Britain*, p. 266; Alan O'Day, 'The Political Organisation of the Irish in Britain, 1867–90', in *The Irish in Britain 1815–1939*, ed. Roger Swift and Sheridan Gilley (London: Pinter, 1989), pp. 193–94.
[34]   'St. Patrick's Day in Birmingham', *BP*, 18 March 1874, p. 8.

local Land League, an organization campaigning against Ireland's exploitative landlords.[35]

Chamberlain watched these developments with interest, and although he had described Ireland's politicians as a 'scurvy lot' in 1877, he began to court Irish nationalist opinion.[36] During 1878 he voted in favour of establishing a Catholic university in Ireland, and his bid for re-election two years later saw him expressing sympathy with the people of Ireland and describing the reasonable nature of their separatist demands.[37] He pointed out that 'Home Rule is a distinct step in advance in Irish politics' and that England ought to grant justice to one of the 'greatest and bravest of nations', even declaring:

> Bear in mind what is the condition of Ireland at the present time, and how it has been brought to that condition. Ireland was subject for centuries to misrule and oppression and misgovernment, of which every Englishman – I am sure every true-hearted Englishman – would be thoroughly ashamed.[38]

As a result, at the annual St Patrick's Day festivities at the town hall that year, Chamberlain won praise from the Irish nationalists of Birmingham. He wrote a letter that was read out in the hall, stating that he had hoped to be present and expressing his sympathy with the poor of Ireland. However, Chamberlain explained that, with regret, he had decided to 'forego the pleasure of attending' because he wanted to avoid giving the impression that he was treating the gathering as an election rally, and felt that his presence might lead to misunderstanding. The audience greeted such sensitivity and compassion with applause.[39] But by contrast, the Conservative candidate for Birmingham, the 15-stone Colonel Fred Burnaby, entirely misjudged the mood of the event, and, wearing a garish green tie that he evidently felt would prove winning, attempted to address the voters. Although Burnaby made two or three cack-handed efforts to barge in, the chairman Canon Eugene O'Sullivan refused to allow the Tory to enter, and whilst the audience hooted approval, explained how unfairly partisan

---

35 'St. Patrick's Anniversary', *BP*, 18 March 1878, p. 5; Fanning, 'The Irish in England', p. 387.

36 Quoted by Chambers, *The Chamberlains*, p. 26.

37 Chambers, *The Chamberlains*, pp. 27–28.

38 Quoted in 'The Birmingham Election', *BP*, 17 March 1880, p. 5.

39 'Election Notes', *BP*, 18 March 1880, p. 5.

the situation would be if Burnaby gained a platform when Chamberlain had so graciously refrained from speaking.[40]

The voters duly re-elected Chamberlain as Liberal MP later in the year, and in office he did show a genuine commitment to Ireland, shocking the Tories with his expressions of sympathy and understanding for the country.[41] In a speech at Birmingham in October 1880 he asserted that now 'there was a Government which was more friendly to Irishmen than any Government which had existed for many years', and maintained that the administration had:

> Pledged up to the eyes to do justice to Ireland. They were bound, if possible, to find some means of giving to the 600,000 tenants in Ireland some right and interest in the soil which they tilled, which should not be in the power of absentee landlords.[42]

In 1879 Chamberlain had even met with Charles Stewart Parnell, the man who would chair the Irish parliamentary party at Westminster from 1880, to see if a solution to this vexed area of policy might be found. Chamberlain wished to find a formula that would prove acceptable to all sides and, not least, mark himself out as the leading thinker of the Liberal party.

However, Chamberlain's ideas about Irish government were doomed to failure. Although Parnell liaised with Chamberlain in 1879, the Birmingham man had misunderstood the Irish leader's aims, believing that Ireland's key demands revolved around land reform and the devolution of local government, and that if these injustices were remedied there would be little appetite for Home Rule.[43] Between 1882 and 1885 Chamberlain continued to consult Parnell about Irish reforms, although the Birmingham MP relied on second-hand information, using another Irish MP called William O'Shea as an unreliable, and ultimately fateful, go-between.[44] Such Chinese whispers allowed Parnell to keep the endpoint of the process vague in order to improve his negotiating position, with Chamberlain failing to see that Parnell's true goal was to establish an entirely independent, tax-raising parliament in Dublin, something which Chamberlain and many other British MPs believed anathema. Nevertheless, as

---

40   Ward, *City-State and Nation*, p. 81; 'St. Patrick's Day Celebration in Birmingham', *BP*, 18 March 1880, p. 5.

41   Marsh, *Joseph Chamberlain*, p. 151.

42   Joseph Chamberlain, BL, Copy of speech delivered in Birmingham on 26 October 1880, ADD MS 44,125, fol. 42.

43   Chambers, *The Chamberlains*, p. 28.

44   Ward, *City-State and Nation*, p. 94.

Chamberlain worked on formulating some definitive Irish proposals he felt that he had maintained Parnell's endorsement and, filled with naïve enthusiasm, even planned to make a tour of Ireland in 1885 to drum up support for these carefully crafted ideas.[45] Yet when the Birmingham politician finally unveiled his reforms, known to history as the 'Central Board' solution, he met with derision from all sides.[46] Parnell saw that the ideas stopped short of the independent Irish parliament he wanted, whilst British imperialists felt Chamberlain gave too much ground and simply encouraged agitation for independence. It dawned on Chamberlain that Parnell had actually been playing a clever tactical game all the time, stringing along the English MP to see how far the new proposals might advance Ireland down the road to independence, and Chamberlain felt deeply wounded when Parnell's *United Ireland* newspaper now denounced the Englishman for selfishly using the Irish issue as a springboard to high office. Whatever about Chamberlain's motivations, he had shown far greater creativity and commitment to the question of Ireland's governance than any other minister, resisted his colleagues' demands for repressive measures in Ireland, and even assisted with the negotiations to release Parnell from jail in 1882.[47] With all of this hard work now thrown back in Chamberlain's face, he decided to change tack. No longer would he attempt to conciliate the ungrateful Irish nationalists, but instead believed that they 'must stew in their juice'.[48]

Killing Home Rule

In September 1885, Chamberlain decided to hit back at Parnell by giving a widely reported speech at Warrington in which he spoke of his downright opposition to Home Rule and to the Irish leader, as well as indicating that those in favour of Irish independence were outnumbered by eight to one, drawing attention to Ireland's demographic and military weakness.[49] In response, Irish nationalists denounced Chamberlain's speech, with Dublin's *Freeman's Journal*

---

45   'The Ministerial Crisis', *Manchester Guardian*, 4 February 1886, p. 6.

46   The 'Central Board' solution would have involved elected Irish county councils sending representatives to a chamber in Dublin, from where various Irish government departments, such as education and communication, could be controlled. H. C. G. Matthew, *Gladstone: 1875–1898* (Oxford: Clarendon Press, 1995), p. 207; Jackson, *Home Rule*, p. 54.

47   Chambers, *The Chamberlains*, pp. 52–55, 64; Robert Kee, *The Laurel and the Ivy: The Story of Charles Stewart Parnell and Irish Nationalism* (London: Hamish Hamilton, 1993), pp. 470, 478, 489.

48   Quoted by Chambers, *The Chamberlains*, p. 68.

49   'A Foe to Parnell's Plans', *New York Times*, 9 September 1885, p. 5; 'The Ministerial

asserting that 'We are not sorry that he has thrown off the mask; we know him now for an avowed foe'.[50]

Nevertheless, the general election two months later pushed the issue of Ireland to the top of the British political agenda. When the votes were counted, Parnell's Irish parliamentary party had gained the balance of power between the Liberals and Conservatives, and, in this situation, MPs at Westminster could scarcely avoid the issue of Ireland.[51] The veteran Liberal, William Gladstone, subsequently became prime minister, and displayed a somewhat different approach to that of Chamberlain, believing that Ireland should be granted independence and that Parnell could still prove a useful collaborator, with Gladstone and Parnell even making arrangements to establish a Dublin parliament. Yet Gladstone also knew that the radical wing of the party demanded representation in the cabinet, and so grudgingly invited Chamberlain to become president of the Local Government Board. The Birmingham MP had actually asked for a more prestigious job as secretary of state, and felt embittered and insulted by Gladstone's behaviour at this time, but nevertheless accepted the proffered cabinet post after making clear that Home Rule remained unacceptable.[52]

In Birmingham, the official Irish-born population had dipped from 11,332 in 1861 to 7,086 in 1881, although the town now housed many second-generation Irish families who increasingly mixed with English townsfolk.[53] Indeed, whilst earlier observers had noted that those from Ireland tended to keep apart from the rest of Birmingham, one observer feared that by the early 1870s the Irish had intermingled with others and now lacked 'coherent union' and political force.[54] However, Chamberlain's hostility to Home Rule served to unite local Irish nationalists, with a large and excitable crowd congregating at the town hall for the St Patrick's Day celebrations in 1886. Whereas Birmingham's prominent MP had once won praise from this assembly, its members now lambasted his ideas and personality, with one of the speakers remarking that Ireland would never flourish until the re-establishment of a Dublin parliament. Another orator then mentioned Chamberlain by name, eliciting hisses from the audience, and

Crisis', *Manchester Guardian*, 4 February 1886, p. 6; 'Liberal Demonstration at Warrington', *BP*, 9 September 1885, p. 5.

50   *Freeman's Journal*, 9 September 1885, p. 4.

51   Jackson, *Home Rule*, p. 55.

52   Chambers, *The Chamberlains*, p. 88; Ward, *City-State and Nation*, p. 98.

53   Davis, *The Irish in Britain*, p. 120.

54   *Reports from Commissioners: Poor Laws (Ireland)*, pp. 475, 480; Heinrick, *A Survey of the Irish in England*, p. 41.

describing the MP as a 'cute man' who 'had in times past for the purposes of his own kept his feelings towards Ireland back'. The crowd then cheered as, in response to Chamberlain's threat of military force, the onstage rhetorician declared, 'Let him now do his best. They had fought in the past, and could fight in the future'.[55]

Nine days later, prime minister Gladstone finally announced to ministers his intention of establishing a parliament in Ireland. An appalled Chamberlain declared his resignation from the cabinet, and left the room.[56] It was now the turn of his supporters to mobilize in Birmingham, with a great number of people in the town knowing little about Irish affairs but feeling the need to retain faith in the MP who had proved Moses-like in leading local residents to a promised land described by one American observer as 'the best-governed city in the world'.[57] Chamberlain exploited such feelings by arranging to speak about Ireland to Birmingham's Liberals in the town hall, a venue that conjured up memories of his earlier mayoral successes. After all, this building sat in the midst of the area immeasurably improved during his term of office, and many of those in the hall arrived at the venue by walking up the road jokingly known as 'Rue Chamberlain' (Corporation Street), or by passing the adjacent Chamberlain fountain that commemorated his achievements.

Furthermore, in addressing the town hall, Chamberlain spoke at the venue that had often been commandeered by Irish nationalists in recent years for Home Rule meetings, and he now relished the chance to take to the stage and deliver the counterblast, encouraging jeers at any mention of the Irish parliamentary party and laughter at Parnell's name. Chamberlain said nothing to the audience about his own 'Central Board' proposals for Ireland, which he realized were unlikely to inspire great enthusiasm, but instead appealed to British patriotism, hoping that just as he had already become closely connected with Birmingham's newfound self-esteem, he might also associate himself with a broader sense of imperial pride. He duly received applause, cheers, and a public vote of support from the assembly, as he warned that Home Rule would:

> Lessen, if it does not destroy, the power and the influence of that mighty empire which has been built up and left to us as a heritage by our forefathers

55   'St. Patrick's Day Celebrations', *BP*, 18 March 1886, p. 8.

56   Ward, *City-State and Nation*, p. 99; Denis Judd, *Radical Joe: A Life of Joseph Chamberlain* (Cardiff: University of Wales Press, 1993), p. 110.

57   J. Ralph, 'The Best-Governed City in the World', *Harpers Monthly Magazine*, June 1890, quoted in Briggs and Gill, *History of Birmingham*, vol. II, p. 67.

– and which has done so much to promote the civilisation and the freedom of the world.[58]

With such rhetoric, the Birmingham man became the most prominent cheerleader for Unionism, and when he and his fellow travellers quashed Gladstone's Home Rule Bill at Westminster two months later he provoked fury from Irish nationalists, with Parnell hissing at Chamberlain, 'there goes the man who killed Home Rule', and other members of the Irish parliamentary party yelling 'traitor'.[59]

The defeat of the Irish bill meant that Gladstone dissolved parliament, and called a general election for July 1886, which the politicians largely fought over the issue of Home Rule.[60] But the governing Liberals could scarcely consider themselves well-placed for such a battle: the party remained in a state of internecine warfare, with factions supporting either Gladstone and Home Rule, or his ex-minister Chamberlain and Unionism. Chamberlain consequently lost control of the official Liberal organization in Birmingham, and so 24 hours after the parliamentary vote that had defeated the Irish bill, he declared that he would form a rival committee to fight Home Rule, founding in the town a National Radical Union that eventually boasted 15,000 members.[61] Accordingly, he met with supporters at the Midland Institute and wrote to his constituents to explain, 'I believe that the existence of a separate and practically independent Parliament in Dublin will be dangerous to the unity and even to the safety of the United Kingdom'.[62] He also played the 'Orange card' by explaining his desire to protect the Protestants of Ulster from absorption into a separate Irish state that might endanger their liberty and freedom of conscience.[63]

However, the Gladstonian Liberals in Birmingham who disagreed with Chamberlain formed their own local Home Rule Association. Many of the town's Irish residents supported this organization, having been themselves the first to promulgate Home Rule in Birmingham and now feeling deeply angry with Chamberlain, who had exploited some demeaning stereotypes of 'sentimental' and 'fitful' Irish behaviour when last addressing the town hall.[64]

---

58   'Birmingham Liberal Association: Annual Meeting of the "Two Thousand"', *BP*, 22 April 1886, p. 5.

59   Ward, *City-State and Nation*, p. 101.

60   Jackson, *Home Rule*, p. 63.

61   Chambers, *The Chamberlains*, p. 99.

62   Ward, *City-State and Nation*, p. 102.

63   'The Political Crisis', *Manchester Guardian*, 9 June 1886, p. 5.

64   Ward, *City-State and Nation*, p. 108.

With Chamberlain running his Unionist campaign from the town, the members of the Liberal Home Rule Association emphasized their opposition by organizing a meeting along the lines of Birmingham's previous Irish Home Rule events, and although such gatherings had conventionally happened on St Patrick's Day, this time the town hall was booked for a few days before that summer's general election. The Liberal Home Rulers invited the prominent Irish MP, John Redmond, to address this event, and when he arrived he struck a mollifying tone, even suggesting that Chamberlain's evident concern for Ireland could have a beneficial effect on the prospects for Home Rule. But the audience felt little sympathy towards the local man, and jeered every mention of Chamberlain's name.[65] Indeed, some did more than jeer. Chamberlain's brother Arthur complained that the town's Unionists were being hassled in meetings by people from Ireland whom he believed had probably been 'collected in gangs from the lowest quarters of the town and bribed with money or promises of beer', whilst rumours also circulated in Harborne that those Englishmen who opposed Joseph Chamberlain swelled their ranks by rounding up itinerant Irish-born labourers from nearby farms.[66]

In the end, however, Home Rule proved a vote loser in British politics during 1886, and the electorate ousted Gladstone.[67] Chamberlain's Unionists split away from the rest of the Liberal party and instead aligned with the Conservative government, whilst Birmingham consequently became known as 'the Mecca of Unionism' or the 'rock upon which Home Rule was wrecked'.[68] Chamberlain's supporters published volumes of his *Speeches on the Irish Question*, and these books boasted their connection with the city on the front cover: 'Issued under the auspices of the National Liberal Union, Birmingham'.[69] In fact, if Chamberlain had wanted to, he could have brought the local area to support Gladstonian Home Rule, but instead by 1886 he had led the old radical stronghold of Birmingham, which formerly tended towards the left of the Liberal party, into becoming a bastion of Unionism. After this realignment in local politics, the days when the Birmingham Political Union had implored parliament to support Daniel O'Connell seemed to belong to another world

---

65 'Birmingham Home Rule Association: Meeting in the Town Hall', *BP*, 18 June 1886, p. 7.
66 'The Recent Elections to the "Two Thousand"', *BP*, 12 April 1887, p. 4; Arthur Chamberlain quoted by Ward, *City-State and Nation*, p. 108.
67 Matthew, *Gladstone*, pp. 255–56.
68 'Time as Healer in Ireland', *BG*, 20 November 1913, p. 3.
69 Joseph Chamberlain, *Speeches on the Irish Question* (London: Swan Sonnenschein, 1890).

entirely. Instead, the majority of the town's voters appreciated Chamberlain's popular British patriotism, remembered his mayoral legacy with enthusiasm, and went on to support him in further elections in 1892 and 1895, with the Liberal Unionists only losing the Birmingham working-class vote to the Labour party at the end of the Second World War.[70] As the political analyst Henry Pelling writes, 'The existence of continuous working-class support for Unionist candidates was a distinctive feature of Birmingham politics – indeed a unique feature'. And by the end of Chamberlain's political career the MP had 'convinced the electorate that Liberal Unionism was a creed which had something to offer to all classes'.[71]

The Second Home Rule Bill

Nevertheless, the battle over Home Rule continued after the defeat of 1886, with Gladstone feeling a strong spiritual and moral mission to achieve justice for Ireland, and spending his twilight years trying to drum up support for his cause. In Birmingham, the Home Rulers also continued campaigning, and during the spring of 1887 spent time organizing further well-attended rallies addressed by Irish nationalist MPs such as John Dillon and T.P. O'Connor.[72]

Later in the year, Gladstone himself came to speak to Birmingham's Home Rulers at the town hall, with the former prime minister receiving one of the best receptions of his long career.[73] A few days afterwards, he addressed a giant audience of 17,000 in suffocatingly cramped conditions at Bingley Hall, where he ascribed the enormous attendance to the popularity of the Home Rule cause before going on to emphasize Irish grievances and to picture the 'tyrannized' way in which Ireland had been coerced into the Act of Union.[74] At the end of this colossal gathering he showed further empathy with Ireland by travelling to the house of a local MP on the Hagley Road to meet a deputation of Birmingham's Irish residents, some of whom had been part of the large and enthusiastic audience at that year's St Patrick's Day celebration in the town hall, where, under the auspices of the Liberal Home Rule Association, the Irish nationalist MP William O'Brien had delivered a stinging attack on

---

[70]   Ward, *City-State and Nation*, p. 255.

[71]   Henry Pelling, *Social Geography of British Elections: 1885–1910* (London: Macmillan, 1967), p. 182.

[72]   Ward, *City-State and Nation*, p. 108.

[73]   *Manchester Guardian*, 6 November 1888, p. 5.

[74]   *Manchester Guardian*, 8 November 1888, p. 5.

Chamberlain.[75] This delegation now presented an address to Gladstone in which they praised him for having:

> Changed our hatred into friendship, our despair into hope [...] from no other man's hands would the gift we crave [Home Rule] come so acceptably as from yours. That you may be spared to see our cause triumphant under your leadership is the heartfelt prayer of all true Irishmen and of none more than those whom we represent.

In response, Gladstone gave a speech criticizing England's previous brutality in Ireland, celebrating the shamrock, and concluding with the rousing promise that 'The residue of my life is the property of Ireland'.[76]

Yet, ultimately, all this activity would count for nothing, as in the meantime Chamberlain was playing his part in driving a stake through the heart of the Irish parliamentary party at Westminster. In one of the most notorious romances of Irish history, Parnell was conducting a love affair with the wife of Captain William O'Shea, the man who had acted as intermediary between Chamberlain and Parnell. When the Birmingham MP found out, he encouraged O'Shea to publicize Parnell's adultery, telling the captain that the boldest course often proved the wisest, and facilitating a scandal that proved too much for Irish Catholic and English nonconformist opinion to bear.[77] The Irish parliamentary party descended into factional infighting, and when Parnell died at the age of only forty-five in 1891 he knew that however far he had brought the cause of Home Rule, these revelations about his personal life had sundered the well-organized coalition of Irish interests that he had marshalled at Westminster.

The year after Parnell's death, a general election returned Gladstone to office, with the Grand Old Man becoming prime minister for the fourth time at the age of eighty-two. He now depended for his majority on the rudderless group of Irish MPs, and felt dismayed by his small parliamentary majority of only 40, but nevertheless remained committed to Home Rule, and attempted to pass a second bill in 1893.[78] Chamberlain, however, had enjoyed a triumphant election in Birmingham, where his Liberal Unionists comfortably carried all

---

75 *National Liberal Federation: Proceedings in Connection with the Eleventh Annual Meeting of the Federation, Held in Birmingham on Tuesday & Wednesday, November 6th & 7th, 1888* (London: Liberal Publications Department, 1888), p. 159; 'Monday, March 19', *BP*, 19 March 1888, p. 4.

76 *National Liberal Federation*, pp. 159, 163.

77 Kee, *The Laurel and the Ivy*, p. 535.

78 Matthew, *Gladstone*, p. 301.

seven seats that now represented the town, and he vowed to deliver a deathblow to Home Rule, continuing to counter Gladstone's call for Irish justice with an appeal to British patriotism. As parliament debated the bill, hundreds of Irish Home Rulers met for St Patrick's Day at the Birmingham town hall, where they again jeered Chamberlain's name and decried his perceived jettisoning of liberty and true Liberalism. The clergyman who acted as chairman compared Birmingham's earlier radicalism with the town's current Unionism, telling the audience that:

> Mr. Chamberlain's head had been turned by vanity. He was an illustration of the time of decay. Had Birmingham so soon come to the end of her excellence that decay had set in, and she had turned from being the pioneer of justice to be the supporter of oppression? [79]

However, despite the angry words that came from this constituency, after lengthy and acrimonious debates in the Commons, the House of Lords threw out the Home Rule Bill.[80] There was no dissolution of parliament this time, as Gladstone's cabinet could summon little enthusiasm for fighting another election, and the supporters of Home Rule shelved their bill until well into the new century.

The Game of Politics

At this moment of triumph, as the smoke cleared after all the battles over the Home Rule Bill, Chamberlain decided to mock Gladstone and the Irish parliamentary party by writing a play called *The Game of Politics*. Chamberlain had long maintained an interest in drama, writing a number of plays and acting in amateur theatricals as a young man.[81] Now, in 1893, he turned his satirical gaze towards recent political enemies, writing a drama to celebrate the demise of Home Rule and to settle some personal scores.

Chamberlain took his inspiration from recent theatre shows that had featured

[79] 'St. Patrick's Day Celebration', *BP*, 18 March 1893, p. 6.
[80] Jackson, *Home Rule*, p. 84.
[81] In 1856, Chamberlain played the part of 'Mr Rollicksome' for family and friends in a one-act comedy, and went on to write a number of other farces, with titles such as 'Crass Purposes' and 'Charades'. He also turned his hand to a verse tragedy called 'Bluebeard', whilst his amateur acting included roles such as 'Young Wilding' in an 1872 production of Samuel Foote's *The Liar*. Joseph Chamberlain, SCUB, Austen Chamberlain Archive, AC 1/6/2/6, AC 1/6/1/8, AC 1/6/2/1, AC 1/6/2/6.

Irish characters. The first major Irish hit in Birmingham after Chamberlain's arrival had been Dion Boucicault's *The Colleen Bawn*, which opened in New York City during 1860 and then clocked up an impressive run of more than 200 performances in London before arriving at Birmingham's Theatre Royal in May 1861, where the piece played to full houses for more than a month.[82] *The Colleen Bawn* stars the Irish character of Myles-na-Coppaleen, who is a buffoon and an illegal distiller of *poitín*, but is also witty and brave, diving into a lake to save the heroine Eily O'Connor at the play's most famous moment. These characters became well known in Birmingham, where, according to the local newspapers, the drama transfixed the public, forming 'a staple topic of conversation. In omnibuses, dining rooms, shops, and railway carriages, its merits are critically discussed, and young ladies over their wool-work and embroidery descant earnestly on the ill-requited affection of Eily O'Connor'.[83]

Sensitive critics realized that there might be something troubling about such melodramatic fare, and when the *Colleen Bawn* returned to the Theatre Royal in 1862 the reviewer for the *Town Crier* complained of the 'wretched imitation' of vocal accents, 'the miserable travesties' of Irish behaviour, and the general bad taste of the playhouse's depictions of foreignness.[84] Yet despite such concerns about the crudity of the stereotypes employed, Irish melodramas remained popular as they toured around Britain, and in 1863 audiences at Birmingham's Theatre Royal saw Edmund Falconer's *Peep o' Day*, an Irish sensation drama that rode on the coat tails of the *Colleen Bawn*. Indeed, Falconer had been in the original cast for Boucicault's play, and accordingly *Peep o' Day* was also set amongst the peasantry in Ireland, featured a key scene with a heroine being rescued from imminent death, and borrowed the storyline from an earlier novelist, just like Boucicault's work.[85] Yet, although the critic in the *Town Crier* lamented that the Theatre Royal where 'Macready won many a laurel – has degenerated to melodrama', the *Peep o' Day* enjoyed great popular success in Birmingham, and returned in 1867.[86] Meanwhile in 1863 *Colleen Bawn* also reappeared

---

82   *BG*, 8 June 1861, p. 3.

83   'Theatre Royal', *BG*, 25 May 1861, p. 6.

84   *Town Crier*, July 1862, p. 9.

85   In *Peep o' Day* the heroine risks being buried alive rather than being drowned as in *The Colleen Bawn*, and if Boucicault borrowed from Gerald Griffin's *The Collegians*, Falconer based his work on John Banim's two novels *John Doe* and *The Nowlans*. Robert Hogan (ed.), *Towards a National Theatre: The Dramatic Criticism of Frank J. Fay* (Dublin: Dolmen, 1970), p. 109.

86   'The Theatres', *Town Crier*, May 1865, p. 10; 'Our Theatres', *Town Crier*, May 1867, p. 11.

in the town, this time at the New Adelphi Theatre on Moor Street, where again the auditorium was packed on night after night.[87] Boucicault's subsequent Irish work – *Arrah-na-Pogue*, set during the rebellion of 1798 – gave the writer another London success in March 1865, and again the work quickly transferred to Birmingham, attracting good houses once more in November.[88] Of course, by the twentieth century such sensation drama would be all but forgotten, and when in 1986 the Birmingham Repertory Theatre premiered Stewart Parker's play about Boucicault, *Heavenly Bodies*, the actors described the Victorian dramatist being consigned to a 'dark and dacent [*sic*] corner of obscurity'.[89]

Nonetheless, Boucicault's depictions of Ireland enjoyed tremendous popularity during the second half of the nineteenth century, and, in particular, the political debates about Home Rule in the 1880s ensured that Irish topics and settings enjoyed a real vogue at the theatres that had recently sprung up around Birmingham. Of course, such fictional depictions of Ireland often reinforced comforting English assumptions rather than confronting the realities of Irish life, and, in the main, served only to dull the urgency of Ireland's complaints. In Birmingham's theatre, 'Peep o' Day' was a harmless play title rather than the name of a sectarian group whose members violently raided Catholic houses. Similarly, 'Young Ireland' could become the designation, not of a Dublin nationalist group that had once organized rebellion, but of an 1885 comedy show at the Bull Ring's concert hall.[90] When Britain's parliament dissolved because of the Home Rule crisis at Whit bank holiday in 1886, the Bull Ring audience could take comfort from knowing that the beguilingly childlike inhabitants of Ireland remained in need of firm imperial control, as demonstrated by 'The Infant Feeney', a comedian and dancer with an Irish accent who performed that weekend alongside a cross-dressing female singer and troupe of stunt bicyclists.[91] Indeed, in this need for paternal rule the Irish could be likened to other colonial subjects, and in April 1886 audiences arrived at the Bull Ring to see an Easter holiday show given by the Irish-voiced comic duo, Farrell and Willott, who danced, told jokes, and shared the bill with two burlesque actors who gave an 'excruciatingly funny' performance in the 'assumed parts of negroes'.[92]

---

87   'The Theatres', *Town Crier*, December 1863, p. 9.

88   McFeely, 'Dion Boucicault's "The Wearing of the Green"', p. 148; 'The Theatres', *Town Crier*, November 1865, p. 14.

89   Parker, *Plays: 2* (London: Methuen, 2000), p. 93.

90   'London Museum', *BM*, 23 October 1885, p. 1; 'London Museum', *BM*, 12 October 1885, p. 1; Upton, *A History of Birmingham*, p. 130.

91   'Museum Concert Hall', *BP*, 14 June 1886, p. 5.

92   'Museum Concert Hall', *BG*, 27 April 1886, p. 5; *BP*, 27 April 1886, p. 1.

The characters on the Birmingham stage who supposedly came from Ireland during this period often mimicked the worst fecklessness of Boucicault's creations without demonstrating any of Myles-na-Coppaleen's redeeming heroism. Hence in April 1886 audiences at the Grand Theatre watched the bird-brained characters of *Irish Aristocracy* saying:

McCARTHY   Say! Mull is my head big [?]

MULLIGAN   I'll acknowledge that it is considerably swelled. Take no notice old boy, there is nothing in it.[93]

Meanwhile, in July 1899 spectators at the Aston Theatre Royal's musical production of *The Wearing o' the Green* saw the very opposite of British stiff-upper-lipped self-control in the demonstrable Irish weakness for drink:

BIDDY   There's a verse in the bible tells us never to refuse a glass of water to a thirsty man. (*Offers glass to Shamus*).

Barney taking it and putting whiskey in from bottle which he has taken from pocket.

BARNEY   And another verse that tells us to put a drop of whiskey in it.

Gives it to Shamus he drinks and returns glass to Biddy.

BIDDY   Sure whiskey wasn't invented in them days.

BARNEY   Then Heaven be praised I wasn't invented in them days either.[94]

In each case, such plays provided an escape from the difficulties of the real-life Home Rule debates. With Birmingham's town hall hosting visits from lucid and provocative speakers from Ireland, audiences often preferred to ignore such complex arguments and view instead the straightforward stereotypes of the local theatre, where the 'rich oily Hibernian brogue [was] so provocative of mirth'.[95] Popular melodramas such as *The Wearing o' the Green* showed that England and Ireland would in any case be reconciled and unified, with Birmingham audiences

93   Ferguson and Mack, BL, Lord Chamberlain's Collection, *Irish Aristocracy*, 53,352C, fol. 11; 'Grand Theatre', *BG*, 6 April 1886, p. 6.
94   Howard, *The Wearing o' the Green*, scene III, fols 8–9; 'Aston Theatre', *BM*, 25 July 1899, p. 2.
95   'Grand Theatre', *BG*, 6 April 1886, p. 6.

learning that such plays were 'realistic' and 'full of typical scenes of Irish life'.[96] Theatre managers, after all, had to run commercially viable operations, attracting spectators with promises of levity rather than heavyweight political discussion. Consequently, when Chamberlain came to script his own play, he opted to echo the portrayals of Ireland that had recently proven so popular in playhouses throughout the region.

Chamberlain's *The Game of Politics* revolves around a devious MP called Weston, who is evidently modelled on the similar sounding Gladstone. Indeed, the trochaic name that Chamberlain gave to this fictional character (*West*-on) emphasizes the grand old man's preoccupation with Ireland rather than with the north, east, or south of the kingdom. During the play, Weston attempts to destroy the career of another MP called Hartley, a barely disguised version of Chamberlain, and in order to do so Weston co-ordinates the actions of a disruptive political group. Weston directs a group of crazed Irish nationalists to infiltrate and ruin a socialist gathering that Hartley has kindly permitted to take place, with Weston asking a conspirator, 'Could you find a few Irishmen – maddened with a sense of their country's wrongs, & primed with a little of their country's whiskey, to go into the square tomorrow & raise their voices in defence of the liberation of Ireland?'[97] After the real-life demonstrations against Chamberlain during the Home Rule debates, he had developed a low opinion of men and women from Ireland, and when scripting this play he may have been thinking in particular of those men alleged by his brother to have accepted bribes in order to disrupt Unionists at meetings in Birmingham.

Chamberlain also described how Ireland had monopolized political debate in Britain, with one of his English characters declaring:

> Well! I say people are sick of the Irish question. The British public can't stand too much of the same thing, and they've had questions & outrages & Home Rule, & all the rest of it dinned into their ears, until now they care no more for the lot.[98]

Here Chamberlain blamed the failure of Home Rule on that old stage stereotype, the violent and garrulous Irishman, who is embodied most clearly in the play's nationalist MP, O'Halloran. This fictional MP displays a 'good deal of brogue',

---

[96] 'Aston Theatre Royal', *BP*, 25 July 1899, p. 10; 'Aston Theatre', *BM*, 25 July 1899, p. 2.

[97] Chamberlain, *The Game of Politics*, fol. 13.

[98] Chamberlain, *The Game of Politics*, fol. 22.

loves whiskey, and enjoys brutality, supporting attacks on landlords as 'fun' and 'a little rough play'. He also repeats the stock words of Irish characters on the Victorian stage, exclaiming 'whirra', 'baloo', and 'sor', even though Chamberlain, if he had made Gladstone's efforts to know the real-life population from Ireland, might have realized that Irish labourers in Britain often used this language mockingly, and that when workers said 'top of the morning, sor', the last word was an old Irish term for bastard.[99]

In *The Game of Politics*, O'Halloran also accepts bribes, collaborates with criminals, and – whilst paying lip-service to the glory of Ireland – actually prefers living in England. By contrast, the Chamberlain-figure of Hartley behaves with consistent nobility, and at the end of the play Chamberlain's wish fulfilment is fully revealed: Hartley is vindicated and the other characters agree that 'Sooner or later he will be Prime Minister'.[100] Happily for the author, in real life his star was indeed on the rise. In 1895 he told Birmingham that he no longer considered himself bound by the terms Liberal or radical but felt 'proud to call myself a Unionist, and be satisfied with that title alone', before accepting the position of colonial secretary in the administration of the aristocratic Tory, Lord Salisbury.[101] Chamberlain, having completed his journey along the political spectrum from left to right, now decided to unveil *The Game of Politics*, and sent the manuscript to the London actor-manager Herbert Beerbohm Tree to gauge whether the piece might be suitable for production. Beerbohm Tree evidently admired Chamberlain's Unionism, and wrote in reply:

> May I take this opportunity of congratulating you on the splendid issue of your brave and noble action of these last years? There are few now who remain your antagonists, and I am persuaded that history will cast your involvement in gold. It has been a great fight.[102]

However, even such an admirer found himself unable to believe that Chamberlain's play could enjoy success on stage, and after studying the manuscript carefully and stalling for half a year, Beerbohm Tree eventually replied to tell Chamberlain that:

---

[99]   Chamberlain, *The Game of Politics*, fols 3, 22, 19; Declan Kiberd, 'The Fall of the Stage Irishman', in *The Irish Writer and the World* (Cambridge: Cambridge University Press, 2005), p. 25.

[100]   Chamberlain, *The Game of Politics*, fol. 91.

[101]   Ward, *City-State and Nation*, pp. 123–24.

[102]   Herbert Beerbohm Tree, SCUB, Joseph Chamberlain Archive, Letter of 16 August 1895, JC 5/69/1.

Though the dialogue is brilliant, the work is more of a satire than a stage-play – that is to say, the plot is not (from a dramatic point of view) sufficiently progressive – the skeleton of the drama is not strong enough to bear the weight of the flesh and muscle of the dialogue.[103]

Beerbohm Tree went on to state that if Chamberlain's authorship became widely known the drama would triumph in any case, and even offered to help with a rewrite, although this proposal came to nothing. Chamberlain's son Austen later sent the work to Allan Aynesworth, one of the most successful English actors of the day and protégé of Beerbohm Tree, but Aynesworth also replied that the play would be too cumbersome to perform and consequently the piece remained un-staged up to 1993 and unpublished until the present day.[104]

Yet as Joseph Chamberlain's play gathered dust, a literary version of his political travails did come from the pen of Ireland's foremost modernist writer, James Joyce. In Joyce's novel *Ulysses* the main character, Leopold Bloom, remembers being amongst a crowd that jeered Chamberlain when the Birmingham MP came to collect an honorary degree from Dublin's Trinity College in 1899. As Bloom wanders around the Irish capital five years later he feels alienated from nationalism and is repeatedly troubled by the memory of taking part in that demonstration, with a teasing voice asking him 'Who booed Joe Chamberlain?', and his mind wandering back to cries of:

–Up the Boers!
–Three cheers for De Wet!
–We'll hang Joe Chamberlain on a sourapple tree.[105]

Chamberlain had envisioned his Irish opponents as a monolithic mob 'maddened with a sense of their country's wrongs', but Joyce reveals that anti-Chamberlain protestors were scarcely a uniform group, and might include those who, like Bloom, have little time for the pieties of Irish nationalism and disapprove of other anti-Chamberlain demonstrators as 'Silly billies'.[106]

---

[103] Herbert Beerbohm Tree, SCUB, Joseph Chamberlain Archive, Letter of 12 January 1896, JC 5/69/3.

[104] Allen Aynesworth, SCUB, Austen Chamberlain Archive, Letter from Aynesworth, AC 1/5/1–1/6/1/5. 'The Game of Politics' was produced by the Classical Theatre Lab in Sunset-Gower Studios on 14 February 1993, under direction of Alexander Wells. Classical Theatre Lab, SCUB, Joseph Chamberlain Archive, JCL ADD 497.

[105] Joyce, *Ulysses*, pp. 434, 155.

[106] Chamberlain, *The Game of Politics*, fol. 13; Joyce, *Ulysses*, p. 155. For more on Bloom

Of course, Joyce could scarcely have known that Chamberlain had written a withering description of an Irish mob in an unpublished play, but nevertheless *Ulysses* presents an alternative view of such protestors. In *The Game of Politics* Chamberlain showed his Irish antagonists as unruly and dangerous, but when Leopold Bloom remembers an anti-Chamberlain demonstration, the Crown's law enforcers rather than the nationalist crowd bring violence, with Bloom narrowly avoiding being beaten by a mounted policeman. Indeed, in Joyce's view, if anyone ought to be indicted for inspiring bloodshed, that person should be Birmingham's foremost politician himself, and the novel offers some stark criticism of Chamberlain's imperialist policies. Towards the end of *Ulysses*, Bloom's wife remembers an earlier lover who died in the Boer War, and laments that elderly politicians fail to 'fight it out between them instead of [the war] dragging on for years killing any finelooking young man'.[107] The novel exists in a kind of dual timeframe, ostensibly describing the events of 16 June 1904 but often alluding to later historical events, and Joyce knew that when the book appeared in 1922 Molly's description of the conflict that drags on for years would most likely remind readers of the First World War.[108] The writer implied that the kind of imperialism pursued by Chamberlain would ultimately lead to that later, larger slaughter on the Western Front, a connection made more explicit when Bloom overhears an Irish nationalist predicting:

> There would be a fall and the greatest fall in history. The Germans and the Japs were going to have their little lookin, he affirmed. The Boers were the beginning of the end. Brummagem England was toppling already and her downfall would be Ireland, her Achilles heel [...] His advice to every Irishman was: stay in the land of your birth and work for Ireland and live for Ireland.[109]

According to this analysis, the popular imperialism being manufactured like Birmingham's cheapest and most tawdry goods, and directed against Irish nationalists and the Boers, signalled the twilight of empire rather than a triumphant assertion of British power. Although Bloom himself is 'rather

---

and the anti-Chamberlain protestors see John Hannay, 'Coincidence and Converging Characters in *Ulysses*', *ELH* 51:2 (1984), pp. 397–98.

[107] Joyce, *Ulysses*, p. 704.

[108] Robert Spoo highlights the link between Bloomsday and World War One in '"Nestor" and the Nightmare: The Presence of the Great War in *Ulysses*', *Twentieth Century Literature* 32:2 (1986), pp. 137–54.

[109] Joyce, *Ulysses*, p. 599.

inclined to poohpooh the suggestion', those reading the book in 1922 would have realized that Bloom had overheard a comment more astute than his own thoughts, whilst those who read the book after 1945 would have recognized that the remark was more telling than even Joyce himself could have apprehended.[110]

Cultural Nationalism

Shortly after the failure of the second Irish bill, Gladstone retired from leadership of the Liberal party, and in 1898 this great champion of Home Rule died at Hawarden. This was a body blow to the cause of Irish independence, and it would take until 1997 for any other British prime minister to demonstrate such a sense of mission towards Ireland. No subsequent London cabinet, of course, gave any serious consideration to Chamberlain's 'Central Board' solution, although later politicians realized what an opportunity had been lost in rejecting Gladstone's ideas. 'What fools we were,' King George V told Ramsay MacDonald in 1930, 'not to have accepted Gladstone's Home Rule Bill'.[111]

William Butler Yeats famously observed that with the failure of the constitutional Home Rule movement, 'A disillusioned and embittered Ireland turned from parliamentary politics'.[112] Although Yeats undoubtedly over-generalized, his comment does help to explain what now happened to the energies of Irish nationalism in Birmingham. As well as losing the national figures of Gladstone and Parnell in the 1890s, 1892 saw the death of Eugene O'Sullivan, the local priest who had marshalled the town hall meetings and tried to organize Birmingham into effective political support for Home Rule.[113] Although in West Birmingham a doctor from Ireland did unsuccessfully run against Chamberlain in the 1895 general election, the Irish political impetus in Birmingham now largely evaporated, and a speaker at the town hall's St Patrick's Day gathering in 1897 lamented that 'in every crisis of Irish history, just when the Irish people were about to win some cause that they had been suffering for, some unfortunate split would occur, some disunion would arise that would dash the cup from their lips'.[114] Of course, the anti-Boer War meeting in the

---

[110] Joyce, *Ulysses*, p. 600. See also Richard M. Kain, *Fabulous Voyager* (Chicago: University of Chicago Press, 1959), p. 176.

[111] Quoted by Matthew, *Gladstone*, pp. 400, 184.

[112] W. B. Yeats, *Autobiographies: Memories and Reflections* (London: Bracken, 1995), p. 559.

[113] 'St. Patrick's Day Celebrations', *BP*, 18 March 1892, p. 8.

[114] Ward, *City-State and Nation*, p. 125; 'St. Patrick's Day', *BP*, 18 March 1897, p. 5.

town hall on St Patrick's Day in 1900 did revive some of the old passions, and showed how pro-Home Rule energies could still be mustered in the face of Chamberlainite imperialism, but, in the main, Irish nationalists now focused their attention elsewhere.

At a dinner held at the Colonnade Hotel in 1891 a local priest named Canon O'Hanlon told members of the local Irish nationalist population that:

> Irishmen in Birmingham, as Irishmen, did not meet sufficiently frequently in social gatherings. Such meetings would tend to deepen their patriotism, and strengthen the social bonds and perhaps would have the effect of encouraging a larger and more tolerant spirit amongst Irishmen in regard to political questions.[115]

As a result of such thinking, by 1895 the first branch of Birmingham's Gaelic League had formed in Albert Street, although admittedly this activity scarcely compared to the Gaelic League in London, which at this stage already boasted 16 branches. Nonetheless, under the name of the 'Irish National Club' the Birmingham organization aimed to 'build up an Irish Ireland looking within itself for its inspiration and its reward', and in a period of activity during the years before the First World War fostered a much wider range of activities than the Irish language group that had previously operated in Birmingham. For example, the club's secretary, the Small Heath businessman James Doherty, attracted members to Wednesday evening classes on Irish language, history, and music, whilst on Saturdays the organization held Irish dance lessons where men and women took part in jigs, reels, and hornpipes to the accompaniment of fiddles and bagpipes. The club's weekly *céilí* also catered for those who wanted to sing, whilst the hurling team 'Erin's Hope' provided opportunities for the local sportsmen to play opponents from Liverpool, Manchester, and London. More ambitiously, between 1908 and 1914, local enthusiasts organized annual 'Irish Athletic Sports' days, held under Gaelic Athletic Association rules, at Selly Oak's football grounds. At these summer events various kinds of races and competitions took place, as well as music and dancing, with participants committing themselves to 'upholding the Athletic condition of Ireland'.[116] Nationalists in Selly Oak also established a separate branch of the Gaelic League, congregations at St Michael's Church and St Chad's Cathedral occasionally celebrated the Eucharist in the Irish language, whilst the White Horse pub in

---

[115] 'St. Patrick's Day Celebration in Birmingham', *BP*, 18 March 1891, p. 7.
[116] 'Metropolitan Notes of the Month', *Birmingham Catholic Magazine*, May 1914, p. 639.

Moor Street became such a regular watering hole for those from Ireland that the building became known as the 'Irish House'.[117]

A profusion of other St Patrick's Day events now stole attention from the old town hall festivities. For instance, the Irish National Club held its annual banquet at the Colonnade Hotel on St Patrick's Day, incorporating songs and numerous toasts, whilst similar music and speechmaking dominated the yearly dinner held at the Hazelwell Inn for those living in and around Stirchley.[118] A branch of the United Irish League, a political party that operated in Britain between 1900 and 1921, also held annual banquets in the early 1900s at the Royal Hotel on Temple Row as part of a campaign for land redistribution in Ireland.[119] Meanwhile, at St Chad's the cathedral's Catholic Men's Society arranged special concerts on St Patrick's Day, whilst remembering to reassure non-Irish members that the group also planned some activity to commemorate St George in April.[120]

Another Irish society that appeared in Birmingham during this period was the Ancient Order of Hibernians, a group originally established in the USA but with a growing membership of patriotic Irish businessmen in England who felt drawn to the organization's Freemason-style activities.[121] In December 1914 the leaders of the London branch arrived to speak to a meeting in Birmingham, and thus inspired local men to form two divisions in the English midlands.[122] These groups soon set about organizing social activities, and during the following February held an evening of Irish dance in Broad Street, followed in July by a theatrical show entitled 'Uncle John from Ballymuck'.[123] Meanwhile, a nationalist benefit society, the Irish National Foresters, added to the glut of Irish societies in Birmingham by beginning operations here during the opening years of the twentieth century.[124]

---

[117] 'Birmingham's Sons of Erin', *BM*, 15 November 1904, p. 5; Chinn, *Birmingham Irish*, pp. 90–91; 'St. Patrick's Day', *BM*, 17 March 1914, p. 3; Ziesler, 'The Irish in Birmingham', p. 136.

[118] 'Ireland a Nation!', *BP*, 18 March 1908, p. 6; 'Commemoration in Birmingham', *BP*, 18 March 1901, p. 10.

[119] 'St. Patrick's Day', *BP*, 18 March 1903, p. 5.

[120] 'St Chad's Men's Society', *Birmingham Catholic Magazine*, March 1915, p. 75; 'St Patrick's Day Celebrations', *Birmingham Catholic Magazine*, April 1917, p. 91.

[121] Connolly (ed.), *Oxford Companion*, p. 14.

[122] 'Metropolitan Notes of the Month', *Birmingham Catholic Magazine*, January 1915, p. 8.

[123] 'Metropolitan Notes of the Month', *Birmingham Catholic Magazine*, March 1915, p. 74; 'Metropolitan Notes of the Month', *Birmingham Catholic Magazine*, August 1915, p. 233.

[124] 'Metropolitan Notes of the Month', *Birmingham Catholic Magazine*, March 1916, p. 37;

Members of these diverse groups helped to organize the town hall's St Patrick's Day meetings, and, under the influence of so many competing agendas, the gatherings inevitably lost the focus that had been so well demonstrated when the events had been marshalled by Liberal Home Rulers and the Irish parliamentary party.[125] As early as 1905 the local press described the town hall event not primarily as a political meeting but as 'a concert', and that year the gathering consisted of an organ recital followed by a discussion about Irish universities.[126] In 1907, the audience listened to a range of Irish music, heard a nostalgic address on 'the land we left, the land we love, the land we hope to see again', and gave a vote of confidence to the Irish parliamentary party. This motion passed, but it was a sign of uncertainty about the purpose of the event that the vote had to be taken at all: such a ballot would scarcely have been necessary during the bullish anti-Chamberlain meetings of the mid-1880s. In any case, the flow of new arrivals from Ireland had long since been stemmed, and the town's official Irish-born population dropped substantially to 3,161 in 1911.[127] The Irish-born population across the whole of mainland Britain fell during these years, yet the proportional drop in Birmingham was particularly large: across England, Wales and Scotland the Irish-born population declined from a peak of 3.5 per cent of the population in 1861 to 1.3 per cent by 1911, but in Birmingham the Irish-born population fell from a peak of 4.01 per cent in 1851 to 0.38 per cent of the area's residents by 1911.[128] By 1914, when the political path towards Home Rule briefly revived at Westminster, one journalist reported that on St Patrick's Day in Birmingham 'the celebrations among exiled Irish folk are said to be more hearty and more general than they have been for some years', but there was no repeat of concerted political campaigning for Home Rule in the city. Apparently those March celebrations 'had an unusual warmth', although they mainly consisted of 'private and personal' dinners and gatherings, with the local newspaper reminiscing that:

Thomas P. Dooley, *Irishmen or English Soldiers: Times and World of a Southern Catholic Irish Man (1876–1916) Enlisting in the British Army during the First World War* (Liverpool: Liverpool University Press, 1995), p. 49.

[125] 'The Future of Ireland: Speeches at the Town Hall', *BP*, 18 March 1915, p. 6; 'Metropolitan Notes of the Month', *Birmingham Catholic Magazine*, April 1913, p. 127.

[126] 'St. Patrick's Day', *BP*, 18 March 1905, p. 8.

[127] Chinn, *Birmingham Irish*, p. 93.

[128] Birmingham figures are located in the appendix. For national figures see Roger Swift, 'Behaving Badly? Irish Migrants and Crime in the Victorian City', in *Criminal Conversations*, ed. Judith Rowbotham and Kim Stevenson (Columbus: Ohio State University Press, 2005), p. 106.

Years ago there used to be angry scenes at town hall meetings on St. Patrick's Day in Birmingham, and old folks have lively memories of those gatherings and others held on that night in the town. Those days are over, however, and it is difficult to rake up such excitement in these times. St. Patrick's Day no longer rouses very keen emotions either way.[129]

At the end of the First World War, the Liberals came to support the repressive policies of the Conservative coalition government, and this proved the nail in the coffin for Irish support for Gladstone's old party, with the Irish in Britain generally coming to support the Labour party.[130] But as Westminster politicians shelved the issue of Home Rule during the early twentieth century, Irish nationalists in Birmingham abandoned the highly politicized meetings that had once been such a notable feature of life in the town, often preferring to pick up the hurley, violin, or Gaelic language primer.

The Death of Chamberlain

In July 1906 Chamberlain's supporters showed their continuing confidence in him with a weekend of festivities to mark both his seventieth birthday and his thirtieth anniversary as an MP. The celebrations included a civic luncheon, an 80-car motorcade around Birmingham's parks, a firework display, and a rally of 10,000 people at Bingley Hall.[131] But the next day he suffered a severe stroke that paralysed his left side and left him unable to talk. He could no longer continue his active political career, although he still exerted a spectral presence on local politics and voters returned him unopposed at two elections in 1910. Instead, his son and doppelganger, Austen, came to the fore, attempting to step into the old man's political shoes despite never really convincing fitting them, and Joseph's final years were filled with thoughts of Austen's underachievement and the idea that perhaps his other son Neville might instead be the coming man.[132]

Meanwhile, without Joseph Chamberlain's influence, the English population of Birmingham displayed an increasing lack of concern for Ireland. Whilst

---

[129] 'St. Patrick's Day', *BM*, 17 March 1914, p. 3.

[130] Holmes, *John Bull's Island*, p. 133.

[131] Peter Fraser, *Joseph Chamberlain: Radicalism and Empire, 1868–1914* (London: Cassell, 1966), p. 278; Ward, *City-State and Nation*, p. ix.

[132] Ward, *City-State and Nation*, p. 175; Fraser, *Joseph Chamberlain*, pp. 281, 309. When Neville Chamberlain later became British prime minister he made an offer of Irish unity to his counterpart in Dublin, willing to ignore the 'Orange card' played by his father if Ireland would enter the Second World War on the Allied side. Bew, *Ireland*, p. 469.

many had worn shamrock in 1900, by the following year, with the Boer War dishearteningly dragging on and with St Patrick's Day falling on a Sunday, the town remained in far less celebratory mood and the theatres made no attempt to repeat any sing-along jingoism. The local press observed that the feast day created 'scarcely the enthusiasm which was manifested last year' and by 1914 journalists reported that 'during the last few years the shamrock habit has fallen into disuse, and today there were very few people seen in the Birmingham streets wearing it'.[133] In the opening years of the twentieth century, displays of shamrock had instead become restricted to local Irish Catholics, who held special services in the city centre to bless and distribute the leaf.[134]

When a Liberal government, dependent on Irish parliamentary party support, introduced a third Home Rule Bill in 1912, Joseph Chamberlain lay on his deathbed and Birmingham housed less than half the number of Irish-born inhabitants than in the 1880s.[135] Accordingly, the city failed to summon up the kind of energy for the debate that had been seen in the previous century. Yet Austen Chamberlain did glimpse the opportunity to prove himself a worthy heir to his father's Unionist legacy, and in 1913 invited Edward Carson, the recent founder of the Ulster Volunteer Force, and Andrew Bonar Law, the opposition Conservative leader, to speak at Birmingham's Hippodrome theatre. Austen, however, had little idea about how to address the Irish issue, other than by reiterating his father's 'Central Board' scheme that had bitten the dust almost thirty years earlier, and the Hippodrome felt trapped in a time warp as Bonar Law also dwelt on the past, declaring that because of Joseph Chamberlain no Unionist could fail to feel at home in Birmingham, with Edward Carson following suit and giving fulsome praise to the dying man.[136] Joseph Chamberlain's last words to his son Austen were to instruct the younger man 'to stand firm and to do what [he] could to protect those Loyalists'.[137]

---

[133] 'Commemoration in Birmingham', *BP*, 18 March 1901, p. 10; 'St. Patrick's Day', *BM*, 17 March 1914, p. 3.

[134] 'Metropolitan Notes of the Month', *Birmingham Catholic Magazine*, April 1914, p. 599.

[135] In 1881 the Irish-born population of Birmingham had been 7,072, but by 1911 had reduced to 3,165, the lowest number of Irish-born residents since the government began keeping such records at the start of the 1840s. See Clare Roche, 'Home from Home? Irish Women in Birmingham' (unpublished master's thesis, University of Birmingham, 1997), p. 47.

[136] 'Home Rule Bombshell: Self-Rule All Round', *BG*, 20 November 1913, p. 1; 'Three Leaders, Three Nevers', *BG*, 22 November 1913, p. 1.

[137] Quoted by Chambers, *The Chamberlains*, pp. 107–8.

But it was clear at the Hippodrome that, without Joseph Chamberlain himself, Birmingham could no longer claim to be positioned anywhere near the cutting edge of debates about Ireland, Liberalism, or the union.

On the other side of the political tracks, the local Home Rulers also failed to rekindle the kind of passions seen in the 1880s. In November 1913 the man who had become leader of the Irish parliamentary party, John Redmond, came to speak at Birmingham's town hall for the first time in almost thirty years, but must have been disappointed with what he now found.[138] On the stage of the town hall, one Birmingham Home Ruler reflected that 'The old bitter spirit has gone'. Other half-hearted comments followed, and by the end of the evening, when a deputation of local Irish men and women came to meet and deliver a speech in praise of Redmond, the politician declared bluntly that he 'did not know that in Birmingham particularly the Irish were as well organized as they were elsewhere', and advised that 'this would be a good time for them to re-form their ranks and strengthen their organisation'.[139]

During the following year, the outbreak of the First World War again torpedoed the passage of the Home Rule Bill at Westminster. The MP for Kerry, John Boland, did attend Birmingham's 1916 St Patrick's Day event with the optimistic message that 'now that Home Rule was on the statute book they knew the long struggle for Irish freedom had come to a successful close'.[140] But in Ireland another group of nationalists decided that they could no longer stomach such stalled constitutional attempts to reach independence. The next month, Pádraic Pearse and Thomas Clarke took matters into their own hands and led a group of advanced nationalists in an armed uprising at the centre of Dublin. Whilst the Irish capital burned, in Birmingham the variety show *When Irish Eyes are Smiling* played at Bordesley's Palace Theatre, depicting the harmless and happy femininity of Ireland with 'an Irish beauty chorus'.[141] The *Birmingham Daily Mail* had already carried an article declaring that the 'stage Irishman today, however, is dead' and that 'it is no longer regarded as funny to exclaim "begorra" or to be called a "broth of a boy"'.[142] Now, in 1916, the reality of the rebellion highlighted just how absurdly out of touch such music-hall fare could be, with the wider population of Birmingham tiring of the Irish

---

138 'Time as Healer in Ireland', *BG*, 20 November 1913, p. 1. The Irish labour leader James Larkin also appeared at the town hall that year, seeking support for striking Dublin workers. 'The "Rebel" and His Creed', *BG*, 13 October 1913, p. 4.

139 'Time as Healer in Ireland', *BG*, 20 November 1913, p. 3.

140 'Celebration in Birmingham', *BP*, 18 March 1916, p. 10.

141 'Bordesley Theatre', *BM*, 2 May 1916, p. 5.

142 'The Stage Irishman', *BM*, 10 April 1907, p. 7.

caricatures of the Victorian era. When the Grand Theatre, by this time stripped of its aesthetic pretensions and instead tarted up as a music hall, presented three supposedly alcoholic Irish policemen at the start of 1916, the *Birmingham Daily Mail* complained about the 'old-fashioned' nature of the work.[143] Two months later, when the playhouse gave slapstick portrayals of Ireland's evictions and drunkenness in the revue *Irish and Proud of It*, the same newspaper complained that the material was 'not new', whilst the *Birmingham Post* expressed weariness at the old stereotypes, noting dryly, 'one realises that it is possible to have too much all Irish'.[144] In any case, the writing was on the wall for such mass entertainment after the opening in 1910 of Birmingham's first cinema, the Electric Theatre in Station Street. Within the next 12 months the Electric brought seven imitators in its wake, and by the end of the First World War the Grand Theatre began a sad decline into picture house and then dance hall.[145] However, if audiences in Birmingham could no longer be tempted to watch comic portrayals of Ireland at the Grand, if the old debates about Home Rule felt increasingly irrelevant, and if the Irish population of Birmingham appeared to be shunning politics, a new chapter in the cultural life of the city was just beginning. Next door to the Electric cinema a small new playhouse called the Birmingham Repertory Theatre had begun to show a new and original kind of work, which, although bearing little resemblance to the old variety hall productions, again drew inspiration from Ireland.

---

143 'Irish Players at the Grand', *BM*, 18 January 1916, p. 7.

144 'Birmingham Amusements', *BM*, 21 March 1916, p. 5; 'The Variety Theatres', *BP*, 21 March 1916, p. 3.

145 Norris, *Birmingham Hippodrome*, p. 7; Salberg, *Ring Down the Curtain*, pp. 69–70.

5

Riot at the Rep

*Except in London at the Stage Society and at the Liverpool
Playhouse, where Mr. Armstrong has done such fine work, there
are no audiences in Great Britain to compare with those of the
Birmingham Repertory for real critical intelligence.*

W. G. Fay [1]

*If anyone had told me twenty years ago that [...] this theatrical
monstrosity would be first performed, and promptly performed, in
Birmingham, I should have marked off that prophet as the most
extravagant lunatic in the world.*

G. B. Shaw [2]

Mob Clamour

On Tuesday, 15 May 1917, the thirty-four-year-old British poet John Drinkwater realized he had a problem. As manager of the relatively new Birmingham Repertory Theatre, he entered the auditorium to watch that evening's show, sat in his brown leather seat, and must have looked on in horror as rioting erupted all around him.

The Repertory Theatre was attempting to perform a triple-bill of plays that had opened at the venue on the previous Saturday. Although the first two evening performances had been well received, Drinkwater presumably began watching the third show on Tuesday with feelings of trepidation. That evening,

[1]   W. G. Fay and Catherine Carswell, *The Fays of the Abbey Theatre: An Autobiographical
Record* (London: Rich and Cowan, 1935), p. 288.
[2]   L. W. Conolly (ed.), *Bernard Shaw and Barry Jackson* (Toronto: University of Toronto
Press, 2002), p. xi.

about an hour before the actors emerged onstage, the theatre had received an anonymous tip-off about a planned interruption. For Drinkwater, the 100 seats sold to a single customer began to look less like a windfall for the theatre, and more like an ominous sign of organized chaos.[3]

When the curtain rose on the first play of the night, Lady Gregory's *The Workhouse Ward*, a number of shouts came from the balcony, although nobody made enough noise to halt the production entirely. The most notable heckle came when one actor delivered a line referring to heaven, prompting an elderly woman with an Irish accent in the audience to shout back, 'You will go to hell!'[4] The second piece on the bill, Gilbert Cannan's *Everybody's Husband*, proceeded with occasional hissing, but the protestors in the audience bided their time, waiting to vent their full anger on the third play of the evening, J. M. Synge's *The Tinker's Wedding*.[5] During this final piece, each time the theatre's hapless actors tried to speak, members of the audience aimed a volley of catcalls, jeers, and missiles at the stage. Eggs and coins rained down, and the actors ducked and dodged to avoid injury.

John Drinkwater knew that Synge's works carried with them the sulphurous whiff of controversy ever since the premiere of the Irish writer's earlier piece *The Playboy of the Western World* at Dublin's Abbey Theatre in 1907 had been greeted by rioting in the auditorium and fighting in the streets, with many feeling that Synge had insulted Ireland's rural peasantry and cast a slur on the virtue of Irish women. On that occasion W. B. Yeats, the famous poet and Abbey director, dealt with the disturbances, calling the police into his playhouse and addressing the tumultuous audience from the stage.[6] In 1917, Drinkwater, also a poet and theatre manager, now fancied himself as Birmingham's version of Yeats. Half a dozen constables arrived at the Repertory Theatre, as Drinkwater demanded that the curtain be lowered and the house lights turned up, before launching himself onto the stage.[7] He then glowered disapprovingly at the audience members, lectured them on the importance of free speech, and paraphrased Yeats by telling them that J. M. Synge was a genius whose work would continue to thrive in the

---

3   Bache Matthews, *A History of the Birmingham Repertory Theatre* (London: Chatto and Windus, 1924), pp. 70–71.

4   'A Repertory Riot', *BG*, 16 May 1917, p. 2.

5   Trewin, *The Birmingham Repertory Theatre*, p. 45.

6   For more on the Abbey riots see Nicholas Grene, *The Politics of Irish Drama: Plays in Context from Boucicault to Friel* (Cambridge: Cambridge University Press, 2002), pp. 77–109.

7   Trewin, *The Birmingham Repertory Theatre*, p. 45.

theatre.[8] Drinkwater then asked the Birmingham rioters to appoint one person to explain the exact nature of the problem, clearly believing that a calm and rational discussion between the two parties would pour oil on troubled waters and allow the production to continue in a civilized and gentlemanly fashion.

The protestors, of course, took no notice. And Drinkwater was no Yeats. After a brief pause whilst one of the leading agitators gamely rose to respond, the rioters continued in even better voice than before. Drinkwater yelled that the play would nevertheless continue, only to find himself slapped down by the riposte, 'very well, but no one will hear a word'. The agitators then started to bellow songs that drowned out the scripted dialogue, whilst the actors onstage continued with Synge's drama through a clumsy combination of lip-reading and guesswork. Although some spectators decided to abandon this dumb show, the majority of those who refrained from rioting simply stayed put, apparently enjoying the unexpected turn of events.[9] Unlike the earlier *Playboy* riots in Dublin, women dominated the Birmingham disturbance, with an octogenarian grandmother amongst the most active agitators, shouting and gesticulating with exceptional vigour. The more enraged audience members clawed at the walls of the playhouse, tearing out lumps of plaster to pelt at the stage. An assortment of ever more varied flotsam and jetsam rained down on the actors, who at one point unnervingly found a knife flying towards them. Luckily this blade hit no one, although a few moments later one of the protestors was considerate enough to hurl a roll of bandages at the cast.[10]

The performance continued in this vein until the end of the piece, which concluded with one of the fictional characters threatening to call the police. If any of those in the audience could have heard the dialogue by that point, they might have appreciated the irony that although Synge's characters fear the long arm of the law, in real life the agitators inside the Birmingham playhouse showed little anxiety about being arrested. The handful of outnumbered constables looked on helplessly, concentrating on stopping only the most extreme acts of violence, and as the show ended a number of the protestors tried storming the stage door to attack the retreating actors, who must have wondered whether it would be possible to escape unscathed.[11]

Nevertheless, the lead actor and director of the piece, Maire O'Neill,

8   'Trouble at the Birmingham Repertory Theatre', *BM*, 16 May 1917, p. 3.

9   Matthews, *A History of the Birmingham Repertory Theatre*, p. 72.

10   'A Repertory Riot', *BG*, 16 May 1917, p. 2; Trewin, *The Birmingham Repertory Theatre*, p. 46.

11   Trewin, *The Birmingham Repertory Theatre*, p. 46.

remained undaunted. In 1907 she had been J. M. Synge's fiancée and acted the incendiary part of Pegeen Mike in Dublin's notorious production of *Playboy*, so in 1917 felt unfazed by the déjà vu of audience fury. Synge himself had succumbed to lymphoma in 1909, but before he died O'Neill had listened carefully to his opinions about *The Tinker's Wedding* and helped him to redraft the work, acquiring an extremely detailed knowledge about which parts of the play might rile spectators.[12] Now that audience members had indeed taken offence, she viewed the situation at the Repertory Theatre with wry amusement. When one of the Birmingham rioters hurled a large latchkey at her, she picked it up, demonstrably stuffed it into her pocket, and retorted, 'One of you won't get in tonight'. Having mocked the protestors, the next day she decided to have her own fun at the expense of the Repertory Theatre, which, after the riot, tried to prevent organized groups from again commandeering the auditorium by forbidding the sale of more than four seats to any single customer. When a woman wearing a shawl and speaking in a gruff Irish accent appeared at the box-office grille to request 40 tickets, the terrified staff panicked and yelled for help, before the potential rioter unveiled to reveal herself as the grinning Maire O'Neill.[13] Indeed, O'Neill had so much fun with this production that she returned to Birmingham the following year to star in a production of Synge's *Deirdre of the Sorrows*, and would return again in 1933 to act in the British premiere of a Denis Johnston play, *The Moon in the Yellow River*.[14]

However, others who had been in the auditorium viewed the situation more seriously. In the aftermath, the local police constables advised the Birmingham Repertory Theatre to halt the production with immediate effect. But John Drinkwater remained obstinate, and decided to follow the earlier example of Yeats in Dublin by holding firm and continuing to stage Synge's work for the rest of the week. Employees at the theatre braced themselves for further disruption during the following day's matinee, but found to their great relief that the play provoked no repeat protest. At the start of Wednesday night's performance John Drinkwater stood on the stage and denounced the protestors' 'cowardly' act of attacking the cast, declaring that he and his staff were not disposed 'to allow mob clamour to dictate to them what they should or should not put on at that theatre'.[15]

---

[12]   J. M. Synge, *The Collected Letters of John Millington Synge*, 2 vols, ed. Ann Saddlemyer (Oxford: Clarendon Press, 1984), vol. II, p. 2.

[13]   Trewin, *The Birmingham Repertory Theatre*, pp. 45–46.

[14]   'The Repertory Theatre', *BP*, 24 November 1918, p. 5; 'An Irish Play at the Repertory Theatre', *BP*, 27 November 1933, p. 4.

[15]   'Repertory Riot', *BG*, 17 May 1917, p. 3.

This time the audience refrained from barracking Drinkwater. Tuesday's protestors had stayed away, feeling they had made their point and having little appetite for further mayhem. After all, theatregoing in late-Victorian Birmingham had been repeatedly marked by chaos, with the Bull Ring's concert hall frequently witnessing invasions by drunken hooligans who gathered on the corner of Park Street and reduced performances to brawls, even leaving a barman dead in 1890.[16] By contrast, those who had protested against Synge's play gathered at St Michael's Catholic Church, and had been egged on by their priest Joseph Hogan, who explained afterwards:

> The demonstrators in Tuesday night went merely with the intention of protesting against the play's presentation, and that anything was thrown on to the stage must have been due to the excitement of the moment. Those who created the opposition never went with the slightest intention of harming anyone. Now that they have made their protest they are content to leave the matter, and any opposition which might occur during the remainder of the week will not have my sanction or approval. But I warn the management of the Repertory Theatre that if the play is ever brought to Birmingham again we shall organize a week's campaign against it.[17]

The argument now moved away from the playhouse and into the pages of the local press, where the coverage proved a real boon for the theatre by providing free advertising that ensured packed houses for the rest of the run.[18]

Why Riot?

After the Dublin disturbances that greeted *The Playboy of the Western World*, any playhouse manager who chose to stage one of Synge's works knew that the author's reputation would in all likelihood precede the show. The Abbey Theatre company had visited a number of British venues in 1906, but the players' first Birmingham performance came in May 1907, only four months after the hullaboo over Synge in Ireland, and the city's press excitedly anticipated the arrival of the work that had recently created such a furore.[19]

---

16   Upton, *A History of Birmingham*, p. 130.
17   'Repertory Riot', *BG*, 17 May 1917, p. 3.
18   Matthews, *A History of the Birmingham Repertory Theatre*, p. 72.
19   'Birmingham Amusements', *BM*, 24 May 1907, p. 5. In 1906 the Abbey company had visited Manchester, London, Leeds, Cardiff, Glasgow, Aberdeen, Newcastle, Edinburgh, and Hull. Between 1903 and 1905 the Irish players had also visited Oxford, Cambridge,

The actors played for a week at the Midland Institute, but although the Abbey
had originally decided to stage Synge's *Playboy* during the second half of this
visit, the company opted to change the bill after arriving in Birmingham.[20]
Once here, the Abbey company perhaps realized that Chamberlain's city might
be an inappropriate place to perform this notorious work and so removed the
play from the bill, as they did in Glasgow, although the drama played to great
acclaim in London.[21] Thus in Birmingham, instead of seeing Synge's play, the
audience saw four shorter pieces by Yeats and the Irish writer Lady Gregory.
This may explain why the *Birmingham Daily Mail* praised the Abbey's 'success'
and 'achievement' on the first day of the visit, but after the programme
had been changed, lambasted the company's 'Novelty that is dull and dead
[and] does not please'.[22] When the Abbey subsequently travelled to the Irish-
American areas of Boston, New York, and Philadelphia between 1911 and
1913 the company did include *Playboy* in the programme, but then found
Synge's work repeatedly interrupted by various outraged protestors. The
Irish leader Eamon de Valera later received a number of letters from Irish-
Americans who complained about the Abbey Theatre's touring productions of
Playboy, including two missives from congressmen who wrote to criticize the
'humiliating' representation of Ireland.[23] The Liverpool Repertory Theatre
also withdrew a Saturday matinee of Synge's *Playboy* in 1913 in deference
to local Irish opinion, but the Abbey cast generally learned to play on and
accept the repeated barracking with good humour.[24] On one occasion,
when a Dublin actor found eggs thrown at him he noted happily that 'they
were fresh ones', and when the battle-hardened Abbey players returned to
Birmingham in 1913 they had little to fear from protestors, so performed

and London. See Richard Cave, 'The Abbey Tours in England', in *Irish Theatre on Tour*, ed.
Nicholas Grene and Christopher Morash (Dublin: Carysfort, 2005), p. 12.

20   'Irish National Drama', *BM*, 28 May 1907, p. 5.

21   Neil Blackadder, *Performing Opposition: Modern Theater and the Scandalized Audience*
(Westport: Praeger, 2003), p. 102.

22   On the first day of the Birmingham visit, Monday 27 May, the actors performed a
bill of four plays: Synge's *Riders to the Sea*, Yeats's *The Hour Glass*, and Lady Gregory's *The
Rising of the Moon* and *Spreading the News*. On Tuesday the company replaced the planned
performance of Synge's *Playboy* with another four short pieces, giving Yeats's *A Pot of
Broth* and *On Baile's Strand*, and Gregory's *The Rising of the Moon* and *Hyacinth Halvey*. 'Irish
National Drama', *BM*, 28 May 1907, p. 5; 'Irish Drama in Birmingham', *BM*, 29 May 1907,
p. 2.

23   Lionel Pilkington, *Theatre and the State in Twentieth-Century Ireland: Cultivating the People*
(London: Routledge, 2001), p. 115.

24   Belchem, *Irish, Catholic and Scouse*, p. 214.

Playboy at the Midland Institute.[25] This time Birmingham enthused over the script and the players, encouraging the company to bring Synge's work back to the city the following year. Although *Playboy* could have been potentially problematic, the Birmingham press noted that the actors played the work as a 'sentimental rather than as ironic comedy', and that as a result 'the satire passes harmlessly'.[26] In any case, the Abbey company balanced such mockery with forthright nationalist politics elsewhere on the Birmingham programme: *The Rising of the Moon* told of an Irish policeman rediscovering his long-forgotten rebel sympathies, and *Cathleen ni Houlihan* concluded stirringly with the men of Killala rushing to fight for Irish liberty.[27]

As the Abbey players had been so well received at Birmingham in 1913 and 1914, few expected to see rioting when one of the company's actors, Maire O'Neill, accepted the invitation to produce *The Tinker's Wedding* with the Birmingham Repertory Theatre in 1917. After all, the region had seen numerous demeaning Victorian stereotypes of onstage Irish behaviour, whilst London had already shown that an English city with a far larger number of arrivals from Ireland could successfully carry off the very play that would prove so inflammatory. In addition, the death of Joseph Chamberlain and the fall in size of the Irish-born population had cooled the temperature of the Irish debate in Birmingham, and at the start of the play's run a critic for the *Birmingham Mail* had even written:

> One wonders why Synge's little masterpiece has been so neglected on the stage; it has never been done here before, and seldom seen elsewhere until a recent production by the London Stage Society. One can imagine a certain prejudice in Catholic Ireland and a certain discretion in Protestant Ulster, but that it has not flourished in the neutral air of our own land is surprising.[28]

---

25   Quoted by Blackadder, *Performing Opposition*, p. 106. For more on the Abbey tours to America see Paula M. Kane, '"Staging a Lie": Boston Catholics and the New Irish Drama', in *Religion and Identity*, ed. Patrick O'Sullivan (London: Leicester University Press, 1996), pp. 111–45; 'Midland Institute', *BP*, 27 May 1913, p. 12.

26   'The Irish Plays', *BM*, 19 May 1914, p. 2; 'Birmingham Amusements', *BP*, 19 May 1914, p. 6.

27   *Birmingham Weekly Mercury*, 16 May 1914, p. 12.

28   'The Tinker's Wedding', *BM*, 14 May 1917, p. 6. Oddly, in the decade after the riot Andrew E. Malone also asserted that '*The Tinker's Wedding*, can be played in Birmingham or Boston but never in Dublin', in *The Irish Drama* (New York: Benjamin Blom, 1965 [1929]), p. 245.

Yet despite such nonchalance, Birmingham's Irish Catholics could scarcely be expected to welcome a script by Synge that lampooned their religion. *The Tinker's Wedding* shows two unruly Irish tinkers planning to marry but being thwarted by a greedy and gluttonous priest who makes unreasonable financial and material demands in exchange for conducting a wedding service.[29] As the play continues, this cleric becomes ever more grasping and threatens vicious punishments for non-payment, only ceasing to denounce the tinkers when they gag him, tie him up, and leave him on the ground with his head in a sack. Synge himself had realized the potential impact of this depiction, and felt that if the play appeared in Dublin it could have created a greater brouhaha than even *Playboy* had done, believing that if some of his own family found *The Tinker's Wedding* they would probably set fire to the script.[30] Indeed, in November 1906 an Irish group in Liverpool had already halted another play that associated the name of St Patrick with a pig, whilst in February 1914 a theatre audience in county Mayo partly fulfilled Synge's prediction by incinerating the property of a troupe presenting a demeaning portrayal of a Catholic cleric in a different Irish play.[31] Yeats feared that Synge's take on priestly behaviour might provoke similar disorder, and so the Abbey Theatre declined to produce *The Tinker's Wedding*.[32] Instead the Afternoon Theatre Company eventually gave the first performance in 1909 as a one-off show in London, and by 1917 no theatre had produced the work as part of a regular programme, with the play having to wait until September 1963 before appearing on the stage of any theatre in Dublin.[33]

---

[29]   J. M. Synge, *Collected Plays and Poems and the Aran Islands*, ed. Alison Smith (London: Everyman, 1996), p. 55.

[30]   See Synge, *Collected Letters*, vol. I, p. 130; vol. II, pp. 23, 127, 145.

[31]   In Liverpool protestors interrupted Calder O'Beirne's performance of *The Boys of Wicklow*, whilst the Mayo rioters interrupted J. O. Hannay's *General John Regan* and set fire to the white collar of the onstage cleric. Belchem, *Irish, Catholic and Scouse*, p. 212; Joan FitzPatrick Dean, 'The Riot in Westport: George A. Birmingham at Home', *New Hibernia Review* 5:4 (2001), p. 9.

[32]   Lady Augusta Gregory, *Our Irish Theatre: A Chapter of Autobiography* (Gerrards Cross: Smythe, 1972), p. 91.

[33]   The play was first produced by Herbert Beerbohm Tree — see *Irish Playography Project* <http://www.irishplayography.com/search/play.asp?play_id=2190> [accessed 22 May 2008] — and in January 1917 Maire O'Neill also gave a one-off performance at the Court in London. In 1963 Liam Miller finally directed a version of *The Tinker's Wedding* in Dublin, at the Pike Theatre. Trewin, *The Birmingham Repertory Theatre*, p. 45; Synge, *Collected Letters*, vol. II, p. 128.

Yet Drinkwater and the Repertory Theatre decided against exercising the Abbey Theatre's caution with *The Tinker's Wedding*, even though Birmingham's history might have indicated the need for kid-glove treatment. After all, the city had been the place where the vituperative preacher William Murphy and his fellow speakers had so famously denounced the Catholic clergy, and although this had happened fifty years before, the *Birmingham Illustrated Weekly Mercury* published an account of these disturbances shortly before the Repertory Theatre's production, observing that the riots of the 1860s 'left a bitter feeling even to this day'.[34] As late as 1928 the Irish MP Timothy Michael Healy recalled how Murphy's mockery of the confessional had brought chaos.[35] In the years since the Murphy affair, Irish Catholics in Birmingham had also been piqued by Joseph Chamberlain, whose Unionist campaign saw him playing the 'Orange card' and describing Protestants as 'the most intelligent, the most enterprising, and the most loyal portion of the Irish people'.[36] The Repertory Theatre's presentation of Synge's malicious priest therefore touched a raw nerve, and inspired protestors in the theatre to respond by singing Irish nationalist songs and Catholic hymns, pairing 'A Nation Once Again' with 'Gloria Maria'.[37]

Most importantly, Birmingham now contained a group of men and women who felt ready to make a stand for Ireland. The rioters initially decided to organize in opposition after seeing the early newspaper reviews of the drama, which delightedly told of Synge's 'outraged priest' who is 'fat and middle-aged, and mean'.[38] As one of Birmingham's clerics later explained:

> Irish Catholics had too great an esteem for their priests to allow them to be made the vehicle of comic episodes. The ordinary Englishman enjoyed a laugh at a burlesque parson on the stage, but no Irishman could indulge in this sort of thing.[39]

After reading the newspaper descriptions, the would-be protestors congregated in St Michael's Church in Moor Street under the guidance of Joseph Hogan, an Irish-born and Irish-speaking priest who worked at that chapel for a number

---

34   *Birmingham Illustrated Weekly Mercury*, 18 May 1916, p. 2.

35   T. M. Healy, *Letters and Leaders of My Day*, 2 vols (London: Thornton Butterworth, 1928), vol. I, p. 23.

36   'The Political Crisis', *Manchester Guardian*, 12 June 1886, p. 5.

37   'Trouble at the Birmingham Repertory Theatre', *BM*, 16 May 1917, p. 3.

38   'The Tinker's Wedding', *BM*, 14 May 1917, p. 6; 'Repertory Theatre', *BP*, 14 May 1917, p. 3.

39   'Repertory Riot', *BG*, 16 May 1917, p. 3.

of years and had become a figurehead for local Irish Catholics. He held special
services in his church to mark St Patrick's Day, and encouraged the formation
of new patriotic Irish societies in the region, as well as presiding over that year's
St Patrick's Day dinner held at the Imperial Hotel.[40] In general, he believed that
somebody needed to fan 'to flames the dying embers of Irish Nationality' in the
city, and lamented that those who attended the St Patrick's Day celebrations
carried out few patriotic activities throughout the rest of the year.[41] He declared
that 'the main features of our race are becoming slowly but surely absorbed by
the foreign environment in which we are living. Our people are simply losing
their national identity'.[42]

When Hogan visited London he felt impressed by the activities of the Irish
population there, and from April 1913 he worked to establish a new Irish club in
Birmingham.[43] His 'Irish Institute' finally opened in February 1918 with a *céilí* at
the Temperance Hall in Temple Street.[44] In the ensuing months, members went
on to enjoy dances, dinners, lectures, and rambles, as well as various informal
gatherings.[45] However, as time went on the club failed to gain wider popularity,
largely due to Hogan's insistence that the Martineau Street headquarters of the
institute should remain alcohol-free. He wrote:

> I have no desire to run a saloon. The Irish Institute is a movement to
> preserve and develop the higher characteristics of race among the Irish
> people of the city; and it is not my belief that beer and billiards do tend to
> improve the spirit of nationality among us.[46]

---

40   'Metropolitan Notes of the Month', *Birmingham Catholic Magazine*, April 1914, p. 599;
'Metropolitan Notes of the Month', *Birmingham Catholic Magazine*, January 1915, p. 8; 'St.
Patrick's Day Celebrations', *BP*, 19 March 1917, p. 3; 'St Patrick's Day Celebrations',
Birmingham Catholic Magazine, April 1917, p. 91.

41   'Metropolitan Notes of the Month', *Birmingham Catholic Magazine*, December 1918,
p. 228; 'Irish Notes and Comments', *Birmingham Catholic Magazine*, April 1919, p. 81.

42   'An Appeal to the Irish Men and Women of Birmingham', *Birmingham Catholic
Magazine*, March 1918, p. 60.

43   'Metropolitan Notes of the Month', *Birmingham Catholic Magazine*, May 1913, p. 167;
'Metropolitan Notes of the Month', *Birmingham Catholic Magazine*, July 1914, p. 719.

44   'The Irish Institute', *Birmingham Catholic Magazine*, February 1918, p. 29.

45   'Irish Notes', *Birmingham Catholic Magazine*, December 1919, p. 241; 'Irish Notes
and Comments', *Birmingham Catholic Magazine*, May 1919, p. 99; 'Irish Notes', *Birmingham
Catholic Magazine*, March 1920, p. 57.

46   'Irish Notes and Comments', *Birmingham Catholic Magazine*, November 1919,
pp. 217–18.

Instead, Hogan wished to focus on the 'language, literature, music, history, and drama' of Ireland.[47] Yet whilst this may have been a principled approach, running the institute without a bar meant that the venture failed to last beyond the 1920s, as fewer and fewer people felt drawn to socialize in the centre's teetotal environment.

When the Birmingham Repertory Theatre presented Synge's drama about how the men, women, and priests of Ireland shared an enthusiasm for alcohol, Hogan and his supporters inevitably reacted with anger. After all, Hogan insisted that no Irish resident of Birmingham 'should go about unwashed, or in dirty, untidy clothes, in rags and tatters, with boots unpolished and buttons missing. Such slovenly ways, whether in men or women, do harm to Ireland by exposing our people to contempt'.[48] Hogan must therefore have found that reports of the theatre's wild Irish tinkers cast an intolerable slur on Ireland, and deplored the licentiousness on display at the playhouse. Indeed, this Birmingham cleric had spent the first part of the First World War worrying about the prevailing moral climate that greeted Irishwomen who travelled to the city, and he directed the newly arrived female munitions workers towards the protection of St Brigid's Hostel in Digbeth.[49] Thus, although Hogan personally steered clear of the playhouse, he encouraged and gave his blessing to the group that set about planning the relatively well-organized protest against *The Tinker's Wedding* at the Repertory Theatre.

The night after the meeting in Father Hogan's church, the protestors gathered in the theatre, where they saw Maire O'Neill playing the part of an elderly and light-fingered Irishwoman, stumbling onto the stage and drunkenly singing:

And when he asked him what way he'd die,
And he hanging unrepented,
'Begob', says Larry, 'that's all in my eye,
By the clergy first invented'.[50]

47   'Irish Notes', *Birmingham Catholic Magazine*, December 1919, p. 241.

48   Although these words have no author ascribed to them, Hogan's numerous similar contributions to the publication make him the likely author. 'Some Irish-Ireland Principles', *Birmingham Catholic Magazine*, June 1917, p. 143.

49   J. Hogan, 'St. Michael's, Moor Street', *Birmingham Catholic Magazine*, March 1920, pp. 95–96; 'St Patrick's Day Celebrations', *Birmingham Catholic Magazine*, April 1917, p. 91.

50   Synge, *Collected Plays*, p. 44. In fact, this was O'Neill's second appearance on the stage that evening: she had first entered as Mrs Donohue in Gregory's *The Workhouse Ward*. 'Repertory Theatre', *BP*, 14 May 1917, p. 3.

Though the protestors may scarcely have realized, this accusation that priests had simply invented the sacrament of penance recalled the old allegations made in Birmingham by William Murphy in his much repeated talk on the Catholic confessional, and Synge's couplets chimed with the rhymes that Murphy had used to insult the sacrament in the 1860s.[51]

The protestors therefore became noisy and agitated when Maire O'Neill's character, Mary, first appeared, singing this song before the onstage priest. Unfortunately for the theatre, Drinkwater tried to quell the riot by inviting an audience member to debate with him, but the rioter who spoke up proved lucid and articulate. The protestor explained his annoyance at the 'untrue and unfavourable' portrayal of the clergy, and gained sympathy by courteously apologizing for interrupting the audience's entertainment.[52] By the time that this spokesman had said his piece, Drinkwater realized that the opposition inside the playhouse had simply been fortified. The impromptu discussion had reminded any protestors distracted by other aspects of the evening to refocus on Synge's treatment of the Catholic priest, and the demonstrators accordingly roared down any further perceived anti-clericalism. Indeed, the protests reached a crescendo a few moments later when Mary offered the fictional churchman a drink from her cup by saying, 'let you drink it up now, for it's a middling drouthy man you are at all times'.[53] The protestors, newly alive to insults about the clergy, understood only too well the mischievous ambiguity of Synge's choice of the word 'drouthy', which ostensibly signified that the priest was thirsty but also carried the implication that he craved alcohol, and the audience noise grew louder and louder until pandemonium broke out when the cleric finally went to gulp from Mary's can.[54] A few moments later things grew worse when, even for those who could not hear a word of the dialogue, Mary hinted that she might start having sex with the onstage cleric, touching him and promising to sing to him 'unto the dawn of day'. The fact that this potential priest-seducer was a drunken atheist called Mary, the most sacred of all female Catholic names, only exacerbated the insult, with her manhandling

---

51   For instance, Murphy had told Birmingham that, in the confessional, Catholic priests gave the following advice about sex: 'A place being selected your powers to expend, / In close embrace cohere till you perfectly spend'. William Murphy, *The Confessional Unmasked: Showing the Depravity of the Roman Priesthood, the Iniquity of the Confessional and the Questions Put to Females in Confession* (London: Protestant Electoral Union, 1865[?]), p. 55; 'Mr William Murphy in Birmingham', *BG*, 22 June 1867, p. 5.

52   Matthews, *A History of the Birmingham Repertory Theatre*, p. 71.

53   Synge, *Collected Plays*, p. 44.

54   'A Repertory Riot', *BG*, 16 May 1917, p. 2.

of the cleric parodying the sanctified image of the pietà.[55] In horrified response, the rioters started singing in praise of the Catholic icon, blotting out O'Neill's blasphemy with a reassertion of the virgin's sanctity and purity.

Of course, by allowing the evening to culminate with a mixture of hymn singing and threats of violence, the rioters risked reinforcing the very stereotypes they wished to dispel, with the *Birmingham Gazette* explaining to its readers that the protest was 'so thoroughly Irish that it would be a mistake to take it too solemnly'. 'This curiously complicated controversy is not an English quarrel', the newspaper continued, 'and so while asking our Irish friends to remember that liberty of art is one of the main essentials of political freedom, we shall wisely remember that the Irish passion for religion and a row is a charming Celtic characteristic'.[56]

Once the playhouse had finally cleared of actors and audience, a real-life priest stepped into the fray. The next day's *Birmingham Post* published Father Hogan's warning that any future production of this work would result in extended protests in Birmingham, provoking John Drinkwater to retort that the play had now been added to the repertory of the theatre in spite of what Hogan thought, and that the piece would be repeated whenever Drinkwater liked. However, although the playhouse manager appeared bullish, the Birmingham Repertory Theatre never revived *The Tinker's Wedding*, even though the other two plays performed alongside Synge's work soon reappeared on the stage.[57]

Father Hogan also complained that a double standard operated in the city, with the behaviour of 'Catholic Ireland in Birmingham' judged more harshly than that of the English population.[58] But Maire O'Neill rebutted this interpretation, telling the *Birmingham Gazette* 'that those who made the loudest protests on Tuesday were obviously not Irish'.[59] In response, the following day's newspaper contained a furious reaction from 'an Irishman, who has been resident in Birmingham for twenty years, and who took a leading part in the protest'. He contradicted O'Neill, claiming rather 'that those who were loudest in the protest were Irish, and "all credit was due to them"'.[60] However, in response, a correspondent who had been absent from the playhouse on the night

55   Synge, *Collected Plays*, pp. 46, 58–59.
56   'The Passer-By', *BG*, 16 May 1917, p. 2.
57   The theatre restaged *Workhouse Ward* the following year and *Everybody's Husband* in 1923.
58   'The Freedom of the Drama', *BG*, 22 May 1917, p. 2.
59   'Miss Maire O'Neill at the Repertory', *BG*, 14 May 1917, p. 2; 'Repertory Riot', *BG*, 17 May 1917, p. 3.
60   'The Tinker's Wedding', *BG*, 18 May 1917, p. 3.

of the riot declared, 'I have a suspicion that the typically Irish were but poorly represented amongst the brawlers of the balcony on Tuesday night. I fancy the native soil of most of them was nearer Birmingham than Dublin'.[61]

This debate came near to the heart of the matter. In 1917, the idea of Irishness in Birmingham proved particularly contentious, as the relationship between Ireland and Britain had entered a period of considerable flux and uncertainty. A number of those with Irish connections in the city enlisted by choice in the British war effort, with the three Birmingham residents named McDermott who fought in the conflict, for instance, joining up by 1915, as well as the three O'Briens.[62] From January 1916, any unmarried men born in England to Irish families were compelled to join the army after ministers introduced conscription to the country. Yet Irish opinion in Birmingham and elsewhere remained far from united. Irish Unionists generally supported the war effort, seeing in the fighting an opportunity to show their loyalty and utility to London, but the situation proved more complicated amongst nationalists. On the one hand, John Redmond had vowed that his Irish parliamentary party would support the Allies, believing that the sight of Irishmen fighting alongside British troops would allow Ireland to win a place at the eventual peace conference and then to claim Home Rule.[63] But on the other hand, increasing numbers of nationalists wanted to do exactly the opposite and fight against rather than alongside the English, with the Rising of Easter 1916 promoting the rebel maxim that 'England's difficulty is Ireland's opportunity'. In retrospect, the division between the two nationalist positions had already been displayed in Birmingham, with those who gathered to see the leader of the Irish parliamentary party at the town hall in 1913 noticing that on the platform alongside him sat Roger Casement, a figure who proclaimed that Ireland should support Germany.[64] After the Easter Rising, Britain executed Casement for attempting to ship German guns to Ireland, and Redmond's endorsement of this death sentence offered a vivid demonstration of the deep cleft in Irish nationalism.[65]

---

[61] *BG*, 19 May 1917, p. 4.

[62] BCL, Local Studies Collection, The National Roll of the Great War, 505,224, pp. 279, 303.

[63] *Catholic News*, 3 June 1916, p. 8.

[64] Casement is likely to have been in the city because his humanitarian work in the Congo had been sponsored by the Birmingham businessman, William Cadbury. See Brian Inglis, *Roger Casement* (Harmondsworth: Penguin, 2002), p. 121.

[65] Redmond wrote, 'With regard to Casement and the other real ringleaders, they will have to be deal with in the most severe manner possible'. Quoted by Denis Gwynn, *The Life of John Redmond* (New York: Books for Libraries, 1971), pp. 475–76.

Yet in the wake of the Easter Rising, nationalist Ireland gradually began to sympathize with Casement rather than with Redmond, and if the rebellion remained deeply unpopular whilst being fought, the harsh British response triggered a belated wave of support for the revolutionary cause. As popular opinion shifted, the way ahead looked foggy in Ireland, and appeared particularly confusing to the Irish-born residents of Birmingham and their descendants, who felt out of touch with recent developments, torn in their loyalties, and wary of rocking the wartime boat in England. Patriotic Irish nationalists living in Birmingham wondered whether to cheer the rebel philosophy that was increasingly popular in Ireland, or support the trench warfare apparently being fought for the freedom of small nations with the help of so many Irish-born soldiers. An indication of how Irish Catholic opinion in Birmingham was shifting can be found in the *Birmingham Catholic Magazine*, which in the immediate aftermath of the Easter Rising condemned 'the misguided action of a few', but in the wake of the reprisals began to criticize Britain's 'wholesome severity', and later printed poetry in praise of Irish nationalist martyrdom.[66] Father Joseph Hogan went through a similar change of heart. Straight after the revolt he attempted to mollify hostile imperial opinion and reaffirm Ireland's loyalty to the war effort by organizing an Irish Soldiers' Flag Day in Birmingham, which took place only six weeks after Dublin conflagration.[67] This street collection raised more than £1,000, yet three years later Hogan was praising the rebels rather than the men of the king's regiments, writing of the revolutionaries:

> They were called 'dreamers' by many of us, who, at the time, did not understand their aims. Their efforts produced little effect. The people had pinned their faith to the politicians. [...] Then the desperate deed was done. To save *the soul* of Ireland the dreamers died. Standing against the wall at dawn they shed their blood. Instantly the scales fell from the eyes of the people. They saw the precipice at their feet. They pulled up sharply. The country was saved.[68]

---

66 'From the Editorial Chair', *Birmingham Catholic Magazine*, May 1916, p. 86; 'From the Editorial Chair', *Birmingham Catholic Magazine*, June 1916, pp. 109–10; 'Terence MacSwiney', *Birmingham Catholic Magazine*, November 1920, p. 211.

67 *Catholic News*, 3 June 1916, p. 8.

68 'Metropolitan Notes of the Month', *Birmingham Catholic Magazine*, September 1916, p. 189; J. B. H., 'Irish Notes and Comments', *Birmingham Catholic Magazine*, August 1919, p. 160.

Yet the Easter Rising had at first simply thrown all the old certainties of Irish politics into confusion, with Birmingham's Irish nationalists scarcely feeling themselves united around a common cause. In previous years, many had been able to join together under the banner of Home Rule at the town hall, but no such unifying idea could now be wheeled out, and formally organized Gaelic sports events were abandoned in Birmingham for about two decades after the rebellion.[69] March 1917 saw St Patrick's Day marked at the town hall by an apolitical concert and dance, with participants eschewing the piquant speeches and discussions that had once been central to this gathering in favour of an anodyne address that praised the 'never-ceasing love St Patrick has for Ireland and for Irishmen'.[70] In such an unsettled atmosphere, Catholicism instead of Home Rule looked likely to provide something for many of the Irish in Birmingham to champion and to defend, with Synge's demeaning portrayal of a priest thus functioning as a lightning rod that distracted away from the wider bewilderments that followed in the wake of the Easter Rising, and allowing one Irish group to express solidarity in shared religious convictions instead of political ideologies.

William Butler Yeats

It was fitting that the Birmingham Repertory Theatre should have become embroiled in this debate about Irish identity in 1917, as the playhouse had been heavily influenced by Dublin in the first place. The theatre owed its creation to the wealthy local man Barry Jackson, who always felt destined for the stage. Before his birth in 1879, his mother and father had greatly admired the theatrical performances of the acclaimed Irish actor born in Birmingham, Barry Sullivan, who appeared at nearby Stratford-upon-Avon five months before Jackson's birth.[71] The young Barry Jackson scarcely surprised his parents, therefore, when he followed his namesake's example, and at the turn of the century began staging a number of private theatricals for the family. By 1904 Barry Jackson had started to take his hobby more seriously, and formed an amateur theatre

---

69 Ziesler, 'The Irish in Birmingham', p. 138.

70 'St. Patrick's Day Celebrations', *BP*, 19 March 1917, p. 3; 'St Patrick's Day Celebrations', *Birmingham Catholic Magazine*, April 1917, p. 91.

71 Trewin, *The Birmingham Repertory Theatre*, p. 3. Barry Sullivan had in fact been christened 'Thomas Sullivan' at St Peter's Church in Birmingham in 1822, but decided to add his mother's maiden name, 'Barry', to his own because it allowed him proudly to show his descent from the ancient Irish family of De Barry. Sillard, *Barry Sullivan*, vol. I, p. 2.

company around himself in Moseley.[72] He and his collaborators, who began styling themselves 'the Pilgrim Players', knew that they could scarcely compete with the kind of theatricals that played for thousands of people at venues such as the Grand Theatre or the Theatre Royal. Such shows had ornate costumes, star turns, and highly decorative sets, but Jackson assembled a cast of unknown amateurs and encouraged them to act in his wealthy family's home, where the most advanced technical resource at his disposal was a set of ordinary dining-room lights and an empty space.

In 1907 the Pilgrim Players acted a version of the sixteenth-century drama, *The Interlude of Youth*, as a private production in Jackson's home. A local vicar saw this play and invited the group to perform in his church, which sat in the midst of a central Birmingham slum. Inauspicious though this setting might have been, the vicar exerted an important influence on the group's development, encouraging the Pilgrim Players to think about the ideas of William Poel, an actor and director who had long been experimenting with simple stage settings and attempting to escape the familiar extravagances of nineteenth-century performances of Shakespeare.[73] The Pilgrims felt inspired by Poel, and produced the rarely seen *The Two Gentlemen of Verona* on a stage lit starkly by two amber lights and with no changes of scene, realizing that they might be able to make a virtue of necessity and understanding that it could be a positive advantage to produce drama with a plain dignity, devoid of scenic contrivances and technological wonders.[74]

At the same time, a similar aesthetic outlook motivated the Abbey Theatre in Dublin. William Butler Yeats and Lady Gregory established the Abbey as a home of Irish national drama that would oppose the values of the commercial theatre, and whereas Dublin's large theatres staged patriotic melodramas for noisy spectators, Yeats wished to make his playhouse the home of poetic utterance, with no need to cater for the tastes of a mass audience. The founders of the Dublin theatre issued an initial statement to declare that 'We hope to find in Ireland an uncorrupted and imaginative audience trained to listen by its passion for oratory [...] not the home of buffoonery or easy sentiment, as it has been represented, but the home of an ancient idealism'.[75]

By May 1907 the Abbey Theatre had grown successful and toured mainland

---

72   Matthews, *A History of the Birmingham Repertory Theatre*, p. 2.

73   Trewin, *The Birmingham Repertory Theatre*, p. 8.

74   The actors staged *The Two Gentlemen of Verona* in the Edgbaston Assembly Rooms, which became the company's home between 1908 and 1912. Trewin, *The Birmingham Repertory Theatre*, p. 10.

75   Quoted by Morash, *A History of Irish Theatre*, p. 116.

Britain, yet after the Dubliners' first visit to Birmingham that year one of the founder members of the company commented that:

> The Birmingham critics were by no means kind, a novel experience for us in England. They could not make us out at all. However, our visit had one very good result. It inspired Barry Jackson and some of his friends to imitate us.[76]

The Irish group had indeed fired the imagination of Jackson by advocating the same dramatic principles that his troupe felt drawn towards. Like the Pilgrim Players, the now flourishing Dublin theatre company had initially possessed no permanent home and played on tiny stages, with audience members sitting almost at eye level with the actors.[77] Encouragingly, Jackson could see that the Pilgrims now closely resembled the formative Abbey Theatre, and in order to gain further insight into this Dublin forerunner he went to watch the Abbey star (and sister of Maire O'Neill) Sara Allgood playing Isabella in Poel's 1908 production of *Measure for Measure* at Stratford.[78] This production was given by the new Manchester theatre company founded by the heiress who had bankrolled the Abbey Theatre in the first place, and Jackson realized that he had the opportunity to do in Birmingham what she had done in Dublin. The Abbey Theatre's example, bewitchingly illustrated by Sara Allgood, showed Jackson the possibility of producing excellent drama without having to rely on the audiences and acclaim of London, and when Jackson's company initially issued a manifesto in the Birmingham local press the statement praised provincial towns that had refused to 'accept the London theatre as the sole arbiter and source of supply in dramatic matters', adding that 'Dublin has made a distinct and valuable contribution to the modern stage with its National Irish Theatre'.[79]

Meanwhile, at the start of the twentieth century, John Drinkwater lived in Birmingham, where, T. S. Eliot-like, he spent his time working as a clerk whilst maintaining a deep fascination with literature and drama, and inevitably gravitated towards Jackson. Drinkwater soon became a core member of the Pilgrim Players by acting, writing play-scripts, and taking the position of secretary to the amateur group, whilst in his spare time he also wrote and

76   Fay and Carswell, *The Fays of the Abbey Theatre*, p. 226.

77   Morash, *A History of Irish Theatre*, p. 140.

78   Trewin, *The Birmingham Repertory Theatre*, p. 11.

79   '"The Pilgrim Players": New Birmingham Society', *BP*, 16 December 1907, p. 4.

studied poetry, learning to appreciate the 'surely maturing brain work' of W. B. Yeats. Drinkwater also read Yeats's plays, and realized that they contained both fine language and the simplicity of staging appreciated by the Pilgrim Players. When Drinkwater published his own volume of poems in 1908 he decided to send a copy to his hero Yeats. The Irishman sent back two polite replies in the spring of 1909, apologizing for a delay in response caused 'by the illness & death of my friend JM Synge'.[80]

Despite this bad news, Drinkwater felt greatly encouraged by these letters, and decided to send the Abbey Theatre management a description of the Pilgrim Players and a request that the Birmingham company might perform Yeats's play, *The King's Threshold*, which had been written seven years earlier. Yeats soon assented, declaring 'I shall be very curious to know what you do with the King's Threshold': he was, after all, preparing a revival at the Abbey Theatre after what he felt was a previously unsuccessful production there.[81] His approval of the Birmingham staging delighted Drinkwater, who took the main part and eagerly invited Yeats to attend the show.[82] Unfortunately Yeats was unable to attend, but expressed his enthusiasm for Birmingham's new theatrical venture, writing 'I have a great desire to see your Company play'.[83]

Accordingly, Yeats arrived with his suitcases in Birmingham in April 1910, when he came to watch the Pilgrim Players' version of *Measure for Measure*, in which Barry Jackson took the role of the Duke and Drinkwater played Angelo. Yeats enjoyed the production, although the city of Birmingham quite literally left him cold: he stayed in Drinkwater's house, where the temperature dropped so low at night that the shivering Irishman had to drag a pony-skin rug from the floor to place over the icy bed.[84]

Nevertheless, Yeats declared that 'I enjoyed my stay with you very much and your Measure for Measure is still sweet in memory to eye and ear'.[85] He also felt delighted by the way that his 1903 prose work *The Hour Glass* was played by the company, presumably in an informal performance given during this visit. When Yeats subsequently decided to rework the play into a verse version published in 1913 he wrote to Drinkwater to acknowledge that 'I owe to you' the revised play because of the 'fine performance' in

80   W. B. Yeats, NYPL, Berg Collection, folder 940410, letter of March 1909.

81   W. B. Yeats, NYPL, Berg Collection, folder 940410, letter of 29 November 1909.

82   W. B. Yeats, *Collected Works of W. B. Yeats: Volume II, the Plays*, ed. David R. Clark and Rosalind E. Clark (New York: Scribner, 2001), p. 843.

83   W. B. Yeats, NYPL, Berg Collection, folder 940410, letter of 31 March 1910.

84   Trewin, *The Birmingham Repertory Theatre*, p. 12.

85   W. B. Yeats, NYPL, Berg Collection, folder 940411, letter of 28 April 1910.

Birmingham.[86] Yeats also told the Birmingham company that 'I shall be delighted if you revive *The Hour Glass*, for you gave a most excellent performance of it. May I make one suggestion: not to correct anything you have done, but to ask you to hide my errors'.[87] And accordingly the Birmingham players staged a version of *The Hour Glass* in March 1917, shortly before their controversial Synge performance brought riots to the city.

Yeats and Drinkwater also discussed the potential for a collaborative production being staged by the Birmingham and Dublin theatre groups. However, Yeats's Dublin colleague Lady Gregory threw cold water on this plan, and so Yeats made a different offer to Drinkwater: the Abbey players would be touring to give a season at the Royal Court Theatre in London later in 1910, and so Yeats asked Birmingham's Pilgrim Players to travel down and perform *The King's Threshold* as part of the same bill. He wrote, 'later on, I would like a joint performance at Manchester because I want to create the precedent with my own people of your people working with them'.[88]

Jackson's company felt thrilled to receive Yeats's invitation, and Drinkwater replied:

> I can assume now that all our people feel very greatly honoured by your invitation [...] They are all very keen, and want to begin rehearsals at once. Will you now let me know as soon as possible whether the performances can be arranged, as we should wish to leave nothing undone that would justify your kindness? [...] Your visit was a great treat to us, and your commendation of the Pilgrims was most encouraging.[89]

The Pilgrim Players therefore gave three shows in London, followed on each occasion with a performance by the Abbey players. Yet, although the Birmingham cast performed with gusto, the Irish actors waiting in the wings remained unimpressed by this interpretation of Yeats's work, and the London critics panned the Pilgrim Players, taking little account of the fact that the amateur company could scarcely compare with the high standard of the professional Dubliners.[90] Yeats himself had lost his initial enthusiasm for the Birmingham company, considering the Pilgrim Players' production a failure,

---

86   W. B. Yeats, NYPL, Berg Collection, folder 940413, letter of 20 October 1913.

87   W. B. Yeats, NYPL, Berg Collection, folder 940413, undated letter.

88   Yeats, folder 940411, letter of 28 April 1910.

89   John Drinkwater, NYPL, Berg collection, folder 6488889, letter of 1 May 1910.

90   Trewin, *The Birmingham Repertory Theatre*, p. 12.

and noting, 'I think you all or nearly all speak well, you have in other words the very thing that most players lack, but you all require more intensity of acting'.[91] Nevertheless, Drinkwater and Jackson felt grateful to Yeats, deeply impressed by the Abbey, and determined to emulate Ireland's success with a similar theatrical renaissance in Birmingham.

Drinkwater planned to re-stage *The King's Threshold*, and Yeats offered to come along, but in the meantime the Birmingham company decided to produce another of Yeats's dramas, *Deirdre*, which had first been performed by the Abbey Theatre in 1906. This time, rather than travelling to London, the Pilgrim Players took the production to the Liverpool Repertory Theatre, and here they received a far better reception than they had been afforded in the capital. The *Liverpool Courier* said that the company, performing for the first time as 'The Pilgrim Players: the Birmingham Repertory Company', produced work 'Quite excellently', and added:

> Deirdre was played with great appreciation of the wavering emotions of the part – passion, fear, pleading, icy resolve – and with very considerable nervous power. One of the musicians had beauty of voice and face. And there was always the charm of Mr. Yeats's poetry, so full of the sense of a mystic, shadowy twilight.[92]

However, Yeats himself had reservations about this production. Although he originally told Drinkwater that the Birmingham company was 'quite welcome to do Deirdre', after the Liverpool production the author now wrote:

> I see you performed Deirdre in Liverpool. I wonder what it was like. I did not think any of your women good enough when I was in Birmingham, but they must have come on considerably since. Please don't give any more performances of any play of mine without arranging with me personally.[93]

Nonetheless, following the critical success of this performance, Barry Jackson began ploughing £100,000 of his own money into a new permanent home for the company, a 464-seat building in Station Street which would be England's

---

91   W. B. Yeats, NYPL, Berg collection, folder 940411, letter of 14 July 1910.

92   Quoted by Matthews, *A History of the Birmingham Repertory Theatre*, p. 39; and Trewin, *The Birmingham Repertory Theatre*, p. 15.

93   W. B. Yeats, NYPL, Berg collection, folder 940411, letter of 3 December 1911, and folder 940412, letter of 3 May 1912.

first purpose-built repertory playhouse, and would impress newspaper writers from as far away as the USA.[94] Yeats had found a benefactress with loose purse strings to enable him to open the 525-seat Abbey Theatre in 1904, and the Birmingham Repertory Theatre now mimicked the Irish enterprise by relying on the private wealth of Barry Jackson, who inherited a family fortune from the Maypole Dairies, gaining the theatre impresario the nickname of 'butter king' of Birmingham.[95] Those who had recently launched similar repertory ventures in other British towns had struggled to find the right kind of venue: with Manchester's actors setting up in the cavernous old Gaiety Theatre in 1907, Liverpool's company gradually working up to full-scale operations in an former variety hall in 1911, and Glasgow's troupe leasing the unmodified Royalty Theatre with the support of local industrialists in 1909.[96] But thanks to Jackson's philanthropy, Birmingham could emulate the purpose-built Irish model and welcome audiences in the hall of the butter king.

At the same time as Jackson organized the construction work, Drinkwater wrote plays for the new theatre, inspired by the scripts that Yeats had created for Dublin's audiences. When Birmingham's actors had performed the Irishman's play *Deirdre* to acclaim in Liverpool they told the story of an embittered high king threatened by a younger rival who wins the affections of the monarch's wife.[97] John Drinkwater, having fallen under Yeats's spell, wrote the drama *Rebellion* for the new Birmingham Repertory Theatre and largely recycled Yeats's storyline, with both plays culminating in the suicide of the unfaithful wife when she realizes that her lover is doomed. Indeed, if anyone who watched the first performance of *Rebellion* at Birmingham in May 1914 had also seen the local company's earlier Yeats production, they may have realized that at some points Drinkwater followed *Deirdre* so closely that it looked as though the Birmingham poet had simply decided to give fuller form to some of the briefly sketched images in the Irishman's earlier, shorter work.[98]

---

[94]   S. A. Eliot, Jr., 'Germany's Theatrical Invasion: The Birmingham Repertory Theatre, a la Teuton, Unique Among England's Playhouses', *Boston Evening Transcript*, 24 May 1913, in NYPL, Lincoln Center Library, MWEZ+NC 27,695, folder 1910–1919.
[95]   Michael Holroyd, *Bernard Shaw: The One-Volume Definitive Edition* (London: Vintage, 1998), p. 510.
[96]   George Rowell and Anthony Jackson, *The Repertory Movement: A History of Regional Theatre in Britain* (Cambridge: Cambridge University Press, 1984), pp. 37, 46, 48.
[97]   Yeats, *Collected Works*, vol. II, p. 178.
[98]   It is worth comparing the following passages: John Drinkwater, *The Collected Plays of John Drinkwater*, 2 vols (London: Sidgwick and Jackson, 1925), vol. I, pp. 56, 68–70, 92; Yeats, *Collected Works*, vol. II, pp. 191, 200.

Of course, Drinkwater knew Yeats's other verse plays as well, and the tyrannical king of *Rebellion* evidently owes something to the title character that Drinkwater encountered when performing in Yeats's *The King's Threshold*. Another of Yeats's dramatic works, the once controversial piece *The Countess Cathleen*, was in 1913 the first of the many plays that Drinkwater himself produced in the Repertory Theatre, a performance that won plaudits from the *Birmingham Post*, although this version appalled Yeats himself.[99] Yet Drinkwater continued to follow the Irish poet's example, writing a number of other verse dramas with mythological settings at this time, such as *Cophetua* (1911), *The Storm* (1915), *The God of Quiet* (1916), and *X=O: A Night of the Trojan War* (1917).[100] The Repertory Theatre staged Drinkwater's *The God of Quiet* in autumn 1916 and his *Cophetua* the following year, and under his supervision the theatre brought other new verse dramas to the Birmingham stage, premiering Lascelles Abercrombie's *The End of the World* in September 1914 and Gordon Bottomley's *King Lear's Wife* in September 1915, with the latter proving highly controversial for vivid descriptions of brutality and for having 'dragged Shakespeare into the Divorce Court'.[101] If English verse drama had long struggled to escape the shadow of Shakespeare, Drinkwater used Yeats's example in order to put Birmingham at the centre of a brief flourishing of modern poetic plays.

Although in 1907 the Pilgrim Players' original aims had stated that 'attention will, for the most part, be confined to old English plays', Jackson and Drinkwater's admiration for the Abbey Theatre brought a number of recently written Irish works to the boards of the new Birmingham playhouse.[102] The new Repertory Theatre opened in February 1913, and Drinkwater's production of Yeats's *The Countess Cathleen* appeared during the following month, with Jackson's troupe then producing Lady Gregory's *The White Cockade* in May.

---

99   'Repertory Theatre', *BP*, 31 March 1913, p. 5. After this production, Yeats wrote, 'Verse plays if not played well injure everybody though the author most [...] Your "King's Threshold" failed in London despite much good work because this was not subjective passion but I thought "The Countess Cathleen" ultimately lacked even this vitality, movement, external life. This lack of life made the whole thing seem "arty"'. W. B. Yeats, NYPL, Berg collection, folder 940412, letter of October 1913.

100   Drinkwater unsuccessfully attempted to have *Cophetua* staged by the Abbey Theatre, but Yeats dismissed the idea and offered distinctly lukewarm praise to the work: 'I [...] enjoyed [reading] it very much. I think it should play well and make an impressive pageant, as well as climaxing as a play should'. Yeats, folder 940412, letter of 3 May 1912.

101   Bottomley's description is quoted by Robert H. Ross, *The Georgian Revolt: Rise and Fall of a Poetic Ideal 1910–22* (London: Faber, 1967), pp. 152–53.

102   '"The Pilgrim Players": New Birmingham Society', *BP*, 16 December 1907, p. 4.

In November the theatre lent its stage to a visiting company whose actors performed a scathing play about Belfast's Orange Order by the Abbey playwright St John Ervine.[103] Such performances passed without incident in Birmingham, with one local newspaper hailing the latter work 'appropriate and welcome'.[104] Consequently, Ireland's Abbey company came to perform for the first time at the new Birmingham Repertory Theatre in 1914 with few misgivings, and Station Street regulars may have felt that some of the nationalist work presented by these Dubliners had been cut from the same cloth as Drinkwater's play *Rebellion*, which played at the Repertory Theatre until three days before the Abbey actors arrived, and echoed the potentially subversive theme of *Cathleen ni Houlihan* in depicting insurgency against an existing king.

Abandoning Ireland

However, when war broke out in 1914 there was no chance that the Repertory Theatre could again stage plays such as *Rebellion* alongside *Cathleen ni Houlihan*, and indeed neither of these plays would ever appear again on the Station Street stage. The playhouse quickly became a centre of English patriotism, with some actors enlisting straight away, other men in the company devoting their Sundays to making shells at the nearby aluminium works, and Barry Jackson joining the navy, resulting in his absence from the theatre during the riot over *The Tinker's Wedding*.[105] Upon the outbreak of war John Drinkwater took to writing partisan verses, praised Rupert Brooke's sacrifice, and took a broadly Redmondite line by asserting that the Irish should fight alongside the English. In his volume *Swords and Ploughshares* Drinkwater threatened Germany that:

> From Derry to Cork, from Thames to Dee,
> With Kentish Hob and Collier Tyne,
> They come to travel the Dover sea,
> A thousand thousand men of the line.[106]

However, the Easter Rising troubled Drinkwater by suggesting that at least some of those from 'Derry to Cork' might resist being co-opted into the lines of the empire's fighting men. He later reacted with admiration to the poetry

---

103 St John G. Ervine, *Four Irish Plays* (Dublin: Maunsel: 1914), p. 116.

104 'An Ulster Play', *BG*, 18 November 1913, p. 4.

105 Trewin, *The Birmingham Repertory Theatre*, pp. 31, 17a, 45.

106 John Drinkwater, *Swords and Ploughshares* (London: Sidgwick and Jackson, 1922), p. 46.

of the Irishman Francis Ledwidge, praising the writer for being a 'genius' in verse as well as for enlisting in the British army and dying at the Western Front when only twenty-six.[107] But although Ledwidge saw Germany as an 'enemy of civilisation' he also supported Sinn Féin, and when Drinkwater read the Irishman's lament for one of the executed nationalists of the Dublin insurrection, the Birmingham poet commented tersely that 'The political equation in the matter does not concern us here'.[108]

After Easter 1916 Drinkwater may have realized that including plays from the Abbey Theatre in Birmingham's repertoire would be a more complicated affair now that increasingly large swathes of the Irish population felt determined to fight free from Britain, but at first the Repertory Theatre tried gamely to carry on as before, and even in the 12 months after the 1917 riots Station Street audiences could have seen plays by Synge, Yeats, and Gregory. But as the Anglo-Irish War began in January 1919 one Birmingham newspaper remarked that 'never have Irishmen been more hated in England than Irishmen are hated to-day', and Jackson's theatre could hardly afford to play something like *Cathleen ni Houlihan* or *Rebellion* at the same time as real-life Irish insurgents were using guerrilla tactics to sever the connection with the British Crown.[109]

In the first four years of the new Birmingham theatre in Station Street, local audiences watched 13 productions of plays by Synge, Yeats, and Gregory. But after 1917 the Repertory Theatre produced plays by these writers only six times in half a century.[110] Jackson's theatre did stage occasional comedies about Ireland in the ensuing years, but scarcely with the same frequency or enthusiasm as in earlier times, and with local critics giving a distinctly frosty reaction. The *Birmingham Post* criticized the theatre's 1927 version of Synge's

---

[107] John Drinkwater, *The Muse in Council* (London: Sidgwick and Jackson, 1925), p. 202; Robert Welch (ed.), *The Oxford Companion to Irish Literature* (Oxford: Clarendon Press, 1996), p. 305.

[108] Drinkwater, *The Muse in Council*, p. 211.

[109] F. G. Masterman, 'A New Star Chamber: The Irish Deportations', *BG*, 17 March 1923, p. 4.

[110] The closest that the Repertory Theatre came to reviving any earlier Yeatsian enthusiasms came in June 1921, when Station Street staged an opera by the English composer Rutland Boughton, based on a play by Scottish writer William Sharp (the pseudonymous Fiona Macleod), which was based upon Irish legendary stories of Tara. 'The Immortal Hour', *BM*, 24 June 1921, p. 4. Information about performances in 'Performing Arts', *Arts and Humanities Data Service* <http://ahds.ac.uk/ahdscollections/docroot/birminghamrep/birminghamrepsearch.jsp> [accessed 22 May 2008].

The Well of the Saints by saying 'it belongs to a generation that is dead'; the newspaper condemned the 1928 production of Shaw's *John Bull's Other Island* as 'ancient history'; and asked of the half-hearted 1930 staging of Synge's *Playboy*, 'Was this the play that cleft a thousand skulls?'[111] The newspaper even reviewed a Lennox Robinson play that had an English setting by mocking the fact that Irish plays all looked interchangeable and indistinct: '"It's a quare thing," says somebody or other, no matter who, in some Irish play or other, no matter which'.[112] Thus, although in 1933 the theatre did stage the British premiere of Denis Johnston's *The Moon in the Yellow River*, featuring an IRA bomber, the playhouse generally avoided dealing with Irish themes and issues until after the Second World War.[113] Indeed, books about Irish drama often describe the fact that in 1928 the Abbey Theatre spurned Seán O'Casey's play about World War One, *The Silver Tassie*, but if O'Casey himself is to be believed, the work suffered an initial rejection at the hands of the recently knighted Barry Jackson.[114] According to O'Casey's third-person account, despite Yeats having begged to have the play for the Abbey:

Sean had promised the first glimpse of the play to Sir Barry Jackson, had sent him the manuscript, and had forgotten about it. Then one day Sir Barry came bustling into the house when he and Eileen were busy trying to make the debts they owed meet and marry the money they had in hand. Sir Barry was in a hurry, a panting hurry; he sat down on a chair in a hurry, first setting down a burnished bowler hat on the table in a hurry, and arranging a pompous-looking umbrella to a stately stand in a corner in a hurry too.

– You've written a fine play, he said; a terrible play! An impossible play for me. I dare not put it on – an English audience couldn't stand it. There's the script. I'm grateful to you for letting me read it. His hand shot out for the burnished bowler hat. I must go now. The play would lacerate our feelings; it would be unbearable. Goodbye; and he

---

[111] 'The Repertory Theatre', *BP*, 1 February 1927, p. 5; 'The Repertory Theatre', *BP*, 2 April 1928, p. 6; 'Synge's Comedy at the Repertory', *BP*, 17 November 1930, p. 11.
[112] 'The Birmingham Repertory Theatre', *BP*, 8 February 1926, p. 12.
[113] The Birmingham Repertory Theatre staged Irish plays more frequently in the late 1940s and 1950s. These productions included George Shiels' *A New Gossoon* in November 1950; a revival of Johnston's *The Moon in the Yellow River* in May 1954; Donagh MacDonagh's *Happy as Larry* in September 1956; and Joseph O'Conor's *The Iron Harp* in October 1957.
[114] Trewin, *The Birmingham Repertory Theatre*, p. 84.

hurried out to his waiting car, and vanished: a plain man in a plain van rushing from life. The next morning, the plain van slid up to the door, and the plain man slid into the house, and hurried to the stately umbrella still standing in the corner. My umbrella – I forgot it yesterday; and the plain man vanished into the plain van again, and Sean saw him no more.[115]

With the Birmingham Repertory Theatre having grown wary of Irish drama, perhaps Jackson's caution was unsurprising. After all, O'Casey's latest play took no more care with Britain's Glorious Dead than his earlier work had taken with Ireland's Bold Fenian Men, and Jackson knew that staging *The Silver Tassie* could potentially inspire protests by affronted English patriots as well as by Irish nationalists who loathed the dramatist because of previous writing that did not fear to speak of Easter week. The Birmingham Repertory Theatre had witnessed rioting in response to Ireland's last controversial playwright in 1917, and now opted to play safe, with no Birmingham audience able to see a play by O'Casey in Station Street until 1945, when the theatre gave a version of the writer's earlier work *Juno and the Paycock*. In 1949 the playhouse then produced Paul Vincent Carroll's play *Shadow and Substance*, which perhaps offered an oblique commentary on the riots of 1917: Carroll's script depicts an Irish mob being driven wild by an unflattering depiction of a parish priest, and a fictional author being pelted 'with sticks and stones'.[116]

After 1917 John Drinkwater also proved wary of Yeats, steering clear of the Irishman's political commitments and instead praising Yeats as a poet who created works of 'enchanting sensibility' or 'intellectual passion'.[117] The publication of Yeats's *Four Plays for Dancers* in 1921 confirmed that Drinkwater and Yeats had moved in different directions. Yeats had composed his most recent collection in an increasingly stark Noh style, but Drinkwater had, by contrast, abandoned verse drama in favour of prose plays about long-dead historical characters, achieving a first real success with *Abraham Lincoln* in 1918, followed by *Oliver Cromwell* and *Mary Stuart* in 1921. Yeats's volume of Noh plays may also have depicted a rebel from the Rising of 1916, but Drinkwater avoided commenting on Irish politics, writing a defensive introduction to *Oliver Cromwell* that explained how the piece was intentionally far from factually 'exhaustive'

---

115 Seán O'Casey, *Autobiographies*, 2 vols (London: Macmillan, 1963), vol. II, p. 271.

116 Paul Vincent Carroll, BCL, Birmingham Repertory Theatre Archive, *Shadow and Substance* Prompt Book, p. 72.

117 Drinkwater, *The Muse in Council*, pp. 45, 61.

and how readers would search in vain for details such as how 'Cromwell wore dirty linen and behaved like a maniac in Ireland'.[118] On performance, the *Birmingham Gazette* duly complained that *Oliver Cromwell* showed nothing of 'the Cromwell of Drogheda' nor the 'Cromwell who was used for centuries by Irish mothers to frighten their naughty children'.[119]

Although the theatre generally became more tight-lipped about Irish politics than it had been in its early years, behind the scenes the playhouse did attract some practical assistance from Ireland after the First World War. When Station Street's regular producer, H. K. Ayliff, temporarily moved to London in March 1926, Barry Jackson invited one of the founders of the Abbey, W. G. Fay, to work in Birmingham as a six-month replacement. At this time, the conflict with Germany had destroyed much of the impetus behind the British repertory theatre movement, yet Fay stayed at Station Street for two and a half years, and greatly enjoyed his time in Birmingham, where he helped to ensure that Jackson's theatre continued to thrive. Fay gave public lectures about drama, collaborated with Jackson in producing five plays that had never been seen on any stage before, and employed a company of gifted young actors that included Peggy Ashcroft, Ralph Richardson, and the young Laurence Olivier. The Irishman later praised Station Street for educating its audience in 'critical values', commenting that 'Just as the Abbey Theatre taught the public and press what an Irish play should be, so the Birmingham Repertory Theatre on a larger scale has given its public a real knowledge and understanding of the modern drama'.[120]

As well as Fay, another Irishman came to stamp his mark on the Birmingham playhouse in the 1920s. From 1917 the Dublin émigré George Bernard Shaw began to occupy the place in Drinkwater's mind once occupied by Yeats, with the Birmingham writer now striving to emulate Shaw and dedicating *Oliver Cromwell* to the bearded Irishman. This change of style was a considerable shift for Drinkwater, with Yeats's stark, mythological verse plays contrasting with the wordy realism of Shaw's socially engaged drama.[121] Yet Barry Jackson was

---

118 Drinkwater quoted by H. R. Hall, *Notes to "Oliver Cromwell", A Play by John Drinkwater* (London: Sidgwick & Jackson, 1939[?]), p. 1.

119 'At the Play. "Oliver Cromwell"', *BG*, 6 March 1923, p. 4.

120 Fay and Carswell, *The Fays of the Abbey Theatre*, pp. 288–90.

121 By the end of the 1920s, Drinkwater would in turn discover a love for the work of James Joyce, helping the ailing Irish writer to find an ophthalmologist in England and praising Joyce's experimental *Anna Livia Plurabelle* as 'one of the greatest things in English literature'. Quoted by Richard Ellmann, *James Joyce* (rev edn; Oxford: Oxford University Press, 1983), pp. 616–17.

discovering similar preferences, making Shaw the most frequently performed playwright in Station Street's history, and forming a working partnership with the writer that had great influence on the theatre of the English midlands.[122] In the ensuing years, Shaw gave assistance during Jackson's directorship of Stratford's Shakespeare Memorial Theatre, the two men collaborated on staging influential festivals of drama in Malvern, and Jackson helped coax Shaw back to playwriting after a five-year hiatus. Initially, Shaw and Jackson had met in the spring of 1923, when Jackson suggested that the Birmingham Repertory Theatre might give the first British performance of Shaw's lengthy play cycle, *Back to Methuselah*.[123] At first Shaw thought that Jackson might be mad, but after the successful performance in October 1923 Shaw's wife wrote that the premiere at Birmingham had been 'probably the crown of G. B. S.'s career' and that, despite the torrential rain that poured down outside the playhouse, visiting the English midlands felt 'like a lovely, elusive dream'.[124]

Shaw pointed out to the staff at the Birmingham Repertory Theatre that staging his work had the potential to bankrupt the playhouse, mockingly commenting that 'if somebody is to be ruined, I had rather it were B. J. than anyone else'.[125] But Barry Jackson himself felt delighted to land this prize, seeing his theatre growing in stature by staging an ambitious new work by such a famous writer. Furthermore, as Jackson aimed to sidestep the troublesome kind of Irish theatricals that had contributed to the venue's original formation, he was able instead to present the work of an Irish dramatist who advised the playhouse with this production, 'don't mix up dramatic entertainment in the theatre with politics'.[126] Shaw's plays generally made little direct mention of Ireland, and his latest offering even sounded a reassuring death knell for Irish nationalism. The fourth part of *Back to Methuselah* presents Galway in the year 3000 AD, where an elderly British man in Gladstonian costume describes the

122 Between 1913 and 1971 George Bernard Shaw works were staged at Station Street for 114 separate runs, compared to Shakespeare's 111. Information in 'Performing Arts', *Arts and Humanities Data Service* <http://ahds.ac.uk/ahdscollections/docroot/birminghamrep/birminghamrepsearch.jsp> [accessed 22 May 2008].

123 Conolly (ed.), *Bernard Shaw and Barry Jackson*, pp. xix–xxvi.

124 Quoted by Conolly (ed.), *Bernard Shaw and Barry Jackson*, p. xi.

125 George Bernard Shaw, NYPL, Lincoln Center Library, Billy Rose Theatre Collection, Cyril Phillips papers regarding the Birmingham Repertory Theatre, T-MSS 2001–057, folder 1, letter of 12 July 1923.

126 George Bernard Shaw, NYPL, Lincoln Center Library, Billy Rose Theatre Collection, Cyril Phillips papers regarding the Birmingham Repertory Theatre, T-MSS 2001–057, folder 1, letter of 17 August 1923.

ultimate fate of the Irish race. At some point in the past, he explains, like Rome under Constantine the British decided to move the centre of their empire to the East, shifting their capital from London to Baghdad. When this migration happened, the inhabitants of Britain told their 'oppressed but never conquered' neighbours in Ireland, 'At last we leave you to yourselves; and much good may it do you'. Those in Ireland feared that they would be ruined if left alone and decided to emigrate as well, travelling to help all those other countries in the world still fighting for national independence. From Tunis to Tripoli, these emigrants from Ireland assisted the wretched of the earth, who considered the formerly oppressed Irish the very incarnation of 'all that is adorable in the warm heart and witty brain'. But finally, once all the national grievances in the world had been set to rights, the newly liberated nations began to view the Irish as a 'pestilence' or at best 'intolerable bores'. Faced with such hostility, the Irish eventually decided to return to Ireland. However, on arrival, although the older men and women flung themselves down to kiss the ground of Ireland, the younger generation looked with gloom at the deplorably rocky landscape. The following day the entire race opted to quit Ireland for England, never admitting to being Irish again. Consequently, within one generation the Irish vanished from the face of the Earth, leaving the world a 'tame dull place'.[127]

After the Synge riots, those managing the Birmingham Repertory Theatre hoped that Irish passions would soon transform into such tame dullness, and as the company sought to disavow the playhouse's youthful enthusiasms the words of *Back to Methuselah* must have resonated pleasingly with Barry Jackson, who ensured that in the real world behind the curtains, just as in the fiction before the footlights, controversial Irish ideas ceased to exert very much influence at Station Street. Indeed, for any English patriots watching Shaw's play in 1923, the idea that the Irish would feel 'damned' and compelled to emigrate in the absence of imperial domination provided a crumb of comfort at a time only a few months after the Southern Irish Free State had, finally and after much bloodshed, gained autonomy from Westminster. For those who had simply grown weary of the terrible conflicts of the previous years, Shaw also offered the welcome prospect of divisive nationalism becoming an anachronism, with his character from the year 3000 exclaiming, 'what a ridiculous thing to call people Irish because they live in Ireland! you might as well call them Airish because they live in air. They must be just the same as other people'.[128] The critic

---

[127] George Bernard Shaw, *Back to Methuselah* (London: Oxford University Press, 1945), pp. 165–67.

[128] Shaw, *Back to Methuselah*, p. 167.

for the *Birmingham Gazette* gave great praise to this part of *Back to Methuselah*, declaring Shaw's work 'full of vital thought on nationalism and war, and the means of getting rid of them through responsibility'.[129] Yet regardless of Shaw's mollifying prophecies, real life animosities would not be so easily dispelled, as conflict between the English and Irish nations would return to Birmingham in the following decade, and would do so with a bang.

---

[129] EAC, 'At the Repertory', *BG*, 12 October 1923, p. 4.

Engrav'd by W.Ridley, from a Minature by Halpin.

1. The Dublin actor-manager William McCready, pictured in 1794, shortly before he moved to Birmingham and became the first high-profile Irish migrant to settle in the area. (Image courtesy of the National Portrait Gallery, London.)

2. *above* A contemporary illustration of the Murphy Riots of 1867, showing Murphy's supporters attacking houses in the Irish-dominated area of Park Street. (Image reproduced with the permission of Birmingham Libraries and Archives.)

3. *left* Park Street, pictured in the week following the Murphy riots. (Image courtesy of the BirminghamLives Collection (the Carl Chinn Archive).)

4. The Birmingham town hall, a building that has enjoyed a long association with Ireland ever since Daniel O'Connell became the first Irish celebrity to speak here in 1836. The first annual St Patrick's Day celebration was held at the venue in 1869, and the event subsequently provided Irish politicians with a platform for praising Home Rule. Eamon de Valera's visit in 1949 paved the way for the city's modern St Patrick's Day parade. (Image reproduced with the permission of Birmingham Libraries and Archives.)

5. The Grand Theatre in Birmingham, where in 1900 an audience of 2,200 mainly English people gathered to celebrate St Patrick's Day in a way that contrasted with the Home Rule celebrations at the town hall. The audience at the Grand wore shamrock, but sang songs in praise of the British Empire and the Boer War. The theatre was demolished when the area was redeveloped in the 1960s. (Image reproduced with the permission of Birmingham Libraries and Archives.)

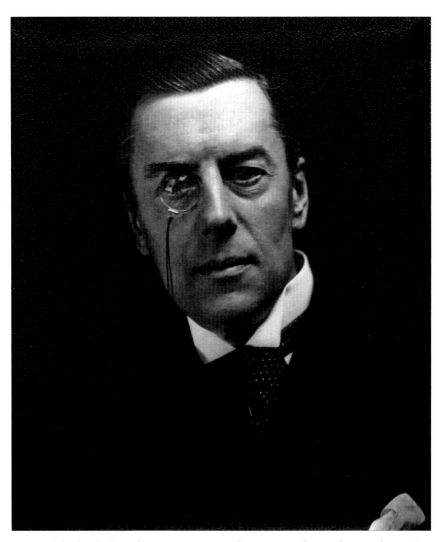

6. Joseph Chamberlain, the prominent Birmingham mayor and MP, whose work gained Birmingham the reputation of being 'the rock upon which Home Rule was wrecked'. This print dates from about the time that he was working to defeat the second Home Rule Bill. (Image courtesy of the National Portrait Gallery, London.)

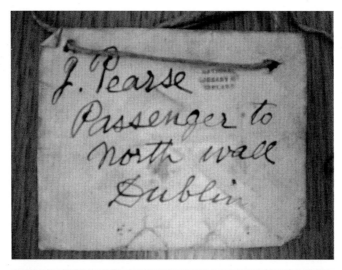

7–8. The luggage labels used by James Pearse when travelling from Birmingham to Dublin. After James settled in Dublin, his son Pádraic went on to become the best known rebel of the 1916 rebellion, acting as Commandant-General of the Army of the Irish Republic and President of the Provisional Government. (Images courtesy of the National Library of Ireland.)

9. The Pearse family in Dublin, from left to right: Pádraic, James, Margaret (seated),
Mary Brigid (on her mother's lap), Willie, and Margaret (seated).
(Image courtesy of the Pearse Museum.)

10. Barry Jackson, the Birmingham man who spent
£100,000 on founding England's first purpose-built
repertory playhouse after seeing the example of
W. B. Yeats and Dublin's Abbey Theatre. Jackson later
worked closely with Irish playwright G. B. Shaw. (Image
reproduced with the permission of Birmingham Libraries
and Archives, and the chairman and trustees of the Barry
Jackson Trust.)

11. The Birmingham
Repertory Theatre in Station
Street, site of the 1917 riot
that saw Irish members of
St Michael's Catholic Church
protesting against J. M. Synge's
controversial play *The Tinker's
Wedding*. (Image reproduced
with the permission of
Birmingham Libraries and
Archives.)

12. The first St Patrick's Day parade in Birmingham in 1952, organized in response to negative newspaper descriptions of Irish living conditions in the city. The event was closely followed by the first London parade, which began 45 minutes afterwards. (Image courtesy of the BirminghamLives Collection (the Carl Chinn Archive).)

13–14. The Birmingham St Patrick's Day parade in 1962 and 1968. In the second photograph, the pole on the council house flies no flag, with officials making sure that this was the case after an earlier controversy about the town hall displaying the Irish tricolour. (Images courtesy of the BirminghamLives Collection (the Carl Chinn Archive).)

15–16. The Irish community in Birmingham increasingly shows dissatisfaction with the situation in Northern Ireland during the late 1960s and early 1970s. Here transport workers go on strike and members of the Campaign for Social Justice in Northern Ireland parade through the city, echoing the protests organized by civil rights groups in Ulster. (Images courtesy of the BirminghamLives Collection (the Carl Chinn Archive).)

17. *above* Levin's furniture store, on the Stratford Road in Sparkhill, is left in ruins by an IRA attack during July 1974. (Image reproduced with the permission of Birmingham Libraries and Archives.)

18. *right* Outside the popular Tavern in the Town pub on 21 November 1974, shortly after the explosion of a 30-pound bomb caused carnage inside the building. (Image reproduced with the permission of Birmingham Libraries and Archives.)

19. The interior of the Mulberry Bush, the pub at the base of the Rotunda building, in the wake of the IRA bombing. (Image reproduced with the permission of Birmingham Libraries and Archives.)

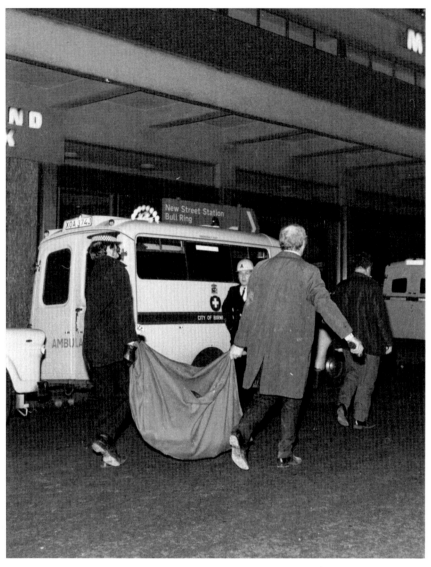

20. Police and rescue workers recover bodies from the destroyed pubs. Four Irish citizens lay amongst the 21 dead, the worst death toll of any IRA attack during the 'Troubles'. (Image reproduced with the permission of Birmingham Libraries and Archives.)

21. The 'Birmingham Six' three days after arriving in Winson Green prison, showing clear
evidence of the torture that they had endured.
Top row from left: Paddy Hill, Hugh Callaghan, Johnny Walker.
Bottom row from left: Richard McIlkenny, Gerry Hunter, Billy Power.
(Copyright Press Association Images.)

22. The Birmingham Six celebrate outside the Old Bailey in London, following their release
from jail by the Court of Appeal. They had spent more than sixteen years behind bars.
From left: Billy Power, Richard McIlkenny, Johnny Walker, Gerry Hunter, Paddy Hill, Hugh
Callaghan. (Image copyright Richard Mildenhall/Guardian News & Media Ltd 1991.)

23–24. The Irish Centre in Digbeth, pictured before and after being expanded for the final years of the twentieth century. (First image reproduced with the permission of Birmingham Libraries and Archives.)

25. The revived St Patrick's Day parade moves through Digbeth in 2001, with the popular 'Dubliner' pub in the background. This postponement of the Dublin parade in this year led Birmingham's organizers to claim their event as the second biggest St Patrick's Day parade in the world, bested only by New York City. (Image courtesy of the BirminghamLives Collection (the Carl Chinn Archive).)

26. The St Patrick's Day parade in 2002. The fire engine and stars-and-stripes flag were designed to show solidarity with the victims of 9/11, and the parade also featured a contingent of fire-fighters from New York. (Image courtesy of the BirminghamLives Collection (the Carl Chinn Archive).)

27–28. The 2009 St Patrick's Day parade: now part of a week-long festival in Birmingham, and the largest community event in the city, with parade attendance estimated at 100,000. The organizers aim to ensure that the event mirrors 'the fantastic diversity of our resident ethnicities'. (Images courtesy of www.bbc.co.uk/birmingham.)

6

War and Immigration

It isn't a case of staying or going. Forced to stay or forced to go.
Never the freedom to decide and make the choice for ourselves. And
then we're half-men here, or half-men away, and how can we hope
ever to do anything [?]

Tom Murphy [1]

Oh Mother dear I'm over here
And I'm never coming back;
What keeps me here is the rake of beer,
The ladies and the crack [sic].

The Dubliners [2]

Summer 1939

In 1939 Birmingham enjoyed one of the sunniest Whit bank holidays in years. Across the city, people lounged over picnics, took lazy walks, and cooled down in the shade. At Birmingham University a lecturer from Belfast, Louis MacNeice, observed that on such restful days in the region, 'the shops empty, shopgirls faces relax', and factory chimneys wait 'on sullen sentry'.[3] Yet, only a

---

1   Tom Murphy, *A Crucial Week in the Life of a Grocer's Assistant*, in *Plays 4* (London: Methuen, 1989), p. 162.

2   Quoted by Des Geraghty, *Luke Kelly: A Memoir* (Dublin: Basement, 1994), p. 40. The singer Ronnie Drew regularly delivered this rhyme at the start of Dominic Behan's song 'McAlpine's Fusiliers' in performances by the folk group The Dubliners.

3   'Birmingham' (written October 1933), in Louis MacNeice, *Collected Poems* (London: Faber, 1966), p. 18. MacNeice's poem in turn inspired Seamus Heaney to write a poem about Newcastle, county Down. See Dennis O'Driscoll, *Stepping Stones: Interviews with Seamus Heaney* (London: Faber, 2008), p. 51.

short time later Hitler would move his troops into Poland and such sleepy city life would seem as unimaginably distant as the long Edwardian summers that preceded the First World War. Indeed, as that very Monday evening came to a close, Birmingham felt a premonitory tremble of the conflicts and tragedies to come, for, although this bank holiday would be forgotten once the Luftwaffe had taken to the skies over the city, that day in 1939 witnessed the first attack on one of Birmingham's entertainment venues by the IRA.

On that Monday, 29 May 1939, those who wanted to rest after a day in the sunshine queued at one of Britain's most modern cinemas, the Paramount Theatre in New Street. The venue had first opened less than two years earlier, and that evening advertised *Hotel Imperial*, a Hollywood film starring the Italian sex symbol Isa Mira.[4] This remade movie, set during the First World War, attracted those who remembered the original 1927 version, as well as those who found a renewed resonance in wartime films during that turbulent summer. But of course most viewers simply came along to see the star, billed in Birmingham as 'the most beautiful woman in Europe and mystery woman of the Balkans'.[5]

At half past nine that evening, the early evening viewers made their way out of the Paramount and brushed past an audience of anything up to 2,440 arriving for the next showing.[6] But the newcomers had no way of knowing that one of those passing by had planted explosives in the cinema. The new audience simply prepared for the titillating sight of Isa Mira disguised as a hotel maid and for the exciting battle scenes featuring Russian and Austrian armies, scarcely realizing that acts of war would erupt in the midst of the auditorium before appearing upon the projector screen.

Moments after the film began, a sharp bang came from an unoccupied seat in the back circle. Viewers started from their seats as a vivid flash of light illuminated the auditorium and flame reached up into the air. One audience member in the front circle attempted to reassure his fellow cinemagoers by calling out for calm and insisting that there was no danger. In the nervous excitement of the moment, some other spectators greeted this statement with ironic laughter, but as it became clear that nobody had sustained injury, the audience mostly returned to, or remained in, the cinema stalls.[7] The

4   Victor J. Price, *Birmingham Cinemas: Their Films and Stars 1900–1960* (Studley: Brewin, 1986), p. 12.

5   Sandra Brennan, 'All Movie Guide', *New York Times* <http://movies2.nytimes.com/gst/movies/movie.html?v_id=95686> [accessed 21 May 2008]; 'Paramount', *BM*, 1 June 1939, p. 1.

6   Price, *Birmingham Cinemas*, p. 12.

7   'Explosions in City Cinema', *BP*, 30 May 1939, p. 1.

Paramount's bewildered assistant manager then appeared on the scene, and appealed to patrons to remain seated, but as he did so, a second device detonated near the cinema's front row. A flash again blanched the auditorium, and for a moment the flames threatened serious harm to a mother and father shielding their son. Other nearby spectators rushed from the area, but most sheltered in the chairs, whilst one of the audience members again tried to prevent panic by shouting, 'Keep your seats. They're only scare bombs'.[8]

More cinema attendants now arrived and dashed around the auditorium, checking for any other incendiary devices, but in the midst of this activity yet another explosion destroyed a chair below the balcony. At this point most of the audience members began to evacuate the venue, with the acrid smell of the charred building wafting after them. But despite the third bang, some people still remained in their seats, and about 100 stoically watched the film through to the end. Some of these spectators even laughed grimly at the finale, a sequence showing the explosions and wreckage of World War One, although perhaps these viewers would have felt less sanguine if they had realized that on the same day an attack on Liverpool's Tatler cinema had left 20 people injured.[9]

In Birmingham, the bomber travelled away from the Paramount and headed to the Gaumont cinema on Steelhouse Lane, leaving more devices that, this time, the local police located and disabled. The following morning, cleaners arriving for work at Birmingham's West End cinema found that a further two charges had detonated there during the night, but the venue's tipping seats had smothered the flames. The janitors hauled away the damaged chairs, and throughout the city cinema staff watched warily for any signs of suspicious behaviour.[10] Some venues paid watchmen to remain on duty throughout the night, as the following hours saw a gas bomb igniting at a picture-house on London's Vauxhall Bridge Road.[11] Cinemagoing had become a nerve-wracking activity during those days, inadvertently preparing audiences for the wartime period ahead when the Birmingham Repertory Theatre would start printing disconcerting air-raid advice in its programmes: 'Keep calm, the performance will go on. You are safer here than in the street'.[12]

Yet Birmingham knew that assailants from Ireland rather than Germany had targeted the cinemas in 1939. When the Irish Free State had been established

8   'Cinema Outrages', *BM*, 30 May 1939, p. 6.

9   'Cinema Outrages', *BM*, 30 May 1939, p. 6.

10   'Bombs in Birmingham Cinemas', *BP*, 31 May 1939, p. 1.

11   'Gas Bomb in Cinema', *BM*, 1 June 1939, p. 10.

12   Programme for Shaw's *You Never Can Tell*, in my own possession.

in the decade before, a treaty had partitioned the island, with Britain retaining control of the new, two-thirds Protestant, Northern Irish state. But this latter province had scarcely enjoyed an easy birth. Michael Collins and the Southern government had attempted to destabilize Northern Ireland from the beginning, with Protestant inhabitants viewing themselves as besieged both by these external forces and by Catholics within the new state.[13] Meanwhile, Northern Catholics felt dissatisfied with the way that the province was set up, as the devolved government in Ulster had a first-past-the-post electoral system modelled on Westminster, which allowed the numerically superior Protestant population to maintain a one-party state, with the Ulster Unionist Party remaining in power for over fifty years.[14]

Such a situation bred sectarianism, and in July 1935 Northern Ireland saw a handful of Protestants and some 2,000 Catholics being forced from their homes, as well as the killing of seven Protestants and three Catholics.[15] Some republicans felt that the Northern Irish province could be abolished through force, particularly as the idea of fighting Britain's troops still had some allure after the Anglo-Irish War of 1919 to 1921, when the notoriously vicious 'Black and Tan' regiments had wreaked havoc in Ireland and had faced retaliation from the newly established IRA. In 1936 the IRA's chief of staff, Seán Russell, consequently sought to regain the initiative by publicly announcing a plan to bomb Britain. But although he garnered enough support from Irish-America to mount operations by the end of 1938, his operatives discovered that the local IRA remained in a poor organizational state upon arriving in various British cities, including Birmingham.[16] Nevertheless, Birmingham's wealth of industrial opportunities meant that, as in the earlier period of Fenian activity, the city again became one of the main manufacturing and distribution centres for Irish revolutionary *matériel*.[17]

On 12 January 1939 the IRA demanded that Britain withdraw troops from the whole island of Ireland, and when the British inevitably failed to comply, attacks followed four days later in London, Liverpool, Manchester, and Birmingham, with devices placed in manhole covers, shop-fronts, and electricity

[13]   Frank Wright shows how the British state ensured Protestant supremacy in the North of Ireland prior to partition, in *Two Lands on One Soil: Ulster Politics before Home Rule* (Dublin: Gill and Macmillan, 1996).

[14]   Thomas Hennessey, *Northern Ireland: The Origins of the Troubles* (Dublin: Gill and Macmillan, 2005), p. x.

[15]   Bew, *Ireland*, p. 460.

[16]   English, *Armed Struggle*, p. 60.

[17]   'More IRA Bombs', *BM*, 10 June 1939, p. 8.

substations.[18] In Birmingham, the IRA began with an abortive attempt to put Hams Hall power plant out of action, followed by assaults on pylons around the city. However, the next Birmingham blast was set off by mistake, when two clumsy bomb-makers accidentally caused an explosion at a flat in Trafalgar Road, and although police carted this duo off to face charges in London, the attacks in Birmingham continued, with incendiary devices placed in city centre litter baskets and then another accidental explosion at a bomb-maker's house in Rubery, followed by the cinema attacks of May.[19] Soon afterwards, Birmingham saw mail bombs and explosions at the city's central post office, but in the wake of these attacks the area experienced a slight lull, before the worst IRA incident of 1939 followed in nearby Coventry at the end of the summer.[20]

On 25 August a nervous IRA operative travelled from Dalkey to Coventry, where he collected a heavy bicycle laden with explosives that he would plant in the unfamiliar English city. However, at 2.30 p.m., as the disorientated cyclist pedalled his way to the chosen site for the attack, he began to struggle with the unwieldy bike, he worried that one of his tyres had started deflating, and then realized that his lack of a wristwatch meant he had no idea how many minutes were left before the ticking package would explode. He panicked, decided to abandon the bicycle and scarper.[21] Half an hour later the device detonated in what was one of the most crowded parts of Coventry, leaving hundreds of shoppers in a hail of flying glass, with 60 injured and five killed. The dead included a fifteen-year-old boy, an eighty-one-year-old pensioner, and a twenty-one-year-old shop assistant, Elsie Ansell, who had been making excited preparations for her marriage a fortnight after the explosion.[22] Her distraught mother had the grim task of identifying Elsie's disfigured body, and managed to do so only by recognizing the engagement ring on the dead woman's finger, before in turn dying in a state of heartbreak shortly afterwards.[23]

The angry backlash against the IRA in the English midlands began immediately, with many people knowing or caring little about the political situation in Ireland and therefore seeing only what therefore seemed to be unprompted and inexplicable violence in the local streets. Across the English

---

18   English, *Armed Struggle*, p. 61.
19   'More IRA Bombs', *BM*, 10 June 1939, p. 8.
20   'IRA Attacks on Postal Services', *BP*, 10 June 1939, p. 1.
21   'Wrong Man Hanged, Says Ex-IRA Bomber', *Sunday Times*, 6 July 1969, p. 1; 'Coventry Bomb Trial', *Manchester Guardian*, 14 December 1939, p. 11.
22   'Bride To Be among Five Killed in Midland Mystery Explosion', *BG*, 26 August 1939, p. 7; 'The Coventry Explosion', *Manchester Guardian*, 12 December 1939, p. 2.
23   'The Condemned Irishmen', *Manchester Guardian*, 6 February 1940, p. 7.

midlands people took to shouting 'Down with the Irish', or 'Come out into the open you Irish bastards', and when one heedless man in Coventry responded with a cry of 'Up the IRA' a crowd seized him and would have thrown him through a window but for the intervention of police officers who managed to bundle him into custody. Four days after the explosions, 2,000 workers in the Baginton aircraft works downed tools and, joined by another 1,000 anti-IRA protestors, marched through Coventry, only being placated when the local police chief constable assured them that he 'was not an Irishman and had never been to Ireland'.[24] As anti-Irish prejudice spread, local industrial managers worried about tensions between Irish and English workers, and one MP observed that 'Because of the IRA bomb outrages, employers are prejudiced against men with Irish names who are seeking work'.[25] Five days after the Coventry explosions a mob almost lynched a man with an Irish accent in Liverpool when he tried to buy a balloon as a gift for his landlady's child. Unfortunately, balloons had been used by the IRA to contain explosives, and after making his purchase in all innocence, the man needed police assistance to escape the ensuing hue and cry.[26] Ultimately, in this feverish atmosphere, the British authorities arrested, tried, and executed two Irish republicans deemed guilty of the Coventry bombing, hanging thirty-two-year-old Peter Barnes and twenty-nine-year-old Jimmy McCormack in Birmingham's Winson Green prison on 7 February 1940.[27] But – *plus ça change* – neither of the men had committed the act for which they had been convicted. Although McCormack had helped prepare IRA explosives, he had not planted the device in Coventry, whilst the allegation that Barnes had transported the material for bomb-making was treated with disbelief by those acquaintances who knew Barnes as the husband who had previously nursed a dying wife with great gentleness. In a speech from the dock, Barnes declared, 'Later I am sure it will come out that I had neither hand, act, or part in it', and the real bomber duly made a confession to the *Sunday Times* in 1969.[28]

---

[24]   '3,000 Coventry Workers in Anti-IRA Demonstration', *BG*, 29 August 1939, p. 4.

[25]   'Police Search for IRA Terrorists', *BP*, 12 June 1939, p. 1.

[26]   'Anti-IRA Crowd Attacks Shop: Baton Charge', *BG*, 31 August 1939, p. 7.

[27]   English, *Armed Struggle*, pp. 61–62; 'The Executed I.R.A. Men', *Manchester Guardian*, 8 February 1940, p. 7; 'Defence Opened in Bomb Murder Trial', *Manchester Guardian*, 13 December 1939, p. 9.

[28]   'Two Death Sentences', *Manchester Guardian*, 15 December 1939, p. 7; 'Wrong Man Hanged', *Sunday Times*, 6 July 1969, p. 1.

Brendan Behan

At the start of 1940, various Irish voices had been raised in protest against the Birmingham hangings. Kathleen Clarke, who as a child had seen her uncle framed on explosives charges in Birmingham, now acted as mayor of Dublin, and appealed to her counterpart in Coventry for leniency.[29] The playwright Seán O'Casey wrote to the British government on the eve of the executions to point out that 'by no means [is it] certain that these men had any direct hand in the fatality' and so appealed to ministers to 'hold your hand and spare the lives of these two men'.[30] Meanwhile the sixteen-year-old Brendan Behan, who would later inherit O'Casey's literary mantle, learned of the hangings in an English jail where the teenager had ended up after making a cack-handed attempt at bombing Liverpool.

In 1939, Behan's seventy-seven-year-old grandmother, Mary Furlong, had travelled from Ireland to Birmingham where her son worked as groundsman at Villa Park.[31] She strongly sympathized with the radical republican cause, and lodged in a three-bedroomed semi-detached house at 84 Cliff Rock Road in Rubery, where the IRA man Martin Clarke spent his time manufacturing explosives. However, shortly after her arrival, disaster struck when some of the ammunition in the house accidentally ignited, and three detonations shattered the windows, blew large holes in Clarke's bedroom floor, and started a serious fire. When local policemen arrived they discovered an Aladdin's cave of bomb-making equipment, and arrested Clarke and Furlong on the spot, even though Furlong attempted to do her bit by hiding two sticks of gelignite between her breasts and, when caught, claiming that she had on her person nothing more incriminating than some cubes of sugar.[32]

Furlong's subsequent courtroom defiance in turn inspired her grandson Brendan to attack England, and in a highly idiosyncratic mission he headed for Liverpool, where he intended to destroy battleships in Birkenhead, but only succeeded in being arrested for possession of explosives.[33] After receiving his

---

[29] 'The Condemned Irishmen', *Manchester Guardian*, 6 February 1940, p. 7.

[30] 'The Condemned Irishmen: Appeal for Reprieve', *Manchester Guardian*, 6 February 1940, p. 9.

[31] This woman was Behan's mother's mother-in-law from a first marriage. Colbert Kearney, *The Writings of Brendan Behan* (Dublin: Gill and Macmillan, 1977), p. 16; Ulick O'Connor, *Brendan Behan* (London: Hamish Hamilton, 1970), p. 38.

[32] 'Explosives Charges', *BM*, 6 June 1939, p. 10; 'Explosives Charge', *BM*, 13 July 1939, p. 13.

[33] Belchem, *Irish, Catholic and Scouse*, p. 313.

borstal term on Ash Wednesday 1940, he heard from a friendly warder about the execution of Barnes and McCormack, which had been carried out on the same day as Behan's sentencing. Barnes had appeared on the scaffold in a state of collapse and received an embrace of support from McCormack, who attempted to reassure his fellow prisoner right up to their final moments, shouting to Barnes 'I'll see you in a minute' as the hangman sprung the trap.[34] Such details haunted Behan, and he made his literary debut in 1942 with a short autobiographical piece called 'I Become a Borstal Boy', set on the day of the hangings and recounting how, on hearing the news from Winson Green, he called to his fellow jailed Irishmen, 'We will recite the *De Profundis* for the repose of the souls of our countrymen who gave their lives for Ireland this morning in Birmingham Jail'.[35]

Behan subsequently reworked this story, transforming it into his famous 1958 memoir *Borstal Boy*, in which he again described his capture against the background of the events in Coventry and Birmingham. In this version of the story, the police who arrest and interrogate Behan are enraged by the deaths in Coventry, whilst the bomber manqué dwells upon the condemned men in Birmingham:

> I knew the man that had planted the bomb and it was neither of the men that had been sentenced. But that would not matter very much to the English. The men that had most to do with it were back home in Ireland [...] I could see the logic of saying to any IRA man, 'You may not be the one that planted the bomb, but you have planted others and anyway you are all in this conspiracy together and if we can't get the ones that caused this explosion you'll bloody well do as well the next [...]'.[36]

In *Borstal Boy*, the warders and other prisoners then mock Behan about the hangings, and as he awakens on the morning of his trial he dwells on events in Birmingham rather than his own fate. But whereas the earlier short work 'I Become a Borstal Boy' had pictured Behan himself leading the prayers for those executed, when he rewrote this story in *Borstal Boy* he described shying away from another Irish prisoner's attempts to celebrate the hanged men.[37]

---

34   Séamus de Búrca, *Brendan Behan: A Memoir* (Dublin: Bourke, 1985), p. 20.

35   Brendan Behan, 'I Become a Borstal Boy', in *After the Wake*, ed. P. Fallon (Dublin: O'Brien, 1981), p. 25.

36   Brendan Behan, *Borstal Boy* (London: Arrow, 1990), pp. 24, 115.

37   Behan, *Borstal Boy*, pp. 116–17, 133–35.

In the late 1940s Behan attempted to persuade the British government to allow him back into the country by asking the authorities to overlook 'that which is past and, I should hope, forgotten'.[38] But it is clear that for Behan the past had not been at all forgotten, and that those Birmingham executions were developing into a key theme in his dramatic work. In 1947 a group of IRA sympathizers in Dublin arranged a concert to remember McCormack and Barnes, and as part of this commemoration Behan scripted a play called *Gretna Green* or *Ash Wednesday*, which was apparently set in an English prison on the eve of a double hanging.[39] However, a heavy snowfall ruined the performance in Dublin's Queen's Theatre on 23 February by keeping the audience away, and matters scarcely improved when Behan turned up too drunk to read the part he had assigned himself.[40] Nevertheless, this inauspicious evening did prefigure some of Behan's later and more successful work. Although the script no longer survives, that production in snowbound Dublin reportedly focused on the feelings of four onstage characters towards the plight of two men sentenced to execution, and thus gave Behan the starting point for his play *The Quare Fellow*, which revolves around the reaction of a group of prisoners and warders to another hanging. In this latter piece, Behan gives an outright condemnation of capital punishment, and also dwells on the kind of eleventh-hour compassion that marked McCormack's behaviour towards Barnes on the scaffold.[41] When Behan wrote a later play, *An Giall* ('the hostage'), he again called to mind his feelings in 1940, portraying a group who hold captive a British soldier in retaliation for a young republican due to be hanged in Belfast jail.[42] In both of these extant scripts, the hanging occurs offstage and the theatre audience witnesses the responses of those wanting to hear about the death, with Behan continuing to remember his own reaction to the Birmingham executions and repeatedly dramatizing that anxious wait for news. When the Birmingham Repertory Theatre came to stage Behan's *The Quare Fellow* in September 1964, the city's theatre critics had of course forgotten all about the events of

---

38   Behan's letter of 17 February 1948, quoted by Colin Holmes, 'The British Government and Brendan Behan, 1941–1954: The Persistence of the Prevention of Violence Act', *Saothar* 14 (1989), p. 125.

39   John Brannigan, *Brendan Behan: Cultural Nationalism and the Revisionist Writer* (Dublin: Four Courts Press, 2002), p. 80.

40   Details of *Gretna Green* are found in de Búrca, *Brendan Behan*, p. 20.

41   See, for example, Brendan Behan, *Complete Plays* (London: Methuen, 2001), pp. 45–46, 60, 114, 100–1.

42   Brendan Behan, *An Giall and The Hostage*, trans. Richard Wall (Gerrards Cross: Colin Smythe, 1987), p. 45.

twenty-five years before, and praised Behan's description of capital punishment for offering an indictment 'against society for its indifference to things done in its name'.[43]

World War Two

Yet if events in the English midlands in the late 1930s inspired Behan's writing, the IRA activities exerted little discernible impact upon the political situation of Britain and Ireland.[44] By the time the IRA leader Seán Russell died in 1940, the greatest effect of the bombings had probably been to alienate many of Birmingham's Irish residents from republicanism. For the time being, the wider public of Birmingham also had little time to spend thinking about the IRA, as scares about the Germans became the city's dominant worry.

In September 1939, many of the Irish-born residents of Birmingham felt little desire to enlist in the British army or to witness the pyrotechnics of the Luftwaffe at first hand, and so when Neville Chamberlain declared war on Germany a large number caught the train back to Ireland. However, this return often proved temporary, as the economic climate in the Southern Irish state felt so uncongenial that many preferred to risk the wartime hazards of England rather than languish at home without work or money, and the Dublin government tacitly approved this emigration, with ministers struggling to tackle the cost of spiralling unemployment. But although there had previously been a tradition of free movement between the two countries, the British government decided to control this process more tightly after the fall of France: now wartime migrants from suspiciously neutral Éire required permission from a British employer, the Dublin government, as well as Britain's ministry of labour. On arrival at the British port these Irish workers were reminded that they were obliged to take up the job specified on their visa, and once in the district where they were to live they had to register with the police.[45] Nevertheless, the British government needed labour from Éire, and during the war, or 'the Emergency' as it became known in Southern Ireland, around a sixth of that country's working population left home, with Whitehall estimating that Britain

---

43   'On this Week at Birmingham', *Stage*, 15 October 1964; M. F. H., '"The Quare Fellow" a Moving Play', *Stratford Herald*, 25 September 1964; and Andy Sims, 'Behan: Pathos Lost', *Redbrick*, 7 October 1964. All located in Birmingham Repertory Theatre, BCL, Birmingham Repertory Theatre Archive, January 1962–July 1966, vol. 117(A).

44   English, *Armed Struggle*, p. 62.

45   Holmes, *John Bull's Island*, p. 195.

and Northern Ireland hosted up to 120,000 of these economic migrants.[46] Such a large number of men travelled from Southern Ireland to take up employment in Birmingham during 1940 that the Unionist MP for Yardley complained to the London parliament about the injustice of allowing them to take jobs from serving British soldiers. Yet Birmingham firms including ICI and Austin still decided to send recruiting agents across the Irish Sea during the following year, and the British government was organizing large-scale recruitment in Southern Ireland by 1942.[47]

As the rate of emigration increased, most boats sailing from Dublin filled with young men, and two-thirds of those who left at this time were less than thirty years old.[48] On arrival in Britain, the newcomers usually found work in construction, although 42,665 men and women opted to enlist in the British armed forces, with some achieving a measure of celebrity in Britain for displays of bravery. In August 1943 the *Birmingham Mail* praised the twenty-five-year-old maintenance engineer Jeremiah O'Brien, who saved lives and prevented a major explosion during a German raid on his factory, whilst in spite of Whitehall's customary caution in praising Irish-born war heroes, Churchill used a 1945 radio broadcast to laud Sergeant Pat Keneally, an Irish-born soldier who had lived in Birmingham before joining up and showing heroism in the North African campaign.[49]

However, others in Ireland still remembered the situation in the North, the history of colonization, and the brutality of the Anglo-Irish War, and thought that Britain now deserved a good dose of the same medicine. Britain's wartime recruitment of Irish workers also caused consternation in some parts of Éire.[50] Organizations like the IRA gave little practical help to Germany, but many in Ireland felt something along the lines of 'I hope England will be nearly beat'.[51] Those from Ireland who earned their living in Birmingham may have felt less nonchalant about the vicissitudes of the Allied campaign, but many believed that the conflict constituted somebody else's fight, and a number shared the tacit hope that the British empire would receive a bloody nose. Yet, although many

46   Clair Wills, *That Neutral Island* (London: Faber, 2007), pp. 49, 310, 314.

47   Sutcliffe and Smith, *History of Birmingham*, p. 44.

48   Wills, *That Neutral Island*, p. 314.

49   Bew, *Ireland*, pp. 472, 479; Alertus, 'Things Talked About', *Sunday Mercury*, 3 June 1945, p. 5. The activities of other Irishmen from Birmingham who fought in the war can be found in BCL, Local Studies Collection, Irish Studies Box 2, folder labelled 'World War II', A8 941.5.

50   Holmes, *John Bull's Island*, p. 198.

51   Wills, *That Neutral Island*, pp. 36–37.

Irish people remained suspicious of the British *en masse*, the new arrivals often grew to like the individuals encountered in Birmingham. Anne Bennett's novel about wartime Birmingham, *Pack Up Your Troubles*, attempts to highlight such paradoxical feelings in describing one Irish Catholic grudgingly volunteering to help the war effort:

> And then the priest got going on about the war and all, saying everyone had to do their bit and pull together to beat the enemy – God that stuck in Brendan's craw, for hadn't the bloody English been the enemy of Ireland for generations? Eventually, for the sake of peace, for the priest, when he put his mind to it, was a greater nag than any woman, he'd agreed to go bloody fire watching a few nights after work.[52]

At the end of the war, emigrants continued to travel in large numbers across the Irish Sea, with Birmingham stationing a recruiting officer to Dublin in order to tempt Stakhanovist workers to England.[53] Birmingham had one of the largest municipally organized bus operations in the world, and set up a centre in Dublin that attracted more Irish labour than any other transport department in Britain.[54] Yet if the 'Emergency' had seen boats filling with men, increasingly large numbers of women also made the journey to Holyhead once restrictions on migration were lifted in peacetime, with many travelling to work as bus conductors, nurses, and factory assistants. Indeed, between 1946 and 1951, 1,365 women left Ireland for every 1,000 men who travelled.[55] In 1955, Birmingham advertised 5,000 employment vacancies for women and 2,000 for 'girls' under eighteen, and as one twenty-five-year-old women who had emigrated from Roscommon to Sparkhill explained:

> In the rural areas of Ireland, especially the West, it's extremely difficult to find a decently paid job at all. Unless you've had a very good education the only kind of job available is shop work or hotel work, and even then there's a great deal of competition. Ireland has so few industries that it's virtually impossible to find employment in factories unless you happened

52   Anne Bennett, *Pack Up Your Troubles* (London: Headline, 2000), p. 130.

53   'Mr De Valera Criticises Midland Cities: Irishmen Said to Be Living in "Appalling" Conditions', *BP*, 29 August 1951, p. 1.

54   'Birmingham Has Jobs For Irish Workers ... But No Houses!', *Sunday Independent*, 15 August 1954, located in NAI, Department of Foreign Affairs, Position of Irish Workers in Birmingham, 402/222.

55   Diarmaid Ferriter, *Judging Dev* (Dublin: Royal Irish Academy, 2007), p. 286.

to live in a big town. In a place like Birmingham there's no problem in getting a job at all.[56]

Men arriving in Birmingham could easily find jobs in some of the less pleasant manufacturing industries, as well as in the transport and building sectors; and as time went by, the city offered increasing opportunities to work in retail and catering. As a result, between 1951 and 1961 the number of overseas immigrants to Birmingham nearly doubled, with 15,500 West Indians and 7,000 from India-Pakistan arriving, alongside 22,000 from the island of Ireland.[57] Indeed, by 1961 Birmingham's census enumerators recorded the city's highest ever Irish-born population, with the figure reaching 58,961, or 5.31 per cent of the area's overall population. Yet, whilst Birmingham changed and expanded, life in Southern Ireland felt increasingly impoverished and desperate. As more young Irish-born men and women raised their children in Balsall Heath, schoolteachers taught fewer pupils in Roscommon and shopkeepers served fewer customers in Mayo. Those in rural Ireland often felt trapped, with scant opportunity to find employment, make money, or meet someone to marry. In this country of dead-end jobs, poverty, and enforced celibacy, life in Britain or the USA could be imagined as an exciting and glamorous alternative, as portrayed in Tom Murphy's play, *A Crucial Week in the Life of a Grocery Assistant*, where the character John Joe Moran dreams about living at 'Two-two-two A, Tottenham Court Road, Madison Square Gardens, Lower Edgbaston, Upper Fifth Avenue, Camden Town, U.S.A., S.W.6'.[58] However, the reality of life for emigrant or seasonal labourers in England often proved far from comfortable, as they had to endure cramped and dirty lodging houses, casual racism, and a lack of the familial and religious support networks that existed back home. When a 1967 Gallup Poll in Britain asked 'Do you think that the country has been harmed through immigrants coming to settle here from Ireland?' only 16 per cent said that the Irish presence had been beneficial, whereas 22 per cent claimed the migrants had been harmful. Meanwhile, a 1971 survey of ethnic jokes from the Independent Television programme 'The Comedians' showed that anti-Pakistani jokes came first, but mockery of the 'thick Paddies' came second.[59] One Birmingham immigrant described 'missing Ireland so much, it was

---

56   Nesta Roberts, 'Irish Girls in England', *Manchester Guardian*, 7 April 1955, p. 14; Pat Bolton, 'Is There Green in Her Eye?', *Midland Catholic Pictorial*, January 1960, p. 2.

57   Cherry, *Birmingham*, p. 204.

58   Murphy, *Plays 4* (London: Methuen, 1997), p. 116.

59   Both surveys are described by Holmes, *John Bull's Island*, p. 233.

unbelievable. I used to count the seconds sometimes till I went back home', and indeed the torrid conditions encountered by the Irish in Birmingham during this period inspired two writers to create some of the most brutal drama seen on the British stage in the 1960s.[60]

Tom Murphy and David Rudkin

In the mid-1930s, a working-class Protestant woman from Milford in Ulster met a Revivalist pastor from Sussex who had come to Northern Ireland on a 'crusade'. The pair married, and in 1938 the pastor was sent to preach in the Black Country, so they set up home in Birmingham with their two-year-old son, David Rudkin. A number of their Ulster relatives also followed this trio to the city shortly afterwards, and the clan stayed in Birmingham during the war, although, in Rudkin's words, 'never became self-consciously part of the "Irish community" in Birmingham, perhaps because that was mainly Catholic and Republican'.[61] After the war the family moved back and forth between rural, fiercely Loyalist Ulster and urban, war-damaged Birmingham a great deal, so that Rudkin ended up spending about a third of his childhood and adolescence in county Tyrone, speaking with an accent that other pupils mocked when he enrolled at one of the local King Edward's schools in Birmingham.[62] He later went up to study at Oxford, but during a summer vacation of at the end of the 1950s he returned to work as a fruit-picker in an orchard near Birmingham, and subsequently described how:

> It was only a couple of miles, as the crow flies, from the Longbridge Austin motor works; if you cycled, as I did, over the rim of hill at the southern perimeter of Birmingham. [...] I reported for duty at the foreman's farmhouse [...] Later in the morning we were joined by an Irish tramp, in broken shoes without socks, a long ragged herring-bone overcoat, and wearing dark glasses, and a teacloth on his head. His name was Roche.

60   Larry Finglass's words quoted in *Birmingham Voices: Memories of Birmingham People*, ed. Lucy Harland and Helen Lloyd (Stroud: Tempus, 1999), p. 82.
61   I am grateful to David Rudkin for providing most of the factual details in this paragraph, and for quoted remarks made in personal correspondence during March 2008.
62   Rudkin has commented that at school his speech was actually mocked most by a Catholic boy from Dublin. For more on Rudkin's background see David Rabey, *David Rudkin: Sacred Disobedience* (Aberystwyth: Harwood, 1997), p. 197; and Marilynn J. Richtarik, *Acting Between the Lines: The Field Day Company and Irish Cultural Politics 1980–1984* (Oxford: Clarendon Press, 1994), p. 191.

Suddenly a play was there: in all dialects and various coloured forms of speech around me.[63]

The real-life situation that Rudkin found during his summer work echoed elements of the his childhood, when he had discovered the clash between two different cultures when moving between Ulster and Birmingham, later believing himself to have lived two entirely different lives and having spoken with two different voices. When bad weather prevented Rudkin from returning to his part-time job one day, he decided instead to write about what he had seen whilst fruit picking, creating his debut play, *Afore Night Come*, which depicts a labourer with an Irish accent called Roche arriving for work in a nearby orchard and becoming a target for English joking and racism. But although the dramatic script is rooted in real-life experience, *Afore Night Come* culminates in a brutal fictional denouement. Roche's colleagues call him 'the playboy of the bleeding Western world', and like Synge's title character, the fictional Roche is garrulous, roams around without permanent employment, and has a marked tendency to confabulate.[64] But whereas Synge had shown the 'playboy' winning adulation upon appearing in a new community, in Rudkin's play the vagrant arrives in a Black Country orchard only to be bullied, mocked, and eventually murdered with knives and a hayfork.

In *Afore Night Come* Roche is lazy and arrogant, and his poetic pretensions win him the nickname 'Shakespeare' from his colleagues. But a large part of the workers' antagonism towards him derives from their disgust at Southern Ireland's neutrality during the recent struggles with Germany. As one of the fruit pickers, Jumbo, asks:

Where was Shakespeare during the war? I seen the Jerries trying to kill our cities night upon night [...] Seen a kid's hand once; all on its own, in the dust [...] And Shakespeare: was in the little Emerald Isle. Cowering, in the little bloody Emerald bloody Holy Isle.

Another worker adds, 'Yeah. Clapping their hands and laughing and saying now it's bloody England's turn. Getting what she asked for after nineteen twenty bloody three', prompting Jumbo to respond, 'Need a good bombing in Ireland, that's what I say'.[65] By the end of the play, when the workers finally slaughter

---

63 David Rudkin, *Afore Night Come* (London: Oberon, 2001), pp. 4–5.

64 Rudkin, *Afore Night Come*, p. 58.

65 Rudkin, *Afore Night Come*, pp. 80–81.

Roche, a helicopter spraying lethal pesticide hovers overhead, suggesting that the murderers are indeed taking revenge for Southern Ireland's absence during the deadly aerial attacks of the Second World War.

The Royal Shakespeare Company first produced *Afore Night Come* in London in 1962, a few months after another debut play, by the twenty-six-year-old Galway man, Tom Murphy, had premiered in the English capital. Like Rudkin, Murphy worked as a schoolmaster in the early 1960s, and came from a family that knew all about immigration to Birmingham. Indeed, four of Murphy's brothers and two of his sisters left Ireland to work in the city.[66] In time, Murphy himself came to Birmingham, although he lived for most of the 1960s in London, noting that 'there was no such concentration of Irish people to encounter there, as was the Birmingham experience'. He has observed that Birmingham 'is the only industrial city in the UK that I have any experience of, the only one I know where Irish working-class men concentrated and lived in ghetto-like communities'.[67] Murphy became fascinated by these communities, observing that those who had left home often felt 'they were people who didn't belong in England' but when they returned to Ireland 'they found they didn't quite belong here either'.[68]

When back in Galway, Tom Murphy recalled these observations whilst writing his first play, *A Whistle in the Dark*, set amongst labourers from the West of Ireland living in Coventry, an area in which Murphy had never actually set foot, and that he constructed from his experience of neighbouring Birmingham. The main character of the work, Michael, has married an Englishwoman called Betty, or 'Brummy' as he insists, but their domestic life is shattered by the arrival of his violent younger brothers and father from Mayo, who drink, fight, smash Michael's possessions, and make an assortment of threats against Betty. As a result of the brothers' behaviour, at the end of the play Betty abandons her marriage and Michael murders his youngest sibling.

Murphy had been inspired to write the play after one of his brothers told him about a vicious family of Irish brawlers in Birmingham, one of whom was said to carry part of another man's ear in a matchbox. This gruesome story fascinated Murphy, and triggered the drama, in which both the family and the earlobe are fictionalized. But in scripting this play Murphy made no attempt

66   Some commentators have written that Murphy's father also worked and lived in Birmingham, although this is not the case.

67   I am grateful to Tom Murphy for providing most of the factual details in this paragraph, and for quoted remarks made in personal correspondence during March 2008.

68   Quoted by Nicholas Grene (ed.), *Talking about Tom Murphy* (Naas: Carysfort, 2002), p. 96.

to create a photographic impression of what he had encountered in the English midlands. Rather, he engaged with a particular kind of oral storytelling that had developed amongst Irishmen in the Birmingham area. As Murphy says, there were 'stories, a mythology about fighting men and fighting prowess. And a new pocket of vocabulary, fanciful, to be enjoyed [...] I saw little violence but I heard a lot of talk about it'. Consequently, in writing the play, Murphy recorded for the first time the stories, gossip, and mythology savoured by Irish who spent their days in the pubs and on the building sites of the city.

Perhaps unsurprisingly, those who saw Murphy's work as a true-to-life portrayal of the Irish in England, rather than as something rooted in the lively conversation of Birmingham's Irishmen, reached some damning conclusions about the work. When Murphy submitted the play to Dublin's Abbey Theatre in 1961 the managing director, Ernest Blythe, saw the drama as a demeaning insult to the nation and sent back a rejection slip along with an abusive note. The next year Blythe saw the play's Dublin premiere at the Olympia Theatre, and declared 'I never saw such rubbish in my life' loudly enough to be reported in the following day's newspapers.[69] Conversely, when the world premiere occurred in September 1961 at the Theatre Royal in London's East End, the play became a hit and transferred to the commercial West End the following month, with some literal-minded British critics confirming Ernest Blythe's fear that the play might bolster British bigotry. Felix Barker, for instance, declared:

> If there's a single Irishman who hasn't been deported from England by next weekend I shall write to the Home Secretary [...] In *A Whistle in the Dark* by Thomas Murphy he will see just what bog vipers we are nursing in our bosom.[70]

Meanwhile, Kenneth Tynan, who had never met the author, wrote, 'Thomas Murphy is the kind of playwright one would hate to meet in a dark theatre. I have always been obscurely frightened of loudly singing Irishmen, and of Irish debaters'.[71]

Nevertheless, the bleakness of Rudkin and Murphy's plays marked an important moment in British and Irish theatre. In 1964 the director Peter Brook introduced the Royal Shakespeare Company to the ideas of the neglected

---

69   Quoted by Fintan O'Toole, *Tom Murphy: The Politics of Magic* (Dublin: New Island, 1994), pp. 7, 54.

70   Quoted by O'Toole, *Tom Murphy*, p. 10.

71   Quoted by Grene (ed.), *Talking about Tom Murphy*, pp. 195–96.

French theatre practitioner Antonin Artaud, who advocated purging Western society of materialism through exposure to violent myth. Rudkin and Murphy produced their works shortly beforehand and heralded this new approach on the British stage, and although neither writer knew of Artaud at the time, the ceremonial and cultish killings that conclude *Afore Night Come* and *A Whistle in the Dark* echo the Frenchman's call for a return to a drama of ritual and cruelty, revealing 'a bloodshed of images'.[72] In addition, the theme of Tom Murphy's first play gave the writer a rich seam of material for his own future work, with his subsequent scripts often revolving around the idea of exile. In particular, his later Abbey Theatre drama *The House* again includes the emigrant's experience of the English midlands, describing the effect on an Irish rural community of the summer return home of those men earning money abroad in the 1950s.[73] One of these returnees, Peter, arrives from Birmingham with 'a bastard accent', an English wife, and children who have no experience of their father's home. Peter earnestly attempts to raise his children according to the Catholic faith of his Southern Irish homeland, and on first arriving declares, 'I love my country! Here, mate! This land!' Yet the longer he remains, the more he feels alienated by friends and family. When he shows photographs of his wedding at St Chad's Cathedral to his mother she thinks he is showing pictures taken in a photographic studio, worries about whether his children are baptized, and mistakenly believes her son has married his landlady.[74] In real life, many of those who came to Birmingham from Ireland felt similarly rootless and worried about intermarriage, with newspapers warning that 'Irish should marry Irish' and Catholic priests advising that 'there is no excuse for mixed marriages. You can always find a nice Irish companion'.[75] Peter feels infuriated by the 'poxy pack of fuckers' who make such comments about his wife's nationality, and he begins to demonstrate that he now feels more at home in England than in his country of birth, increasingly using the telltale English appellation 'mate', and by the end of the drama declaring his enthusiasm for the return journey to Birmingham.[76]

---

72   Antonin Artaud, *Collected Works Volume Four* (London: Calder, 1999), p. 62.

73   As with David Rudkin's play, *The House* echoes Synge's *The Playboy of the Western World*. In both *The House* and Synge's work a main character called Christy arrives in an isolated Irish community, breaks the heart of a rural spinster, and becomes associated with a murder.

74   Tom Murphy, *The House*, in *Plays 5* (London: Methuen, 2006), pp. 194, 197, 226–27.

75   Pat Bolton, 'Is There Green in her Eye?', *Midland Catholic Pictorial*, January 1960, p. 2; '60,000 Birmingham "Exiles" Celebrate St. Patrick's Day', *BG*, 17 March 1952, p. 5.

76   Tom Murphy, *Plays 5*, p. 248.

Eamon de Valera

Of course, during the mid-twentieth century, the Irish living in and around Birmingham knew little about what was said of them in the theatres of London. The performances with which the majority of those who came to the city from Ireland remained most familiar were those of the Catholic Church, and religious pageants and parades had become an increasingly familiar sight in Birmingham during the first half of the twentieth century.[77] For a number of years, local Catholics had joined in processions on the feast of *Corpus Christi*, with the Archbishop of Birmingham also ensuring that the relics of St Chad would be paraded around the city in May 1919, an occasion on which a souvenir programme highlighted the saint's connection with Ireland.[78] In the following decade, such Catholic gatherings escalated in scale after the Anglican Bishop Ernest Barnes of Birmingham criticized the Catholic concept of the Eucharist, causing a Mass scheduled for the Catholic Young Men's Society to become a giant rally, with almost 1,500 men turning out to show support for the Catholic sacrament. The year afterwards, these men congregated again to demonstrate against an unrepentant Barnes, and the gathering had a specifically Irish tone, as it came at the start of the month during which Catholics celebrated the centenary of emancipation and was advertised as 'an act of thanksgiving for the passing of the Roman Catholic Emancipation Act'.[79] For the Irish members of the congregation, the modern struggle against the local Anglican hierarchy resonated pleasingly with Daniel O'Connell's earlier campaign, and the monsignor who co-ordinated the rally took care to remind a preparatory meeting that Catholicism was the religion handed down by St Patrick in Ireland.[80]

Even after Bishop Barnes had died in 1953, Catholic men continued to gather at the cathedral every Easter Monday, and whilst such rallies developed in Birmingham, in Ireland, Catholic marches took on increasingly

---

[77]   The 1951 census shows that of the 36,000 Irish-born residents of Birmingham, 8,000 came from the predominantly Protestant North and 27,000 from the mainly Catholic South (1,000 failed to align with either). R. J. Smith, *Migration in Post-War Birmingham* (Birmingham: Birmingham University, 1969), p. 22.

[78]   The programme appealed to the Irish in Birmingham by describing the role played by monks from Ireland in Chad's education. 'Irish Notes and Comments', *Birmingham Catholic Magazine*, June 1919, p. 119; Christine Ward-Penny, *Catholics in Birmingham* (Stroud: Tempus, 2004), p. 17.

[79]   'Catholic Demonstration', *BM*, 1 April 1929, p. 2.

[80]   'The Catholics and Dr Barnes', *BP*, 18 March 1929, p. 13.

political overtones. Following the 1916 rebellion, many Irish towns and villages organized a series of annual Easter processions to celebrate Pádraic Pearse and his comrades, with such events usually taking the form of a parade to the local graveyard where the participants gathered to say the rosary in the Irish language. In 1929 the Dublin government co-ordinated a far grander procession in the Southern Irish capital, with proud speeches and marching troops, and in the ensuing years ever more elaborate commemorations took place, particularly after the election of the sole surviving leader of the rebellion, Eamon de Valera, to the post of Irish prime minister in 1932. From 1935 de Valera presided over ceremonies on a grand scale at the General Post Office, with thousands of marchers, the crackle of gunfire, and flypasts by the Irish air force.[81]

By January 1949 many of those who had come to Birmingham from Ireland had been influenced both by the growing public pageantry around St Chad's and by the politicized marches in Irish towns, and so organized a giant procession to welcome de Valera himself to the city. During the previous years, Birmingham's town hall had seen large crowds attracted to St Patrick's Day music concerts, featuring dancers, pipers, and harpists, and with figures such as the Primate of All-Ireland and the Irish leader William Cosgrave sending messages of goodwill to these events.[82] Now de Valera came in person to the venue, intending to speak against partition. He had visited a number of English cities to criticize the division of Ireland, but Birmingham provided the biggest reception to meet him, with the welcome party swelling to such a size that de Valera's own participation needed revising at the last moment. The organizers had arranged for their guest to arrive at the Bull Ring at 4 p.m. on Sunday, 30 January and then to lead a parade to the town hall, but they changed the plan when it became clear that a giant crowd had choked all routes to and from the proposed starting point. Eventually a pipe band led a shuffling parade along New Street and Corporation Street to the town hall, whilst a car whisked de Valera to the indoor venue by another route. Meanwhile, all four sides of the town hall became thronged by people excitably singing songs, wearing rosary beads, and waving flags. When this assembly finally caught a glimpse of de Valera's beaky features, he found himself mobbed, managing only with great difficulty to extricate himself from the 5,000 supporters chanting 'We want Dev'. Then, inside the hall, another 2,500 ticket-holders cheered and applauded

---

81   James Moran, *Staging the Easter Rising: 1916 as Theatre* (Cork: Cork University Press, 2005), p. 69.

82   'St. Patrick's Day in Birmingham', *BP*, 18 March 1929, p. 13; 'St. Patrick's Day Concert in Birmingham', *BP*, 18 March 1930, p. 7; 'St. Patrick's Day Parades in Ireland', *BP*, 18 March 1931, p. 7.

and declared, 'We want to be on good terms with the people of Britain. We want to see the old quarrel ended, but so long as this partition of our country lasts it never can be ended'.[83]

De Valera felt impressed by this hero's welcome, and remained concerned with the welfare of those who had given him such a rousing reception. Indeed, the secretary of the department for external affairs, Seán Murphy, later wrote a note to a colleague, observing that 'of course you will remember' that de Valera 'was very much interested' in the Irish of Birmingham.[84] De Valera felt particularly stirred a few months after the parade when he received an alarming but accurate report about local living conditions by Maurice Foley, a young second-generation Irishman who was then engaged as a Christian youth worker in the city. Foley cared passionately about social justice; indeed he would later become Labour MP for West Bromwich in 1963, going on to become a minister for race relations and for Africa. He was even touted as a future British prime minister at one point, before leaving parliament to work for Africa on behalf of the European Community.[85] But before all this, Foley wrote his report on Birmingham that described those from Ireland living in 'grossly over-crowded, ill-kept, dirty' accommodation, paying an 'exorbitant' amount of rent, with some men on shift work sleeping during the day in beds which others would occupy during the night.[86]

After the Irish ambassador in London had passed the report from Foley to de Valera in July 1951, confirming that the work needed 'serious consideration' and was likely to prove 'objective, trustworthy, and not exaggerated in any way', the premier decided to inform both the British government and the Catholic Church about the situation.[87] The Archbishop of Birmingham, Joseph Masterson, who claimed Irish ancestry and spent much time in Ireland, vainly

---

83   '"Dev" Speaks – 5,000 Are Turned Away', *BG*, 31 January 1949, p. 1.

84   Seán Murphy, NAI, Department of Foreign Affairs, Position of Irish Workers in Birmingham, Seán Murphy's note of 18 October 1955, 402/222.

85   Tim Dalyell, 'Maurice Foley', *Independent*, 14 February 2002, <http://www.independent.co.uk/news/obituaries/maurice-foley-729746.html> [accessed 21 May 2008]; Delaney, *The Irish in Post-War Britain*, pp. 97–98.

86   Maurice Foley, NAI, Department of Foreign Affairs, Position of Irish Workers in Birmingham, Report by Maurice Foley, 402/222.

87   NAI, Department of Foreign Affairs, Position of Irish Workers in Birmingham, Note from London embassy to department of external affairs on 23 July 1951, 402/222. For comments on Foley's report see Tim Pat Coogan, *De Valera: Long Fellow, Long Shadow* (London: Hutchinson, 1993), pp. 662–63; Delaney, *The Irish in Post-War Britain*, p. 98; and Ferriter, *Judging Dev*, pp. 285–88.

asked the Dublin government to set up a consul in Birmingham, and warned immigrants, 'it is so easy to be led astray [...] Birmingham at present is a materialist's paradise'.[88]

De Valera himself delivered a speech in Galway to highlight the plight of those who worked in the English midlands. He mentioned Birmingham, Wolverhampton, and Coventry as particular areas for concern, and went on to describe one particular unnamed city, 'where there was already an estimated shortage of 60,000 houses, [and] over 100,000 new workers have come – half of whom are Irish – for whom no proper accommodation has been provided'. De Valera stated that here in one instance 50 men from Ireland had crammed into a single lodging house, and declared, 'The accommodation shortage is exploited by avaricious landlords, and the prestige of our people generally suffers by the suggestion that "anything is good enough for the Irish"'.[89] Journalists had little difficulty in recognising that de Valera's description pointed to the situation in Birmingham, where the council house waiting list stretched to roughly 60,000 names at this time.[90] Indeed, the *Irish Independent* printed many of the specific details about Birmingham from the Foley report.[91] British newspapers such as *The Times*, *Mirror*, and *Mail* also took up the story, whilst one Irish journalist warned that, 'This city with its back to back houses was no place for children from any of the four green fields of Ireland', continuing, 'I want to say to the youngsters who may be contemplating setting out for Birmingham "for God's sake stay at home for the present anyway"'.[92]

But de Valera's words provoked angry anti-Irish commentary in Birmingham's newspapers, which detested the imputation that local residents had proved grasping and exploitative. The chairman of the city's health committee acknowledged that those from Ireland frequently suffered from cramped accommodation, but told the *Birmingham Post*, 'More often than not the landlord is one of their own countrymen'.[93] The *Birmingham Gazette* reported that city officials believed such overcrowding 'was the Irishmen's own fault', and went on to quote one Ulsterman in Birmingham who distanced himself from Southern Ireland's migrants by saying:

---

[88]   'Mgr. Joseph Masterson', *Tablet*, 5 December 1953, p. 558; NAI, Department of Foreign Affairs, Position of Irish Workers in Birmingham, 402/222.

[89]   'Mr De Valera Criticises Midland Cities', *BP*, 29 August 1951, p. 1.

[90]   'Irish Exploited in Midlands', *BG*, 30 August 1951, p. 1.

[91]   'Irish Workers in England Degraded', *Irish Independent*, 30 August 1951, p. 5.

[92]   Terry Ward, 'A City to Avoid', *Irish Press*, 30 January 1953, located in NAI, Department of Foreign Affairs, Position of Irish Workers in Birmingham, 402/222.

[93]   'Mr De Valera Criticises Midland Cities', *BP*, 29 August 1951, p. 1.

The people living in that type of conditions are the sort of people who like those conditions. They come from the backwoods of Ireland, where their parents have brought up a dozen or more children in tiny cottages. They have never known anything better, and that is what they prefer.

The *Gazette* also published the opinion of an English probation officer, who proclaimed that arrivals from Ireland 'live in very overcrowded conditions in lodgings because they prefer it that way. They like to spend their money on beer'.[94] De Valera himself reacted by declaring, 'That my statement has caused anger to certain people does not surprise me, but their anger is certainly not greater than mine when I read the report'.[95]

In response to such negative press coverage, during the following spring Irish-born men and women in Birmingham, as well as their descendants, arranged the city's first ever St Patrick's Day parade. The organizers sought to dispel the pessimistic popular conceptions of Ireland by showing to a wider audience the kind of music and festivity that had so often been witnessed on St Patrick's Day at the town hall, where a 'musical promenade' had been incorporated into proceedings as the concerts became less politicized after the First World War.[96] In the USA, of course, the Ancient Order of Hibernians had been organizing parades of more than 20,000 marchers since the 1860s, and Irish-Americans had since become rich, influential, and on the verge of occupying the White House.[97] Those in Birmingham now aimed to emulate their transatlantic cousins, and on Sunday, 16 March 1952, 10,000 men, women, and children, as well as a sizeable contingent of nuns, duly assembled in central Birmingham's West End cinema car park and started singing the Irish national anthem. The West End cinema itself had in fact been targeted by IRA bombers in 1939, but the organizers of the 1952 parade hoped to trigger an entirely different set of associations. In a study of the pageantry of ancient Rome, Mary Beard has pointed out that the meaning of a procession 'regularly "feeds off" the buildings and landscapes by which it passes', and something similar happened in 1950s Birmingham, as many of those who walked the 35-minute St Patrick's Day route remembered that the parade followed part of

94 'Irish Exploited in Midlands', *BG*, 30 August 1951, pp. 1, 5.

95 Coogan, *De Valera*, p. 664.

96 'Irish Notes', *Birmingham Catholic Magazine*, March 1919, p. 55; 'Metropolitan Notes of the Month', *Birmingham Catholic Magazine*, March 1920, p. 49.

97 Indeed, the first records of a St Patrick's Day parade in New York date back to 1766. See John T. Ridge, *The St. Patrick's Day Parade in New York* (New York: St. Patrick's Day Parade Committee, 1988), pp. 35, 4.

the same route as the attempted procession that had welcomed de Valera to the city.[98] Participants would also have recalled that Irish labourers had helped with the construction and repair of many of these roads, and may have found a redemptive significance in the event as the parade approached a conclusion at St Chad's Cathedral. The academic Domenico Pietropaolo has emphasized that a public procession is rather 'like a rubber chain, capable of being stretched and reshaped without loss of continuity and without threat to its identity as a single longitudinal form', and the Irish parade accordingly twisted and turned through the city, halting and speeding up at different moments, and even at one point threatening to go into reverse when a group of kamikaze nuns managed to loose clutch control and roll their car backwards into the marchers behind.[99] Nevertheless, along the way many spectators watched and applauded as the kilted Birmingham Irish Pipe Band led a snaking column of marchers onto New Street, Corporation Street, and then Bull Street, with many participants wearing the shamrock, or tricolour rosettes emblazoned with the legend 'Together we stand'.[100]

For all the rhetoric of togetherness, of course, the event clearly equated Irishness with Catholicism, and gave scant thought to Birmingham's Irish Protestants. At St Chad's Cathedral the venue's largest ever congregation crammed in to hear Mass said by Father Seán Connellan, a priest from Rathkeale who had become parish priest at St Anne's in Digbeth, where his brother Colm had joined him as curate.[101] Seán also reported on conditions in the city to the Irish government, acted as secretary to local Irish groups, and arranged for the *Irish Press* to go on sale at Birmingham's newsagents.[102] As he said Mass, 8,000

98   Mary Beard, *The Roman Triumph* (Cambridge, MA: Harvard University Press, 2007), p. 92.

99   Domenico Pietropaolo, 'Spectacular Literacy and the Topology of Significance: The Processional Mode', in *Petrarch's Triumphs: Allegory and Spectacle*, ed. Konrad Eisenbichler and Amilcare A. Ianucci (Ottawa: Dovehouse, 1990), p. 364. I am grateful to Elizabeth Moran for telling me about the nuns.

100   'Irish Urged to Boycott Bad Lodgings: St. Patrick's Parade and Service in Birmingham', *BP*, 17 March 1952, p. 5; '60,000 Birmingham "Exiles" Celebrate', *BG*, 17 March 1952, p. 5.

101   John Joseph Roche, 'The First St. Patrick's Day Parade in England', in *A Great Day: Celebrating St. Patrick's Day in Birmingham*, ed. Gudrun Limbrick (Birmingham: St. Patrick's Festival, 2007), p. 27. Despite Roche's title, the parade in Birmingham was not the first such parade in England: there had been unruly parades in Liverpool to celebrate the feast day during the previous century. See Belchem, *Irish, Catholic and Scouse*, p. 125.

102   NAI, Department of Foreign Affairs, Position of Irish Workers in Birmingham, 402/222.

people packed the main building, the crypt, and the schoolyard adjoining the Cathedral, with another 2,000 standing on the pavement and hearing the service relayed through a loudspeaker. In response to the controversy about lodgings, Seán Connellan told his congregation to 'Blacklist the house where you have met bad conditions. Publish it, tell your friends you have found a place that is unsatisfactory', and he continued in a more mollifying vein than de Valera, saying, 'Credit is due to the people of Birmingham because they have taken in such a surplus population [...] If you keep looking you will find nice places'.[103] The whole point of the celebration was to boost the self-esteem of the Irish Catholic population, and Seán Connellan bragged that the Irish in Birmingham now included 100 priests, 100 teachers, 300 nuns, 300 doctors, 1,000 transport workers, 1,500 nurses, as well as university professors, police officers, firemen, and thousands of industrial and other workers, with the clergyman concluding that the Irish could therefore make Birmingham the greatest Roman Catholic city in the world.[104]

Indeed, so popular was the idea of Birmingham's parade that the Irish in London followed the suggestion almost immediately, and organized a procession in the capital that began a deferential 45 minutes after the march in the English midlands.[105] The Birmingham event also impressed the local council, which especially opened 12 restaurants to enable the city's celebrations to continue throughout that night, although many of those in the parade needed little encouragement to carry on the festivities, with St Patrick's dances being organized that evening in halls and ballrooms across the region.[106]

Irish Eyes Are Smiling

After this successful parade, the Irish Catholics of Birmingham began to manifest an increasing sense of self-confidence. On the following St Patrick's Day, the Lord Mayor of Dublin presented his counterpart in Birmingham with a tricolour flag, and Irish colours flew over the Birmingham town hall for the first time.[107] De Valera also dispatched one of the members of his parliament to a special Irish banquet in Birmingham's Grand Hotel, bearing the leader's message of personal appreciation for the work being done by those from Ireland now living in the city. An indication of exactly what work those in Birmingham were doing

---

103 '60,000 Birmingham "Exiles" Celebrate', *BG*, 17 March 1952, p. 5.
104 'Irish Urged to Boycott Bad Lodgings', *BP*, 17 March 1952, p. 5.
105 'Irish Urged to Boycott Bad Lodgings', *BP*, 17 March 1952, p. 5.
106 'Gala Night for Irish "Exiles"', *BG*, 18 March 1952, p. 6.
107 'St. Patrick's Day but Something is Missing', *BM*, 17 March 1962, p. 1.

could be seen in that year's elaborate procession, where participants wearing their smartest clothes carried colourful banners boasting of local affiliations and achievements. The men and women who usually ran the city's transport service abandoned their buses to walk beneath a first banner; visitors from nearby towns such as Coventry, Wolverhampton, and Nottingham marched under a second; and Birmingham's nurses followed behind a third. Then came the Irish language association; the 'Holy Family Confraternity' whose male adherents endeavoured to spread praise of Jesus, Mary, and Joseph; and next the orderly marchers of the teetotal Pioneer Association, which claimed hundreds of abstemious members in the district. Following on, the more energetic part of the parade included the women sportsmen of the *Camogie* Association; representatives from the 27 Gaelic Athletic Association clubs in the area; members of the rapidly expanding St Anne's *Céilí* Club; and, finally, pupils from a range of local Irish dancing schools. All the while, six bands accompanied the march from the West End car park to St Chad's, with the Lord Mayor of Birmingham himself receiving the procession.[108]

In previous years, many of those who arrived in Birmingham had made their way to the Irish Immigrants' Association at St Anne's Church in Digbeth, but the organizers of the St Patrick's Day parade now decided to campaign for a dedicated building in Birmingham that would welcome such newcomers, and in 1955 circulated a petition during the parade to endorse this proposal.[109] At the Mass that concluded the march the Archbishop of Birmingham, whose presbytery had frequently been disturbed by those searching for 'digs', threw his support behind the idea, praising the 'heroic' efforts of those who had already helped the recent arrivals, and urging everyone else to lend a hand.[110] In consequence, within two years the Irish Welfare Centre had opened near the Bull Ring in Moat Lane, remaining closely allied to the Church, and assisting arrivals from Ireland to find accommodation and employment. For a number of years the building proved a first port of call for many newcomers to the city, as well as providing a headquarters for a number of Birmingham's

---

[108] 'St. Patrick Parade in Birmingham', *BP*, 16 March 1953, p. 7. The parade continued to include Birmingham's Lord Mayor in future years. For example, in 1960 Aer Lingus sent one of its glamorous air hostesses to pin shamrock on a delighted Lord Mayor's lapels. 'Great Day for the Irish', *BP*, 18 March 1960, p. 7.

[109] Valentin Iremonger, NAI, Department of Foreign Affairs, Position of Irish Workers in Birmingham, Follow-up Report on 26 and 27 June 1956, 402/222.

[110] 'Irishmen Asked to Help Immigrants: Birmingham Appeal by Dr Grimshaw', *BP*, 18 March 1955, p. 7.

Irish societies.[111] The Welfare Centre also incorporated a shop, with windows displaying crucifixes and religious statues, commemorative ornaments bearing images of John F. Kennedy, and books about various rebels.[112] Indeed, the Birmingham novelist David Lodge would later satirize the kind of assistance given by such Church-related welfare organizations in his novel *Small World*. Lodge describes an academic from Ireland arriving for a university conference in 'Rummidge', a fictional version of Birmingham, and encountering a local priest in a nearby church:

> A light was burning above a confessional bearing the name of 'Fr Finbar O'Malley,' and within a few minutes Persse had unburdened his conscience and received absolution. 'God bless you, my son,' said the priest in conclusion.
>
> 'Thank you, Father.'
>
> 'By the way, do you come from Mayo?'
>
> 'I do.'
>
> 'Ah. I thought I recognized the sound of Mayo speech. I'm from the West myself.' He sighed behind the wire grille. 'This is a terrible sinful city for a young Irish lad like yourself to be cast adrift in. How would you like to be repatriated?'
>
> 'Repatriated?' Persse replied blankly.
>
> 'Aye. I administer a fund for helping Irish youngsters who have come over here looking for work and think better of it, and want to go back home. It's called the Our Lady of Knock Fund for Reverse Emigration.'[113]

In reality, as the rate of migration slowed in the 1960s, the Irish Welfare Centre increasingly focused on the needs of those who had settled in Birmingham, and in 1962, for example, the centre used the annual parade to raise funds for those couples from Ireland wanting to swap rented accommodation for permanent homes in the city.[114] With the post-war arrivals putting down roots in Birmingham, the number of city children born to parents who had travelled from Ireland reached a peak in 1964 and 1965, when midwives delivered 4,525 babies to families with an Irish-born mother and father, and 2,707 to

---

[111] *Midland Catholic Pictorial*, January 1960, p. 2.

[112] Martin Davies, 'The Flow is Slowing Down', *BM*, 27 October 1965, p. 10.

[113] David Lodge, *Small World* (Harmondsworth: Penguin, 1985), pp. 49–50.

[114] 'Housing Plan to Aid Irish', in McKenna, 'The Irish in Birmingham: A Scrapbook', fol. 28.

couples with one Irish-born parent, making up one in every six births in the region.[115] In that year one local newspaper estimated that, overall, every tenth person in Birmingham could claim Irish identity by birth or extraction, and described how those who came from Ireland had reached positions of local significance, including a magistrate and three council members.[116] In 1955 the Irish government instructed Valentin Iremonger, a junior official in the London embassy and a noted poet, to travel to Birmingham and prepare another report on conditions in the city, allowing the Irish prime minister John Costello to reassure the Dublin parliament that housing accommodation in Birmingham for Irish workers had improved.[117] The trip led Iremonger to observe that the situation was 'not so bad as it was five or six years ago', and may have encouraged him to spend the subsequent years translating Dónall Mac Amhlaigh's Irish-language work *Dialann Deoraí* ('Diary of an Exile'), which gives an account of an unskilled navvy's life in the post-war English midlands.[118]

Nevertheless, when Iremonger described the situation to the Dublin government he relied on the reports of clergymen and referred to the population that was Irish and Catholic rather than Birmingham's smaller group of Irish Protestants. In 1961, after the Republic of Ireland's tricolour had flown over the town hall on St Patrick's Day for seven years, some of those from Ulster did request that Birmingham should fly the red and white banner of St Patrick instead, and the council initially agreed to rotate between the two flags. However, officials soon received complaints about this change, and so exasperatedly abandoned plans to fly anything at all on the day, eventually opting instead to fly the Irish tricolour on 27 July, the date on which Southern Ireland became a republic.[119]

Of course, not all of the Irish Catholics of Birmingham felt and believed

---

[115]   Corporate Statistician, *Ethnic Origins of Birmingham Children 1966–81*, 'The Nationality of Children Born in 1964', table 11, and 'Trends, The Nationality of Children Born in 1965'.

[116]   Martin Davies, 'The Flow is Slowing Down', *BM*, 27 October 1965, p. 10.

[117]   'Irish in City Now Better Housed', *Evening Dispatch*, 27 June 1956, located in NAI, Department of Foreign Affairs, Position of Irish Workers in Birmingham, 402/222. Another question about conditions for the Irish in Birmingham was asked by deputy Seán Flanagan on 26 June 1956; see NAI, Department of Foreign Affairs, Position of Irish Workers in Birmingham, 402/222.

[118]   Dónall Mac Amhlaigh, *An Irish Navvy: The Diary of an Exile*, trans. Valentin Iremonger (London: Routledge, 1966); Delaney, *The Irish in Post-War Britain*, pp. 101–2.

[119]   'St. Patrick's Day but Something is Missing', *BM*, 17 March 1962, p. 1; 'Tricolour Will Fly in City on July 27', *BM*, 14 March 1966, p. 5.

the same things, with some developing sympathies that were distinctly frowned upon by the Church. For example, the Connolly Association operated amongst the Irish in Britain, drumming up anti-partition sentiment and promoting socialism, and gaining a reputation as a Communist front organization.[120] Valentin Iremonger recorded that the Birmingham members of this leftwing group held weekly meetings, met trains arriving in the city in order to enlist new recruits, and sold the association's newspaper inside the pubs and outside the church doors of the region. Indeed, the Dublin government came to suspect that some of the complaints about living conditions that it received from the Irish in Birmingham might be traced back to the Connolly Association's agitation rather than to a sense of genuine grievance.[121] For the Church, the fear was that such socialist tendencies might lead towards 'godless' communism, and at the start of the 1960s some of the Irish in Birmingham had indeed forsaken the scapular and beads for the hammer and sickle. The Dublin communist Seán Ó Maolbhríde had clashed with the Irish Church and found his teaching career in Ireland's schools curtailed as a result, so instead settled with his wife and two children at King's Heath in Birmingham. Here the family accepted as lodger another Dubliner, who had left home in a spectacularly unsuccessful attempt to find employment on an English building site. However, although this failed labourer, named Luke Kelly, would never develop a career in construction, he did enjoy discussing communism with Ó Maolbhríde, and singing with the local labour-movement choir, the Birmingham Clarion Singers.[122] Later in the decade Luke Kelly would achieve fame as one of Ireland's best balladeers, but Birmingham had an early chance to hear that distinctive voice, as he performed with the Clarion group at, for example, the October 1962 Trades Union Festival, giving socially-aware folk and classical songs that prepared the way for his renowned recordings of leftwing works such as 'Joe Hill' and 'Molly Maguires'.[123]

Less politicized Irish Catholics held dances at an assortment of Birmingham parishes, as well as at other locations under the auspices of societies such as the Gaelic Athletic Association and Gaelic League, with such groups becoming

---

120 Holmes, *John Bull's Island*, p. 134.

121 Iremonger, NAI, Department of Foreign Affairs, Position of Irish Workers in Birmingham, Follow-up Report on 26 and 27 June 1956; and material from June 1956, 402/222.

122 Geraghty, *Luke Kelly*, p. 40.

123 I am grateful to Annie Smith and the Birmingham Clarion Singers for this information. 'Joe Hill' and 'Molly Maguires' can be found on *Luke Kelly: The Collection*, audio CD, Outlet music, 1999.

particularly numerous in the area of Sparkhill, where the first-generation Irish comprised 17 per cent of the overall population by 1967, and ran a thriving centre of shops, cafés, and pubs.[124] Anyone walking through this part of Birmingham could easily locate a nearby pub balladeer, a cheap weekend ticket to Dublin, or an Irish newspaper, and would not have to wander very far before finding advertisements for dances at the Harp social club, posters promoting Irish concerts in the town hall, and notices about Gaelic football games played at Glebe Farm.[125] Indeed, when a newspaper for the Irish in Britain, the *Irish Post*, first appeared in 1970, the Sparkhill MP Roy Hattersley made sure to pander to his constituents by appearing on the 'Nationwide' television programme to praise the publication.[126] Meanwhile, Sparkhill's English Martyrs church attracted one of the largest Irish-born congregations in the country, with so many packing into services that overflow Masses had to be held in adjacent school and parish buildings, forcing parishioners to become some of the most punctual churchgoers in Britain, with anyone who failed to arrive 15 minutes early forfeiting the chance of finding a seat.[127]

At this time, many of those who came to Birmingham from Ireland socialized in local county associations, which organized song and dance evenings, pub quizzes, and transport to Ireland, as well as arranging sick visiting, charity collections, and opportunities for the jobless to meet prospective employers.[128] In 1958 the separate associations representing Ireland's 32 counties banded together to create the All Ireland Counties Association, and campaigned in the 1960s for a social club to cater for those of Irish birth and descent.[129] The Association's members felt inspired by Liverpool's Irish Centre, which in the mid-1960s had been set up in Mount Pleasant and provided a focus for all kinds of cultural activities including Irish language classes, dancing, and drama. Liverpool's ambitious centre also organized talent contests, evenings of music

---

[124] Parishes holding Irish dances included St Anne's, St Francis's, St Augustine's, Erdington Abbey, St Catherine's, Sacred Heart, St Chad's and St Vincent's. Maurice Foley, NAI, Department of Foreign Affairs, Position of Irish Workers in Birmingham, Report by Maurice Foley, 402/222; Rex and Moore, *Race, Community, and Conflict*, p. 47.

[125] Brendan Farrell, 'Man in the Midlands', in *A History of the* Irish Post: *The Voice of the Irish in Britain*, ed. Martin Doyle (London: Smurfit, 2000), p. 37.

[126] Martin Doyle, 'The History', in *A History of the* Irish Post: *The Voice of the Irish in Britain*, ed. Martin Doyle (London: Smurfit, 2000), p. 15.

[127] Rex and Moore, *Race, Community, and Conflict*, p. 150.

[128] Rex and Moore, *Race, Community, and Conflict*, pp. 153–54.

[129] Martin Davies, 'Self Help with the Housing Problem', *BM*, 29 October 1965, p. 12; 'Big Drive for an Irish Club', *BM*, 25 August 1966, p. 5.

or debate, and a film group, whilst the venue's library contained many books in Irish and the centre had even staged an art exhibition.[130] Indeed, by 1966 the Liverpool centre could boast an annual profit of several thousand pounds, and now acted as guarantor for the Irish Community Centre in Birmingham. Although the Birmingham version never reached the heady heights of its Liverpool parent, the new centre opened in Digbeth on 13 May 1968 and survives to the present day, having hosted dinners, evenings of folk music, and events such as the 'Miss Ireland in Birmingham' pageant. Following the example of the successful St Patrick's Day parade, the centre's managers wished to continue forging a positive impression of Irishness in the area, and initially decreed that anyone made bankrupt, found guilty of conduct 'unworthy of a gentleman', or failing 'to uphold the honour of Ireland' could be expelled from the club.[131]

Meanwhile, the council tore down the original Irish Welfare Centre in 1973 as part of the wholesale redevelopment of the city, and the staff relocated to Shadwell Street.[132] The opening of the new premises and the demolition of the old site seemed to mark the end of an era, with many of those who had journeyed from Ireland to Birmingham no longer feeling marginalized, but full of optimism. The city now boasted nine Irish-born councillors, and those of Irish birth and descent saw that the social success and proud hybrid identity of the Irish in the USA might provide a model for Birmingham's upwardly mobile population, raising money in 1968 for a 23-foot tribute to John F. Kennedy that was made from mosaic tiles and placed in the sunken pedestrian area next to St Chad's.[133] One new arrival from Northern Ireland, the fifteen-year-old Paddy Hill, fatefully travelled over to join his father in Birmingham during 1960, and later remembered:

He told me it was a tremendous city, with plenty of work and the religious troubles of Belfast nonexistent. He really loved it, and I could tell from that moment there was never going to be any prospect of us all returning to

130 John Daniels, 'If Birmingham's Irish Think Big', in McKenna, 'The Irish in Birmingham: A Scrapbook', fol. 46.
131 Ziesler, 'The Irish in Birmingham', p. 247; 'Go Ahead for New Irish Centre', *BM*, 19 December 1966, p. 7; '"My Life in Peril": Irish Centre Girl Quits', *BM*, 16 May 1974, p. 5; 'Britain's New Generation of Irish', *BM*, 19 September 1973, p. 12; John McCarthy, 'Carnival Time with a £1,000 target', *BM*, 2 February 1973, p. 16.
132 John McCarthy, 'Extra "Time" for Centre', and Barry Dillon, 'Bishop Sings Centre's Praises', in McKenna, 'The Irish in Birmingham: A Scrapbook', fols 65, 71.
133 '10 Years On ... Tribute to a President', *BM*, 22 November 1973, p. 17.

Belfast as a family. If I were to go back, it would have to be on my own. In fact, my dad did not set foot in Belfast again, and I never heard him utter a word of regret at leaving.[134]

The *Birmingham Mail* now mocked the old stereotype of the 'fighting drinker', and instead pointed out that people from Ireland were statistically less likely to be arrested for drunkenness or violence than the overall population of Birmingham.[135] By the start of the 1970s, the same newspaper estimated that 100,000 Irish-born men and women and their immediate descendants lived in Birmingham, and between 1967 and 1973 the *Mail* ran a separate column advertising Irish events in the city.[136] After all, if the first generation of post-war immigrants often wished to attend a variety of familiar parish clubs or drinking dens such as the Garryowen in Small Heath, the teenage second generation increasingly wanted to branch out and socialize with a broader mix of people in the area. These youngsters might visit the Mayfair Suite, a relatively upmarket venue near New Street Station that showcased musicians such as the returning Luke Kelly, or might instead attend the rough and ready Shamrock club in Hurst Street where Irish show bands would play.[137] At the same time, the second generation equally enjoyed drinking in pubs with no particular Irish theme, such as the popular and central Tavern in the Town and the Mulberry Bush. Yet although the young drinkers in the city pubs could scarcely have realized, time had started running out for this period of easy self-confidence in Birmingham, as the city was about to change, and change utterly.

134 Paddy Joe Hill and Gerard Hunt, *Forever Lost, Forever Gone* (London: Bloomsbury, 1995), p. 20.

135 Martin Davies, 'The Myth of the Fighting Drinker', *BM*, 28 October 1965, p. 10; Martin Davies, 'Self Help with the Housing Problem', *BM*, 29 October 1965, p. 12.

136 The 'Irish Mail' column was written by John McCarthy. See for example, John McCarthy, 'Carnival Time with a £1,000 Target', *BM*, 2 February 1973, p. 16. Some footage of the 1970 St Patrick Day procession, with pipe bands, kilts, and babies wrapped in green all-in-ones, can be found in BCL, 'Birmingham St. Patrick's Day Parade '98', video cassette, VB102.

137 'Britain's New Generation of Irish', *BM*, 19 September 1973, p. 12.

7

The Pub Bombings

*'The IRA hurt my sister,' he said to Cicely. It was a simple
statement of fact; the best he could do.*

Jonathan Coe[1]

*I suppose you believe a policeman's word over mine. Oh aye. Isn't
that how the Birmingham Six went down?*

Martin McDonagh[2]

8.17 p.m. and 8.19 p.m.

On the evening of 21 November 1974, twenty-three-year-old Eugene
Reilly met his younger brother, twenty-year-old Desmond, by New Street
Station. Their parents, John and Bridget Reilly, had moved from Donegal to
Birmingham two decades earlier, and the sons had recently moved out of the
family home. Yet both brothers had remained in the nearby suburbs, with
Eugene now living in Saltley, and Desmond having married and settled in
Erdington. Indeed, Desmond and his wife now anticipated a new family of
their own, excitedly preparing their Erdington home for the arrival of a first
child in March.

When the brothers met in the city centre on that Thursday, they tried to
decide where to go for a drink, and settled by chance on the Tavern in the Town,
a pub in New Street only two minutes' walk from the railway station.[3] Eugene
and Desmond took their seats beneath the beamed ceiling of this busy bar,

1   Jonathan Coe, *The Rotters' Club* (London: Penguin, 2004), p. 348.
2   Martin McDonagh, 'The Beauty Queen of Leenane', in *Plays: 1* (London: Methuen,
1999), p. 53.
3   'Two Irish Brothers Died Together', *BP*, 26 November 1974, p. 7.

which by quarter past eight had filled with about 100 other young customers, the majority aged between eighteen and twenty-four.[4] Here, amidst the concrete columns and the clatter of conversation, nothing seemed particularly out of the ordinary. A twenty-year-old barman made his way to the doorway, a young woman edged towards the bar, whilst outside the pub the number 90 bus trundled around Smallbrook Ringway. A jukebox blared out 'When will I see you again?'[5]

Yet the next moment, a massive explosion rocked the building. Unseen by Desmond, Eugene, and the other drinkers, a 30-pound bomb had been wired to two ticking alarm clocks and placed in a briefcase at the far side of the bar.[6] On detonation, shards of debris strafed the area, leaving scores of people charred and lacerated or with garments ripped off by the impact. For those unfortunate enough to be wearing synthetic clothing, the material melted in the heat and caused appalling burn injuries. Even those on the bus outside were left bleeding.[7] Then the ceiling collapsed, plunging the scene into darkness and sending up clouds of concrete dust. As the initial noise subsided, tortured screaming and groaning came from those deafened, blinded, and half-suffocated in the ruins, with some of the victims who had been drinking and joking only moments before now scrabbling and clawing at the debris in a desperate attempt to retrieve the broken bodies that protruded from the rubble.[8]

A number of passers-by heard the cacophony and rushed to help, crunching through ankle-deep glass and ruined fragments of pub paraphernalia in order to reach those inside. Taxi drivers from New Street Station ferried the injured away in makeshift ambulances, and then police officers set about retrieving the dead.[9] Local constables collected body parts in red canvas sacks, but had to abandon these efforts when the whole building looked in danger of collapse.[10] After a pause, the recovery operation then continued into the night, as police began contacting the relatives of the dead. The newspapers subsequently

---

[4]   Chris Mullin, *Error of Judgement: The Truth About the Birmingham Bombings* (4th edn; Dublin: Poolbeg, 1997), p. 5.

[5]   'Only One Way to Describe the Scene – Carnage', *BM*, 22 November 1974, p. 31; 'Belfast-Type Horror Strikes Birmingham', *BM*, 22 November 1974, p. 3; '"Attack on People Disastrous and Appalling" Say Police', *BM*, 22 November 1974, p. 3; Harland and Lloyd (eds), *Birmingham Voices*, p. 124.

[6]   Mullin, *Error of Judgement*, p. 7.

[7]   Harland and Lloyd (eds), *Birmingham Voices*, p. 126.

[8]   'Only One Way to Describe the Scene – Carnage', *BM*, 22 November 1974, p. 31.

[9]   'Belfast-Type Horror', *BM*, 22 November 1974, p. 3.

[10]   'Only One Way to Describe the Scene – Carnage', *BM*, 22 November 1974, p. 31.

reported that, amidst this horror, John Reilly found himself asked to identify the body of his son Eugene. Although John must have felt stunned by this loss, he believed that at least his younger son Desmond had spent the day safely working away from Birmingham and so would have been spared injury. But when John arrived at the mortuary he found that the first body presented to him belonged to Desmond, and soon realized that both brothers had perished alongside one another.[11]

The city's sense of shock was multiplied by the fact that the Tavern in the Town explosion had been Birmingham's second deadly bombing of the evening. Three hundred yards away, a bar called the Mulberry Bush sat at the foot of the rotunda building, a prestigious decade-old office block that symbolized Birmingham's progress and modernity. Although this pub had a mezzanine level, most customers congregated in a section that made up the Rotunda's curving and intimate basement, little realizing what a death trap would be created here by a bomb large enough to blow the stairs away, blast a 40-inch-wide hole in the concrete floor, and echo a deep and ominous thud in the Tavern in the Town just moments before the second bomb.[12]

Amidst the chaotic events of the evening, the earliest hint about the attacks came only a few minutes before that explosion in the Mulberry Bush. At 8.11 p.m. the office shared by the *Birmingham Post* and *Birmingham Evening Mail* received a phone call from a man using the IRA codeword, warning that devices had been planted at the tax office in New Street and at the Rotunda. But the caller failed to specify how long was left until detonation, and six minutes later the police who had begun searching the Rotunda felt the first dull shudder of devastation.[13]

That evening another bomb left in the doorway of Barclays Bank on Hagley Road failed to explode, and a number of hoaxers then phoned the police with a range of terrifying but disingenuous warnings.[14] Nevertheless, the two successful detonations had strewn severed limbs and corpses into the pubs and streets of the city, injuring 162 people and killing 21, the worst death toll as a result of any operation planned by the IRA.[15] One of the responding surgeons in Birmingham commented that 'you could be forgiven for thinking that roast

---

11   'Two Irish Brothers Died Together', *BP*, 26 November 1974, p. 7.

12   Mullin, *Error of Judgement*, p. 5.

13   McGladdery, *The Provisional IRA in England*, p. 90; Mullin, *Error of Judgement*, p. 3.

14   'Belfast-Type Horror', *BM*, 22 November 1974, p. 3.

15   Gareth Parry, 'Bombs Hit Two Pubs', *Guardian*, 22 November 1974, p. 1; Mullin, *Error of Judgement*, p. 9. Prior to that point the biggest atrocity of the 'Troubles' was the fifteen killed in McGurk's bar in North Belfast in 1971, and the worst death toll came

beef was cooking' in the casualty ward, where 'the smell of burns was still there long after these people had been removed. You want to put drips on an arm and it isn't there. You look for a leg and there isn't one'.[16]

The Birmingham Campaign

The pub bombing formed part of a concerted campaign in the English midlands during the early 1970s, and, just as had been the case in the late 1930s, the situation in Ulster motivated the attacks. Ever since the 1920s, Northern Ireland had been governed by the implicitly anti-Catholic Ulster Unionist Party, been policed by an overwhelmingly Protestant armed force, and had seen town councils such as Derry/Londonderry and Dungannon systematically gerrymandered.[17] Catholics also felt discriminated against in terms of employment, with the state's prime minister in 1932 declaring 'Roman Catholics were endeavouring to get in everywhere. He would appeal to Loyalists therefore, wherever possible, to employ good Protestant lads and lassies'.[18] Indeed, the 1971 census figures revealed just how divided the province had become, with Catholics far more likely to work in those industries that had low social prestige and high unemployment, such as construction, whilst Protestants dominated those areas with greater pay and status.[19]

When 1968 saw ideas of radicalism spreading across Europe and the USA, Catholics in the Northern Irish state organized a series of civil rights marches to highlight their predicament. Indeed, those who arranged the important Belfast-to-Derry/Londonderry march in January 1969 consciously emulated the Selma-to-Montgomery protest four years earlier, with those struggling for civil rights in Northern Ireland and in the USA copying tactics and sharing a common political vocabulary.[20] When riots followed across Derry/Londonderry and Belfast, London politicians felt compelled to act, and by 1969 the British army had deployed to separate the warring communities. Nationalist areas at first welcomed these troops, but the reception soon soured, and by 1971 Northern Ireland saw murders, gun battles, and Protestants and Catholics being forced

---

twenty-four years after the Birmingham attacks, when 29 died in the Real IRA's attack on Omagh. See Charles Reiss, 'A Tactical Dilemma', *BP*, 23 November 1974, p. 6.

[16]   Quoted by Mullin, *Error of Judgement*, p. 7.

[17]   Hennessey, *Northern Ireland*, pp. xi–xiii.

[18]   Basil Brooke, quoted by Hennessey, *Northern Ireland*, p. xiii.

[19]   Bew, *Ireland*, pp. 488, 491.

[20]   Brian Dooley, *Black and Green: The Fight for Civil Rights in Northern Ireland and Black America* (London: Pluto, 1998), p. 4.

from their homes. The presence of the British army on the streets served to foster an atmosphere of violence and retaliation, particularly after 30 January 1972, when the British Parachute Regiment ran amok in Derry/Londonderry on 'Bloody Sunday' and killed 14 unarmed civilians. By March of that year, the British government had decided to impose direct rule, a situation that for some recalled the situation in Ireland during the Anglo-Irish War earlier in the century. With the British army on the streets, 1972 and 1973 saw over a quarter of all killings from political violence during the thirty years of 'Troubles', with Catholic civilians making up 254 and Protestant civilians 125 of the 759 deaths.[21] Birmingham came under attack after a number of republican dissidents felt disappointed that the IRA had done little to protect Northern Irish Catholics, and formed the Provisional IRA in order to retaliate and take the war to the enemy, with this organization soon becoming the dominant IRA group. After 'Bloody Sunday', IRA members sought an effective response, and in early 1973 the organization's leadership, realizing that bombs in English locations would generate far more media attention than attacks in Northern Ireland, formally sanctioned the idea of extending the campaign to England.[22]

In Birmingham, a number of people had attempted to initiate public discussion about the political situation in Ireland during the years before the bombings. Many of those in Birmingham's first- and second-generation Irish population expressed sympathy with the Catholic population of Ulster, and Birmingham boasted various anti-partition groups from the early 1950s, as well as a branch of Sinn Féin from the mid-1960s.[23] In August 1969, when the Falls and Crumlin Road areas of Belfast experienced severe inter-communal violence, more than 30 evicted Catholic families fled to Birmingham where churches made appeals to house the refugees and where the newly formed local 'Irish Civil Rights Group' set about organizing support for Catholics.[24] That month the recently-founded Birmingham division of the 'Campaign for Social Justice in Northern Ireland' also organized a march of 2,000 people from the Irish Community Centre in Digbeth through the middle of the city, with many participants wearing black armbands, and with the parade interspersed by sit-down demonstrations and chants of 'British troops out, IRA in'. Some participants also circulated leaflets asking Birmingham's men to

21   Bew, *Ireland*, pp. 506, 508, 510.
22   English, *Armed Struggle*, p. 163.
23   NAI, Department of Foreign Affairs, Position of Irish Workers in Birmingham, 402/222; Davies, 'The Flow is Slowing', *BM*, 27 October 1965, p. 10.
24   '"Find Homes for Irish Refugee Families" Call in Churches', *BP*, 25 August 1969, p. 12; 'Call for Strike by City's Irish', *BM*, 28 August 1969, p. 5.

join the IRA.[25] As the situation in Ulster deteriorated, Irish feelings of anger increased in Birmingham, so that by 1970 the city had its own branch of the Sinn Féin support organization *Clann na hÉireann* (Party of Ireland), which considered running an electoral candidate in Sparkhill. That year Birmingham also welcomed the young civil rights campaigner and recently elected republican MP Bernadette Devlin, who addressed a large two-hour rally at Digbeth's civic hall and led a march along New Street, as well as visiting the Catholic teacher training centre, Newman College, where students voted to 'adopt' the interned lecturer Desmond O'Hagan.[26] After her visit, *Clann na hÉireann* organized a 'smash internment' rally in the Bull Ring, and local newspapers reported that republicans had begun raising funds outside Catholic churches.[27]

During this period, Birmingham's branch of Sinn Féin also operated quite openly and organized into five lodges or *cumman*, each with 15 or 20 members who spent time selling newspapers and organizing more radical protests. In January 1973, for example, these *cumman* occupied the *Aer Lingus* offices in Bennetts Hill, protesting against the arrest in Southern Ireland of the Sinn Féin president and the IRA chief of staff.[28] Elsewhere, in March 1974, between 3,000 and 4,000 attended a service in Small Heath to commemorate Dublin's 1916 Easter Rising, whilst the Clancy brothers also celebrated the golden jubilee of the rebellion with a concert in the New Street Odeon.[29] Another 1,000 people joined Sinn Féin in January 1973 to parade from Small Heath to Digbeth in order to commemorate the first anniversary of 'Bloody Sunday', with a colour party wearing the IRA uniform and carrying republican flags in sight of local police officers. Indeed, when the superintendent in charge of the parade's security checked if the marchers were ready to begin he was told that they remained waiting 'for the colour party'. 'Oh', he replied, 'it's nice to see the coloured people getting involved'.[30]

By this time, even the yearly St Patrick's Day parade was falling under suspicion as 'a Republican parade', with some marchers noticing that they

[25]   'IRA Call for Volunteers during Midland March', *Sunday Mercury*, 17 August 1969, p. 3.

[26]   'Irish May Seek Candidate to Fight Midland MP', *Sunday Mercury*, 25 January 1970, p. 3.

[27]   'Irish Internee is "Adopted"', *Sunday Mercury*, 24 October 1971, p. 6; 'Republicans Plan Fund-Raising at Midland Churches', *Sunday Mercury*, 24 October 1971, p. 6.

[28]   'Irish Protestors Occupy Office', *BP*, 2 January 1973, p. 5.

[29]   'Longer Arms of the Law', *BP*, 30 November 1974, p. 6; 'Odeon New Street', *BM*, 14 March 1966, p. 2.

[30]   Quoted by Mullin, *Error of Judgement*, p. 279.

were being photographed by shadowy figures within the Rotunda building.[31] But of course those from outside the Irish population also wished to debate the situation in Ulster, and when the Birmingham Repertory Theatre settled into a new, high-profile building off Broad Street in 1972, David Edgar's new play *Death Story* was the second production on the smaller of the venue's two stages.[32] Edgar gave a modernized version of *Romeo and Juliet* in which the Montagues are not a family but the original social group living in an area that has since been inhabited by another community called the Capulets.[33] The Capulets have taken control of most local businesses, but all too familiar violence has ensued, with stones being thrown, homemade bombs detonated, and civilians driven out of their homes. The Capulet's antagonists are known as the 'Montags', a name echoing the derogatory nickname 'Taigs' that Ulster's Protestants had started using to describe Catholics, and, more provocatively for a Birmingham audience only a few months after the events of 'Bloody Sunday', an external army that attempts to separate Montague from Capulet only ends up inflaming the situation. An army captain asks his intelligence captain:

> Did you seek to provoke violence in order to make martial law inevitable? Was the plan meant to go wrong? ... I think you're in shit up to your elbows, Captain. I've no idea whether you were part of it or not, but I'm almost certain that your operation was even nastier than I thought.[34]

Edgar's drama appeared in the new theatre's studio space, but when the playhouse came to stage another piece about Ireland in the larger 900-seat auditorium during the following year, commercial demands dictated that there should be no repeat of Edgar's disturbing suggestion that the British army might be blamed for the recent violence. In May and June 1973, the theatre dealt with Ireland in music-hall mode when staging Brendan Behan's *The Hostage*, a comic piece that Joan Littlewood considerably adapted

---

31   Jim Gilraine, 'It's No Holiday', in *A Great Day: Celebrating St. Patrick's Day in Birmingham*, ed. Gudrun Limbrick (Birmingham: St. Patrick's Festival, 2007), pp. 43–44; Queenie Mulvey, 'We've Come a Long Way' in *A Great Day: Celebrating St. Patrick's Day in Birmingham*, ed. Gudrun Limbrick (Birmingham: St. Patrick's Festival, 2007), p. 59.

32   Conolly (ed.), *Bernard Shaw and Barry Jackson*, p. 200.

33   For an intelligent discussion of the limitations of applying the paradigm of *Romeo and Juliet* to the Northern Irish situation see Joe Cleary, *Outrageous Fortune: Capital and Culture in Modern Ireland* (Dublin: Field Day, 2007), pp. 254–56.

34   David Edgar, BCL, Shakespeare Collection, *Death Story*, S345.92F, fols 3, 43.

for English tastes from Behan's original Irish-language play *An Giall*. The knockabout action of the performance at the Repertory Theatre reassured the local audience that republicans posed little real-life threat, with the *Birmingham Post* declaring the production 'warm hearted, lively and extremely funny', whilst the *County Express* giggled at the 'Comic soldiers of the IRA' who 'rush around yelling, screaming, swilling Guinness, shooting off guns'.[35] Of course, the city would feel less sanguine about Irish nationalists by the end of the year, and as the explosions came closer to home the local council gave hints about cuts to the arts budget, with the Birmingham Repertory Theatre understanding the implication and generally avoiding plays dealing with Ireland throughout the 1970s and 1980s.[36]

Yet whilst audiences applauded the Repertory Theatre's clownish soldiers in June 1973, outside the playhouse Birmingham's non-fictional IRA was recruiting willing operatives to start attacking the area by the end of August.[37] The local republican leaders had lived in the city for a long time and were largely men in their thirties, but they enlisted younger enthusiasts living in Birmingham and also controlled a subsidiary operation in Manchester.[38] By the time of the pub bombings the following year, the Birmingham IRA had grown skilled at manufacturing devices from batteries and alarm clocks, and had launched more than 30 attacks in and around the city.[39] The first explosion targeted the Poplar Road branch of Lloyd's bank in Solihull on 29 August 1973, with the IRA giving no warning but only damaging the bank's doors and brickwork.[40] The following day, republicans struck Birmingham's city centre with three lunchtime bombs, destroying a shoe shop and slightly damaging a card store and bookshop.[41] Forty-eight hours later, the IRA placed devices that failed to explode in Sherlock Street and Calthorpe Road, although the next week a bomb wrecked two shops in Sutton Coldfield, followed by a charge that damaged part of an electronics factory in Witton.[42]

---

[35]   A. J. W., 'Comic Soldiers of the IRA', *County Express*, 11 May 1973, p. 11.
[36]   Claire Cochrane, *The Birmingham Rep: A City's Theatre 1962–2002* (Birmingham: Sir Barry Jackson Trust, 2003), pp. 212–15; 'CBSO and Rep Warned: Axe your Budget', *BM*, 3 April 1974, p. 9.
[37]   English, *Armed Struggle*, p. 169.
[38]   Mullin, *Error of Judgement*, p. 286.
[39]   'Months of Death and Devastation', *BP*, 23 November 1974, p. 4.
[40]   'Bomb Blast at Solihull Bank', *BP*, 30 August 1973, p. 1.
[41]   '15 Outrages over Seven Months', *BP*, 8 April 1974, p. 3.
[42]   'Testimony on Terror', *BP*, 21 September 1973, p. 1; 'Midnight Bombers Strike at Factory', *BP*, 17 September 1973, p. 1.

A teenage boy had suffered injuries in the Sutton Coldfield incident, but so far the Birmingham campaign caused no casualties. By contrast, the IRA in London had killed two people and injured almost 300 between March and September 1973.[43] However, on 17 September a bomb on Edgbaston's Highfield Road caused the IRA's first death in the English midlands, as a young army bomb disposal expert, Ronald Wilkinson, who had planned to go on holiday with his wife that day, instead found himself called in to investigate a suspect package. As he attempted to make the device safe it detonated in his face, blowing him into the air and causing the severe head and chest injuries from which he died six days later.[44] In response to the first IRA killing in the English midlands, St Chad's Cathedral, which had long been associated with Irish worship and festivities, led special prayers to 'Convert the minds of those who are causing injuries and fear on our streets'.[45] Down the road at the Irish Community Centre, the founding chairman Dermot O'Riordan and the manager Nancy McCann tried to ban IRA sympathizers, and both decided to resign when these efforts at first failed to garner support from the rest of the centre's organizational committee. O'Riordan, himself a former Royal Air Force sergeant, remained adamant that 'We are a social club and don't allow arguments on politics or religion'.[46]

After the death of Wilkinson, the local IRA bombers themselves paused. From the start of the bombing campaign, the commander of the Birmingham organization had given strict orders that only property should be targeted, and cancelled operations if he suspected his volunteers had touched even a drop of alcohol. But 1974 a new leader took control, and during that year the organization adopted a less cautious approach.[47] As the city greeted New Year with frost and freezing fog, two five-pound bombs, the largest seen in the region, exploded almost simultaneously in the middle of Birmingham, mauling Colmore Circus and New Street Shopping Centre.[48] More ominously, on 7 April, at the same time as co-ordinated strikes on Manchester, London, and New Street Station, the IRA attacked the Birmingham rotunda with bombs three times larger than anything previously used by the organization in the

---

43 'Testimony on Terror', *BP*, 21 September 1973, p. 1; McGladdery, *The Provisional IRA in England*, pp. 236–37.

44 'Officer Critical after Five-Hour Operation', *BP*, 17 September 1973, p. 1; 'Bomb Blast Officer Dies', *BP*, 24 September 1973, p. 1.

45 'Officer Critical after Five-Hour Operation', *BP*, 17 September 1973, p. 1.

46 '"My Life in Peril"', *BM*, 16 May 1974, p. 5.

47 Mullin, *Error of Judgement*, pp. 286–87.

48 '15 Outrages over Seven Months', *BP*, 8 April 1974, p. 3.

English midlands. An explosion at Lloyd's bank in the foyer of the rotunda showered glass into the New Street crowds, and tore through the roof of the parking bay with such force that for almost two weeks afterwards structural engineers feared that the whole skyscraper might collapse.[49]

On 14 July the IRA returned to the rotunda, detonating explosives on the roof of Lloyd's bank that smashed shop windows along New Street.[50] The campaign then intensified during the summer in response to the death of nationalist hunger striker Michael Gaughan, with the IRA incinerating furniture stores in Sparkhill, attacking business premises in Aston, and, in an echo of 1939, leaving devices at five nearby cinemas. Although the Birmingham organization suffered a number of arrests in August, the late summer and autumn saw this branch of the IRA leaving explosives at Moseley's timber yards, aiming car bombs at establishment figures, and targeting local governmental offices.[51] For the IRA, these activities all constituted part of a long war, which offered some redress for the brutalities and injustices of the Northern Irish state, and, by making the public of cities such as Birmingham feel continually unsafe, potentially lessened Britain's enthusiasm for control over the province.

James McDade

But, on 14 November 1974, the IRA suffered a casualty of its own. On that day, a bomb pulverized the Conservative club in Manor Road, Solihull, and an incendiary device set light to Sheepcote Street timber yard.[52] At the same time, twenty-eight-year-old James McDade travelled to Coventry, intending to destroy the telephone exchange, but carrying a malfunctioning bomb. As he clutched the device tight to himself, it exploded prematurely, scattering parts of McDade's body over a wide area, leaving only his burnt clothes and the print on his dismembered thumb by which to identify him.[53]

McDade had been in Birmingham for the past five years, and at the time

---

49   'Hunt Is on for Brains Behind the Bombings', *BP*, 8 April 1974, p. 1.

50   Jeffrey Berliner, 'Midnight: Bombers Hit Birmingham Again', *BP*, 15 July 1974, p. 1.

51   Mullin, *Error of Judgement*, pp. 282–83; 'Months of Death and Devastation', *BP*, 23 November 1974, p. 4; 'Hospitals Rocked as Midnight Bombers Hit Birmingham Bank', *BP*, 6 November 1974, p. 1.

52   'Fires Hit Furniture Stores', *BP*, 23 November 1974, p. 4.

53   'Birmingham Man Identified from Thumbprint and Clothing Only', *BM*, 22 November 1974, p. 2.

of his death lived with his pregnant wife – an English Protestant – and his
two-year-old son on Ivy Avenue in Balsall Heath.[54] Although he was demonized
by English newspapers and lionized by IRA supporters after his death, the reality
of his life probably lay somewhere between these two poles. 'Jamsie' had a fine
singing voice, and was well known and popular in Birmingham's Irish pubs
for his impersonations of Jim Reeves and Johnny Cash. But he sometimes gave
vent to a fierce temper: he had brawled with local Asians, had been evicted
by his mother-in-law, and was even rumoured to have beaten his wife.[55] In
Ardoyne, McDade and his fellow Catholics had experienced discrimination,
unemployment, and an electoral system that consistently worked against them.
But the real turning point for McDade came in December 1971, when British
paratroopers shot dead his brother Gerry in a raid on a Belfast club.[56]

When in turn James McDade died, IRA supporters in Birmingham
intended to laud him as the latest in a long line of martyrs who had sacrificed
everything for Ireland. On the death of Michael Gaughan earlier in 1974,
thousands of supporters gathered in Kilburn, including those dressed in the
IRA uniform of dark suit and sweater, black beret, and sunglasses.[57] The IRA
now wanted to organize a similar commemoration in Coventry, but when
the organization approached the Archbishop of Birmingham with the request,
the cleric adamantly refused. After all, he had been deeply embarrassed to
find that two priests from the English midlands had officiated at Gaughan's
London funeral, one of whom was the hunger striker's cousin, Father Michael
Connolly.[58] Even worse, the Coventry priest Father Patrick Fell (born an
English Protestant) had been found guilty in Birmingham of conspiring to cause
explosions for the IRA, and the archbishop detested the thought that republican
bombers should be finding succour in the Church, warning that 'Anyone guilty

---

54 'Two Men Taken off Plane as McDade's Body Flown Out', *BM*, 22 November 1974,
p. 3; Hill and Hunt, *Forever Lost, Forever Gone*, p. 44.

55 The rumours that McDade beat his wife are reported both by Nora Power, the wife
of the wrongly convicted Billy Power, and by another member of the 'Birmingham Six',
Paddy Hill. See Nora Power's view in Mullin, *Error of Judgement*, p. 15, as well as Hill and
Hunt, *Forever Lost, Forever Gone*, p. 36.

56 Mullin, *Error of Judgement*, p. 16.

57 'Will IRA Dare to Flout the Prelate?', *BM*, 18 November 1974, p. 1.

58 Connolly had run St Joseph's Catholic Church in Wolverhampton and had already
incurred the wrath of Enoch Powell for inflaming an Irish crowd at Digbeth. After
leading the mourning for Gaughan, Connolly finally gained the career-ending censure of
the Archbishop. Peter Chippindale, 'Archbishop Sacks Priest for IRA Funeral Speech',
Guardian, 12 June 1974, p. 28.

of such violence is guilty of grave sin'.[59] As for McDade's funeral arrangements, the archbishop allowed only that a prayer at the graveside should be said 'in the hope that the person responsible had time to repent before death', and a Church spokesman reiterated that no priest in the archdiocese should dare to contradict this order.[60]

Nevertheless, a few days after McDade's death, funeral notices began appearing in Birmingham's Irish pubs and clubs, declaring that 'On November 21 at 3.30 the remains of our comrade, James McDade, will be escorted from Coventry to Birmingham and on to Belfast. We consider it the duty of all Irish people to be present at Coventry mortuary'.[61] In spite of the hieratic injunction, two Roman Catholic priests conducted this short service at Coventry mortuary, behind one of the largest security operations ever seen in the area, as more than 1,300 police officers struggled to keep IRA sympathizers away from members of the National Front and Ulster Defence Association.[62] At the memorial service a lone piper played the lament and mourners placed two wreaths on the coffin, whilst the protestors sang 'go home you bums' to the tune of 'Auld Lang Syne', and others chanted 'IRA out', or threw bags of flour at the hearse.[63] The convoy and police escort then drove from Coventry to Birmingham airport, where handlers loaded the coffin onto a British Airways flight for Belfast, but learned that Loyalist ground staff had refused to unload the dead man at the other end, so instead transferred the funeral party onto an *Aer Lingus* plane bound for Dublin (much to the subsequent embarrassment of the Irish government, which questioned why the funeral party had arrived in the South of Ireland at all).[64] When the plane finally prepared to leave Birmingham the local policemen breathed a momentary sigh of relief, as, despite some arrests earlier in the afternoon, the day appeared to have gone relatively smoothly. Only then, however, did the officers start to hear reports about a terrible disturbance in the centre of the city, and began to realize that the most difficult part of their day's work had yet to begin.

---

[59]   'Will IRA Dare to Flout the Prelate?', *BM*, 18 November 1974, p. 1; Mullin, Error of Judgement, p. 279; Hill and Hunt, *Forever Lost, Forever Gone*, p. 39.

[60]   'Heartsearching', *BP*, 19 November 1974, p. 4.

[61]   Mullin, *Error of Judgement*, p. 17; Louis Blom-Cooper, *Victims of Circumstance: The Birmingham Six and Other Cases* (London: Duckworth, 1997), pp. 43–44.

[62]   'Bomber: Big Police Net', *BM*, 21 November 1974, p. 1; 'Two Men Taken off Plane', *BM*, 22 November 1974, p. 3; 'Belfast-Type Horror', *BM*, 22 November 1974, p. 2.

[63]   Mullin, *Error of Judgement*, p. 33.

[64]   *BM*, 22 November 1974, p. 2.

Backlash

The pub blasts of 1974 prompted a widespread sense of crisis amongst the Irish in Birmingham. After all, the list of those injured included names such as Patrick Farrell, Michael O'Brien, Patricia O'Connell, Bernadette O'Connor, Collette Twomey, and Bridget O'Gorman, and in total an estimated 35 Irish citizens were maimed, whilst four Irish citizens lay amongst the 21 dead.[65] 'I have been in this country for nine years since I was 11 and I say today that I am ashamed to be Irish', declared one man who had been drinking inside one of the bars at the time of the explosions. 'I think the IRA are a load of dirty, stupid bastards to pick on innocent people out for a quiet drink'.[66] In Ireland the press was equally condemnatory: the *Irish Independent* spoke of the 'shock and revulsion of the Irish people', whilst the *Irish Times* condemned the 'merciless, psychopathic brutality' of the IRA, 'a group of Irish men and women who have consistently shamed themselves and their country'.[67] Even the *Irish Press*, whilst reminding its readers that the 'people in Belfast have endured horrors like Birmingham for many years', condemned the bombings as 'cruel and wrong', alongside a stark picture of two bodies lying in the debris.[68]

The night after the bombings, Irish councillors in Sparkhill pledged to help ban militant republicanism in Britain, and students at Birmingham Polytechnic who previously pledged funds to the IRA now publicly rescinded that support.[69] The prominent Sinn Féin member Brendan Magill, who had travelled with McDade's body from Birmingham to Dublin, castigated the bombers' actions as 'disgraceful', whilst the IRA saw a propaganda catastrophe unfolding and refused to admit responsibility, claiming instead that another group must have conducted the attack.[70] Three days afterwards an official statement proclaimed, 'It has never been and is not the policy of the IRA to

---

[65]   'Police Release Names of 167 Casualties', *BP*, 23 November 1974, p. 7; McGladdery, *The Provisional IRA in England*, p. 90.

[66]   Reported by Wendy Hughes, 'Bars Deserted in Frightened Rush for Home', *BP*, 23 November 1974, p. 9.

[67]   'Inhuman', *Irish Independent*, 23 November 1974, p. 3; 'The Mark of the Beast', *Irish Times*, 22 November 1974, p. 15.

[68]   'Mourning for Many', *Irish Press*, 22 November 1974, p. 10.

[69]   'Irish Support Call for Ban on the IRA', *BP*, 23 November 1974, p. 9; 'Row over Call to Back Irish Terror Tactics', *BM*, 26 November 1974, p. 7.

[70]   'Bombs Shatter Crowded Pubs in Birmingham', *Guardian*, 22 November 1974, p. 28; McGladdery, *The Provisional IRA in England*, p. 90.

bomb non-military targets without giving adequate warning to ensure the safety of civilians'.[71]

The fruit of the 1952 St Patrick's Day procession now withered on the vine, as those who had grown self-confident and voluble now became paranoid and persecuted. The day after the bombings, Edgbaston's Conservative MP, Jill Knight, pointed the finger of blame towards previous local Irish activities, declaring 'It is an outrage that people of this sort should be allowed to hire civic halls in Birmingham to plot and plan their raids'.[72] British newspapers similarly complained of excessive leniency in allowing previous 'IRA meetings and parades in the Birmingham area'.[73] The prime minister and Tory opposition leader had in fact been in Dublin on the day of the explosions, attending the state funeral of former Irish president Erskine Childers, but in the week after the bombings both British politicians helped to pass legislation making IRA membership illegal, allowing police to hold republican suspects without charge, and – until an eleventh-hour change – including a clause allowing judges to assume that anyone possessing IRA-related documents must have joined the outlawed organization.[74] Even the left-leaning *Guardian* newspaper approved of such increased surveillance of Sinn Féin's 'fringe sympathisers', declaring that 'infringement of their privacy is a small price to pay'.[75] In this atmosphere many Irish-born people felt worried by any earlier sympathies they may have shown towards the nationalist cause, and fretted about previous political conversations with workmates, attendance at Irish events, or possession of republican pamphlets, all of which might be viewed in a newly incriminating light. Families in Birmingham with Irish connections felt a sense of guilt by association, with British newspapers confirming that the bombers were most likely 'first or second generation Irish, men and women who have lived in England for years, and who are sufficiently established in the community to have safe refuges and in some cases to be entirely indistinguishable from English people'.[76]

As a result, 1974 saw many of the Irish-born population of Birmingham and their families go to ground, and the night after the attack the management of the Irish Community Centre cancelled a scheduled dance and left the building

71   'Pub Bombs: Six Men Will Appear in Court Today', *BP*, 25 November 1974, p. 1.
72   Simon Hoggart, 'Jenkins Gets Hanging Call', *Guardian*, 22 November 1974, p. 1.
73   'Savagery and the Law', *Guardian*, 22 November 1974, p. 14.
74   'The Angry City', *BP*, 25 November 1973, p. 6; Mullin, *Error of Judgement*, pp. 10–11.
75   'Savagery and the Law', *Guardian*, 22 November 1974, p. 14.
76   Peter Chippindale, 'Sinister Precedent Feared', *Guardian*, 23 November 1974, p. 1.

in semi-darkness with the doors locked. Those running the centre issued a statement to say:

> Our Irish community shares in the horror of the events of last night in Birmingham and offers sincere sympathy to the people of Birmingham – particularly to the families and friends of those killed and injured as a result of this terrible act. No words of ours can represent the utter revulsion we feel at this terrifying and unbelievable act of madness.[77]

The centre's founding chairman, Dermot O'Riordan, also declared, 'People should realise that most of the Irish population here have absolutely nothing to do with the IRA', although such statements did little to assuage local anger.[78] The centre's president – an assistant priest from Westport in Mayo, Father Brendan O'Malley – continually answered the phone to fend off promises of violence against the club. Very soon after the bombings, one man called to threaten vengeance for the death of a friend in the blasts, whilst a white paper bag with 'get home Irish bastards' was pushed through the letter-box.[79] Indeed, despite O'Malley's best efforts, revenge attackers ignited petrol over the building's roof within hours of the explosions, and by the end of the following week had firebombed the venue on two occasions.[80]

The first signs of an anti-Irish backlash came on the evening of the bombing, when youths in the city centre streets began chanting anti-Irish slogans, and the English Catholic priest of Sacred Heart chapel in Aston found his presbytery under assault from petrol bombs, presumably in response to James McDade's marriage at the church four years earlier.[81] The next day many Irish-born residents of Birmingham stayed indoors or avoided going about their usual business, and a number encountered threats and abuse. For example, one seventy-nine-year-old man who had spent the last sixty years in England ventured out to buy a Calor gas canister that he desperately needed for cooking, but had to retreat from local shops with insults ringing in his ears when bystanders heard his accent, whilst in another part of the city a local baker

[77] John Solan, 'A Stone Shatters the Apprehensive Silence', *BP*, 23 November 1974, p. 9.
[78] 'Don't Take Law into Own Hands – Jenkins', *BP*, 23 November 1974, p. 1.
[79] 'Years of Work Ruined in Two Minutes', *Irish Times*, 23 November 1974, p. 10.
[80] 'It Feels Bad to Be Irish in Birmingham', *Observer*, 24 November 1974, p. 5; Wendy Hughes, 'Backlash Hampering Police – Warning', *BP*, 25 November 1974, p. 5.
[81] 'Belfast-Type Horror', *BM*, 22 November 1974, p. 2; 'Bombs Shatter Crowded Pubs', *Guardian*, 22 November 1974, p. 28.

allegedly refused to serve Bridget Reilly, little knowing that she had lost both of her sons in the blasts.[82] Other families received abusive letters in the post, and immediately after the explosions such tension built up amongst the night-workers at the giant Longbridge car plant that by the morning there were fights amongst Irish and English workers, with 1,500 employees eventually marching out of the factory to chant anti-IRA slogans in the street outside. One English worker said:

> You could cut the atmosphere with a knife from the time we clocked-in. One lad had a daughter injured and other victims are friends or relatives of the people here. Some bloody stupid Irishman started shouting the odds for the IRA and got a clout in his teeth. The trouble soon spread and there were more fights. This stopped the assembly line for about an hour before we decided to walk out.

The trouble then spread to another five Rover factories, with one elderly man who took part in the walk-out declaring, 'Anyone with an Irish accent would be well advised to keep his mouth shut. If he can't do that, he should stay at home'.[83] Workers in other factories also downed tools, staff at British Airways refused to take planes to Ireland, and the National Front demanded the restoration of capital punishment.[84] Meanwhile 300 workers at the city's fruit and vegetable markets refused to handle any Irish goods, and one Bull Ring trader voiced the feelings of many when he declared: 'Send all the Irish back to Ireland. Get them out of the country. Of course we could carry on without them, we would be better off without them'.[85]

Police, politicians, and priests now appealed for calm, on 24 November using London Weekend Television to exonerate the wider Irish community, but the situation deteriorated further over the weekend as the anti-Irish fire-bombers discovered new targets for revenge, burning lorry cabs at Gallagher's construction firm in Small Heath, attacking members of the Boundary Club in Acocks Green with several petrol bombs, and causing £5,000 worth of

---

82   Maureen Mitchell, news interview, BBC, 18 November 2004, available at 'Irish Quarter' <http://www.irishquarterbirmingham.com/news.htm> [accessed 21 May 2008]. See also 'Irish Support Call for Ban on the IRA', *BP*, 23 November 1974, p. 9.

83   'Walk-Outs Hit Car Factories after Clashes between Workers', *Irish Times*, 23 November 1974, p. 10.

84   'Don't Take Law into Own Hands', *BP*, 23 November 1974, p. 1.

85   'Irishmen Picked Up Boarding Ulster Ferry', *Guardian*, 23 November 1974, p. 1; Dennis Barker, 'Aftermath of Vengeance', *Guardian*, 23 November 1974, p. 11.

damage to the College Arms pub in Erdington, where a barman had recently refused to serve a British soldier in uniform.[86] The city also saw attacks on the Holy Family Catholic Church in Small Heath and St Gerard's Catholic School in Castle Vale, with lunchtime drinkers at a pub in Greet beating three men with Irish accents so severely that one of the trio was left in hospital.[87] Indeed, almost every Irish-born person then living in Birmingham has stories about how they altered their behaviour at this time, either by avoiding pubs and social events, using a disguised accent, or issuing apologies to English friends and workmates.

One of the worst incidents reported at this time involved Thomas Burnside, a press-operator at Longbridge who had left Belfast in 1966 and whose sleeping children were almost killed by a petrol bomb that set fire to their bed in Wellhead Lane, Perry Barr, and then by a second paraffin attack on the house during the following week.[88] Burnside's traumatized wife declared, 'I have no idea why anyone should pick on us. The letters say that we are IRA sympathisers but that is just not true and we deplore the bombings in Birmingham'.[89] Of course, although such attacks were perpetrated by those who objected to the IRA, such retribution followed exactly the same logic as the original pub bombings, as the cultural critic Seamus Deane pointed out:

> The rage is directed against those who killed the people in Birmingham – and those who did so are not the actual bombers themselves but the whole community of people from whom the bombers come […] This is precisely the rationale behind the bombings themselves. The British are killers, as their record shows in Northern Ireland now and in Ireland as such. Therefore, British people should be killed – as well those in the pub as anyone else. It doesn't matter that they are not in the SAS or among those who actually planted bombs or fired guns in Northern Ireland. They are from that constituency.[90]

A worker in Birmingham assessed the situation more bluntly: 'We, the Irish

---

86   'Firebombers in Attack on Night Club', *BM*, 27 November 1974, p. 12; '"Stay Calm" Plea by Police', *BM*, 28 November 1974, p. 7.

87   Hughes, 'Backlash Hampering Police', p. 5.

88   'Family in Fire Bomb Terror', *BM*, 26 November 1974, p. 1.

89   'New Fire Attack on Irish Family', *BM*, 2 December 1974, p. 1.

90   Seamus Deane, 'A State of Injustice', in *The Birmingham Six: An Appalling Vista* (Dublin: LiterÉire, 1990), p. 36.

get it both ways. We get the backlash and we're in as much danger from the bombs as the English'.[91]

Years later, Jonathan Coe would include a fictionalized account of this anti-Irish retaliation in a story stretched across two novels, the 2001 work *The Rotters' Club* and the 2004 sequel *The Closed Circle*. The first book begins by showing how the pub bombings cut so many young lives prematurely short, as one of Coe's characters sits in the Tavern in the Town and prepares to propose marriage:

> 'Look, love, you know what I think about you, don't you?'
>
> Lois didn't answer. She just looked back at him, her eyes staring to brim over.
>
> 'I love you,' said Malcolm. 'I'm crazy about you.' He took a long breath, an enormous breath. 'I've got to say something to you. I've got to ask you something.' He grasped her hand, and squeezed it tightly. As if he would never let go.[92]

However, at that point the bomb detonates nearby. Malcolm is killed, and Lois remains permanently traumatized by the explosion. In this, Coe reflects the real-life experience of Derek Blake, whose memories of that fateful visit to the Mulberry Bush had been published in a 1995 memoir. Blake recalled that he had gone to the pub with his fiancée Pam Palmer to discuss their wedding plans, but that:

> Everything went black and the whole place seemed to come in on me as the ceiling collapsed. I tried to get to Pam to see if she was alright. I could not move and I could not hear my own voice, even though I was shouting. It was not until three days afterwards I was told Pam had died. There we were, going to talk about our future together, and the next second there was no future. Everything was over. I wanted to die too.[93]

Yet, whilst Coe acknowledges the horror of the attacks in his fictional version, his carefully structured story is also at pains to describe the subsequent sufferings of the Irish inhabitants of Birmingham. The brutality of the bombing is balanced by Coe's description of how, in the aftermath, the city sees vicious assaults on workers at Longbridge and 'Micks being beaten up all over the

---

91   Quoted by McGladdery, *The Provisional IRA in England*, pp. 93–94.

92   Jonathan Coe, *The Rotters' Club* (London: Penguin, 2004), pp. 103–104.

93   Quoted by Hill and Hunt, *Forever Lost, Forever Gone*, p. 54.

place'. Coe also depicts the divorce of an Irish-born man and an Englishwoman, whose son as a result gains an anglicized name and a disturbing enthusiasm for far-right extremism.[94] Thus Coe carefully delineates English and Irish victims of the bombings, and reveals how the aftershocks might affect a range of people who were nowhere near the explosions at the time. In addition, Coe, writing years after the event, avoids any simplistic notions of causality by placing the bombing in a broader history of colonialism, and even attempts to convey a sense of redemption and reconciliation in the city. If the start of his work shows a potential marriage being ruined by an Irish-made bomb, then at the end of *The Rotters' Club* another marriage is saved by an Irish-made novel, as one character recovers his wife's affections thanks to the help of James Joyce's *Ulysses*, with *The Rotters' Club* concluding in a description of erotic happiness that self-consciously parodies the unpunctuated and sexually explicit stream-of-consciousness famously delivered by Joyce's Molly Bloom.[95]

However, when the BBC decided to screen a television adaptation of *The Rotters' Club* in 2005, the broadcaster opted to leave out much of the balancing detail that Coe included in the original book.[96] The Welsh nationalist who, in the novel, explains England's history of colonialism becomes, in the televised adaptation, a sullen figure who simply dislikes the English because he 'has strong views about most things'. Similarly, the schoolboy whose Irish and English parents divorce in Coe's novel is transformed in the television version into a straightforwardly comic, English figure whose peculiar behaviour is entirely unrelated to the pub bombings.

The BBC adaptation also offers a considerably sanitized version of some of the grislier moments of *The Rotters' Club*. Coe's original novel describes Malcolm's ruined body in the aftermath of the explosion at the Tavern in the Town, but the television version instead shows the attack in a stop-frame sequence that simply pictures an unharmed Malcolm flying through the air. Similarly, the reprisals at Longbridge that follow the explosions are more ambiguous in the televised adaptation than in the novel: Coe's original story makes plain that murderousness comes in the wake of the bomb attacks, but BBC viewers could believe that the aftermath was marked only by some severe

---

94   Coe, *The Rotters' Club*, pp. 236, 290; Jonathan Coe, *The Closed Circle* (London: Penguin, 2005), pp. 365–66, 375–76.

95   Indeed, Coe's Benjamin Trotter provides a 13,955-word sentence, surpassing the famous 4,391-word sentence of Molly Bloom. NW, 'Diary', *Guardian*, 1 December 2007, review section, p. 15.

96   *The Rotters' Club*, adapted by Dick Clement and Ian La Frenais, BBC2, 26 January 2005, 2 February 2005, 9 February 2005.

bullying.[97] In excising some of the more violent features of Coe's novel, the 2005 adaptation thus provided a rose-tinted view of the 1970s, in which the IRA could be lumped together in a nostalgic medley of 'Prog Rock', 'Blue Nun', and 'Smash'. Shortly after the BBC broadcast this version of *The Rotters' Club*, London would suffer a co-ordinated series of Islamist suicide bombings on the underground transport network, and for an audience in the age of al-Qaida, the televised IRA attacks of *The Rotters' Club* encouraged thoughts of a supposedly gentler and simpler time.

The 'Birmingham Six'

In real life, the rush to vengeance in 1974 had one further tragic consequence, and one that, over time, came to overshadow the actual bombings. In the years before the IRA attacks, James McDade had not been the only Catholic to move to Birmingham in order to escape the troubled Ardoyne district. Indeed, when he arrived in England he found numerous acquaintances dotted about the city, and at first he lodged in Aston with his old childhood friend, Gerry Hunter, before staying for a short time with another schoolmate, Billy Power, who had moved to Handsworth to escape unemployment: and these three men often joined together to do painting jobs around Birmingham. On about six occasions, McDade also encountered one of his brother Joe's old schoolboy companions, Paddy Hill, and sometimes met with the less-familiar family friends Hugh Callaghan and Richard McIlkenny, who introduced McDade to the Derry/Londonderry man, Johnny Walker. All of these men drank in the Crossways pub in Perry Common, but were scarcely a tight-knit group, with the other six remaining unaware that 'Jamsie' had secretly become an IRA operative.[98]

McDade's sudden death of course laid bare his IRA activities, and in response five of his Birmingham acquaintances decided to travel to the funeral in Belfast, wishing to show solidarity with his bereaved family.[99] Hunter, Power, Hill, McIlkenny, and Walker therefore set off from the city centre shortly before

---

[97]   Some viewers may however have picked up a hint about murder from the casting of the televised version. The key revenge-attacker was played by Andrew Tiernan, an actor who had recently come to fame in Birmingham as a particularly bloody Banquo in a well-known television adaptation of *Macbeth* set in Ladywood. *Macbeth on the Estate*, dir. Penny Woolcock, BBC2, 5 April 1997.

[98]   Mullin, *Error of Judgement*, pp. 14–15, 19, 26; *World in Action: The Birmingham Six – Their Own Story*, prod. Eamon T. Connor, Ian McBride, and Charles Tremayne, Granada, 18 March 1991; Hill and Hunt, *Forever Lost, Forever Gone*, pp. 32–36.

[99]   *World in Action: The Birmingham Six.*

the pub explosions, and by the time that the men made an attempt to board their ferry at Heysham a national manhunt was underway for the bombers, with the five consequently finding themselves stopped by police officers, transported to Morecambe police station, and finally subjected to a test that revealed that two of the five had been in contact with explosives.

The next day, police picked up the gently spoken Hugh Callaghan, who had accompanied the other five to New Street Station for a farewell drink at the outset of their Belfast trip. With all six now in custody, the police unleashed Birmingham's feelings of outrage upon the prisoners, knocking teeth from skulls, extinguishing cigarettes on bare flesh, and conducting mock executions. Officers then forced the detainees to sign false confessions, before bringing all six back to a brutal reception at Winson Green prison, where the beatings intensified, and where officers took turns to assault the six with particular sadism. Outside, a 500-strong mob shouted and jeered abuse.[100] When police drove the captives along Steelhouse Lane this crowd surged forward, chanting anti-Irish slogans, and although police kept the protestors away from the accused men, local gossip as well as the clear bruises on the men's faces indicated the treatment being meted out behind closed doors.[101] Eventually the six faced a 45-day trial, at the end of which they each received terms of life imprisonment, with the judge declaring that he sentenced the men 'on the clearest and most overwhelming evidence I have ever heard'. Meanwhile the Birmingham homes occupied by the families of the six were ransacked, robbed, and daubed with graffiti declaring 'hang IRA bastards'.[102] Paddy Hill's father, a former member of the British army who had lived in Birmingham for years, was badly beaten up for being a 'bomber's father' and would never work again.[103] 'I only had the prison population to put up with', Hugh Callaghan later reflected, 'I thought about my wife. I said, well, she has to face the whole wide world out there'.[104]

Of course, a terrible error had been made. Although the courtroom jury had reached a guilty verdict, the men who became known as the 'Birmingham Six' had nothing whatsoever to do with the bombings. A local group called 'Rough Justice' realized the truth, as did the jailed Irishmen's fellow prisoners, but the mind of the general public had quickly been decided, with popular

---

[100] 'Gun Guard as Six Face Court', *BM*, 25 November 1974, p. 1.

[101] Pauline Hepburn, 'Jeers as Accused Six Go to Court', *BP*, 26 November 1974, p. 7.

[102] Mullin, *Error of Judgement*, pp. 60, 68, 108, 57, 63, 144–47, Justice Bridge quoted on 233, 171.

[103] Hill and Hunt, *Forever Lost, Forever Gone*, p. 227.

[104] Broadcast as part of *World in Action: The Birmingham Six*.

opinion set so resolutely that in 1985 the editor of the *Birmingham Post* could state that he had never seriously heard the suggestion that the verdict was wrong.[105] Only in the second half of the 1980s did popular attitudes begin to shift and change, as television producers created a widespread feeling of unease about the convictions. In 1985 Chris Mullin, the editor of the British leftwing *Tribune* magazine and son of an Irish-born mother, re-examined the 'Birmingham Six' affair for Granada Television's investigative programme, *World in Action*, and began to expose the faults in the legal case, with a broadcast of 28 October 1985 highlighting the deeply flawed nature of the 'scientific' evidence on which the prosecution had relied.[106] The *World in Action* team asked two independent scientists to replicate the tests that had connected the convicted men with nitro-glycerine, and found that the same positive result could have been gained from contact with a wide range of common substances, including the playing cards, train tables, and cigarettes that the six had handled on the evening of the arrests.[107] The television programme also featured a senior IRA figure giving the first public acknowledgement of the organization's responsibility for the bombings, with the declaration that 'The volunteers who did carry out those operations are freely walking about today'.[108]

Although most of Britain had considered the conviction of the six men to be a cut-and-dried case before the *World in Action* exposé, the programme's broadcast attracted renewed attention to these prisoners. In July the following year, Chris Mullin published his book *Error of Judgement*, arguing powerfully that a miscarriage of justice had occurred, and in December he wrote a letter to the *Birmingham Post* appealing for any policemen with information about the events of 1974 to speak with him. A disaffected ex-officer duly came forward to admit that the six had been tormented with sleep deprivation, attack dogs, and firearms, giving Mullin the material for a second *World in Action* programme, which appeared on British television screens on 1 December 1986.[109]

With the media spotlight turning back to the imprisoned men, the events of 1974 began to receive wider discussion and reappraisal. The Belfast playwright Stewart Parker, for example, wrote the 1987 play *Pentecost* in which he depicted a

---

[105] *World in Action: The Birmingham Six*; Mullin, *Error of Judgement*, p. 247.

[106] Andrew Roth, 'Ask Aristotle about Chris Mullin', *Guardian*, 16 March 2001, <http://politics.guardian.co.uk/profiles/story/0,,458072,00.html> [accessed 21 May 2008].

[107] Lawrence Howard, *Terrorism: Roots, Impact, Responses* (London: Praeger, 1992), p. 131.

[108] Quoted by Mullin, *Error of Judgement*, p. 304.

[109] David Spark, *Investigative Reporting: A Study in Technique* (Oxford: Focal, 1999), p. 189; Mullin, *Error of Judgement*, p. 269.

Northern Irish Protestant returning to the province in May 1974 after setting up home in Birmingham. Anyone in Parker's audience who was aware of the recent television documentaries about the 'Birmingham Six' would have realized the irony of Parker's setting: although the play's Ulster character believes he has put the 'Troubles' behind him by moving to Birmingham, such a relocation would offer no respite from the conflict in 1974. Indeed, Parker's fictional character travels back to Northern Ireland via a delayed ferry sailing from Heysham, the same trip that the Birmingham 'bombers' attempted to make on the night of their arrest.

Meanwhile, at Westminster the home secretary referred the case of the 'Birmingham Six' back to the Court of Appeal, where a hearing opened in November 1987. However, the court continued to trust in the original evidence and the Crown counsel criticized a media campaign led by 'irresponsible journalists who have espoused a cause'.[110] 'The hallmarks of that campaign', the court heard, 'are extremely careful selection of the material which is ventilated in public and a complete failure to scrutinize the allegations and assertions made by the six men who were convicted'. When the new verdict came at the end of January 1988, the judges duly declared, 'We have no doubt that these convictions are both safe and satisfactory', with the *Daily Express* declaring 'Justice Has Been Done' and the *Sun* editorializing, 'If the *Sun* had its way, we would have been tempted to string 'em up years ago'.[111] Nevertheless, 175 Westminster MPs, who now included Chris Mullin amongst their number, tabled a motion expressing 'widespread disquiet' over the verdict, and the Irish government expressed 'deep regret' at the court's decision. In addition, editorials criticizing the judgement appeared in the *Independent* and the *Economist*, whilst in *The Times* the journalist Robert Kee wrote that the judges had simply acted 'to protect the name and past performance of British justice rather than to uphold it by seeing that justice was done'.[112] The *Daily Mirror* subsequently ran a two-page story on the families of the six, praising those wives and daughters who 'confronted the might of the British legal and political systems'.[113]

With the judicial system seemingly incapable of granting justice, campaigners looked to television as an alternative court of appeal. The punk-folk band The Pogues included the song 'Streets of Sorrow/Birmingham Six' on their album

---

[110]   Quoted by Howard, *Terrorism*, p. 131.

[111]   Quoted by Mullin, *Error of Judgement*, pp. 340, 351.

[112]   Quoted by Mullin, *Error of Judgement*, p. 352.

[113]   Noreen Taylor, 'Women Who Wait in Hope: Crying out for Freedom', *Daily Mirror*, 2 February 1990, pp. 18–23.

If I Should Fall from Grace with God, and attempted to perform the song on the Channel 4 programme *Friday Night Live* on 15 April 1988, with the lyrics:

> There were six men in Birmingham
> In Guildford there's four
> That were picked up and tortured
> And framed by the law
> And the filth got promotion
> But they're still doing time
> For being Irish in the wrong place
> And at the wrong time.[114]

As the group started to sing, the television editors mysteriously cut to an advertising break, and the Independent Broadcasting Authority subsequently banned the song from being transmitted again, ruling that the work contained 'lyrics alleging that some convicted terrorists are not guilty and that Irish people in general are at a disadvantage in British courts of law'.[115] But at Granada the makers of *World in Action* responded to the courtroom verdict by making a compelling drama-documentary titled *Who Bombed Birmingham?*, which operates in a dual timeframe, portraying the events of 1974 alongside a reconstruction of the recent investigations by Chris Mullin. By the time of the broadcast on 28 March 1990, the convicted men had been in prison for almost sixteen years, and *Who Bombed Birmingham?* was perhaps the most influential part of the campaign to free the six, catalyzing popular opinion in Birmingham. In particular, the film shows the hypocrisy of those in the British judicial system who had long realized and concealed the innocence of the prisoners, and concludes by revealing the names of those IRA operatives believed to have been behind the attacks on Birmingham, a disclosure that irritated Mullin at the time of the original broadcast. The programme also emphasizes the aging of the unjustly convicted men by utilizing a range of wigs, makeup, and clever cutting between scenes, and so in 1990 encouraged those who watched the piece to see that the guilty verdict needed to be overturned as a matter of urgency.[116]

In the opening minutes, the programme gives a haunting depiction of the Birmingham bombings, showing a policeman frantically scrambling to clear the

---

114 Lyrics quoted by Cleary, *Outrageous Fortune*, p. 278.

115 'The Pogues Fall from Grace with Government', *New Musical Express*, 19 November 1988, p. 3.

116 *Who Bombed Birmingham?*, by Rob Ritchie, dir. Mike Beckham, Granada, 28 March 1990.

streets after the attack on the Mulberry Bush, only to become engulfed himself by the second blast. Such horror is framed by depictions of the six innocent men as they travel away from Birmingham, with their behaviour entirely contrasting with that of the grim IRA bombers. Instead, the 'Birmingham Six' are depicted as family men, who wave to their wives and kiss their children prior to the arrests, and who interact with one another in a jovial and jocular fashion. The main prisoner depicted is Richard McIlkenny, nicknamed 'the bishop' because of the religious faith he shows by, amongst other things, reading from Isaiah 9:7 about 'justice and righteousness', and in leading prayers to 'guide the decision of this court and to bless the efforts of our barristers'. Yet McIlkenny and the other prisoners are also shown enduring horrendous brutality, being beaten and dunked into filthy water, with their teeth and blood dropping out onto the prison floor. By contrast with this *Via Dolorosa*, the West Midlands police force appears as a scheming mob whose machinations parallel those of the IRA. Indeed, when the policeman in charge of the investigation is shown swigging whiskey, he mirrors the IRA bombers of the film who attack the pubs whilst nervously drinking alcohol.

Unsurprisingly, British prime minister Margaret Thatcher felt furious with this campaign, and on the day after the first broadcast of *Who Bombed Birmingham?* she retorted:

> Most of us recall the scenes of that terrorist act, and the great tragedy will live with some families for ever. But we do not conduct trial by television. The place to put any new evidence is with the police [...] There has already been one rehearing by the Court of Appeal, which gave a very detailed judgment [...] A television programme alters nothing. We do not have trial by television, and the day we do, the rule of law will have left this country for good.[117]

The Conservative MP Ivan Lawrence felt similarly enraged, and told the House of Commons that 'the innocence of the Birmingham Six was not demonstrated by an emotional and misleading television programme in which one of the most absurd propositions was that a conspiracy was conducted by police officers'.[118]

---

117 Margaret Thatcher, 'Terrorists (Extradition)', *Hansard House of Commons*, 29 March 1990 <http://www.publications.parliament.uk/pa/cm198990/cmhansrd/1990-03-29/Orals-2.html> [accessed 22 May 2008] (column 668).

118 Ivan Lawrence, 'Business of the House', *Hansard House of Commons*, 29 March 1990 <http://www.publications.parliament.uk/pa/cm198990/cmhansrd/1990-03-29/Debate-2.html> [accessed 22 May 2008] (column 685).

Nevertheless, the 'Birmingham Six' now stood on a much firmer footing as a result of the *World in Action* intervention, with the docudrama being transmitted in Ireland and the USA. Later in the year, Granada continued to exert pressure by transmitting on 23 July a meeting between Mullin and a man in Donegal who admitted having planted the bombs sixteen years before.[119] Other British television producers now followed Granada's lead by making drama-documentaries about the equally innocent 'Guildford Four' and 'Maguire Seven', with the BBC also commissioning a programme about the suffering experienced by the families of the 'Birmingham Six'.[120] In this climate, many people who had previously felt little sympathy towards those six prisoners now started to believe that the men ought to be released without delay.

Meanwhile, after November 1974 the IRA avoided any further operations in Birmingham. Republicans did shoot dead a British soldier at nearby Lichfield railway station in June 1990, and in April 1997 police officers found explosive devices at two of Birmingham's motorway junctions, whilst the final death throes of the 'Troubles' in November 2001 saw a hard-line splinter group called the Real IRA making a bungled attempt to detonate a car bomb in the city centre.[121] But the area never again became the target of an IRA campaign. By July 2002 the IRA had issued an apology to all civilian victims of its violence, and Sinn Féin marked the thirtieth anniversary of the pub bombings by stating that the attacks were wrong and should never have happened.[122] On the British side, prime minister Tony Blair apologized for his country's inaction during the potato famine. Yet for many people, such words could scarcely make amends for the errors and brutalities of the previous decades.[123] For families of those who had been killed or maimed on that cold November night in 1974, for the innocent men who had subsequently wasted so many years in jail, and for those Irish-born men and women who encountered so much distrust and hostility in Birmingham, the only hope was that history would never be repeated.

---

[119]   Mullin, *Error of Judgement*, p. 377.

[120]   Lance Pettitt, *Screening Ireland: Film and Television Representation* (Manchester: Manchester University Press, 2000), p. 248; Alan F. Parkinson, *Ulster Loyalism and the British Media* (Dublin: Four Courts Press, 1998), p. 79.

[121]   McGladdery, *The Provisional IRA in England*, p. 255.

[122]   '1974 Pub Bombings "Were Wrong"', BBC news website, <http://news.bbc.co.uk/1/hi/northern_ireland/4023451.stm> [accessed 22 June 2007] (para. 1 of 12).

[123]   Neil Ferguson and others, 'The IRA Apology of 2002 and Forgiveness in Northern Ireland's Troubles: A Cross-National Study of Printed Media', *Peace and Conflict: Journal of Peace Psychology* 13:1 (2007), pp. 106–107.

Conclusion: St Patrick's Day

The case of the Birmingham Six may have to be reconsidered.

Lord Tom Denning[1]

Ooh ah, Paul McGrath,
Say ooh ah Paul McGrath.

Supporters of Aston Villa FC[2]

The Bleak 1980s

On Sunday, 17 March 1996, Birmingham witnessed the first St Patrick's Day parade to be held in the city streets for many years. At first, a few hundred people congregated in St Catherine's Catholic Church, where priests said Mass for peace in Ireland. By the time the service had finished, however, about 5,000 people had gathered in glorious sunshine nearby, where decorated floats and marchers in fancy dress assembled for the procession. The organizers wished to show how Ireland was emerging from a difficult past, and so began the outdoor proceedings by hushing those assembled on the tarmac into observing a minute's silence for victims of the 'Troubles'. The atmosphere then brightened, as marchers took up positions behind county banners just as had happened in the city's parades during the 1950s and 1960s, and then the entire gathering processed along Bradford Street, accompanied on a civic bus by the waving Lord Mayor.[3] Finally, after snaking through the city, this green, white, and orange jamboree arrived at Highgate Park,

---

1   Spoken on 20 October 1989, quoted by Mullin, *Error of Judgement*, p. 369.

2   Chanted during Paul McGrath's career at Villa Park, 1989 to 1996.

3   Maureen Messent, 'St Patrick's Day Parade Back in Style: Irish Make a Day of It', *BM*, 18 March 1996, p. 9.

where the parade concluded with a carnival of pipe music, Irish dancing, and traditional song.[4]

Many of those who had lived in the central urban area at the time of the 1974 pub bombings had since moved to the more affluent outlying districts, and some felt extremely emotional to see such a high-profile reunion in the heart of the city.[5] After all, it had been more than two decades since the previous St Patrick's Day procession in the conurbation, and the local television presenter Miriam O'Reilly now spoke of the region being 'restored', whilst the local priest from Mayo, Joe Taaffe, declared that 'this is a resurrection of the Irish in Birmingham'.[6]

If this churchman was correct, then the resurrection had taken a very long time to arrive, as Birmingham had become a particularly cold and unwelcoming place for those from Ireland after 1974. Although the reprisal attacks gradually petered out, a sullen feeling of hostility remained, and anyone with a discernibly Irish voice entering one of the city's pubs might be subject to stop and search measures, could be arrested without charge under emergency rules, and might find fellow drinkers making aggressive jokes.[7] Local Conservative MPs suggested that those from Ireland should be denied the right to vote during elections, and the Archbishop of Birmingham acknowledged that 'If you have an Irish accent, you are at once a suspicious person'.[8] In this atmosphere, the organizers of the St Patrick's Day parade had abandoned the festivities during January 1975, noting that a cancellation had been made necessary by 'the unrest at the moment in Birmingham'.[9] Few had the stomach for the inevitable confrontations that such an event would entail, and so the organizing parade committee dissolved. Children marched in a 'mini-parade' around the Irish Community Centre in the ensuing years; some Irish men and women joined in with English May Day festivities instead; and a procession in support of the IRA hunger striker Bobby Sands took place in 1983, although this latter event attracted only half of the anticipated 1,000 supporters, and those who did turn up found themselves locked in a threatening stand-off with a group of right-wing

4   Jon Hurt, 'Irish Celebrations Return to Streets of Birmingham', *BP*, 18 March 1996, p. 6.

5   Williams, Dunne, and Mac an Ghaill, *Economic Needs of the Irish Community*, p. 12.

6   Hurt, 'Irish Celebrations Return', p. 6.

7   Chinn, *Birmingham Irish*, p. 164.

8   'War of Words over Plan to Axe Irish Vote', *BP*, 18 March 1980, p. 7; Archbishop quoted by McGladdery, *The Provisional IRA in England*, pp. 93–94.

9   Gudrun Limbrick, 'A Difficult Decision', in *A Great Day: Celebrating St. Patrick's Day in Birmingham*, ed. Gudrun Limbrick (Birmingham: St. Patrick's Festival, 2007), p. 64.

skinheads.[10] Many of the Irish-born residents of Birmingham instead adopted the attitude described by Seamus Heaney in Northern Ireland, 'Whatever you say say nothing'.[11]

Furthermore, as Ireland and Irishness endured censure in Birmingham, the entire city also suffered from a severe crisis of confidence. By the second half of the twentieth century the region had grown over-reliant upon automobile manufacture, but whereas this industry had once looked futuristic and dynamic, the 1970s saw the arrival of high oil prices and recession. Birmingham had coped admirably with previous downturns, but the area's economy now lacked the diversity of earlier times, and when the motor trade collapsed, local unemployment soared to almost double the national average and to almost three times that average in the inner city.[12] An urban landscape that had been entirely reshaped for automobiles during the previous years only served to highlight Birmingham's car-dependent folly, with an inner ring road having been carved through the heart of the city, demolishing some of the most distinctive and architecturally significant buildings in the area, and leaving Birmingham's central commercial district choked by a 'concrete collar'. Indeed, the city's dark pedestrian underpasses now provided an ideal working environment for local muggers, whilst other new civic spaces proved entirely devoid of charm, with buildings such as New Street Station and the Central Library having been concreted together regardless of the need to let in light. Poverty only exacerbated racial tensions, and the Handsworth riots of 1985 drew attention to the appalling discrimination and inequality faced by the West Indian inhabitants of the city, whilst the Irish continued to maintain a low profile as reports of the 'Troubles' brought back painful local memories. Inevitably, ever greater numbers of residents decided that enough was enough, and the Birmingham population plummeted throughout the 1970s and 1980s.[13]

During this period, the Irish songwriter Pete St John wrote the ballad 'Dublin in the Rare Oul Times', offering an implicit comparison between the Irish capital and England's industrial midlands. In the song, the narrator laments

---

10   'Hunger-Strike March Passes off Peacefully', *BP*, 2 May 1983, p. 3; Limbrick, 'A Difficult Decision', p. 64.

11   Seamus Heaney, *North* (London: Faber, 1975), p. 57.

12   Peter J. Larkham, *Discovering Cities: Birmingham* (Sheffield: Geographical Association, 2003), p. 22; Cherry, *Birmingham*, p. 207.

13   Whereas 1,113,000 people had lived in the city in 1951, Birmingham's population fell to less than one million by 1987. Upton, *A History of Birmingham*, p. 213; Cherry, *Birmingham*, p. 204.

urban Ireland's pell-mell rush to modernize, whilst remembering how his one-time lover ran away with an English rival:

> I lost her to a student chap,
> With skin as black as coal.
> When he took her off to Birmingham,
> She took away my soul.[14]

Such lyrics typified Irish attitudes towards Birmingham in the wake of the pub bombings, a place of profound loss and disappointment, encapsulated here by the repeated 'he took'/'She took' of the stanza. For an audience listening in the mid-1980s, the crude racial characterization of the song was also likely to summon up televised images of the racism and rioting experienced by Britain's black communities, whose members in those days appeared unfamiliar and even threatening to some in white Ireland. In addition, those who listened to the remainder of the ballad heard of Dublin being transformed into a place of 'grey unyielding concrete', and if this encouraged them to consider that the future Irish city might one day resemble Birmingham, that prospect could scarcely be regarded with relish.

Elsewhere, in Stewart Parker's play *Pentecost*, a Protestant character who has left Belfast to live in Birmingham noticeably avoids praising his new home:

RUTH   Birmingham [...] Do you really like it there?

PETER   It's a lot bigger.

RUTH   It's where all the roads are, isn't it [?][15]

Peter may be scathing about Ulster and its divisions, but his evasive reply indicates that Birmingham is far from being an idyllic alternative.

The novelist William Trevor reflected at greater length on the bleak welcome that faced exiles from Ireland coming to the English midlands during this period. In the 1980s the stalled Southern Irish economy continued to drive large numbers of men and women to England, and Trevor's 1994 novel *Felicia's Journey* describes the title character travelling from Ireland to a nondescript destination in the Birmingham area as part of a vain attempt to locate the father

---

14   'Dublin in the Rare Oul Times' on *Luke Kelly: The Collection*.
15   Parker, *Plays: 2*, p. 219.

of her unborn child. However, the English environment that Felicia finds is unremittingly inhospitable:

> Now, there is a plain, similar architecture everywhere, shops and office blocks laid out in a grid of straight lines, intersections at right angles. Wide pedestrian walkways were planted in the 1950s with shrubs and flowers in long, raised central beds; and the new town's architects included burgeoning arcades, and hanging baskets on the street lights. Since then the soil has soured in the long raised beds; heathers have died there, leaving only browned strands behind, among which beer cans and discarded containers of instant food provide what splashes of colour there are.[16]

Trevor's novel attempts to describe the dispiriting predicament of this generation of Irish exiles. Felicia has difficulty in understanding the English accent, falls victim to a delusional psychopath, and eventually ends up living on the streets. Yet the Ireland that she leaves behind is scarcely more welcoming, as the country's puritanical religious codes condemn her for being unmarried and pregnant, her father remains obsessed by outmoded republican battles, and when the local canning factory closes she loses a rare opportunity for employment. Consequently, by the end of the novel, Felicia is neither able to return to Ireland nor to settle properly in the English midlands, and so she remains destitute, her teeth rotting within her head.

Changing Perceptions

Yet although life in Birmingham scarcely proved pleasant for many of those who settled during the 1980s, the city did begin to show the first signs of change and renewal during this decade. Town planners started to realize the mistakes of the previous generation and to consider a new set of architectural arrangements, with the Central Area Local Plan of 1984 recognizing that the inner city consisted of districts with distinctive and valuable characteristics, including a heritage quarter around the Irish area of Digbeth. The Highbury Initiative that followed in 1988 saw the decision to break the stifling grip of the inner ring road, and during the following year the council lowered Paradise Circus so that pedestrians could walk between Chamberlain Square, Centenary Square, and an extremely ambitious new building, the International Convention Centre.[17]

---

16   William Trevor, *Felicia's Journey* (Harmondsworth: Penguin, 1995), pp. 3, 8.

17   Upton, *A History of Birmingham*, p. 231.

This £180 million construction opened in 1991 and quickly became one of England's leading business buildings, incorporating the acoustically impressive Symphony Hall concert venue, neighbouring a new national sports arena, and welcoming president Bill Clinton for a meeting of world leaders within seven years of opening.

In the years after the pub bombings, those from Ireland also made occasional attempts to lighten the gloom. For instance, during the late 1970s a dinner dance and evening banquet continued to mark St Patrick's Day for some in central Birmingham, in 1975 the traditional music group 'The Chieftains' gave a concert at Digbeth, and in 1977 Dominic Behan gave a talk and Seán Cannon played the guitar at a cultural event in Handsworth. During 1983 the musical acts De Dannan and Foster and Allen turned out for an Irish festival on Broad Street, which was accompanied by an exhibition from the National Library of Ireland about the Irish language.[18] However, the local Irish population struggled to shake off the prevailing mood of melancholy, and even Behan's arrival in Handsworth had hardly inspired tremendous feelings of pride and self-worth, as he chose to deliver a lecture on 'the dearth of literature emanating from the Irish proletariat in Britain'.

Nevertheless, the city's perception of Ireland did begin to change during the 1980s, due at least in part to the efforts of two local Catholic priests. The first, Father Patrick O'Mahony from Cork, co-ordinated a series of remarkable humanitarian campaigns from Our Lady of the Wayside Church in Shirley, with his work appearing in the media. He established the first church-sponsored Amnesty International group, sent millions of pounds' worth of aid to disaster areas around the globe, and conducted the everyday business of his parish in the midst of hundreds of tea chests being packed full of emergency medicines and supplies. In addition, O'Mahony focussed on making improvements within the city, using his membership of the multi-cultural panel of the Birmingham Community Relations Council to ensure that immigrants from across the world could gain places at local schools, distributing food parcels to the local poor, and writing a major study on ethical investment that embarrassed the Birmingham archdiocese into changing a number of financial

18   Limbrick, 'A Difficult Decision', p. 64; 'Arts Review/Parliament', *BP*, 18 March 1975, p. 2; John Bright, 'Irish Festival', *BP*, 4 August 1977, p. 4; 'B'ham Hosts First Irish Festival', *BM*, 21 May 1983, p. 4. John Fitzgerald of the Minstrel Music shop at the Irish Community Centre organized the exhibition on the Irish language. BCL, Local Studies Collection, Irish Studies Box 2, programme for the 1989 Birmingham Centenary Irish Festival, A8 941.5.

holdings.[19] This Cork priest scarcely embodied a country of sectarianism and aggression, but instead consistently emphasized internationalism and humanitarianism.[20] Indeed, when he died at the end of 1991, the *Independent* printed an appropriate tribute by a local Anglican, who said, 'never losing his Irish charm (and it is in Irish ground that he will be buried), he was the most Christ-like priest and the most catholic human being I have had the privilege to call my friend'.[21]

At the same time as O'Mahony worked in Shirley, the Mayo priest Joe Taaffe helped to rebuild the self-respect of the Irish in the centre of Birmingham. Taaffe encouraged the Irish to meet together at pensioners' clubs, adult education groups, and traditional dancing classes, whilst also working hard to improve the material situation of many who had arrived from Ireland, taking charge as director of the Irish Welfare Centre and organizing housing schemes that helped numerous new arrivals to find accommodation and to integrate into the city.[22]

Father Taaffe also chaired the 'Birmingham Campaign for the Birmingham Six', organizing meetings, fundraising, and petitions that endorsed the television campaign and made the general public increasingly queasy about the convictions.[23] An indication of the city's changing mood came in 1987 when Chris Mullin received a letter from one of those who had been in the Tavern in the Town during the bombing, but who now declared:

> I am writing to you in a somewhat futile attempt to rid myself of an awful feeling that a gross miscarriage of justice has not only occurred, but been upheld by our courts. I can remember the attitude when they were convicted. I was actually subpoenaed to the trial, but I felt I could not stand the ordeal of looking them in the face. I hated all of them. It was many years before I could think objectively about Irish people. My irrational feelings were

[19]   'Monsignor Patrick O'Mahoney [*sic*]', *Daily Telegraph*, 2 January 1992, p. 17.

[20]   In one of O'Mahony's books, for instance, he describes how, during a period of early childhood in London, 'I asked my mother to explain why we were so different from the majority, both in nationality and religion. She was at pains to underline that we were first of all people sharing a common humanity'. Patrick J. O'Mahony, *The Fantasy of Human Rights* (Great Wakering: Mayhew-McCrimmon, 1978), p. 13.

[21]   Paul Oestreicher, 'Mgr Patrick O'Mahony', *Independent*, 30 December 1991, p. 17.

[22]   'Big Hearts of Ireland', *BM*, 17 March 1987, p. 7; Maureen Messant, 'A Little Bit of Ireland Celebrates Its Jubilee', *BM*, 16 March 1982, p. 6; Chinn, *Birmingham Irish*, p. 169.

[23]   Hill and Hunt, *Forever Lost, Forever Gone*, p. 210.

exactly the mood in which these men were convicted. Normal housewives attacked an Irishman in a local Woolworths. Stones were thrown through an Irish neighbour's window. I am as ashamed of my uncivilised feelings as I am of our British justice.[24]

As attitudes began to change in this way, the local cultural landscape began to grow more amenable to Irish themes and issues. The 1989 festivities that marked the hundredth anniversary of Birmingham's inauguration as a city saw a celebration of Irish language and music at the Stockland Green Leisure Centre, as well as the Birmingham Conservatoire Symphony Orchestra's premiere of Andrew Downes's *Centenary Firedances*, an orchestral piece performed for 30,000 people in Cannon Hill park, for which Downes, himself of Irish extraction, included the bodhrán alongside the sounds of African-Caribbean and Indian music to highlight the diversity of the city.[25] These celebrations also saw the Birmingham Repertory Theatre launch the much-hyped production of *Heartlanders*, a community play featuring 300 amateur actors and scripted by the Belfast-born playwright Anne Devlin together with Stephen Bill and David Edgar.[26] This drama illustrates how residents of the modern, multicultural city might live in harmony, describing a heavily pregnant character from Ireland called Rose Devine who meets with characters from Jamaica, Wales, India, and England, before finally delivering her baby at the same time as the simultaneous arrival of Christmas and Diwali.[27] As if to illustrate this theme of reconciliation in real life, the first day of that performance also saw the release of three of the 'Guildford Four', who were also wrongly convicted of terrorism in 1974, and amongst the first public words of this trio were 'Let's hope the Birmingham Six are soon freed'.[28] Now English and Irish politicians, as well as the judge who previously dismissed the appeal of the six, called insistently for the Birmingham case to be reopened.[29]

---

[24]   Quoted by Mullin, *Error of Judgement*, pp. 353–54.
[25]   BCL, Programme for the 1989 Birmingham Centenary Irish Festival. I am grateful to Andrew Downes for information about *Centenary Firedances*.
[26]   BCL, Birmingham Repertory Theatre Archive, John Adams's souvenir programme for *Heartlanders*.
[27]   Stephen Bill, Anne Devlin, and David Edgar, *Heartlanders* (London: Hern, 1989), p. 91.
[28]   Mullin, *Error of Judgement*, p. 367.
[29]   Nigel Hastilow, 'Spotlight Turns on Police Liars', *BP*, 20 October 1990, p. 1; Nigel Hastilow and Michael Higgins, 'Denning Admits to Error over Six', *BP*, 21 October 1989, p. 1.

As public opinion shifted, a very different kind of performer helped to promote Ireland in the city. In 1989 Aston Villa Football Club signed Paul McGrath, a Republic of Ireland international who had recently appeared at the European Championships, the first major soccer finals for which an Irish squad had ever qualified.[30] Previously, Southern Ireland's fans had no world-class team of their own to support, but now they had a group of players that proved capable of beating even the well-regarded English side. And if those living in the Republic felt proud of the national team, those of Southern Irish descent in Birmingham felt particularly enthusiastic about the side, as the squad clearly depended on an inclusive sense of the nation in order to achieve success, with the team featuring the children and grandchildren of those who had left Ireland, as well as the London-born Dubliner, McGrath himself.

At the end of McGrath's first season in Birmingham he travelled with his Villa teammate Tony Cascarino to play for the Republic at the World Cup, becoming one of the tournament's stars and one of Ireland's first celebrities from a mixed-race background. Even those amongst the city's English population began to view McGrath as a hero, as his return from the World Cup saw him guide Aston Villa to some of the best seasons of the club's recent history, and long uneven lines of fans in Birmingham waved tricolour flags and adopted Irish crowd chants in support of the player, who became professional footballer of the year in 1993. His well-publicized struggles with alcohol in places such as Mere Green's Barley Mow only served to increase his prestige amongst supporters, for whom he took on something of the patina of George Best.[31] Indeed, some fans took to wearing replica shirts labelled with McGrath's number five and the moniker 'God'. Meanwhile, those successful years at the club saw McGrath joined at Villa by the Republic's future manager Steve Staunton, the Glasgow-Irish Ray Houghton, and the London-Irish Andy Townsend, with Southern Ireland's next World Cup exploits in 1994 seeing Townsend holding the captaincy and Houghton scoring a spectacular solo goal against Italy. As England had failed to qualify for this tournament, many non-Irish soccer fans in Birmingham transferred their allegiance to the familiar faces of the Republic team, and so, remarkably, in a city where groups had chanted anti-Irish slogans just thirty years earlier, pub customers could now hear lusty cries of support for Ireland during the televised matches. In addition, the local Gaelic Athletic Association also celebrated a victory at this

---

30   Anton Rippon, *The Aston Villa Story* (Derby: Breedon, 1993), p. 223.
31   Paul McGrath and Cathal Dervan, *Ooh Ahh Paul McGrath: The Black Pearl of Inchicore* (London: Mainstream, 1994), pp. 160, 170.

time, having moved to a splendid new facility near Birmingham airport, *Páirc na hÉireann*. Although such plans had been shelved for many years, the hurlers and Gaelic footballers of the region now had a top-class venue in which to play, and by the start of the twenty-first century local Irish organizations estimated that some 1,200 schoolchildren from across Birmingham regularly played Gaelic football.[32]

Of course, the situation in Birmingham reflected a far broader Irish renaissance in the 1990s, as the 'Celtic Tiger' economy began to roar, and as various aspects of Ireland's culture became correspondingly fashionable and marketable. When Ireland hosted the Eurovision song contest in 1994 the event became overshadowed by the show-stopping 'Riverdance' interval performance, which starred an Irish-American dancer who had been living in Birmingham, Jean Butler; and by the following year this ten-minute piece had swollen into a vapid if lucrative touring show.[33] Later in 1995, Butler was joined in this show by Colin Dunne, a dancer who had won nine world championship titles for Irish dancing, who took over the lead role in the show from Michael Flatley. In the 1970s, at the age of ten, Dunne had appeared on *Blue Peter*, and when asked 'Where are you from?' by the presenter Lesley Judd, he replied 'Birmingham'. 'And where did you learn to dance?' she continued. 'Birmingham', he answered again. Indeed, Dunne had been born into a Wexford family in the city, and went on to work in Birmingham as an accountant, but by the start of the 1990s abandoned the offices of Arthur Andersen to tour instead with various Irish musicians and to work with Jean Butler, ultimately achieving transatlantic stardom through 'Riverdance' and subsequent imitative shows.[34]

At the same time, pop music proved one of Ireland's most successful exports, and groups such as U2, Boyzone, and The Corrs performed at Birmingham's 12,000-seat National Exhibition Centre. Meanwhile, those watching British television in the 1990s noticed that, as the *Birmingham Post* put it, 'Everywhere

---

32   Farrell, 'Man in the Midlands', p. 37; Chinn, *Birmingham Irish*, p. 164; 'Birmingham's Irish Community', *Birmingham Irish Quarter* <http://www.irishquarterbirmingham.com/community.htm> [accessed 11 December 2007] (para. 5 of 6).

33   Aoife Monks, *Comely Maidens and Celtic Tigers: Riverdance and Global Performance* (London: Goldsmiths, 2007), p. 2.

34   Brendan McCarthy, 'Reel Lives', *The Tablet*, 28 February 2009, p. 29; Colin Dunne, 'Biography', *Colin Dunne Official Website* <http://www.colindunne.com/biog.php> [accessed 2 March 2009]; Eddie Dunne, 'There's No Dancing with a Broken Leg', in *A Great Day: Celebrating St. Patrick's Day in Birmingham*, ed. Gudrun Limbrick (Birmingham: St. Patrick's Festival, 2007), p. 71.

you turn, there's another new Irish comic popping up', with such figures as Dermot Morgan, Graham Norton, and Dylan Moran becoming household names across the islands.[35] In the cinema, films such as *The Commitments* (1991) and *Into the West* (1992) promoted Irish humour and legend, with audiences in Birmingham finding particular resonance in these portrayals of Dublin's gritty urban landscape. Although quite unthinkable only ten years earlier, the fashionable Irishness of the mid-1990s meant that a child living in Birmingham could be teased for being insufficiently Irish rather than for being a 'Mick', with the title of 'Plastic Paddy' now taunting the wannabes of the second, third, and fourth generation.[36]

By this stage, one of the most well known of these 'diasporic' Irish men and women was the Labour MP for Ladywood, Clare Short. The Irish women of Birmingham from earlier times have tended to disappear from the archives, but there would be little chance of this happening to Short, who won her parliamentary seat in 1983, resigned as a front-bencher over the Prevention of Terrorism Act and over the First Gulf War, and became secretary of state for international development by 1997. Quite aside from her political work, Short's family history neatly encapsulates the long and intermingling history of the Irish in Birmingham. Her mother was the great-granddaughter of a man from county Clare who escaped the potato famine in the nineteenth century by fleeing to Birmingham, where his descendents have lived ever since. But Short's father was a twentieth-century migrant from Crossmaglen in Armagh, who arrived to Britain to train as a teacher. Each of his seven children, of whom Clare Short is the second, was born and grew up in Birmingham, and Short herself has commented on the way that this background affected her high-profile political role, saying:

> My father's objection to the behaviour of the UK in Ireland and throughout the Empire helped to shape my view of international affairs. My mother's liberation-theology style Catholicism and both of their firm commitments to social justice were also influential. I think my Catholic background also led to a belief that politics should be a moral crusade.[37]

This awareness of her own heritage certainly affected the controversial note

---

35   Andy Tipper, 'Comics with the Gift of the Gab', *BP*, 17 March 1997, p. 9.

36   Killeen, 'Culture, Identity and Integration', p. 260.

37   I am grateful to Clare Short for providing most of the factual details in this paragraph, and for quoted remarks made in personal correspondence during April 2009.

that she sent to Zimbabwe's agriculture and land minister in 1997, noting that 'My own origins are Irish and, as you know, we were colonised, not colonisers'.[38] And her Irish-inflected knowledge of Britain's problematic military history was revealed by her high-profile clash with Tony Blair over the Second Gulf War, which ultimately led to her resignation as a minister in 2003.

Of course, Ireland's increasing popularity in England during the 1990s owed much to the 'moral crusade' of other politicians: those who were playing out an endgame in Northern Ireland. On 31 August 1994, the IRA declared 'a complete cessation of military operations', and although the organization carried out further attacks in 1996 after growing frustrated at the perceived prevarication of John Major's British government, republican leaders increasingly talked of peace.[39] As a result, the ceasefire resumed in July 1997 and Belfast witnessed the Good Friday agreement in April 1998. By this time Birmingham had, of course, already seen one major wrong set right, as the 'Birmingham Six' celebrated their release from jail on 14 March 1991, watched by millions of people on television news bulletins. Following five years of high-profile campaigning, one final legal appeal had been launched on behalf of the men, and after more than sixteen years in jail those wrongly convicted of killing 21 people were granted their freedom by the Lord Justice at the Old Bailey, who expressed his desire 'to quash these convictions and perhaps in doing so to express our society's deep regret to these men that it has taken sixteen years for this injustice to be recognized'.[40] Now, in a reversal of the mob that bayed for blood in 1974, many supporters gathered in the street outside the court, alongside the massed ranks of press photographers. As the international media looked on, the relatives of the six appeared in the road, running, embracing, and cheering with delight, followed a few moments later by the freed men themselves, with Paddy Hill punching the air and telling reporters that 'every dog has its day'. Father Joe Taaffe then emerged from the crowd, to be embraced by Gerry Hunter and Paddy Hill, before Chris Mullin then herded the group into waiting limousines.[41] By the end of this month, one final *World in Action* television programme had given the released men the chance to tell their own story, with John Walker, now an old man, reflecting:

---

38   Chris McGreal, 'There Are Many Villains to Blame for Zimbabwe's Decade of Horror', *Guardian*, 13 April 2008 <http://www.guardian.co.uk/world/2008/apr/13/zimbabwe> [accessed 7 April 2009] (paras 1 and 2 of 27).

39   English, *Armed Struggle*, p. 285.

40   Quoted by Mullin, *Error of Judgement*, p. 398.

41   '37 Words Lead to Freedom', *BP*, 15 March 1991, p. 3.

I never seen my children growing up. What hurts me most, like, my boy was getting around that age of eleven years old, I started taking him down to the football, to watch the Villa. We weren't doing too well at the time, we were in the third division, and I was getting to go with my son, getting to know him. I've lost all that.[42]

The sad dignity of Walker and the other released men provided a deeply affecting broadcast, signalling the end of the city's once rabidly anti-Irish atmosphere. Indeed, by the thirtieth anniversary of the pub bombings, attitudes towards Ireland in the city had changed so radically that the local memorial service saw a wreath laid by Mike Nangle, an ex-Lucas worker from county Armagh who had received abuse in the 1970s, but who had now been elected as Birmingham's first Irish-born Lord Mayor.[43]

The Gaelic Revival

With the release of the 'Birmingham Six' and the IRA declaring ceasefires, the Irish-born population and their descendants in the city felt the burden of 1974 finally being lifted. Many felt the desire to demonstrate that, just as the released men had proudly appeared before the crowds and television cameras, so the wider group of local Irish residents could now emerge from the shadows and join in the civic life of Birmingham. Consequently, the city council – under some pressure from Father Joe Taaffe – finally agreed to reinstate the St Patrick's Day parade in 1996, although the route steered well clear of New Street and the Rotunda out of respect for those who had died in the pub bombings. When the march set off from St Catherine's Church to Highgate Park, Joe Taaffe accompanied the parade from an open-top bus, where he stood, waving, alongside Birmingham's mayor. Sadly, Taaffe died during that summer, but the following year the city repeated the parade, which began with two minutes' silence in memory of the priest.[44] Throughout those early years the parade rapidly grew in size and became increasingly well organized. The 1996 procession had largely consisted of an *ad hoc* collection of a dozen haphazard trucks watched by about 5,000 people, but by 1998 a crowd estimated at more than 30,000 packed the route to Highgate Park to see a number of carefully drilled floats and musicians parading

---

42 Broadcast as part of *World in Action: The Birmingham*.
43 'Irish Paid Price for Pub Bombs', *BP*, 20 April 2006 <http://icbirmingham.icnetwork. co.uk/birminghampost/news/tm_method=full%26objectid=16969420%26siteid=50002-name_page.html> [accessed 11 December 2007] (para. 5 of 30).
44 Maureen Messant, 'Here's to St Pat!', *BM*, 17 March 1997, p. 13.

through the streets.[45] The organizers heralded the procession as the largest St Patrick's Day event in Britain, only outranked globally by the celebrations in Dublin and New York City, and whilst such claims are difficult to verify the mass participation in Birmingham's parade did seem remarkable to those who had lived through the 1970s, scarcely imagining that so many in Birmingham could ever be attracted to an event where participants played republican ballads and hoisted pictures of Pádraic Pearse and Thomas Clarke.[46]

During the following years the event swelled yet further, with the participation of legions of pipe bands, majorettes, set dancers, *camogie* teams, and piano-accordion players; and at the start of the new millennium, newspaper and television reporters consistently estimated the attendance at around 80,000.[47] As the 1990s drew to a close, the march itself formed only one part of a week-long celebration involving a fun fair, street market, and entertainment area in Digbeth near the Dubliner, a pub that had opened next to the Irish Community Centre earlier that decade and regularly hosted evenings of Irish music and dancing. During the yearly St Patrick's celebrations, the Dubliner found itself submerged by a great deal of green kitsch that often aimed to emulate the energies of Irish-America, but Birmingham also looked back to the rural country that many had left behind in the 1950s, and hence the parade featured horses and donkeys, milk churns, and bales of hay, with participants encouraged to 'come as you came' by dressing in the kind of clothes worn upon first arrival in Birmingham.

Of course, such nostalgia increasingly contrasted with the reality of life in the modern Irish state, which experienced a bewilderingly fast transformation

---

[45]   Hurt, 'Irish Celebrations Return', p. 6.

[46]   Kirsty Wigglesworth, 'When Irish Eyes are Smiling', *BP*, 16 March 1998, p. 5; Maureen Messent, 'Invasion of the Emerald Army!', *BM*, 15 March 1999, pp. 8–9. Indeed, the large Tyrone banner – with its images of the Dublin GPO as well as Pearse, Clarke, James Connolly, and Seán McDermott – won the prize for 'best banner' at the 1996 parade. See Dave Chambers, 'Birmingham's County Show', in *A Great Day: Celebrating St. Patrick's Day in Birmingham*, ed. Gudrun Limbrick (Birmingham: St. Patrick's Festival, 2007), p. 38.

[47]   Both the Birmingham Post and the BBC have repeatedly given the estimated figure of 80,000. The *Birmingham Post* did give a lower estimate of between 60,000–75,000 attendees in 2000, but the newspaper also gave the larger estimate of 100,000 people attending the 2002 parade which, following 9/11, was led by a group of New York firemen. The BBC also estimated the attendance at 100,000 in 2005. See, for example, 'St Patrick's Festival', <http://www.bbc.co.uk/birmingham/entertainment/local_events/st_patrick_parade/> [accessed 17 June 2009].

during the final part of the twentieth century. In those giddy boom years, Ireland apparently proved ideally suited for the new online world of international business, and between 1987 and 2001 the annual growth rates of Irish Gross National Product exceeded 7 per cent and sometimes approached double digits.[48] Those who had arrived in Birmingham from Ireland during earlier times looked on in amazement as relatives back home began to enjoy an enviable lifestyle of foreign holidays and expensive cars, whilst at the same time many old certainties and assumptions about the country began to crumble. The Irish constitution no longer laid claim to Northern Ireland, the government legalized divorce, and laws on homosexuality became more liberal than those in England. Next, euros replaced punts, miles became kilometres, and barmen banished smokers onto the street. The pace of change may have felt dizzying, but at least those in Birmingham found it easier to keep abreast of life in Ireland than ever before, with a monthly newspaper called *The Harp* explicitly addressing Irish issues in and around Birmingham from 2001, and new technology facilitating increasingly close contact with Ireland. In the 1990s, when workmen laid cable television through much of the city for the first time, subscribers watched RTÉ programmes on the Tara television channel, and after Tara stopped broadcasting, viewers could swap to high-speed internet connections that gave direct access to RTÉ and also allowed those sitting at computers in Birmingham to hear Irish radio stations, read Irish newspapers, or discover the latest score from Croke Park. No longer was it necessary for friends to pass around outdated copies of the *Western People* if they wanted to know what was happening at home. Meanwhile, the expansion of Ryanair's operations from Elmdon may have been environmentally disastrous, but did make Dublin less than an hour's journey away for those who could never previously afford the air fare, with the Irish capital feeling as close to Birmingham as cities such as Luton, Liverpool, or London.

Of course, it was not only Birmingham that now sent planeloads of passengers to Dublin. One of the greatest changes to life in Ireland at the end of the twentieth century was that a country so long dominated by emigration became, almost overnight, a land of mass immigration. Applications for asylum had numbered less than 50 per year at the start of the 1990s, but reached an annual figure of nearly 11,000 by the turn of the millennium.[49] Residents of Birmingham, of course, already knew a thing or two about living in a

---

[48]   R. F. Foster, *Luck and the Irish: A Brief History of Change 1970–2000* (London: Allen Lane, 2007), p. 7.

[49]   Foster, *Luck and the Irish*, p. 34.

multicultural environment. Since the mid-twentieth century, those in areas like Sparkhill had dwelt in lodging houses alongside other immigrant groups, with Irish pubs nestling between Pakistani grocery stores and West Indian cafés.[50] Indeed, in the 1950s, when such a thing would have been widely disapproved of in Ireland, St Paul's Church Hall in Balsall Heath had hosted social evenings where people from the West Indies and from Ireland danced together in mixed couples, and for those already accustomed to such life, twenty-first century Ireland's multiculturalism might have been noteworthy but could scarcely seem particularly daunting.[51]

For some, what proved more difficult to accept was that many who had left Ireland for Birmingham during the previous decades now faced severe financial hardship, having completely bypassed the boom. A 1998 report found that such people had the worst physical and mental health of any minority in Britain, and had become the only migrant group whose life expectancy actually deteriorated on arrival in the country. The 2001 census showed that almost three-quarters of Birmingham's self-declared 'White Irish' ethnic group were aged over thirty-nine and that 'Nearly 31% of households lack central heating, and 50% do not have a car. About 20% are not in good health and the percentage with limiting long-term illness is high'.[52] Many such elderly Irish men and women felt cut off from the wealthy modern Ireland and abandoned to an existence of relative poverty in Birmingham. In sympathy, Irish president Mary Robinson, who visited the city in 1996, attempted to highlight the plight of such emigrants by keeping a lighted candle at the window of her official residence, and when the Irish agriculture minister, Joe Walsh, later attended the Birmingham's St Patrick's Day parade he praised those who left Ireland in 1950s and 1960s, saying, 'We appreciate the sacrifices people made to send money home to their families in Ireland in those early difficult days [...] We are now a country of opportunity and it's largely thanks to them.'[53]

The other major losers from the process of change in Ireland were those in the Catholic priesthood, who found themselves confronted by a deeply

---

50   Colin McGlashan, 'How Ghettoes Came to Britain', *Observer*, 12 February 1967, p. 5.

51   'From Kingston or Kerry – It Makes No Difference', *Manchester Guardian*, 13 October 1956, p. 5.

52   Dunne, *An Unconsidered People*, p. 239; Birmingham City Council, *2001 Population Census in Birmingham*, p. 8.

53   Walter, *Outsiders Inside*, p. 12; Walsh quoted by Poppy Brady, 'Dancing in the Rain', *BM*, 15 March 2004, p. 26.

damaging series of sex scandals. Of course, when Birmingham's Irish parade began in the 1950s, the event culminated with a service at St Chad's where almost the entire 10,000-strong gathering squeezed into and around the cathedral.[54] But by the end of the century, well-publicized revelations about the sex lives of clerics like Eamonn Casey, Michael Cleary, and Brendan Smyth had helped to destroy much of the Church's standing in Ireland. Similarly, in the late 1980s and early 1990s, police investigated a number of priests from the Birmingham archdiocese for the sexual abuse of children, and after one particular clergyman was sentenced to almost eight years in prison for conducting such assaults, a 1993 BBC *Everyman* documentary revealed that the local Church had taken no action despite receiving complaints about this cleric from concerned parents many years earlier. The Archbishop of Birmingham (and patron of the Irish Welfare Centre), Maurice Couve de Murville, appeared on the television programme, but he seemed uneasy and distracted when challenged to explain why the allegations had not been passed on to the police, and why the paedophile priest in question had instead been moved to another parish where incidents of abuse continued. In the face of such public woes, the archbishop himself opted for early retirement, and the Pope's children abandoned the pew in increasing numbers.[55] Accordingly, although the revived parade of the 1990s did begin near St Catherine's Church on Bristol Street, where clergymen continued to celebrate Mass before the march began, those who attended this service represented only a tiny fraction of the tens of thousands who packed the parade route. By the end of the first decade of the twenty-first century only a handful of people could be found at this morning Mass, despite the service being advertised in the *Irish Post* as the start of the festivities, and the priests and nuns appearing at the parade itself were most likely groups of lay men and women in fancy dress.[56] The shifting priorities of those in attendance could be found, for example, in the introduction to the parade programme for 2009, which explained that:

> Parade day – starts for some in a sincerely religious manner with a traditional mass. The parade does not discriminate however and many of our more secular supporters take alternative spiritual fulfilment in the

54 'Irish Urged to Boycott Bad Lodgings', *BP*, 17 March 1952, p. 5.

55 Paulinus Barnes, 'The Most Rev Maurice Couve de Murville', *Independent*, 9 November 2007 <http://www.independent.co.uk/news/obituaries/the-most-rev-maurice-couve-de-murville-399611.html> [accessed 22 May 2008] (paras 8–10 of 13).

56 Enda Mullin, 'Two Wheels and the Truth', *The Harp*, April 2007 <http://www.theharpnews.com/issues/april_07/news_story_3.html> [accessed 11 December 2007].

local hostelries [...] [The festivities] will feature blistering performances from the likes of The Destroyers and the Scarlet Harlots.[57]

With religious devotion proving less of a draw, the organizers of the revived Birmingham parade now had the chance to develop a new kind of rhetoric to attract participants. The planners attempted to avoid the earlier implication that Irishness incorporated Catholicism and excluded local Irish Protestants, who had kept a particularly low profile during so much of the twentieth century but had suffered equally from the racism and hostility that came in the aftermath of the pub bombings. Indeed, developing a more inclusive language became a real necessity to ensure the survival of the parade, as those who had arrived from Ireland in the 1950s and 1960s began to die off in ever greater numbers, causing the Irish-born population of Birmingham to shrink considerably during the 1990s.[58] At the 1999 procession Len Cale, who took the part of St Patrick, asserted that the parade constituted an occasion for 'everyone in Birmingham, whether they're Irish or not', whilst Birmingham's mayor spoke on local radio to advertise the event to anyone sitting at home regardless of nationality.[59] After all, as early as 1838 the preacher Thomas Finigan had noted how 'English, Scotch, and Irish' all joined together to celebrate the feast day, although by the turn of the millennium the exhortations to Birmingham-wide participation took a cue not from local history but from the global festivities promoted by Guinness and the 'Irish' theme pub.[60] Indeed, the boom years in Ireland saw a revolutionary growth in St Patrick's celebrations across the world, with historians Mike Cronin and Daryl Adair pointing out that 'with the expansion of Irish bars across the world, especially in Britain, Guinness began linking the consumption of its famous drink with the celebration of Ireland's patron saint'. According to Cronin and Adair, these pub- and club-centred celebrations:

> May well be part of a wider process in Britain where various ethnic groups are now openly celebrating their ethnicity [...] Placed alongside St Patrick's

---

[57]   *St Patrick's Day Magazine* (Birmingham: Moda Media, 2009), p. 3.

[58]   The 1991 census records 38,290 Southern Irish-born people living in Birmingham, but by 2001 that figure had reduced to 22,828 (although 31,467 still declared that their ethnic group was Irish). Birmingham City Council, *Ethnic Groups in Birmingham, 1991 Census Topic Reports* (Birmingham: Birmingham City Council, 1998[?]), p. 11; Birmingham City Council, *2001 Population Census in Birmingham*, table 2.11 and table 3.1.

[59]   BCL, Local Studies Collection, 'Birmingham Irish Community Forum, St. Patrick's Day Parade 1999', video cassette.

[60]   Finigan, Journal of Austin Finigan, fol. II–54.

Day, the Notting Hill Carnival, the various Asian Diwali events, Jewish New Year, and even the growth of the Highland Games, all demonstrate that ethnic festivals have been central to the gradual acceptance that Britain is a multi-cultural society.[61]

Birmingham itself had by now become an excitingly diverse city, boasting large and vibrant communities from Jamaica and other parts of the Caribbean, Kashmiris from Mirpur, Hindus from Gujeratand, and Sikhs from the Punjab; and consequently the St Patrick's Day parades of the new millennium saw increasing efforts to advertise the cavalcades as events for 'Brum's Irish population and people of all cultures'.[62] After all, local wags had long joked: 'I'm Birmingham through and through, I wear a shamrock in my turban'.

Accordingly, the 2008 festivities featured a group of Sikh musicians and the 2004 parade starred the local African-Caribbean dance group 'Golden Storm', whose members had already performed at the Handsworth carnival and felt enthusiastic about participating in the St Patrick's Day event because one of the troupe had family connections to Connemara.[63] By 2009 the parade included a West Indian carnival float, samba drummers, members of the Chinese and Polish community groups, and American civil-war re-enactors. The programme for that year repeatedly emphasized that 'being Birmingham's biggest community event means that we increasingly mirror the fantastic diversity of our resident ethnicities as we welcome guest appearances from other communities'.[64] From 1998 the parade committee also invited the Irish lesbian, gay, and bisexual group *Cáirde le Chéile* ('Friends Together') to march under a flag and banner at the event.[65] The future dynamism of the parade, and perhaps the event's access to corporate and local government funding, depends on continuing to celebrate what is distinctly Irish whilst at the same time developing a cross-community

---

61   Mike Cronin and Daryl Adair, *The Wearing of the Green: A History of St Patrick's Day* (London: Routledge, 2002), pp. 240, 199.

62   Carl Chinn, 'The Many Cultures that Make Up Brum', *BM*, 15 March 1999, p. 9; 'St Patrick's Parade 2007', BBC news Web site, <http://www.bbc.co.uk/birmingham/content/articles/2007/03/08/st_patricks_day_preview_feature.shtml> [accessed 11 December 2007] (para. 3 of 6).

63   Poppy Brady, 'Going Down a Storm ...', *BM*, 15 March 2004, p. 30. Interviews with some of Birmingham's mixed race Irish population can be found in Killeen, 'Culture, Identity and Integration', p. 261.

64   *St Patrick's Day Magazine*, p. 25.

65   Rory Murray, 'Cáirde le Chéile', in *A Great Day: Celebrating St. Patrick's Day in Birmingham*, ed. Gudrun Limbrick (Birmingham: St. Patrick's Festival, 2007), p. 97.

appeal, encouraging interaction between Irish and other groups in Birmingham, and avoiding the kind of time-warped assumptions about Irish identity that have dominated New York's arguments about whether to exclude gay and lesbian groups from St Patrick's Day parades in recent years.

Indeed, as the Birmingham festivities grew and developed, some of the more provocative questions surrounding modern Irish identity were explored at the Birmingham Repertory Theatre. The playhouse had generally avoided dealing with Ireland after the pub bombings, but in 1991 the theatre decided to stage Brian Friel's *Translations*, a play about the confrontation between British army officers and Irish-speaking residents of the Inishowen peninsula in the nineteenth century. The work had been applauded both by the Unionist mayor of Derry/Londonderry and by supporters of Sinn Féin when premiered in Ulster in 1980, and the English playhouse now recreated something of that original production's mood of reconciliation by staging the work just two months after the release of the 'Birmingham Six'.[66]

Translations indeed proved a success with Birmingham audiences, encouraging the Repertory Theatre to stage further productions about Ireland, and in February 1993 the playhouse gave the British premiere of John B. Keane's 1969 play *Big Maggie*, inspiring the critic Michael Coveney to devote nearly half of his weekly *Observer* column to the drama and to give fulsome praise to Gillian Hanna's 'wonderful' performance as Maggie, which he deemed as 'suggestive of a nation poised on the brink of change and confusion'.[67] Although *Big Maggie* may have lost some of its shock value since the 1960s, Keane had set out to challenge conservative attitudes towards family, religion, and sex, and when the theatre staged Synge's *The Playboy of the Western World* in 1994, the actor who had starred in all three of the theatre's recent Irish productions, Seán Cranitch, wrote programme notes suggesting that a successful Irish play could be rooted in Ireland's culture whilst also being provocative and challenging.[68]

Accordingly, the Birmingham theatre then opted to deal with more experimental Irish work. Although it was a new play about the Sikh community, Gurpreet Kaur Bhatti's *Behzti*, that caused riots and brought the small studio to worldwide attention in 2004, the playhouse was, at the same time, using that same theatre space to premiere a range of controversial new plays about Ireland.

---

66   Morash, *A History of Irish Theatre*, p. 240.

67   Michael Coveney, *Observer*, 14 February 1993, quoted by Cochrane, *The Birmingham Rep*, p. 156.

68   BCL, Birmingham Repertory Theatre Archive, programme for *Big Maggie* and programme for *The Playboy of the Western World*.

In February 1999 the theatre premiered Declan Croghan's *Paddy Englishman, Paddy Irishman and Paddy ...?*, a reworking of Seán O'Casey's *The Shadow of a Gunman* in which a bed-sit in Kilburn replaces an urban slum in Dublin, and in which disaffected anti-ceasefire republicans of the 1990s take the place of those fighting the Anglo-Irish War in 1920. Despite the comedy of Croghan's piece, and the concluding message that 'the war is over', the play contained scenes that an audience in Birmingham would find discomforting. Most notably, Croghan depicts a hard-line republican who walks into a nearby pub and commits murder, leaving 'bodies everywhere', and who leaves an explosive device with two panicked flatmates, who in turn discuss how they will 'plant the bomb and then we will phone up and give them a warning'.[69] In Birmingham such black humour inevitably conjured up harrowing memories from the 1970s, and the theatre's decision to premiere Croghan's work in the city indicated that playhouse had abandoned the earlier caution that guided programming through the previous quarter of a century.

As a result of this newfound boldness, in 2005 the theatre staged another new play that sought to analyse the recent peace process. Billy Cowan's *Smilin' Through* depicts a young gay Protestant in East Belfast struggling to make his mother understand that he is in love with a Catholic man, and although the play is set at the time of the Good Friday agreement Cowan shows that any simplistic notions of peace may be illusory. In *Smilin' Through* the old conflicts have simply been realigned, with Catholic-Protestant hostility being channelled into other kinds of persecution. During the play a fiery Presbyterian minister teams up with a bigoted Catholic bishop to denounce a 'sodomite', whilst another homosexual is tarred and feathered by an anti-gay mob, and the Police Service of Northern Ireland colludes in homophobic attacks. In retaliation, homosexuals resort to the old tactics of the 'Troubles', with one man going on hunger strike and another styling himself a member of the Irish Queer Liberation Army, promising to 'use whatever means are necessary to secure our rights to self determination [...] The armalite is the only language the people of this island recognise'.[70] Cowan's tongue-in-cheek work thus made the serious point that, despite all the talk of peace, members of marginalized

---

69   Declan Croghan, *Paddy Irishman, Paddy Englishman and Paddy ...?* (London: Faber, 1999), pp. 55, 59–60. The piece later played at London's Tricycle theatre, a venue that has worked to provide a programme appealing to both Kilburn's African-Caribbean and Irish communities. Margaret Llewellyn-Jones, *Contemporary Irish Drama and Cultural Identity* (Bristol: Intellect, 2002), p. 122.

70   I am grateful to Billy Cowan for providing me with a copy of the play as performed in Birmingham.

groups in Northern Ireland might continue to face bigotry, eviction, and physical abuse.

Equally provocatively, the Repertory Theatre also premiered Kaite O'Reilly's *Belonging* in 2000, a play by a Birmingham writer with Irish-born parents, showing that families such as her own might now feel an entirely confused sense of national identity. The work depicts an elderly couple who arrived in the city long ago, but who in the present day hold differing views about England, with the father of the family regarding Birmingham as his home but his wife wishing to return to Ireland, as her son puts it, to:

> Go back to a place that only exists in the imagination [...] in love with some romantic Ireland, trapped in a nineteen-fifties idyll, that probably didn't even exist then. In fact I know it didn't; Dad couldn't wait to leave the fucking place.[71]

The second-generation members of the household are similarly divided, with the son disavowing his Irish heritage but his sister feeling ferocious loyalty to Ireland, and the tensions in the family come to a head at the time of Birmingham's revived St Patrick's Day march. The matriarch of the family insists on joining the parade, largely to dispel the crippling sense of shame instilled by the pub bombings, as she explains:

> I just want to go home. I've always hated this city. I don't want to be in this country. I've counted the days we were here, desperate to get back where I belong. And I'm going. But first I'm going to walk through this city with my head held high. And if anyone shouts at me to get off the road, I'll tell them your father built the road; that we own the fucking road.[72]

However, by the end of the play, all of her plans are ruined. The family fails to join in the march that her son dismisses as simply meaningless and drunken, and she is finally unable to return to a changed Ireland where, unbeknownst to her, the old family home has been lost prior to the economic boom. O'Reilly thus provided a harsh counterpoint to the euphoric press coverage of the modern St Patrick's Day parade in Birmingham, showing that such a spectacle may not necessarily be a unifying or redeeming cultural festival at all, but one that either drunkenly eschews all meaning, conjures up

---

[71]   O'Reilly, *Belonging*, p. 62.

[72]   O'Reilly, *Belonging*, pp. 76–77.

bitter and upsetting local memories, or simply reveals how the impoverished and infirm emigrants of the 1950s and 1960s had been abandoned by a wealthy and unattainable new Ireland that was leaving the country's earlier incarnation dead, gone, and in the grave.

Yet, despite the reservations expressed by Kaite O'Reilly, outside the theatre Birmingham's Irish parade had become a saleable commodity at the start of the new millennium, co-opted by local businesspeople who wanted to share in the event's perceived success. After all, the Irish procession dovetailed neatly with the ethos of a city now being praised as excitingly cosmopolitan, with the *Lonely Planet* guidebook to Britain declaring that the 'drab, grimy urban basket case' had 'spectacularly reinvented itself as a vibrant, cultural hot spot'.[73] In 1998 Birmingham gained support from the Bank of Ireland and Allied Irish Bank to launch what was claimed as the first Irish business group in Britain, and whose initial meeting was held in a venue named after that one-time antagonist of many of the Irish in the city, the Chamberlain Hotel.[74] Similarly, the UK-wide 'Federation of Irish Societies' opted to hold its millennium congress, attended by Irish president Mary McAleese, in Birmingham's council chamber, with the organizers praising 'this outstanding example of Municipal Victorian architecture'.[75] But such gatherings felt little inclination to dwell on the historical ironies, as Birmingham made a headlong dash to redevelop and renovate in the early years of the new century. The appearance of the iconic new Bullring shopping centre radically altered Birmingham's skyline, a rash of designer clothes stores spread around the Mailbox centre, and restaurants and apartment blocks sprouted along the reclaimed canal basin. Indeed, it took a second-generation Irish writer who grew up in Birmingham, Catherine O'Flynn, to sound a note of cynicism about such developments, with her 2007 novel *What Was Lost* pointing out that although the city's shoppers might now enjoy a great deal of comfort, the staff at such modern retail centres generally enjoyed behind-the-scenes facilities 'of an extremely low level: few toilets, dark interior areas, outdated and ineffective ventilation and heating, bare breeze-block walls, constant sewage odours and significant rat infestation'.[76]

[73] *Lonely Planet Great Britain*, ed. David Else (7th edn; London: Lonely Planet, 2007), p. 408.

[74] Jon Griffin, 'City Group to Support Irish', *BM*, 10 December 1998, p. 43.

[75] BCL, Local Studies Collection, Irish Studies Box 2, Seamus McGarry's programme notes for the 27th congress of the Federation of Irish Societies, A8 941.5.

[76] Catherine O'Flynn, *What Was Lost* (Birmingham: Tindal Street Press, 2007), p. 89. For an analysis of O'Flynn's work see James Moran, 'Swallowed by the Shopping Centre',

Nevertheless, as the city redeveloped, locals realized the power of the green pound, and in the first years of the new century the St Patrick's Day celebrations were trailed at inordinate length on local radio and television, featured in pull-out supplements to local newspapers, and exploited by tie-in offers at the city's shops and bars. In 2003 the parade was combined with the end of the World Indoor Athletics Championships and an enormous pop concert in Centenary Square, in 2005 the parade was diverted to the new Millennium Point development in order to incorporate performances by *Cirque du Soleil*, and by 2006 the St Patrick's Day festivities had reached inside the Bullring mall. Here crowds gathered next to the iconic Selfridges department store to hear Irish music and watch Irish dancing, with the building's famous bobbled exterior turned from purple to green during the city's week-long festivities.[77] When the Birmingham town hall reopened after a multi-million pound refurbishment in October 2007, the venue hosted an Irish music and dancing event as one of the opening concerts, sandwiched in between performances by Christy Moore and by the Celtic Women at the nearby Symphony Hall.

By this time, with Irish celebrations taking place at the designer boutiques and prestigious concert venues of the city centre, some of the older Irish haunts started to look like relics from a bygone age. By 2003 police had restricted the disorderly Garryowen club in Small Heath to opening on only two nights a week, but still found themselves called there on 223 occasions before finally closing the premises two years later.[78] Elsewhere, the popular but dingy Dubliner pub in Digbeth attracted unwelcome publicity in 2004 when police suspected that one customer had murdered another, and the venue inexplicably burned down a few months later.[79] Similarly, the celebrations of St Patrick's

---

Dublin Review of Books 5 (April 2008) <http://www.drb.ie/apr08_issues/swallowed_by_the_shopping.htm> [accessed 21 May 2008].

[77]   Gudrun Limbrick, 'A Record-Breaking Parade – St. Pat at the Point', in *A Great Day: Celebrating St. Patrick's Day in Birmingham*, ed. Gudrun Limbrick (Birmingham: St. Patrick's Festival, 2007), pp. 115–16; Alex Murphy, 'Parade Comes in from the Cold', *The Harp*, April 2006 <http://theharpnews.com/issues/april_06/news_story_3.html> [accessed 11 December 2007].

[78]   David Bell, 'Rowdy Club to Stay Shut', *BM*, 2 September 2005 <http://icbirmingham.icnetwork.co.uk/0100news/0100localnews/tm_objectid=15940723&method=full&siteid=50002&headline=rowdy-club-to-stay-shut-name_page.html> [accessed 11 December 2007].

[79]   'I'll Make Sure Reece Is Brought up to Know Who His Nana Was', *BM*, 21 March 2007 <http://icbirmingham.icnetwork.co.uk/mail/news/tm_method=full%26objectid=18787043%26siteid=50002-name_page.html> [accessed 11 December 2007].

Day at the neighbouring Irish Centre in 2008 concluded with a fight involving a dozen people and one man being stabbed in the head.[80]

Yet the Dubliner soon reopened in a spruced-up incarnation, and during the rebuilding of this charred tavern architects planned extensive reconstruction across the whole of the surrounding area. Indeed, the city council embarked upon the next phase of the region's redevelopment by granting £400 million to revamp Digbeth as the first formal Irish quarter in England. By 2009, the new owners of the Irish Community Centre had set about a long-overdue modernization of the venue, whilst the rundown coach station next door, which had been the initial, dispiriting sight for countless immigrants to the city during the previous half century, was demolished and a more welcoming terminal designed as a replacement.[81] In addition, planners decided to raise and reshape the river Rea as an attractive water feature rather than a grimy ditch, and to place a range of new business developments and housing amidst the existing Irish buildings of the area, hoping to reflect in Birmingham something of the capitalist dynamism that had characterized the previous decade in Ireland.[82]

In order to avoid being accused of creating an 'Irish quarter in name only', developers have also given some consideration to the kind of historical symbols that might be seen in this part of the city, and at the time of writing they are considering whether to relocate the local Irish mosaic of John F. Kennedy to the rebuilt area, as well as whether to name part of the development after that hero of Birmingham's recent dark days, Father Joe Taaffe.[83] Of course, unfortunately, the development of this site has occurred at the very time that the economic boom has finally turned to bust, and although the developers of Digbeth undoubtedly intended to call to mind the 'Celtic Tiger', it may be that Birmingham faces a reminder of the poverty and migration that affected the Irish during the 1950s and 1980s. Nevertheless, when the new quarter is

---

80   Will Oliphant, 'St Patrick's Day Party Double Stabbing', *BM*, 17 March 2008 <http://www.birminghammail.net/news/birmingham-news/2008/03/17/st-patrick-s-day-party-double-stabbing-97319-20635653/> [accessed 6 January 2009].

81   Alison Dayani, 'Fond Farewell for Digbeth Coach Station', *BM*, 19 November 2007 <http:icbirmingham.icnetwork.co.uk/mail/news/centralcity/tm_method=full%26object id=20128012%26siteid=50002-name_page.html> [accessed 11 December 2007].

82   Emma Pinch, 'A Colourful Vision for the Future', *BP*, 15 June 2006 <http://icbirmingham.icnetwork.co.uk/birminghampost/news/tm_method=full%26objectid=17 234538%26siteid=50002-name_page.html> [accessed 11 December 2007].

83   'Renaissance of the Irish Quarter', *Birmingham Irish Quarter* <http://icbirmingham.icnetwork.co.uk/0150business/irishquarter/tm_method=full%26objectid=14670294%26s iteid=50002-name_page.htm> [accessed 11 December 2007] (paras 34 and 38 of 38).

completed it will offer a clear indication of the way in which the reputation of Ireland in Birmingham has been transformed over the past three decades, and although the city has always proved singularly unsentimental about development and change, those who look closely might find that some of the memories from a turbulent history might yet linger in the area for a while still to come.

Appendix: Census Information

Date	Number of Birmingham residents born in Ireland	Total population of Birmingham	Per cent of Birmingham population born in Ireland
1841	4,683	182,922	2.56
1851	9,341	232,841	4.01
1861	11,332	296,076	3.83
1871	9,076	343,787	2.64
1881	7,072	400,774	1.76
1891	5,043	478,113	1.05
1901	4,217	522,204	0.81
1911	3,165	840,202	0.38
1921	6,055	919,444	0.66
1931	6,470	1,002,603	0.65
1941	No census	No census	No census
1951	36,349	1,112,685	3.27
1961	58,961	1,110,683	5.31
1971	57,620	1,014,670	5.68
1981	47,172	996,369	4.7
1991	38,396	961,041	4.0
2001	28,933	970,892	2.98

Census Figures

Whilst these figures indicate general trends in population, the numbers should be treated with some caution. The geographical size of the Birmingham area changes depending on the year of the census, and there are also technical changes in who qualifies as a resident of an area. Furthermore, the figures do not give an indication of the seasonal workers who have lived in Birmingham, those who evaded the enumerators, and the children or descendants of the original migrants. Estimates of a far larger population of Irish in Birmingham have been calculated in Chinn, *Birmingham Irish*, pp. 48–49, and Killeen, 'Culture, Identity and Integration', p. 73. Patsy Davis suggests that multiplying the figures by 2.5 gives a better representation of the true size of the Irish population (Davis, 'Birmingham's Irish Community', p. 38).

Census Information Sources

1841 Census Great Britain, Statements on Population (London: William Clowes, 1841), p. 331; *Census of England and Wales for the year 1861, Vol. III, General Report* (London: Eyre and Spottiswoode, 1863), p. 160; *British Parliamentary Papers, 1871 Census England and Wales, Population 18* (Shannon: Irish University Press, 1970), p. 342; *Census of England and Wales, 1881, Volume III, Ages, Condition as to Marriage, Occupations, and Birthplaces of the People* (London: Eyre and Spottiswoode, 1883), p. 265; *British Parliamentary Papers, 1891 Census England and Wales, 1893–94 [c.7058] Vol. CVI, Population 23* (Shannon: Irish University Press, 1970), p. 275; *Accounts and Papers, Seventy-Seven Volumes (67) Population (England and Wales) Continued: Staffordshire to Yorkshire: Vol. CXXI* (London: HMSO, 1902), p. 69; *1911 Census of England and Wales: 1911, Vol. IX Birthplaces* (London: HMSO, 1913), pp. 260–61; *Census of England and Wales, 1921, County of Warwick* (London: HMSO, 1923), p. 56; *Census of England and Wales 1931, General Tables: Comprising Population, Institutions, Ages and Marital Conditions, Birthplace and Nationality, Welsh Language* (London, HMSO, 1935), p. 213; *Census of England and Wales 1951, County Report, Warwickshire* (London: HMSO, 1954), p. 52; *Census of England and Wales 1961, County Report, Warwickshire* (London: HMSO, 1963), p. 20; *Census of England and Wales 1971, County Report, West Midlands, as Constituted 1st April 1974* (London: HMSO, 1974), p. 10; *Census 1981 County Report, West Midlands Part 1* (London: HMSO, 1982), p. 17; *1991 Census County Report: West Midlands Part 1* (London: HMSO, 1992), p. 81; *Census 2001: Key Statistics for Urban Areas in the Midlands* (London: HMSO, 2004), p. 89.

Bibliography

Bibliography of Published Sources

Archer, William, *William Charles Macready* (London: Kegan Paul, 1890)

Arnstein, Walter L., 'The Murphy Riots: A Victorian Dilemma', *Victorian Studies* 14:1 (1975), pp. 51–71

——, *Protestant Versus Catholic in Mid-Victorian England: Mr. Newdegate and the Nuns* (London: University of Missouri Press, 1982)

Artaud, Antonin, *Collected Works Volume Four* (London: Calder, 1999)

Aston, T. H., *Truth Versus Error: Facts about the Recent Riots in Birmingham* (Birmingham: Underwood, 1867)

Austen, Jane, *Emma*, ed. James Kinsey (Oxford: Oxford University Press, 1995)

Barba, Eugenio, *The Paper Canoe: A Treatise on Theatre Anthropology*, trans. Richard Fowler (London: Routledge, 1995)

Barker, Kathleen, and Joseph Macleod, 'The McCready Prompt Books at Bristol', *Theatre Notebook* 4:4 (1950), pp. 76–81

Beard, Mary, *The Roman Triumph* (Cambridge, MA: Harvard University Press, 2007)

Behan, Brendan, *An Giall and The Hostage*, trans. Richard Wall (Gerrards Cross: Colin Smythe, 1987)

——, *Borstal Boy* (London: Arrow, 1990)

——, *Complete Plays* (London: Methuen, 2001)

——, 'I Become a Borstal Boy', in *After the Wake*, ed. P. Fallon (Dublin: O'Brien, 1981)

Belchem, John, *Irish, Catholic and Scouse: The History of the Liverpool Irish 1800–1939* (Liverpool: Liverpool University Press, 2007)

Bennett, Anne, *Pack Up Your Troubles* (London: Headline, 2000)

Bew, Paul, *Ireland: The Politics of Enmity 1789–2006* (Oxford: Oxford University Press, 2007)

Bill, Stephen, Anne Devlin, and David Edgar, *Heartlanders* (London: Hern, 1989)

Bills, Peter, *Passion in Exile: 100 Years of London Irish RFC* (Edinburgh: Mainstream, 1998)

Birmingham City Council, *2001 Population Census in Birmingham: Cultural Background: Ethnic and Religious Groups, Country of Birth* (Birmingham: Birmingham City Council, [2007])

Birmingham City Council, *Ethnic Groups in Birmingham, 1991 Census Topic Reports* (Birmingham: Birmingham City Council, 1998[?])

'Birmingham's Irish Community', *Birmingham Irish Quarter* <http://www.irishquarter birmingham.com/community.htm> [accessed 11 December 2007]

Bisset, James, *A Poetic Survey Round Birmingham* (Birmingham: Swinney and Hawkins, 1800)

Blackadder, Neil, *Performing Opposition: Modern Theater and the Scandalized Audience* (Westport: Praeger, 2003)

Blom-Cooper, Louis, *Victims of Circumstance: The Birmingham Six and Other Cases* (London: Duckworth, 1997)

Brannigan, John, *Brendan Behan: Cultural Nationalism and the Revisionist Writer* (Dublin: Four Courts Press, 2002)

Briggs, Asa, and Conrad Gill, *History of Birmingham*, 2 vols (London: Oxford University Press, 1952)

British Association for the Advancement of Science, *Handbook of Birmingham* (Birmingham: Hall and English, 1886)

Buckstone, John Baldwin, *The Irish Lion* (London: Chapman and Hall, 1838[?])

'Bunreacht na hÉireann' <http://www.taoiseach.gov.ie/upload/static/256.htm> [accessed 29 January 2010] ('the Nation', Article 2 of 3)

Búrca, Séamus de, *Brendan Behan: A Memoir* (Dublin: Bourke, 1985)

Butler, Cuthbert, *Life and Times of Bishop Ullathorne*, 2 vols (London: Burns, Oates and Washbourne, 1926)

Cashmore, Herbert Maurice, *Birmingham Public Libraries Catalogue of the Birmingham Collection: Supplement 1918–1931* (Birmingham: Public Libraries Committee, 1931)

Cave, Richard, 'The Abbey Tours in England', in *Irish Theatre on Tour*, ed. Nicholas Grene and Christopher Morash (Dublin: Carysfort, 2005), pp. 9–34

Census 1981 County Report, West Midlands Part 1 (London: HMSO, 1982)

Census of England and Wales for the Year 1861, Volume III, General Report, Appendix to the Report (London: HMSO, 1863)

Chamberlain, Joseph, *Speeches on the Irish Question* (London: Swan Sonnenschein, 1890)

Chambers, Dave, 'Birmingham's County Show', in *A Great Day: Celebrating St. Patrick's Day in Birmingham*, ed. Gudrun Limbrick (Birmingham: St. Patrick's Festival, 2007), pp. 36–42

Chambers, Ian, *The Chamberlains, the Churchills and Ireland: 1874–1922* (New York: Cambria, 2006)

Champ, Judith, 'Priesthood and Politics in the Nineteenth Century: The Turbulent Career of Thomas McDonnell', *Recusant History* 18:3 (May 1987), pp. 289–303

——, *William Bernard Ullathorne 1806–1889: A Different Kind of Monk* (Leominster: Gracewing, 2006)

Chapman's Birmingham Directory (Birmingham: Chapman, 1800)

Cherry, Gordon E., *Birmingham: A Study in Geography, History and Planning* (Chichester: Wiley, 1994)

Chinn, Carl, *Birmingham Irish: Making Our Mark* (Birmingham: Birmingham Libraries, 2003)

——, '"Sturdy Catholic Emigrants": The Irish in Early Victorian Birmingham', in *The Irish in Victorian Britain: The Local Dimension*, ed. Sheridan Gilley and Roger Swift (Dublin: Four Courts Press, 1995), pp. 52–74

Clarke, Kathleen, *My Fight for Ireland's Freedom* (Dublin: O'Brien, 1997)

Clarke, Thomas, *Glimpses of an Irish Felon's Prison Life* (Dublin: Maunsel, 1922)

Cleary, Joe, *Outrageous Fortune: Capital and Culture in Modern Ireland* (Dublin: Field Day, 2007)

Cliff, Nigel, *The Shakespeare Riots: Revenge, Drama, and Death in Nineteenth-Century America* (New York: Random House, 2007)

Clifford, James, *The Predicament of Culture: Twentieth-Century Ethnography, Literature, and Art* (Cambridge, MA: Harvard University Press, 1988)

Cochrane, Claire, *The Birmingham Rep: A City's Theatre 1962–2002* (Birmingham: Sir Barry Jackson Trust, 2003)

Coe, Jonathan, *The Closed Circle* (London: Penguin, 2005)

——, *The Rotters' Club* (London: Penguin, 2004)

Collins, Tony, *Encyclopedia of Traditional British Rural Sports* (London: Routledge, 2005)

Connolly, S. J. (ed.), *The Oxford Companion to Irish History* (Oxford: Oxford University Press, 2002)

Conolly, L. W. (ed.), *Bernard Shaw and Barry Jackson* (Toronto: University of Toronto Press, 2002)

Coogan, Tim Pat, *De Valera: Long Fellow, Long Shadow* (London: Hutchinson, 1993)

——, *Wherever Green Is Worn: The Story of the Irish Diaspora* (London: Random House, 2000)

Cooter, Roger, *When Paddy Met Geordie: The Irish in County Durham and Newcastle* (Sunderland: University of Sunderland Press, 2005)

Croghan, Declan, *Paddy Irishman, Paddy Englishman and Paddy ...?* (London: Faber, 1999)

Cronin, Mike and Daryl Adair, *The Wearing of the Green: A History of St Patrick's Day* (London: Routledge, 2002)

Crowley, Brian, '"His Father's Son": James and Patrick Pearse', *Folk Life: Journal of Ethnological Studies* 43 (2004–5), pp. 71–88

Cullen, Fintan, 'Maclise and Shakespeare', in *Daniel Maclise 1806–1870: Romancing the Past*, ed. Peter Murray (Kinsale: Gandon, 2008), pp. 169–79

Cullen, Fintan, and Roy Foster, *'Conquering England': Ireland in Victorian London* (London: National Portrait Gallery, 2005)

Cullinane, John, *Aspects of Irish Céilí Dancing 1897–1997* (Cork: [n. pub.], 1998)

Davis, Graham, *The Irish in Britain 1815–1914* (Dublin: Gill and Macmillan, 1991)

Davis, Leith, *Music, Postcolonialism, and Gender* (Notre Dame: University of Notre Dame Press, 2006)

Davis, Patsy, 'Birmingham's Irish Community and the Murphy Riots of 1867', *Midland History* 31 (2006), pp. 37–66

Dean, Joan FitzPatrick, 'The Riot in Westport: George A. Birmingham at Home', *New Hibernia Review* 5:4 (2001), pp. 9–21

Deane, Seamus, 'A State of Injustice', in *The Birmingham Six: An Appalling Vista* (Dublin: LiterÉire, 1990), pp. 34–38

Delaney, Enda, *The Irish in Post-War Britain* (Oxford: Oxford University Press, 2007)

Delaney, John J., and James Edward Tobin, *Dictionary of Catholic Biography* (London: Hale, 1962)

Dent, Robert K., *Old and New Birmingham: A History of the Town and Its People*, 3 vols (Birmingham: Houghton and Hammond, 1880; repr. Wakefield: EP Publishing, 1973)

Denvir, John, *The Irish in Britain: From the Earliest Times to the Fall and Death of Parnell* (London: Kegan Paul, 1892)

Dibdin, Charles, *The Songs of Charles Dibdin* (London: Howe and Parsons, 1842)

Dobson, Michael, 'Let him be Caesar!', *London Review of Books*, 2 August 2007, pp. 15–17

Dooley, Brian, *Black and Green: The Fight for Civil Rights in Northern Ireland and Black America* (London: Pluto, 1998)

Dooley, Thomas P., *Irishmen or English Soldiers: Times and World of a Southern Catholic Irish Man (1876–1916) Enlisting in the British Army during the First World War* (Liverpool: Liverpool University Press, 1995)

Downer, Alan S., *The Eminent Tragedian: William Charles Macready* (London: Oxford University Press, 1966)

Doyle, Martin, 'The History', in *A History of the* Irish Post: *The Voice of the Irish in Britain*, ed. Martin Doyle (London: Smurfit, 2000), pp. 12–20

Drinkwater, John, *Swords and Ploughshares* (London: Sidgwick and Jackson, 1922)

——, *The Collected Plays of John Drinkwater*, 2 vols (London: Sidgwick and Jackson, 1925)

——, *The Muse in Council* (London: Sidgwick and Jackson, 1925)

Dudley Edwards, Owen, 'The Stage Irish', in *The Creative Migrant*, ed. Patrick O'Sullivan (London: Leicester University Press, 1994), pp. 83–114

Dudley Edwards, Ruth, *Patrick Pearse: The Triumph of Failure* (Dublin: Poolbeg, 1990)

Duggan, G. C., *The Stage Irishman: A History of the Irish Play and Stage Characters from the Earliest Times* (Dublin and Cork: Talbot, 1937)

Dunne, Catherine, *An Unconsidered People: The Irish in London* (Dublin: New Island, 2003)

Dunne, Colin, 'Biography', *Colin Dunne Official Website* <http://www.colindunne.com/biog.php> [accessed 2 March 2009]

Dunne, Eddie, 'There's No Dancing with a Broken Leg', in *A Great Day: Celebrating St. Patrick's Day in Birmingham*, ed. Gudrun Limbrick (Birmingham: St. Patrick's Festival, 2007), p. 71

Egan, Pierce, *Pierce Egan's Book of Sports* (London: Tegg, 1832)

Ellmann, Richard, *James Joyce* (rev edn; Oxford: Oxford University Press, 1983)

Else, David (ed.), *Lonely Planet Great Britain* (7th edn; London: Lonely Planet, 2007)

English, Richard, *Armed Struggle: The History of the IRA* (London: Macmillan, 2003)

Ervine, St John G., *Four Irish Plays* (Dublin: Maunsel: 1914)

Fanning, Peter, 'The Irish in England', *The New Age: A Weekly Review of Politics, Literature, and Art*, 31 July 1913, pp. 386–87

Farrell, Brendan, 'Man in the Midlands', in *A History of the* Irish Post: *The Voice of the Irish in Britain*, ed. Martin Doyle (London: Smurfit, 2000), pp. 35–40

Fay, W. G., and Catherine Carswell, *The Fays of the Abbey Theatre: An Autobiographical Record* (London: Rich and Cowan, 1935)

Ferguson, Neil, and others, 'The IRA Apology of 2002 and Forgiveness in Northern Ireland's Troubles: A Cross-National Study of Printed Media', *Peace and Conflict: Journal of Peace Psychology* 13:1 (2007), pp. 93–113

Ferriter, Diarmaid, *Judging Dev* (Dublin: Royal Irish Academy, 2007)

Fielding, Steven, *Class and Ethnicity* (Milton Keynes: Open University Press, 1992)

Finlay, John, *Miscellanies: The Foreign Relations of the British Empire, the Internal Resources of Ireland, Sketches of Character, Dramatic Criticism, etc, etc, etc.* (Dublin: Cumming, 1835)

Finnegan, Frances, *Poverty and Prejudice: Irish Immigrants in York, 1840–75* (Cork: Cork University Press, 1985)

Fitzpatrick, David, 'Irish Emigration in the Later Nineteenth Century', *Irish Historical Studies* 22 (1980), pp. 126–43

Flick, Carlos, *The Birmingham Political Union and the Movements for Reform in Britain* (Folkestone: Dawson, 1978)

Flynn, Christopher, 'Challenging Englishness from the racial margins: William Macready's *Irishman in London; Or; The Happy African*', *Irish Studies Review*, 16:2 (2008), pp. 159–72

Foster, R. F., *Luck and the Irish: A Brief History of Change 1970–2000* (London: Allen Lane, 2007)

——, *Paddy and Mr Punch* (London: Allen Lane, 1993)

Foucault, Michel, 'Different Spaces', in *Aesthetics, Method, and Epistemology*, ed. James Faubion (London: Penguin, 2000), pp. 175–85

Foulkes, Richard, 'Macready [M'cready], William (1755–1829)', *Oxford Dictionary of National Biography*, ed. H. C. G. Matthew and Brian Harrison (Oxford: Oxford University Press, 2004), vol. XXXVI, pp. 14–15

——, 'Macready, William Charles (1793–1873)', *Oxford Dictionary of National Biography*, ed. H. C. G. Matthew and Brian Harrison (Oxford: Oxford University Press, 2004), vol. XXXVI, pp. 15–23

Fraser, Peter, *Joseph Chamberlain: Radicalism and Empire, 1868–1914* (London: Cassell, 1966)

Gallman, Matthew J., *Receiving Erin's Children: Philadelphia, Liverpool, and the Irish Famine Migration 1845–1855* (Chapel Hill: University of Carolina Press, 2000)

Galloway, Peter, *The Most Illustrious Order of St. Patrick, 1793–1983* (Shopwyke Hall: Phillimore, 1983)

Geraghty, Des, *Luke Kelly: A Memoir* (Dublin: Basement, 1994)

Gillaspie, Jon A., 'Dibdin, Charles', *Oxford Dictionary of National Biography*, ed. H. C. G. Matthew and Brian Harrison (Oxford: Oxford University Press, 2004), vol. XVI, 25–30

Gillow, Joseph, *A Literary and Biographical History, or Bibliographical Dictionary of the English Catholics*, 4 vols (New York: Burt Franklin, 1969)

Gilraine, Jim, 'It's No Holiday', in *A Great Day: Celebrating St. Patrick's Day in Birmingham*, ed. Gudrun Limbrick (Birmingham: St. Patrick's Festival, 2007), pp. 43–44

Goffman, Erving, *The Presentation of the Self in Everyday Life* (New York: Doubleday, 1956)

Greaney, William, *A Guide to St. Chad's Cathedral* (Birmingham: Canning, 1877)

Gregory, Lady Augusta, *Our Irish Theatre: A Chapter of Autobiography* (Gerrards Cross: Smythe, 1972)

Grene, Nicholas, *The Politics of Irish Drama: Plays in Context from Boucicault to Friel* (Cambridge: Cambridge University Press, 2002)

Grene, Nicholas (ed.), *Talking about Tom Murphy* (Naas: Carysfort, 2002)

Gwynn, Denis, *The Life of John Redmond* (New York: Books for Libraries, 1971)

Hall, H. R., *Notes to "Oliver Cromwell", A Play by John Drinkwater* (London: Sidgwick & Jackson, 1939[?])

Handley, James Edmund, *The Irish in Modern Scotland* (Cork: Cork University Press, 1947)

——, *The Irish in Scotland 1798–1845* (Cork: Cork University Press, 1943)

Hanham, H. J., *Elections and Party Management: Politics in the Time of Disraeli and Gladstone* (London: Longmans, 1959)

Hannay, John, 'Coincidence and Converging Characters in *Ulysses*', *ELH* 51:2 (1984), pp. 385–404

Harland, Lucy, and Helen Lloyd (eds), *Birmingham Voices: Memories of Birmingham People* (Stroud: Tempus, 1999)

Hartnoll, Phyllis (ed.), *The Oxford Companion to the Theatre* (London: Oxford University Press, 1957)

Hayton, D. W., 'From Barbarian to Burlesque: English Images of the Irish c.1660–1750', *Irish Economic and Social History* 15 (1988), pp. 5–31

Healy, T. M., *Letters and Leaders of My Day*, 2 vols (London: Thornton Butterworth, 1928)

Heaney, Seamus, *North* (London: Faber, 1975)

Heinrick, Hugh, *A Survey of the Irish in England*, ed. Alan O'Day (London: Hambledon, 1990)

Hennessey, Thomas, *Northern Ireland: The Origins of the Troubles* (Dublin: Gill and Macmillan, 2005)

Herbert, Michael, *The Wearing of the Green: A Political History of the Irish in Manchester* (London: Irish in Britain Representation Group, 2001)

Herring, John Frederick, 'Birmingham, with Patrick Conolly up, and his Owner John Beardsworth (1830)', in *The Tate Gallery: Illustrated Catalogue of Acquisitions 1978–80* (London: Tate Gallery, 1981), pp. 29–30

Heslop, T. P., 'Medical Aspects of Birmingham', in *The Resources, Products, and Industrial History of Birmingham and the Midland Hardware District*, ed. Samuel Timmins (London: Cass, 1967), pp. 689–703

Hill, Paddy Joe, and Gerard Hunt, *Forever Lost, Forever Gone* (London: Bloomsbury, 1995)

Hogan, Robert (ed.), *Towards a National Theatre: The Dramatic Criticism of Frank J. Fay* (Dublin: Dolmen, 1970)

Holmes, Colin, *John Bull's Island: Immigration and British Society, 1871–1971* (Houndmills: Macmillan, 1988)

——, 'The British Government and Brendan Behan, 1941–1954: The Persistence of the Prevention of Violence Act', *Saothar* 14 (1989), pp. 125–28

Holroyd, Michael, *Bernard Shaw: The One-Volume Definitive Edition* (London: Vintage, 1998)

Hopkins, Eric, 'The Birmingham Economy during the Revolutionary and Napoleonic Wars 1793–1815', *Midland History* 23 (1998), pp. 105–20

——, *The Rise of the Manufacturing Town: Birmingham and the Industrial Revolution* (Phoenix Mill: Sutton, 1998)

Hopkins, Gerard Manley, *Further Letters of Gerard Manley Hopkins*, ed. Claude Colleer Abbott (London: Oxford University Press, 1956)

——, *Selected Poetry*, ed. Catherine Phillips (Oxford: Oxford University Press, 1998)

——, *The Letters of Gerard Manley Hopkins to Robert Bridges*, ed. Claude Colleer Abbott (London: Oxford University Press, 1935)

House of Commons, *An Act to Enable His Majesty, His Heirs and Successors to Grant Letters Patent for Establishing a Theatre or Playhouse, under Certain Restrictions, in the Town of Birmingham, in the County of Warwick, Anno Quadragesimo Septimo, Georgii III Regis, Sess. 2, Cap. 44* (London: George Eyre and Andrew Strahan, 1807)

Howard, Lawrence, *Terrorism: Roots, Impact, Responses* (London: Praeger, 1992)

Inglis, Brian, *Roger Casement* (Harmondsworth: Penguin, 2002)

The Irish Miscellany; or Teagueland Jests (London: R. Adams, 3rd ed., 1749)

Irish Playography Project <http://www.irishplayography.com/search/play.asp?play_id=2190> [accessed 22 May 2008]

Jackson, Alvin, *Home Rule: An Irish History 1800–2000* (London: Weidenfeld and Nicolson, 2003)

Jackson, John Archer, *The Irish in Britain* (London: Routledge and Kegan Paul, 1963)

Joyce, James, *Ulysses* (London: Folio Society, 1998)

Judd, Denis, *Radical Joe: A Life of Joseph Chamberlain* (Cardiff: University of Wales Press, 1993)

Kain, Richard M., *Fabulous Voyager* (Chicago: University of Chicago Press, 1959)

Kane, Paula M., '"Staging a Lie": Boston Catholics and the New Irish Drama', in *Religion and Identity*, ed. Patrick O'Sullivan (London: Leicester University Press, 1996), pp. 111–45

Kearney, Colbert, *The Writings of Brendan Behan* (Dublin: Gill and Macmillan, 1977)

Keating, John E., *The Wreck of the Deutschland: An Essay and Commentary* (Kent, OH: Kent State University, 1963)

Kee, Robert, *The Laurel and the Ivy: The Story of Charles Stewart Parnell and Irish Nationalism* (London: Hamish Hamilton, 1993)

Keegan, Alan, *Irish Manchester* (Stroud: Sutton, 2004)

Keegan, Alan, and Danny Claffey, *More Irish Manchester* (Stroud: Sutton, 2006)

Ker, Ian, *John Henry Newman* (Oxford: Oxford University Press, 1988)

Kerr, Barbara M., 'Irish Seasonal Migration to Great Britain, 1800–38', *Irish Historical Studies* 3 (1943), pp. 365–80

Kiberd, Declan, 'The Fall of the Stage Irishman', in *The Irish Writer and the World* (Cambridge: Cambridge University Press, 2005), pp. 21–41

Kiernan, R. H., *The Story of the Archdiocese of Birmingham* (West Bromwich: Wones, 1950)

Kipling, Rudyard, *The Sussex Edition of the Complete Works in Prose and Verse of Rudyard Kipling*, vol. 35 (London: Macmillan, 1939)

Knight, Thomas, *The Honest Thieves: A Farce* (London: G. Cawthorn, 1797)

Krause, David (ed.), *The Dolmen Boucicault* (Dublin: Dolmen, 1964)

Langford, J., *A Century of Birmingham Life; or, A Chronicle of Local Events, from 1741 to 1841*, 2 vols (Birmingham: Osborne, 1868)

——, *Modern Birmingham and Its Institutions*, 2 vols (London: Simkin, Marshall and company, 1873)

Larkham, Peter J., *Discovering Cities: Birmingham* (Sheffield: Geographical Association, 2003)

Lawrence, Ivan, 'Business of the House', *Hansard House of Commons*, 29 March 1990 <http://www.publications.parliament.uk/pa/cm198990/cmhansrd/1990-03-29/Debate-2.html> [accessed 22 May 2008] (column 685)

Lees, Lynn Hollen, *Exiles of Erin: Irish Migrants in Victorian London* (Manchester: Manchester University Press, 1979)

Limbrick, Gudrun, 'A Difficult Decision', in *A Great Day: Celebrating St. Patrick's Day in Birmingham*, ed. Gudrun Limbrick (Birmingham: St. Patrick's Festival, 2007), p. 64
——, 'A Record-Breaking Parade – St. Pat at the Point', in *A Great Day: Celebrating St. Patrick's Day in Birmingham*, ed. Gudrun Limbrick (Birmingham: St. Patrick's Festival, 2007), pp. 115–16

Llewellyn-Jones, Margaret, *Contemporary Irish Drama and Cultural Identity* (Bristol: Intellect, 2002)

Lloyd, David, *Ireland after History* (Cork: Cork University Press, 1999)

Lodge, David, *Small World* (Harmondsworth: Penguin, 1985)

Lowe, W. J., *The Irish in Mid-Victorian Lancashire: The Shaping of a Working-Class Community* (New York: Lang, 1989)

Lynch, Michael, and Damian Smyth, *The Beatles and Ireland* (Cork: Collins Press, 2008)

Lyon, Eileen Groth, *Politicians in the Pulpit* (Aldershot: Ashgate, 1999)

Mac Amhlaigh, Dónall, *An Irish Navvy: The Diary of an Exile*, trans. Valentin Iremonger (London: Routledge, 1966)

MacDonagh, Oliver, *The Emancipist: Daniel O'Connell 1830–1847* (London: Weidenfeld and Nicolson, 1989)

Macintyre, Angus, *The Liberator* (London: Hamish Hamilton, 1965)

MacNeice, Louis, *Collected Poems* (London: Faber, 1966)

MacRaild, Donald M., *Culture, Conflict and Migration: The Irish in Victorian Cumbria* (Liverpool: Liverpool University Press, 1998)
——, *Faith, Fraternity and Fighting: The Orange Order and Irish Migrants in Northern England, c.1850–1920* (Liverpool: Liverpool University Press, 2005)
——, *Irish Migrants in Modern Britain, 1750–1922* (Houndmills: Macmillan, 1999)
——, 'Networks, Communication and the Irish Protestant Diaspora in Northern England, c.1860–1914', in *Irish Migration, Networks and Ethnic Identities Since 1750*, ed. Enda Delaney and Donald M. MacRaild (Abingdon: Routledge, 2007), pp. 163–89
——, 'William Murphy, the Orange Order and communal violence: The Irish in West Cumberland, 1871–84', in *Racial Violence in Britain, 1840–1950*, ed. Panikos Panayi (Leicester: Leicester University Press, 1993), pp. 44–65

Macready, William Charles, *The Diaries of William Charles Macready, 1833–1851*, ed. William Toynbee, 2 vols (London: Chapman and Hall, 1912)

Macready, William Charles, *The Irishman in London; or, the Happy African* (Dublin: Perrin, 1793)

Macready, William Charles, and Andrew Cherry, *The Magic of British Liberty*, in John E. Cunningham, *Theatre Royal: The History of the Theatre Royal Birmingham* (Oxford: Ronald, 1950), pp. 98–108

Malone, Andrew E., *The Irish Drama* (London: Constable, 1929; repr. New York: Benjamin Blom, 1965)

The Man and the City (Birmingham: Silk and Terry, 1906[?])

Marranca, Bonnie, Marc Robinson, and Una Chaudhuri, 'Criticism, Culture, and Performance: An Interview with Edward Said', in *Interculturalism and Performance: Writings from PAJ*, ed. Bonnie Marranca and Gautam Dasgupta (New York: PAJ, 1991), pp. 38–59

Marris, N. Murrell, *Joseph Chamberlain: The Man and the Statesman* (London: Hutchinson, 1900)

Marsh, Peter T., *Joseph Chamberlain: Entrepreneur in Politics* (New Haven: Yale University Press, 1994)

Matthew, H. C. G., *Gladstone: 1875–1898* (Oxford: Clarendon Press, 1995)

Matthews, Bache, *A History of the Birmingham Repertory Theatre* (London: Chatto and Windus, 1924)

McBride, Lawrence W. (ed.), *The Reynolds Letters: An Irish Emigrant Family in Late Victorian Manchester* (Cork: Cork University Press, 1999)

McCarthy, Brendan, 'Reel Lives', *Tablet*, 28 February 2009, p. 29

McCracken, Donal P., *MacBride's Brigade: Irish Commandos in the Anglo-Boer War* (Dublin: Four Courts Press, 1999)

McCulloch, Andrew, *The Feeneys of the Birmingham Post* (Birmingham: University of Birmingham Press, 2004)

McDonagh, Martin, 'The Beauty Queen of Leenane', in *Plays: I* (London: Methuen, 1999), pp. 1–60

McDonnell, Thomas, 'Narrative of a Few Weeks in Ireland', *Catholic Magazine* 4 (1833), pp. 247–53

——, 'O'Connell's Visit to Birmingham', *Catholicon* 1:3 (1836), pp. 135–41

——, 'Renewal of the Magazine', *Catholic Magazine* 5:45 (1834), pp. 609–10

——, *The Case of the Rev. T.M. McDonnell, Late of St. Peter's Mission, Birmingham, Stated by Himself in a Series of Letters: Letter First* (London: Brown, 1842)

——, 'The Rambler', *Catholic Magazine* 5:44 (1834), pp. 595–605

——, 'The Rambler in Ireland', *Catholic Magazine* 5:37 (1834), pp. 109–17

——, 'The Rambler in Ireland', Catholic Magazine 5:42 (1834), pp. 465–71

McDonnell, Thomas, and John Burnet, *Authentic Report of the Discussion which Took Place between the Rev. John Burnet (of Cork), and the Rev. T. M. McDonnell (of Birmingham)* (Birmingham: Hudson, 1827)

McFeely, Deirdre, 'Dion Boucicault's "The Wearing of the Green"', in *Irish Theatre on Tour*, ed. Nicholas Grene and Chris Morash (Dublin: Carysfort, 2005), pp. 139–59

McGladdery, Gary, *The Provisional IRA in England: The Bombing Campaign 1973–1997* (Dublin: Irish Academic Press, 2006)

McGrath, Paul, and Cathal Dervan, *Ooh Ahh Paul McGrath: The Black Pearl of Inchicore* (London: Mainstream, 1994)

McManus, Kevin, *Ceílís, Jigs and Ballads: Irish Music in Liverpool* (Liverpool: Institute of Popular Music, 1994)

McRedmond, Louis, *Thrown Among Strangers: John Henry Newman in Ireland* (Dublin: Veritas, 1990)

'Mgr. Joseph Masterson', *Tablet*, 5 December 1953, p. 558

Miller, D. W., 'Irish Catholicism and the Great Famine', *Journal of Social History* 9 (1975), pp. 81–98

Money, John, 'Taverns, Coffee House and Clubs: Local Politics and Popular Articulacy in the Birmingham Area, in the Age of the American Revolution', *The Historical Journal* 14:1 (1971), pp. 15–47

Monks, Aoife, *Comely Maidens and Celtic Tigers: Riverdance and Global Performance* (London: Goldsmiths, 2007)

Moore, Chris, *United Irishmen: Manchester United's Irish Connection* (Edinburgh: Mainstream, 2000)

Moore, Thomas, *Moore's Irish Melodies: with Symphonies and Accompaniments by Sir John Stevenson*, ed. J. W. Glover (Dublin: Duffy, 1859)

Moran, Dermot, 'Review – A History of Irish Thought', *Notre Dame Philosophical Reviews* (1 September 2003) <http://ndpr.nd.edu/review.cfm?id=1165> [accessed 21 May 2008]

Moran, James, *Staging the Easter Rising: 1916 as Theatre* (Cork: Cork University Press, 2005)

——, 'Swallowed by the Shopping Centre', *Dublin Review of Books* 5 (April 2008) <http://www.drb.ie/apr08_issues/swallowed_by_the_shopping.htm> [accessed 21 May 2008]

Morash, Christopher, *A History of Irish Theatre, 1601–2000* (Cambridge: Cambridge University Press, 2002)

Moynahan, Brian, *The British Century: A Photographic History of the Last Hundred Years* (London: Weidenfeld and Nicolson, 1997)

'Mr. O'Connell', *Catholicon* 1:6 (1836), pp. 289–304

Mullin, Chris, *Error of Judgement: The Truth About the Birmingham Bombings* (4th edn; Dublin: Poolbeg, 1997)

Mulvey, Queenie, 'We've Come a Long Way' in *A Great Day: Celebrating St. Patrick's Day in Birmingham*, ed. Gudrun Limbrick (Birmingham: St. Patrick's Festival, 2007), p. 59

Murphy, James H., *Abject Loyalty: Nationalism and Monarchy in Ireland During the Reign of Queen Victoria* (Cork: Cork University Press, 2001)

Murphy, Tom, *Plays 4* (London: Methuen, 1997)

——, *Plays 5* (London: Methuen, 2006)

Murphy, William, *The Confessional Unmasked: Showing the Depravity of the Roman Priesthood, the Iniquity of the Confessional and the Questions Put to Females in Confession* (London: Protestant Electoral Union, 1865[?])

Murray, Rory, 'Cáirde le Chéile', in *A Great Day: Celebrating St. Patrick's Day in Birmingham*, ed. Gudrun Limbrick (Birmingham: St. Patrick's Festival, 2007), p. 97

Museum of London, 'Irish London' <http://www.museumoflondon.org.uk/English/ Collections/Onlineresources/RWWC/themes/1295/1151> [accessed 4 March 2009]

Nash, Catherine, *Of Irish Descent: Origin Stories, Genealogy, and the Politics of Belonging* (Syracuse: Syracuse University Press, 2008)

National Liberal Federation: Proceedings in Connection with the Eleventh Annual Meeting of the Federation, Held in Birmingham on Tuesday & Wednesday, November 6th & 7th, 1888 (London: Liberal Publications Department, 1888)

Neal, Frank, *Sectarian Violence: The Liverpool Experience, 1819–1914* (Manchester: Manchester University Press, 1988)

Newman, John Henry, *Lectures on the Present Position of Catholics in England* (Notre Dame, IN: University of Notre Dame Press, 2000)

——, *The Letters and Diaries of John Henry Newman, vol. XXIII*, ed. Charles Stephen Dessain (Oxford: Clarendon Press, 1973)

Norman, Edward, *The English Catholic Church in the Nineteenth Century* (Oxford: Clarendon Press, 1984)

Norris, Fred, *Birmingham Hippodrome, 1899–1999* (Birmingham: Birmingham Hippodrome Theatre Trust, 1999)

O'Casey, Seán, *Autobiographies*, 2 vols (London: Macmillan, 1963)

'O'Connell at Oscott', *Catholicon* 1:6 (1836), pp. cxx–cxxii

O'Connell, Daniel, *The Correspondence of Daniel O'Connell*, ed. Maurice R. O'Connell, 8 vols (Dublin: Irish Manuscripts Commission, 1972–80)

'O'Connell's Visit to Birmingham', *Catholicon*, 1:3 (1836), pp. 135–41

O'Connor, Ulick, *Brendan Behan* (London: Hamish Hamilton, 1970)

O'Day, Alan, 'The Political Organisation of the Irish in Britain, 1867–90', in *The Irish in Britain 1815–1939*, ed. Roger Swift and Sheridan Gilley (London: Pinter, 1989), pp. 183–211

O'Donnell, Roderick, *The Pugins and the Catholic Midlands* (Leominster: Gracewing, 2002)

O'Driscoll, Dennis, *Stepping Stones: Interviews with Seamus Heaney* (London: Faber, 2008)

O'Flynn, Catherine, *What Was Lost* (Birmingham: Tindal Street Press, 2007)

O'Keeffe, John, *The Irish Mimic; or, Blunders at Brighton* (London: Longman, 1795)

O'Mahony, Patrick J., *The Fantasy of Human Rights* (Great Wakering: Mayhew-McCrimmon, 1978)

O'Reilly, Kaite, *Belonging* (London: Faber, 2000)

O'Toole, Fintan, *Tom Murphy: The Politics of Magic* (Dublin: New Island, 1994)

Pakenham, Thomas, *The Boer War* (London: Weidenfeld and Nicolson, 1997)

Parker, Stewart, *Plays: 2* (London: Methuen, 2000)

Parkinson, Alan F., *Ulster Loyalism and the British Media* (Dublin: Four Courts Press, 1998)

Paulton, Edward, *The Stone Lady* (New York: French, 1926)

Paulton, Harry, and Edward Paulton, *Niobe, All Smiles* (London: French, 1904)

Paz, D. G., *Popular Anti-Catholicism in Mid-Victorian England* (Stanford: Stanford University Press, 1992)

Pearce, Edward, *Reform!: The Fight for the 1832 Reform Act* (London: Jonathan Cape, 2003)

Pearse, Mary Brigid, *The Home Life of Pádraig Pearse* (Dublin: Browne and Nolan, 1934)

Pearse, P. H., 'Childhood and Youth', in Mary Brigid Pearse, *The Home Life of Pádraig Pearse* (Dublin: Browne and Nolan, 1934)

———, 'O'Donovan Rossa', in *Political Writings and Speeches* (Dublin: Phoenix, 1924), pp. 125–37

———, 'The Coming Revolution' in *Political Writings and Speeches* (Dublin: Phoenix, 1924), pp. 89–99

———, 'The King', in *Plays, Stories, Poems* (Dublin: Talbot, 1966), pp. 45–67

———, 'The Master', in *Plays, Stories, Poems* (Dublin: Talbot, 1966), pp. 69–100

Pelling, Henry, *Social Geography of British Elections: 1885–1910* (London: Macmillan, 1967)

'Performing Arts', *Arts and Humanities Data Service* <http://ahds.ac.uk/ahdscollections/docroot/birminghamrep/birminghamrepsearch.jsp> [accessed 22 May 2008]

Pettitt, Lance, *Screening Ireland: Film and Television Representation* (Manchester: Manchester University Press, 2000)

Pietropaolo, Domenico, 'Spectacular Literacy and the Topology of Significance: The Processional Mode', in *Petrarch's Triumphs: Allegory and Spectacle*, ed. Konrad Eisenbichler and Amilcare A. Ianucci (Ottawa: Dovehouse, 1990), pp. 359–68

Pfister, Manfred, *The Theory and Analysis of Drama*, trans. John Halliday (Cambridge: Cambridge University Press, 1988)

Pilkington, Lionel, *Theatre and the State in Twentieth-Century Ireland: Cultivating the People* (London: Routledge, 2001)

Powell, Walter, and Herbert Maurice Cashmore, *Birmingham Public Libraries Catalogue of the Birmingham Collection* (Birmingham: Cornish Brothers, 1918)

Price, Victor J., *Birmingham Cinemas: Their Films and Stars 1900–1960* (Studley: Brewin, 1986)

'1974 Pub Bombings "Were Wrong"', BBC news Web site, <http://news.bbc.co.uk/1/hi/northern_ireland/4023451.stm> [accessed 22 June 2007]

Pugin, Augustus, *The Collected Letters of A. W. N. Pugin*, ed. Margaret Belcher, 2 vols (Oxford: Oxford University Press, 2001)

Rabey, David, *David Rudkin: Sacred Disobedience* (Aberystwyth: Harwood, 1997)

Redford, Arthur, *Labour Migration in England, 1800–1850* (Manchester: Manchester University Press, 1926)

'Renaissance of the Irish Quarter', *Birmingham Irish Quarter* <http://icbirmingham.icnetwork.co.uk/0150business/irishquarter/tm_method=full%26objectid=14670294%26siteid=50002-name_page.htm> [accessed 11 December 2007]

Report from the Select Committee Appointed to Inquire into the Origin, Nature, Extent and Tendency of Orange Institutions in Great Britain and the Colonies; with the Minutes of Evidence, Appendix and Index. Reports from the Committees: Sixteen Volumes (13) Orange Lodges: Great Britain and Colonies, Session 19 February–10 September 1835 (Vol. XVII) 1835 (London: House of Commons [n.d.])

Reports from Commissioners: Fifteen Volumes (13) Poor Laws (Ireland): Supplement II, Vol. XXXIV, 1836 (Appendix G: Report on the State of the Irish Poor in Great Britain), Evidence Taken 4–7 January 1834 (London: House of Commons [n.d.])

Rex, John, and Robert Moore, *Race, Community and Conflict: A Study of Sparkbrook* (London: Oxford University Press, 1967)

Rhodes, R. Crompton, *The Theatre Royal, Birmingham, 1774–1924: A Short History* (Birmingham: Moody, 1924)

Richtarik, Marilynn J., *Acting Between the Lines: The Field Day Company and Irish Cultural Politics 1980–1984* (Oxford: Clarendon Press, 1994)

Richter, Donald C., *Riotous Victorians* (Athens: Ohio University Press, 1981)

Ridge, John T., *The St. Patrick's Day Parade in New York* (New York: St. Patrick's Day Parade Committee, 1988)

Rippon, Anton, *The Aston Villa Story* (Derby: Breedon, 1993)

Robson, Brian, 'Roberts, Frederick Sleigh', *Oxford Dictionary of National Biography*, ed. H. C. G. Matthew and Brian Harrison (Oxford: Oxford University Press, 2004), vol. XLVII, pp. 156–61

Roche, John Joseph, 'The First St. Patrick's Day Parade in England', in *A Great Day: Celebrating St. Patrick's Day in Birmingham*, ed. Gudrun Limbrick (Birmingham: St. Patrick's Festival, 2007), p. 27

Ross, Robert H., *The Georgian Revolt: Rise and Fall of a Poetic Ideal 1910–22* (London: Faber, 1967)

Rowell, George, and Anthony Jackson, *The Repertory Movement: A History of Regional Theatre in Britain* (Cambridge: Cambridge University Press, 1984)

Rudkin, David, *Afore Night Come* (London: Oberon, 2001)

Salberg, Derek, *Ring Down the Curtain* (Luton: Cortney, 1980)

Samuel, Raphael, 'The Roman Catholic Church and the Irish Poor', in *The Irish in the Victorian City*, ed. Roger Swift and Sheridan Gilley (London: Croom Helm, 1985), pp. 267–300

Semmel, Stuart, *Napoleon and the British* (New Haven: Yale, 2004)

Shaw, George Bernard, *Back to Methuselah* (London: Oxford University Press, 1945)

Sillard, Robert M., *Barry Sullivan and His Contemporaries*, 2 vols (London: Fisher Unwin, 1901)

Skipp, Victor, *Victorian Birmingham* (Birmingham: Studio Press, 1983)

Smith, R. J., *Migration in Post-War Birmingham* (Birmingham: Birmingham University, 1969)

Spark, David, *Investigative Reporting: A Study in Technique* (Oxford: Focal, 1999)

Spoo, Robert, '"Nestor" and the Nightmare: The Presence of the Great War in *Ulysses*', *Twentieth Century Literature* 32:2 (1986), pp. 137–54

St Chad's Cathedral clergy, *A History of St. Chad's Cathedral Birmingham, 1841–1904* (Birmingham: Cornish Brothers, 1904)

——, 'Our Heritage: Pugin & the Hardmans' <www.stchadscathedral.org.uk/heritage.php> [accessed 21 May 2008]

St Patrick's Day Magazine (Birmingham: Moda Media, 2009)

'St Patrick's Festival', BBC news Web site, <http://www.bbc.co.uk/birmingham/entertainment/local_events/st_patrick_parade/> [accessed 17 June 2009]

'St Patrick's Parade 2007', BBC news Web site, <http://www.bbc.co.uk/birmingham/content/articles/2007/03/08/st_patricks_day_preview_feature.shtml> [accessed 11 December 2007]

Steedman, Carolyn, *Policing the Victorian Community: The Formation of English Provincial Police Forces, 1856–80* (London: Routledge, 1984)

Stephens, W. B. (ed.), 'Political and Administrative History: Political History to 1832', in *A History of the County of Warwick: Volume 7: The City of Birmingham* (1964), pp. 270–97 <http://www.british-history.ac.uk/report.aspx?compid=22971> [accessed 22 May 2008]

——, 'Religious History: Roman Catholicism', in *A History of the County of Warwick: Volume 7: The City of Birmingham* (1964), pp. 397–402 <http://www.british-history.ac.uk/report.aspx?compid=22977> [accessed 22 May 2008]

Sullivan, Mary C. (ed.), *The Friendship of Florence Nightingale and Mary Clare Moore* (Philadelphia: University of Pennsylvania Press, 1999)

Sutcliffe, Anthony, and Roger Smith, *History of Birmingham, Volume III, Birmingham 1939–1970* (London: Oxford University Press, 1974)

Swift, Roger, 'Anti-Catholicism and Irish Disturbances', *Midland History* 9 (1984), pp. 94–98

——, 'Behaving Badly? Irish Migrants and Crime in the Victorian City', in *Criminal Conversations*, ed. Judith Rowbotham and Kim Stevenson (Columbus: Ohio State University Press, 2005), pp. 106–25

——, *Irish Migrants in Britain, 1815–1914: A Documentary History* (Cork: Cork University Press, 2002)

Swift, Roger, and Sheridan Gilley (eds), *The Irish in the Victorian City* (London: Croom Helm, 1985)

Synge, J. M., *Collected Plays and Poems and the Aran Islands*, ed. Alison Smith (London: Everyman, 1996)

——, *The Collected Letters of John Millington Synge*, 2 vols, ed. Ann Saddlemyer (Oxford: Clarendon Press, 1984)

Thatcher, Margaret, 'Terrorists (Extradition)', *Hansard House of Commons*, 29 March 1990 <http://www.publications.parliament.uk/pa/cm198990/cmhansrd/1990-03-29/Orals-2.html> [accessed 22 May 2008] (column 668)

Thompson, Dorothy, 'Ireland and the Irish in English Radicalism before 1850', in *The Chartist Experience: Studies in Working-Class Radicalism and Culture, 1830–60*, ed. James Epstein and Dorothy Thompson (Houndmills: Macmillan, 1982)

Townshend, Charles, *Easter 1916: The Irish Rebellion* (London: Allen Lane, 2005)

Trevor, William, *Felicia's Journey* (Harmondsworth: Penguin, 1995)

Trewin, J. C., *Mr Macready: A Nineteenth-Century Tragedian and His Theatre* (London: Harrap, 1955)

——, *The Birmingham Repertory Theatre 1913–1963* (London: Barrie and Rockliff, 1963)

Truninger, Annelise, *Paddy and the Paycock: A Study of the Stage Irishman from Shakespeare to O'Casey* (Bern: Francke, 1976)

Turner, Michael J., *The Age of Unease: Government and Reform in Britain, 1782–1832* (Stroud: Sutton, 2000)

Ullathorne, William, *The Confessional: An Address, Delivered in the Catholic Churches, Walsall* (London: Richardson, 1867)

Underdown, P. T., 'Religious Opposition to the Licensing of the Bristol and Birmingham Theatres', *University of Birmingham Historical Journal* 6 (1957–58), pp. 149–60

Upton, Chris, *A History of Birmingham* (Chichester: Phillimore, 1993)

———, *Living Back to Back* (Trowbridge: Cromwell, 2005)

Walker, Brian, '"The Lost Tribes of Ireland": Diversity, Identity and Loss among the Irish Diaspora', *Irish Studies Review* 15:3 (2007), pp. 267–82

Walter, Bronwen, *Outsiders Inside: Whiteness, Place and Irish Women* (London: Routledge, 2001)

Ward, Roger, *City-State and Nation: Birmingham's Political History 1830–1940* (Chichester: Phillimore, 2005)

Ward-Penny, Christine, *Catholics in Birmingham* (Stroud: Tempus, 2004)

Watson, Samuel (ed.), *Gentleman's and Citizen's Almanack* (Dublin: Powell, 1770)

Watson Stewart, John (ed.), *The Treble Almanack, for the Year MDCCXCVIII* (Dublin: Watson, 1798)

Welch, Robert (ed.), *The Oxford Companion to Irish Literature* (Oxford: Clarendon Press, 1996)

Whelan, Kevin, 'Daniel O'Connell: The Kerry Proteus', in *Daniel O'Connell*, ed. Kevin Whelan (Dublin, Keough-Notre Dame Centre, 2003), pp. 23–29

White, Norman, *Hopkins: A Literary Biography* (Oxford: Clarendon Press, 1992)

Williams, Iestyn, Máiréad Dunne, and Máirtín Mac an Ghaill, *Economic Needs of the Irish Community in Birmingham* (Birmingham: Birmingham City Council, 1996)

Wills, Clair, *That Neutral Island* (London: Faber, 2007)

Wright, Frank, *Two Lands on One Soil: Ulster Politics before Home Rule* (Dublin: Gill and Macmillan, 1996)

Yeats, W. B., *Autobiographies: Memories and Reflections* (London: Bracken, 1995)

———, *The Collected Works of W. B. Yeats: Volume II, the Plays*, ed. David R. Clark and Rosalind E. Clark (New York: Scribner, 2001)

———, *The King's Threshold Manuscript Materials*, ed. Declan Kiely (Ithaca, NY: Cornell University Press, 2005)

Newspaper Sources

'A Foe to Parnell's Plans', *New York Times*, 9 September 1885, p. 5

A. J. W., 'Comic Soldiers of the IRA', *County Express*, 11 May 1973, p. 11

'A Repertory Riot', *BG*, 16 May 1917, p. 2

Alertus, 'Things Talked About', *Sunday Mercury*, 3 June 1945, p. 5

'An Appeal to the Irish Men and Women of Birmingham', *Birmingham Catholic Magazine*, March 1918, p. 60

'An Irish Play at the Repertory Theatre', *BP*, 27 November 1933, p. 4

'An Ulster Play', *BG*, 18 November 1913, p. 4

'Anti-IRA Crowd Attacks Shop: Baton Charge', *BG*, 31 August 1939, p. 7

'Arts Review/Parliament', *BP*, 18 March 1975, p. 2

'Aston Theatre Royal', *BP*, 25 July 1899, p. 10

'Aston Theatre', *BM*, 25 July 1899, p. 2

'At the Play. "Oliver Cromwell"', *BG*, 6 March 1923, p. 4

'"Attack on People Disastrous and Appalling" Say Police', *BM*, 22 November 1974, p. 3

Barker, Dennis, 'Aftermath of Vengeance', *Guardian*, 23 November 1974, p. 11

Barnes, Paulinus, 'The Most Rev Maurice Couve de Murville', *Independent*, 9 November 2007 <http://www.independent.co.uk/news/obituaries/the-most-rev-maurice-couve-de-murville-399611.html> [accessed 22 May 2008]

'Belfast-Type Horror Strikes Birmingham', *BM*, 22 November 1974, p. 3

Bell, David, 'Rowdy Club to Stay Shut', *BM*, 2 September 2005 <http://icbirmingham. icnetwork.co.uk/0100news/0100localnews/tm_objectid=15940723&method=full &siteid=50002&headline=rowdy-club-to-stay-shut-name_page.html> [accessed 11 December 2007]

Berliner, Jeffrey, 'Midnight: Bombers Hit Birmingham Again', *BP*, 15 July 1974, p. 1

BG, 19 August 1776, p. 3

BG, 5 September 1803, p. 2

BG, 10 August 1807, p. 4

BG, 15 January 1838, p. 2

BG, 3 August 1846, p. 3

BG, 16 November 1846, p. 3

BG, 22 February 1847, p. 3

BG, 27 December 1847, p. 3

BG, 10 January 1848, p. 3

BG, 8 June 1861, p. 3

BG, 19 May 1917, p. 4

'B'ham Hosts First Irish Festival', *BM*, 21 May 1983, p. 4

'Big Drive for an Irish Club', *BM*, 25 August 1966, p. 5

'Big Hearts of Ireland', *BM*, 17 March 1987, p. 7

'Birmingham Amusements', *BM*, 24 May 1907, p. 5

'Birmingham Amusements', *BP*, 19 May 1914, p. 6

'Birmingham Amusements', *BM*, 21 March 1916, p. 5

'60,000 Birmingham "Exiles" Celebrate St. Patrick's Day', *BG*, 17 March 1952, p. 5

'Birmingham Has Jobs For Irish Workers … But No Houses!', *Sunday Independent*, 15 August 1954, located in NAI, Department of Foreign Affairs, Position of Irish Workers in Birmingham, 402/222

'Birmingham Home Rule Association: Meeting in the Town Hall', *BP*, 18 June 1886, p. 7

Birmingham Illustrated Weekly Mercury, 18 May 1916, p. 2

'Birmingham, Jan 23, 1832', *BG*, 23 January 1832, p. 3

'Birmingham, July 25, 1803', *BG*, 25 July 1803, p. 3

'Birmingham Liberal Association: Annual Meeting of the "Two Thousand"', *BP*, 22 April 1886, p. 5

'Birmingham Man Identified from Thumbprint and Clothing Only', *BM*, 22 November 1974, p. 2

'Birmingham, Monday, March 31', *BG*, 31 March 1777, p. 3

'Birmingham Reform Meeting', *BG*, 14 May 1832, p. 1

'Birmingham, September 12, 1803', *BG*, 12 September 1803, p. 3

'Birmingham, September 28, 1812', *BG*, 28 September 1812, p. 3

Birmingham Weekly Mercury, 16 May 1914, p. 12

'Birmingham's Sons of Erin', *BM*, 15 November 1904, p. 5

BM, 22 November 1974, p. 2

Bolton, Pat, 'Is There Green in Her Eye?', *Midland Catholic Pictorial*, January 1960, p. 2

'Bomb Blast at Solihull Bank', *BP*, 30 August 1973, p. 1

'Bomb Blast Officer Dies', *BP*, 24 September 1973, p. 1

'Bomber: Big Police Net', *BM*, 21 November 1974, p. 1

'Bombs in Birmingham Cinemas', *BP*, 31 May 1939, p. 1

'Bombs Shatter Crowded Pubs in Birmingham', *Guardian*, 22 November 1974, p. 28

'Bordesley Theatre', *BM*, 2 May 1916, p. 5

BP, 27 April 1886, p. 1

Brady, Poppy, 'Dancing in the Rain', *BM*, 15 March 2004, p. 26

———, 'Going Down a Storm …', *BM*, 15 March 2004, p. 30

Brennan, Sandra, 'All Movie Guide', *New York Times* <http://movies2.nytimes.com/gst/
    movies/movie.html?v_id=95686> [accessed 21 May 2008]

'Bride To Be among Five Killed in Midland Mystery Explosion', *BG*, 26 August 1939, p. 7

Bright, John, 'Irish Festival', *BP*, 4 August 1977, p. 4

'Britain's New Generation of Irish', *BM*, 19 September 1973, p. 12

'Call for Strike by City's Irish', *BM*, 28 August 1969, p. 5

'Carnival Time with a £1,000 Target', *BM*, 2 February 1973, p. 16

'Catholic Demonstration', *BM*, 1 April 1929, p. 2

Catholic News, 3 June 1916, p. 8

'CBSO and Rep Warned: Axe your Budget', *BM*, 3 April 1974, p. 9

'Celebration in Birmingham', *BP*, 18 March 1916, p. 10

Chinn, Carl, 'The Many Cultures that Make Up Brum', *BM*, 15 March 1999, p. 9

———, 'The Voice of the Irish in Brum', *The Harp*, May 2007, p. 23

Chippindale, Peter, 'Archbishop Sacks Priest for IRA Funeral Speech', *Guardian*, 12 June
    1974, p. 28

———, 'Sinister Precedent Feared', *Guardian*, 23 November 1974, p. 1

'Cinema Outrages', *BM*, 30 May 1939, p. 6

'Commemoration in Birmingham', *BP*, 18 March 1901, p. 10

'Coventry Bomb Trial', *Manchester Guardian*, 14 December 1939, p. 11

'3,000 Coventry Workers in Anti-IRA Demonstration', *BG*, 29 August 1939, p. 4

Dalyell, Tim, 'Maurice Foley', *Independent*, 14 February 2002, <http://www.
    independent.co.uk/news/obituaries/maurice-foley-729746.html> [accessed 21 May
    2008]

'Daniel O'Connell, Esq., M. P., in Birmingham', *BG*, 11 March 1844, p. 1

Daniels, John, 'If Birmingham's Irish Think Big', located in BCL, Joe McKenna,
    'The Irish in Birmingham: A Scrapbook 1643–1989', Birmingham Collection 21.7,
    fol. 46

Davies, Martin, 'Self Help with the Housing Problem', *BM*, 29 October 1965, p. 12

———, 'The Flow is Slowing Down', *BM*, 27 October 1965, p. 10

———, 'The Myth of the Fighting Drinker', *BM*, 28 October 1965, p. 10

Dayani, Alison, 'Fond Farewell for Digbeth Coach Station', *BM*, 19 November 2007
    <http:icbirmingham.icnetwork.co.uk/mail/news/centralcity/tm_method=full

%26objectid=20128012%26siteid=50002-name_page.html> [accessed 11 December 2007]

'Defence Opened in Bomb Murder Trial', *Manchester Guardian*, 13 December 1939, p. 9

'"Dev" Speaks – 5,000 Are Turned Away', *BG*, 31 January 1949, p. 1

Dillon, Barry, 'Bishop Sings Centre's Praises', located in BCL, Joe McKenna, 'The Irish in Birmingham: A Scrapbook 1643–1989', Birmingham Collection 21.7, fol. 71

'Don't Take Law into Own Hands – Jenkins', *BP*, 23 November 1974, p. 1

EAC, 'At the Repertory', *BG*, 12 October 1923, p. 4

'Election Notes', *BP*, 18 March 1880, p. 5

Eliot Jr., S. A., 'Germany's Theatrical Invasion: The Birmingham Repertory Theatre, a la Teuton, Unique Among England's Playhouses', *Boston Evening Transcript*, 24 May 1913, in NYPL, Lincoln Center Library, MWEZ+NC 27,695, folder 1910–1919

'Explosions in City Cinema', *BP*, 30 May 1939, p. 1

'Explosives Charge', *BM*, 13 July 1939, p. 13

'Explosives Charges', *BM*, 6 June 1939, p. 10

'Family in Fire Bomb Terror', *BM*, 26 November 1974, p. 1

'Fenianism in Birmingham', *The Nation*, 21 May 1870, p. 629

'"Find Homes for Irish Refugee Families" Call in Churches', *BP*, 25 August 1969, p. 12

'Firebombers in Attack on Night Club', *BM*, 27 November 1974, p. 12

'Fires Hit Furniture Stores', *BP*, 23 November 1974, p. 4

Freeman's Journal, 9 September 1885, p. 4

'From Kingston or Kerry – It Makes No Difference', *Manchester Guardian*, 13 October 1956, p. 5

'From the Editorial Chair', *Birmingham Catholic Magazine*, May 1916, p. 86

'From the Editorial Chair', *Birmingham Catholic Magazine*, June 1916, pp. 109–10

'Funeral of Mr. W. Murphy', *BG*, 19 March 1872, p. 8

'Gala Night for Irish "Exiles"', *BG*, 18 March 1952, p. 6

'Gas Bomb in Cinema', *BM*, 1 June 1939, p. 10

'Go Ahead for New Irish Centre', *BM*, 19 December 1966, p. 7

'Grand Theatre', *BG*, 6 April 1886, p. 6

'Great Day for the Irish', *BP*, 18 March 1960, p. 7

Griffin, Jon, 'City Group to Support Irish', *BM*, 10 December 1998, p. 43

'Gun Guard as Six Face Court', *BM*, 25 November 1974, p. 1

Hastilow, Nigel, 'Spotlight Turns on Police Liars', *BP*, 20 October 1990, p. 1

Hastilow, Nigel, and Michael Higgins, 'Denning Admits to Error over Six', *BP*, 21 October 1989, p. 1

'Heartsearching', *BP*, 19 November 1974, p. 4

Hepburn, Pauline, 'Jeers as Accused Six Go to Court', *BP*, 26 November 1974, p. 7

Hogan, J., 'St. Michael's, Moor Street', *Birmingham Catholic Magazine*, March 1920, pp. 95–96

Hoggart, Simon, 'Jenkins Gets Hanging Call', *Guardian*, 22 November 1974, p. 1

'Home Rule Bombshell: Self-Rule All Round', *BG*, 20 November 1913, p. 1

'Hospitals Rocked as Midnight Bombers Hit Birmingham Bank', *BP*, 6 November 1974, p. 1

'Housing Plan to Aid Irish', located in BCL, Joe McKenna, 'The Irish in Birmingham: A Scrapbook 1643–1989', Birmingham Collection 21.7, fol. 28

'How the Irish Fought at Birmingham', *The Nation*, 6 July 1867, p. 724

Hughes, Wendy, 'Backlash Hampering Police – Warning', *BP*, 25 November 1974, p. 5

——, 'Bars Deserted in Frightened Rush for Home', *BP*, 23 November 1974, p. 9

'Hunger-Strike March Passes off Peacefully', *BP*, 2 May 1983, p. 3

'Hunt Is on for Brains Behind the Bombings', *BP*, 8 April 1974, p. 1

Hurt, Jon, 'Irish Celebrations Return to Streets of Birmingham', *BP*, 18 March 1996, p. 6

'I'll Make Sure Reece Is Brought up to Know Who His Nana Was', *BM*, 21 March 2007 <http://icbirmingham.icnetwork.co.uk/mail/news/tm_method=full%26objectid=18787043%26siteid=50002-name_page.html> [accessed 11 December 2007]

'Inhuman', *Irish Independent*, 23 November 1974, p. 3

'IRA Attacks on Postal Services', *BP*, 10 June 1939, p. 1

'IRA Call for Volunteers during Midland March', *Sunday Mercury*, 17 August 1969, p. 3

'Ireland a Nation!', *BP*, 18 March 1908, p. 6

'Irish Drama in Birmingham', *BM*, 29 May 1907, p. 2

'Irish Exploited in Midlands', *BG*, 30 August 1951, pp. 1, 5

'Irish in City Now Better Housed', *Evening Dispatch*, 27 June 1956, located in NAI, Department of Foreign Affairs, Position of Irish Workers in Birmingham, 402/222

'Irish Internee is "Adopted"', *Sunday Mercury*, 24 October 1971, p. 6

'Irish May Seek Candidate to Fight Midland MP', *Sunday Mercury*, 25 January 1970, p. 3

'Irish National Drama', *BM*, 28 May 1907, p. 5

'Irish Notes', *Birmingham Catholic Magazine*, March 1919, p. 55

'Irish Notes', *Birmingham Catholic Magazine*, December 1919, p. 241

'Irish Notes', *Birmingham Catholic Magazine*, March 1920, p. 57

'Irish Notes and Comments', *Birmingham Catholic Magazine*, April 1919, p. 81

'Irish Notes and Comments', *Birmingham Catholic Magazine*, May 1919, p. 99

'Irish Notes and Comments', *Birmingham Catholic Magazine*, June 1919, p. 119

'Irish Notes and Comments', *Birmingham Catholic Magazine*, November 1919, pp. 217–18

'Irish Paid Price for Pub Bombs', *BP*, 20 April 2006 <http://icbirmingham.icnetwork.co.uk/birminghampost/news/tm_method=full%26objectid=16969420%26siteid=50002-name_page.html> [accessed 11 December 2007]

'Irish Players at the Grand', *BM*, 18 January 1916, p. 7

'Irish Protestors Occupy Office', *BP*, 2 January 1973, p. 5

'Irish Reform Bill', *Birmingham Journal*, 30 June 1832, p. 2

'Irish Support Call for Ban on the IRA', *BP*, 23 November 1974, p. 9

'Irish Urged to Boycott Bad Lodgings: St. Patrick's Parade and Service in Birmingham', *BP*, 17 March 1952, p. 5

'Irish Workers in England Degraded', *Irish Independent*, 30 August 1951, p. 5

'Irishmen Asked to Help Immigrants: Birmingham Appeal by Dr Grimshaw', *BP*, 18 March 1955, p. 7

'Irishmen Picked up Boarding Ulster Ferry', *Guardian*, 23 November 1974, p. 1

'It Feels Bad to Be Irish in Birmingham', *Observer*, 24 November 1974, p. 5

J. B. H., 'Irish Notes and Comments', *Birmingham Catholic Magazine*, August 1919, p. 160

Lennon, Michael J., 'James Pearse', *BP*, 21 August 1947, p. 2

'Liberal Demonstration at Warrington', *BP*, 9 September 1885, p. 5

'London Museum', *BM*, 12 October 1885, p. 1

'London Museum', *BM*, 23 October 1885, p. 1

'Longer Arms of the Law', *BP*, 30 November 1974, p. 6

Manchester Guardian, 6 November 1888, p. 5

Manchester Guardian, 8 November 1888, p. 5

Masterman, F. G., 'A New Star Chamber: The Irish Deportations', *BG*, 17 March 1923, p. 4

McCarthy, John, 'Carnival Time with a £1,000 Target', *BM*, 2 February 1973, p. 16
———, 'Extra "Time" for Centre', *BM*, located in BCL, Joe McKenna, 'The Irish in Birmingham: A Scrapbook 1643–1989', Birmingham Collection 21.7, fol. 71

McGlashan, Colin, 'How Ghettoes Came to Britain', *Observer*, 12 February 1967, p. 5

McGreal, Chris, 'There Are Many Villains to Blame for Zimbabwe's Decade of Horror', *Guardian*, 13 April 2008 <http://www.guardian.co.uk/world/2008/apr/13/zimbabwe> [accessed 7 April 2009]

McGreevy, Ronan, 'Oasis to Come "Home" to Slane', *Irish Times*, 16 October 2008 <http://www.irishtimes.com/newspaper/ireland/2008/1016/1224069691647.html> [accessed 4 March 2009]

'Mechanics Institute', *Birmingham Journal*, 9 January 1830, p. 2

'Meeting in the Town Hall', *Birmingham Journal*, 18 April 1868, p. 3

Messent, Maureen, 'A Little Bit of Ireland Celebrates Its Jubilee', *BM*, 16 March 1982, p. 6
———, 'Here's to St Pat!', *BM*, 17 March 1997, p. 13
———, 'Invasion of the Emerald Army!', *BM*, 15 March 1999, pp. 8–9
———, 'St Patrick's Day Parade Back in Style: Irish Make a Day of It', *BM*, 18 March 1996, p. 9

'Metropolitan Notes of the Month', *Birmingham Catholic Magazine*, April 1913, p. 127

'Metropolitan Notes of the Month', *Birmingham Catholic Magazine*, May 1913, p. 167

'Metropolitan Notes of the Month', *Birmingham Catholic Magazine*, April 1914, p. 599

'Metropolitan Notes of the Month', *Birmingham Catholic Magazine*, May 1914, p. 639

'Metropolitan Notes of the Month', *Birmingham Catholic Magazine*, July 1914, p. 719

'Metropolitan Notes of the Month', *Birmingham Catholic Magazine*, January 1915, p. 8

'Metropolitan Notes of the Month', *Birmingham Catholic Magazine*, March 1915, p. 74

'Metropolitan Notes of the Month', *Birmingham Catholic Magazine*, August 1915, p. 233

'Metropolitan Notes of the Month', *Birmingham Catholic Magazine*, March 1916, p. 37

'Metropolitan Notes of the Month', *Birmingham Catholic Magazine*, September 1916, p. 189

'Metropolitan Notes of the Month', *Birmingham Catholic Magazine*, December 1918, p. 228

'Metropolitan Notes of the Month', *Birmingham Catholic Magazine*, March 1920, p. 49

M. F. H., '"The Quare Fellow" a Moving Play', *Stratford Herald*, 25 September 1964, located in BCL, Birmingham Repertory Theatre Archive, January 1962–July 1966, vol. 117(A)

Midland Catholic Pictorial, January 1960, p. 2

'Midland Institute', *BP*, 27 May 1913, p. 12

'Midnight Bombers Strike at Factory', *BP*, 17 September 1973, p. 1

'Miss Maire O'Neill at the Repertory', *BG*, 14 May 1917, p. 2

'Monday, March 19', *BP*, 19 March 1888, p. 4

'Monday's Post, from the London Gazette', *BG*, 5 September 1803, p. 3

'Monsignor Patrick O'Mahoney', *Daily Telegraph*, 2 January 1992, p. 17

'Months of Death and Devastation', *BP*, 23 November 1974, p. 4

'More IRA Bombs', *BM*, 10 June 1939, p. 8

'Mourning for Many', *Irish Press*, 22 November 1974, p. 10

'Mr De Valera Criticises Midland Cities: Irishmen Said to Be Living in "Appalling" Conditions', *BP*, 29 August 1951, p. 1

'Mr Murphy in Birmingham', *BP*, 19 June 1867, p. 5

'Mr Murphy in Birmingham: Renewed Disturbances Yesterday', *BP*, 18 June 1867, p. 4

'Mr Murphy in Birmingham: Serious Disturbances', *BP*, 17 June 1867, p. 8

'Mr O'Connell in Birmingham', *Birmingham Journal*, 21 January 1832, p. 3

'Mr O'Connell in Birmingham', *BG*, 8 February 1836, p. 4

'Mr O'Connell in Birmingham', *BG*, 18 December 1837, p. 2

'Mr W Murphy in Birmingham', *BG*, 17 June 1867, p. 3

'Mr William Murphy in Birmingham', *BG*, 22 June 1867, p. 5

'Mr William Murphy in Birmingham', *BG*, 29 June 1867, p. 5

Mullin, Enda, 'Two Wheels and the Truth', *The Harp*, April 2007 <http://www.theharpnews.com/issues/april_07/news_story_3.html> [accessed 11 December 2007]

Murphy, Alex, 'Parade Comes in from the Cold', *The Harp*, April 2006 <http://www.theharpnews.com/issues/april_06/news_story_3.html> [accessed 11 December 2007]

'Murphy Bound Over to Keep the Peace', *Manchester Guardian*, 2 September 1868, p. 6

'Museum Concert Hall', *BG*, 27 April 1886, p. 5

'Museum Concert Hall', *BP*, 14 June 1886, p. 5

'"My Life in Peril": Irish Centre Girl Quits', *BM*, 16 May 1974, p. 5

'New Fire Attack on Irish Family', *BM*, 2 December 1974, p. 1

NW, 'Diary', *Guardian*, 1 December 2007, review section, p. 15

'Odeon New Street', *BM*, 14 March 1966, p. 2

Oestreicher, Paul, 'Mgr Patrick O'Mahony', *Independent*, 30 December 1991, p. 17

'Officer Critical after Five-Hour Operation', *BP*, 17 September 1973, p. 1

Oliphant, Will, 'St Patrick's Day Party Double Stabbing', *BM*, 17 March 2008 <http://www.birminghammail.net/news/birmingham-news/2008/03/17/st-patrick-s-day-party-double-stabbing-97319-20635653/> [accessed 6 January 2009]

'On this Week at Birmingham', *Stage*, 15 October 1964, located in BCL, Birmingham Repertory Theatre Archive, January 1962–July 1966, vol. 117(A)

'Only One Way to Describe the Scene – Carnage', *BM*, 22 November 1974, p. 31

'Our Theatres', *Town Crier*, May 1867, p. 11

'15 Outrages over Seven Months', *BP*, 8 April 1974, p. 3

'Paramount', *BM*, 1 June 1939, p. 1

Parry, Gareth, 'Bombs Hit Two Pubs', *Guardian*, 22 November 1974, p. 1

Pinch, Emma, 'A Colourful Vision for the Future', *BP*, 15 June 2006 <http://
    icbirmingham.icnetwork.co.uk/birminghampost/news/tm_method=full%26objectid
    =17234538%26siteid=50002-name_page.html> [accessed 11 December 2007]
'Police Release Names of 167 Casualties', *BP*, 23 November 1974, p. 7
'Police Search for IRA Terrorists', *BP*, 12 June 1939, p. 1
Prentice, David, 'Irish Eyes Smiling as Liverpool Stars Boost Charity', *Liverpool
    Echo*, 5 February 2009 <http://www.liverpoolecho.co.uk/liverpool-fc/
    liverpool-fc-news/2009/02/05/irish-eyes-smiling-as-liverpool-stars-boost-charity-
    100252-22859043/> [accessed 4 March 2009]
'Pub Bombs: Six Men Will Appear in Court Today', *BP*, 25 November 1974, p. 1
'Rebellious Conspiracy in Ireland', *BG*, 1 August 1803, p. 2
'Records of Catholicity in the Midland Districts from Penal Times', *Birmingham Catholic
    Magazine*, September 1913, pp. 353–54
'Records of Catholicity in the Midland Districts from Penal Times', *Birmingham Catholic
    Magazine*, October 1913, p. 389
'Records of Catholicity in the Midland Districts from Penal Times', *Birmingham Catholic
    Magazine*, November 1913, p. 428
'Reform Dinner', *BG*, 1 February 1836, p. 2
Reiss, Charles, 'A Tactical Dilemma', *BP*, 23 November 1974, p. 6
'Repertory Riot', *BG*, 17 May 1917, p. 3
'Repertory Theatre', *BP*, 31 March 1913, p. 5
'Repertory Theatre', *BP*, 14 May 1917, p. 3
'Republicans Plan Fund-Raising at Midland Churches', *Sunday Mercury*, 24 October 1971,
    p. 6
Roberts, Nesta, 'Irish Girls in England', *Manchester Guardian*, 7 April 1955, p. 14
'Row over Call to Back Irish Terror Tactics', *BM*, 26 November 1974, p. 7
Roth, Andrew, 'Ask Aristotle about Chris Mullin', *Guardian*, 16 March 2001, <http://
    politics.guardian.co.uk/profiles/story/0,,458072,00.html> [accessed 21 May 2008]
'Savagery and the Law', *Guardian*, 22 November 1974, p. 14
'Second Reform Meeting at Newhall Hill', *BG*, 14 May 1832, p. 2
Sims, Andy, 'Behan: Pathos Lost', *Redbrick*, 7 October 1964, located in BCL,
    Birmingham Repertory Theatre Archive, January 1962–July 1966, vol. 117(A)
Solan, John, 'A Stone Shatters the Apprehensive Silence', *BP*, 23 November 1974, p. 9
'Some Irish-Ireland Principles', *Birmingham Catholic Magazine*, June 1917, p. 143
'St Chad's Men's Society', *Birmingham Catholic Magazine*, March 1915, p. 75
'St. Patrick Parade in Birmingham', *BP*, 16 March 1953, p. 7
'St. Patrick's Anniversary', *BP*, 18 March 1878, p. 5
'St. Patrick's Day', *BM*, 17 March 1914, p. 3
'St. Patrick's Day', *BP*, 18 March 1897, p. 5
'St. Patrick's Day', *BP*, 18 March 1903, p. 5
'St. Patrick's Day', *BP*, 18 March 1905, p. 8
'St. Patrick's Day but Something is Missing', *BM*, 17 March 1962, p. 1
'St. Patrick's Day Celebration', *BP*, 18 March 1893, p. 6
'St. Patrick's Day Celebration in Birmingham', *BP*, 18 March 1880, p. 5

'St. Patrick's Day Celebration in Birmingham', *BP*, 18 March 1891, p. 7

'St Patrick's Day Celebrations', *Birmingham Catholic Magazine*, April 1917, p. 91

'St. Patrick's Day Celebrations', *BP*, 18 March 1886, p. 8

'St. Patrick's Day Celebrations', *BP*, 18 March 1892, p. 8.

'St. Patrick's Day Celebrations', *BP*, 19 March 1917, p. 3

'St. Patrick's Day Celebrations: Concert at the Town Hall', *BP*, 18 March 1869, p. 8

'St. Patrick's Day Celebrations in Birmingham', *BM*, 19 March 1900, p. 3

'St. Patrick's Day Concert in Birmingham', *BP*, 18 March 1930, p. 7

'St. Patrick's Day in Birmingham', *BP*, 18 March 1874, p. 8

'St. Patrick's Day in Birmingham', *BP*, 18 March 1929, p. 13

'St. Patrick's Day in Birmingham: A Discordant Irish Note', *BG*, 18 March 1900, p. 4

'St. Patrick's Day Parades in Ireland', *BP*, 18 March 1931, p. 7

'State of the Town Yesterday', *BP*, 21 June 1867, p. 4

'"Stay Calm" Plea by Police', *BM*, 28 November 1974, p. 7

'Synge's Comedy at the Repertory', *BP*, 17 November 1930, p. 11

Taylor, Noreen, 'Women Who Wait in Hope: Crying out for Freedom', *Daily Mirror*, 2 February 1990, pp. 18–23

'Terence MacSwiney', *Birmingham Catholic Magazine*, November 1920, p. 211

'Testimony on Terror', *BP*, 21 September 1973, p. 1

'The Angry City', *BP*, 25 November 1973, p. 6

'The Birmingham Election', *BP*, 17 March 1880, p. 5

'The Birmingham Repertory Theatre', *BP*, 8 February 1926, p. 12

'The Catholics and Dr Barnes', *BP*, 18 March 1929, p. 13

'The Catholics of Birmingham – Extraordinary Document', *Freeman's Journal*, 11 November 1841, p. 1

'The Condemned Fenians at Manchester: Disturbances in Birmingham', *Birmingham Journal*, 23 November 1867, p. 8

'The Condemned Irishmen', *Manchester Guardian*, 6 February 1940, p. 7

'The Condemned Irishmen: Appeal for Reprieve', *Manchester Guardian*, 6 February 1940, p. 9

'The Coventry Explosion', *Manchester Guardian*, 12 December 1939, p. 2

'The Executed I.R.A. Men', *Manchester Guardian*, 8 February 1940, p. 7

'The Fenians in London', *The Nation*, 4 June 1870, p. 659

'The Freedom of the Drama', *BG*, 22 May 1917, p. 2

'The Future of Ireland: Speeches at the Town Hall', *BP*, 18 March 1915, p. 6

'The Immortal Hour', *BM*, 24 June 1921, p. 4

'The Irish Institute', *Birmingham Catholic Magazine*, February 1918, p. 29

'The Irish Plays', *BM*, 19 May 1914, p. 2

'The London Hibernian Society', *BG*, 27 April 1846, p. 2

'The Mark of the Beast', *Irish Times*, 22 November 1974, p. 15

'The Mayor and Murphy', *Town Crier*, July 1869, p. 8

'The Ministerial Crisis', *Manchester Guardian*, 4 February 1886, p. 6

'The Passer-By', *BG*, 16 May 1917, p. 2

'"The Pilgrim Players": New Birmingham Society', *BP*, 16 December 1907, p. 4

'The Pogues Fall from Grace with Government', *New Musical Express*, 19 November 1988, p. 3

'The Political Crisis', *Manchester Guardian*, 12 June 1886, p. 5

'The "Rebel" and His Creed', *BG*, 13 October 1913, p. 4

'The Recent Elections to the "Two Thousand"', *BP*, 12 April 1887, p. 4

'The Repertory Theatre', *BP*, 2 April 1928, p. 6

'The Repertory Theatre', *BP*, 1 February 1927, p. 5

'The Repertory Theatre', *BP*, 24 November 1918, p. 5

'The Rev. T. M. MacDonnell', *Freeman's Journal*, 11 November 1841, p. 2

'The Scene outside the Tabernacle', *BP*, 17 June 1867, p. 8

'The Stage Irishman', *BM*, 10 April 1907, p. 7

'The Theatre', *BG*, 15 June 1795, p. 3

'The Theatres', *Town Crier*, December 1863, p. 9

'The Theatres', *Town Crier*, May 1865, p. 10

'The Theatres', *Town Crier*, November 1865, p. 14

'The Tinker's Wedding', *BM*, 14 May 1917, p. 6

'The Tinker's Wedding', *BG*, 18 May 1917, p. 3

'The Variety Theatres', *BP*, 21 March 1916, p. 3

'The Wearing of the Green', *BP*, 18 March 1900, p. 11

'Theatre, Birmingham', *BG*, 15 June 1795, p. 3

'Theatre, Birmingham', *BG*, 8 August 1803, p. 2

'Theatre, Birmingham', *BG*, 30 July 1804, p. 2

'Theatre, Birmingham', *BG*, 1 June 1807, p. 3

'Theatre, Birmingham', *BG*, 20 July 1807, p. 3

'Theatre, Birmingham', *BG*, 17 August 1807, p. 3

'Theatre, Birmingham', *BG*, 24 August 1807, p. 3

'Theatre: Covent Garden', *The Times*, 9 September 1786, p. 2

'Theatre Royal', *BG*, 25 May 1861, p. 6

'Theatre Royal, Birmingham', *BG*, 15 August 1808, p. 5

'Three Leaders, Three Nevers', *BG*, 22 November 1913, p. 1

'Time as Healer in Ireland', *BG*, 20 November 1913, pp. 1, 3

Tipper, Andy, 'Comics with the Gift of the Gab', *BP*, 17 March 1997, p. 9

Town Crier, July 1862, p. 9

Town Crier, October 1865, p. 14

Town Crier, August 1867, p. 6

'Town-Hall Meeting – O'Connell', *Birmingham Journal*, 16 December 1837, p. 1

'Tricolour Will Fly in City on July 27', *BM*, 14 March 1966, p. 5

'Trouble at the Birmingham Repertory Theatre', *BM*, 16 May 1917, p. 3

'Two Death Sentences', *Manchester Guardian*, 15 December 1939, p. 7

'Two Irish Brothers Died Together', *BP*, 26 November 1974, p. 7

'Two Men Taken off Plane as McDade's Body Flown Out', *BM*, 22 November 1974, p. 3

'Walk-Outs Hit Car Factories after Clashes between Workers', *Irish Times*, 23 November 1974, p. 10

'War of Words over Plan to Axe Irish Vote', *BP*, 18 March 1980, p. 7

Ward, Terry, 'A City to Avoid', *Irish Press*, 30 January 1953, located in NAI, Department of Foreign Affairs, Position of Irish Workers in Birmingham, 402/222

Wigglesworth, Kirsty, 'When Irish Eyes are Smiling', *BP*, 16 March 1998, p. 5

'Will IRA Dare to Flout the Prelate?', *BM*, 18 November 1974, p. 1

Wiseman, N., 'To the Editor of the Freeman's Journal', *Freeman's Journal*, 19 November 1841, p. 2

'37 Words Lead to Freedom', *BP*, 15 March 1991, p. 3

'Wrong Man Hanged, Says Ex-IRA Bomber', *Sunday Times*, 6 July 1969, p. 1

'Years of Work Ruined in Two Minutes', *Irish Times*, 23 November 1974, p. 10

'10 Years On … Tribute to a President', *BM*, 22 November 1973, p. 17

'Yesterday's Proceedings', *BG*, 18 June 1867, p. 3

Film, Television, and CD Sources

BCL, 'Birmingham St. Patrick's Day Parade '98', video cassette, VB102

BCL, Local Studies Collection, 'Birmingham Irish Community Forum, St. Patrick's Day Parade 1999', video cassette

Luke Kelly: The Collection, audio CD, Outlet music, 1999

Macbeth on the Estate, dir. Penny Woolcock, BBC2, 5 April 1997

Mitchell, Maureen, news interview, BBC, 18 November 2004, available at 'Irish Quarter' <http://www.irishquarterbirmingham.com/news.htm> [accessed 21 May 2008]

The Rotters' Club, adapted by Dick Clement and Ian La Frenais, BBC2, 26 January 2005, 2 February 2005, 9 February 2005

Who Bombed Birmingham?, by Rob Ritchie, dir. Mike Beckham, Granada, 28 March 1990

World in Action: The Birmingham Six – Their Own Story, prod. Eamon T. Connor, Ian McBride, and Charles Tremayne, Granada, 18 March 1991

Unpublished Sources

Adams, John, BCL, Birmingham Repertory Theatre Archive, John Adams's souvenir programme for *Heartlanders*

'Aug 12 20', NYPL, Lincoln Center Library, MWEZ+NC 27,695, folder marked 'no dates', clipping about Birmingham Theatre marked 'Aug 12 20'

Aynesworth, Allan, SCUB, Austen Chamberlain Archive, Letter from Aynesworth, AC 1/5/1–1/6/1/5

BCL, Local Studies Collection, The National Roll of the Great War, 505,224

——, Local Studies Collection, Two Irish Studies Boxes, LF21.7

——, Local Studies Collection, Irish Studies Box 2, folder labelled 'World War II', A8 941.5

——, Local Studies Collection, Irish Studies Box 2, programme for the 1989 Birmingham Centenary Irish Festival, A8 941.5

——, Local Studies Collection, Irish Studies Box 2, Seamus McGarry's programme notes for the 27th congress of the Federation of Irish Societies, A8 941.5

BCL, St Thomas Bath Row, Marriages vols. 3–5, 1 October 1853–13 July 1868

Beerbohm Tree, Herbert, SCUB, Joseph Chamberlain Archive, Letter of 16 August 1895, JC 5/69/1

——, SCUB, Joseph Chamberlain Archive, Letter of 12 January 1896, JC 5/69/3

Birmingham Repertory Theatre, BCL, Birmingham Repertory Theatre Archive, January 1962–July 1966, vol. 117(A)

Birmingham Repertory Theatre, BCL, Birmingham Repertory Theatre Archive, programme for *Big Maggie* and programme for *The Playboy of the Western World*

Carroll, Paul Vincent, BCL, Birmingham Repertory Theatre Archive, *Shadow and Substance* Prompt Book

Catholic Education Committee, BRCAA, Journal of the Catholic Sunday School Established in Birmingham 1809, Meeting of the committee held on 16 July 1832, P1/60/1

Chamberlain, Joseph, BL, Copy of speech delivered in Birmingham on 26 October 1880, ADD MS 44,125

——, SCUB, Austen Chamberlain Archive, AC 1/6/1/8

——, SCUB, Austen Chamberlain Archive, AC 1/6/2/1

——, SCUB, Austen Chamberlain Archive, AC 1/6/2/6

——, SCUB, Austen Chamberlain Archive, *The Game of Politics*, AC 1/5/1–1/6/1/5

Classical Theatre Lab, SCUB, Joseph Chamberlain Archive, JCL ADD 497

Corporate Statistician, BCL, *Ethnic Origins of Birmingham Children 1966–81*, Birmingham Central Statistical Office, LF 40–41

Davis, Patsy 'Green Ribbons: The Irish in Birmingham in the 1860s: A Study of Housing, Work and Policing' (unpublished master's thesis, University of Birmingham, 2003)

Drinkwater, John, NYPL, Berg collection, folder 6488889, letter of 1 May 1910

Edgar, David, BCL, Shakespeare Collection, *Death Story*, S345.92F

Ferguson and Mack, BL, Lord Chamberlain's Collection, *Irish Aristocracy*, 53,352C

Finigan, Thomas Austin, BCL, Journal of Austin Finigan, MS 3255, no. 12749

Foley, Maurice, NAI, Department of Foreign Affairs, Position of Irish Workers in Birmingham, Report by Maurice Foley, 402/222

Hardman, John, and Company, BCL, The Archives of John Hardman and Company, MS 175

Howard, Walter, BL, Lord Chamberlain's Collection, *The Wearing o' the Green: A Story of the Irish Rebellion*, 53,607

Iremonger, Valentin, NAI, Department of Foreign Affairs, Position of Irish Workers in Birmingham, Follow-up Report on 26 and 27 June 1956, 402/222

Killeen, Nuala Katherine, 'Culture, Identity and Integration: The Case of the Irish in Birmingham' (unpublished doctoral thesis, University of Birmingham, 2002)

McKenna, Joe, 'The Irish in Birmingham 1990', BCL, Local Studies Collection, LF 21.7

——, 'The Irish in Birmingham: A Scrapbook 1643–1989', BCL, Local Studies Collection, Birmingham Collection 21.7

Murphy, Seán, NAI, Department of Foreign Affairs, Position of Irish Workers in Birmingham, Seán Murphy's note of 18 October 1955, 402/222

NAI, Department of Foreign Affairs, Position of Irish Workers in Birmingham, 402/222

NAI, Department of Foreign Affairs, Position of Irish Workers in Birmingham, Note from London embassy to department of external affairs on 23 July 1951, 402/222

Orange Order, BCL, Minute Book of the Orange Order Birmingham, MS 1250/1

Peach, Alex, 'Poverty, Religion and Prejudice in Britain' (unpublished doctoral thesis, De Montford University, 2000)

Pearse, James, NLI, James Pearse's Diary, ACC 5153

——, NLI, Pearse Papers, Account book of James Pearse's sculpting business, MS 21,075

——, NLI, Pearse Papers, Bank books of James Pearse 1889–98, MS 21,076

——, NLI, Pearse Papers, 'England's Duty to Ireland', MS 21,079

——, NLI, Pearse Papers, Envelope addressed to William Pearse, MS 21,078 (1)

——, NLI, Pearse Papers, James Pearse's train ticket from Birmingham to Dublin, MS 21,078 (1)

——, NLI, Pearse Papers, Letter re. James Pearse's conversion to Catholicism, MS 21,077

——, NLI, Pearse Papers, Plans of business premises to be erected in Bristol Street Birmingham, MS 21,078 (3)

Roche, Clare, 'Home from Home? Irish Women in Birmingham' (unpublished master's thesis, University of Birmingham, 1997)

Shaw, George Bernard, NYPL, Lincoln Center Library, Billy Rose Theatre Collection, Cyril Phillips papers regarding the Birmingham Repertory Theatre, T-MSS 2001–057, folder 1, letter of 12 July 1923

——, NYPL, Lincoln Center Library, Billy Rose Theatre Collection, Cyril Phillips papers regarding the Birmingham Repertory Theatre, T-MSS 2001–057, folder 1, letter of 17 August 1923

Walsh, Thomas, BRCAA, letter dated 20 February 1833, B133

——, BRCAA, letter dated 23 August 1834, B185

Yeats, W. B., NYPL, Berg Collection, folder 940410, letter of March 1909

——, NYPL, Berg Collection, folder 940410, letter of 29 November 1909

——, NYPL, Berg Collection, folder 940410, letter of 31 March 1910

——, NYPL, Berg Collection, folder 940411, letter of 28 April 1910

——, NYPL, Berg Collection, folder 940411, letter of 14 July 1910

——, NYPL, Berg Collection, folder 940411, letter of 3 December 1911

——, NYPL, Berg Collection, folder 940412, letter of 3 May 1912

——, NYPL, Berg Collection, folder 940412, letter of October 1913

——, NYPL, Berg Collection, folder 940413, letter of 20 October 1913

——, NYPL, Berg Collection, folder 940413, undated letter

Weinberger, Barbara, 'Law Breakers and Law Enforcers in the Late Victorian City: Birmingham 1867–1877' (unpublished doctoral thesis, University of Birmingham, 1989)

Ziesler, Kaja Irene, 'The Irish in Birmingham 1830–1970' (unpublished doctoral thesis, University of Birmingham, 1989)

Index